NEW DIGITAL MUSICAL INSTRUMENTS: CONTROL AND INTERACTION BEYOND THE KEYBOARD

THE COMPUTER MUSIC AND DIGITAL AUDIO SERIES

John Strawn, Founding Editor
James Zychowicz, Series Editor

DIGITAL AUDIO SIGNAL PROCESSING
Edited by John Strawn

COMPOSERS AND THE COMPUTER
Edited by Curtis Roads

DIGITAL AUDIO ENGINEERING
Edited by John Strawn

COMPUTER APPLICATIONS IN MUSIC:
A BIBLIOGRAPHY
Deta S. Davis

THE COMPACT DISC HANDBOOK
Ken C. Pohlman

COMPUTERS AND MUSICAL STYLE
David Cope

MIDI: A COMPREHENSIVE INTRODUCTION
Joseph Rothstein
William Eldridge, *Volume Editor*

SYNTHESIZER PERFORMANCE AND
REAL-TIME TECHNIQUES
Jeff Pressing
Chris Meyer, *Volume Editor*

MUSIC PROCESSING
Edited by Goffredo Haus

COMPUTER APPLICATIONS IN MUSIC:
A BIBLIOGRAPHY, SUPPLEMENT I
Deta S. Davis
Garrett Bowles, *Volume Editor*

GENERAL MIDI
Stanley Jungleib

EXPERIMENTS IN MUSICAL INTELLIGENCE
David Cope

KNOWLEDGE-BASED PROGRAMMING FOR
MUSIC RESEARCH
John W. Schaffer and Deron McGee

FUNDAMENTALS OF DIGITAL AUDIO
Alan P. Kefauver

THE DIGITAL AUDIO MUSIC LIST:
A CRITICAL GUIDE TO LISTENING
Howard W. Ferstler

THE ALGORITHMIC COMPOSER
David Cope

THE AUDIO RECORDING HANDBOOK
Alan P. Kefauver

COOKING WITH CSOUND
PART I: WOODWIND AND BRASS RECIPES
Andrew Horner and Lydia Ayers

HYPERIMPROVISATION: COMPUTER-
INTERACTIVE SOUND IMPROVISATION
Roger T. Dean

INTRODUCTION TO AUDIO
Peter Utz

NEW DIGITAL MUSICAL INSTRUMENTS:
CONTROL AND INTERACTION BEYOND
THE KEYBOARD
Eduardo R. Miranda and
  Marcelo M. Wanderley, with a
  Foreword by Ross Kirk

Volume 21 • THE COMPUTER MUSIC AND DIGITAL AUDIO SERIES

NEW DIGITAL MUSICAL INSTRUMENTS:
CONTROL AND INTERACTION BEYOND THE KEYBOARD

Eduardo R. Miranda and Marcelo M. Wanderley
With a Foreword by Ross Kirk

∎

Middleton, Wisconsin

Library of Congress Cataloging-in-Publication Data

Miranda, Eduardo Reck, 1963–
    New digital musical instruments : control and interaction beyond the keyboard / by Eduardo Miranda and Marcelo Wanderley.
       p. cm. -- (Computer music and digital audio series)

       ISBN 0-89579-585-X

    1. Electronic musical instruments. 2. Sound--Recording and reproducing--Digital techniques. 3. Computer sound processing.
    I. Wanderley, Marcelo. II. Title. III. Series.
    ML1092.M57 2006
    786.7'192--dc22

                                      2005035245

ISBN-13: 978-0-89579-585-4
ISBN-10: 0-89579-585-X

        A-R Editions, Inc., Middleton, Wisconsin 53562
          © 2006 All rights reserved.
          Printed in the United States of America
          10 9 8 7 6 5 4 3 2 1

Contents

List of Figures ix

Foreword xv

Preface xix

■ **Chapter 1 Musical Gestures: Acquisition and Mapping** 1

    1.1. Introduction 2
    1.2. A Digital Musical Instrument Model 3
    1.3 Physical Gestures 5
    1.4 Gestures in Music 8
    1.5 Gesture and Feedback 11
    1.6 Gesture Acquisition and Mapping 11
    1.7 Further Reading 17

■ **Chapter 2 Gestural Controllers** 19

    2.1 Augmented Instruments 21
    2.2 Instrument-like and Instrument-inspired Controllers 25
    2.3 Alternate Controllers 30
    2.4 Food for Thought: Examples and Discussion 43
    2.5 Haptic Music Controllers: Tactile and Force Feedback 71
    2.6 High-end Motion Trackers 84
    2.7 Collaborative and Web-based Controllers 86

2.8 Adaptive Controllers   92
2.9 Comparing Gestural Controllers   95
2.10 Remarks on DMI Design   98
2.11 Further Reading   99

Chapter 3 Sensors and Sensor-to-Computer Interfaces   103

3.1 Transducers, Sensors, and Actuators   103
3.2 Sensors in Musical Applications   108
3.3 Review of Commonly Used Sensors in Musical Applications   109
3.4 Signal Conditioning   153
3.5 Sensor Interfaces   158
3.6 Examples of Sensor Interfaces   161
3.7 Using Audio Interfaces to Transmit Control Signals   164
3.8 Food For Thought   165
3.9 Further Reading   168

Chapter 4 Biosignal Interfaces   173

4.1 Brief Introduction to Electrodes and Electrical Safety Issues   173
4.2 Examples of Biosignals   175
4.3 Biosignal Conditioning   184
4.4 Protocols for Collecting Training Data   196
4.5 Biofeedback   199
4.6 Examples of Biosignal Systems for Music   200
4.7 Further Reading   215

Chapter 5 Toward Intelligent Musical Instruments   219

5.1 The Legacy of Electroacoustic Music   219
5.2 The Emergence of the Computer   221
5.3 Computer Musicianship   225
5.4 Interactive Musical Evolution with Genetic Algorithms   240
5.5 Improvising with Swarm Intelligence   247
5.6 Further Reading   253

Epilogue	255
References	257
Appendix: The Accompanying CD-ROM	285
Index	287

List of Figures

CHAPTER 1

Figure 1.1: A possible approach to the representation of a digital musical instrument.

CHAPTER 2

Figure 2.1: Comparing controllers with respect to their resemblance to existing acoustic instruments.

Figure 2.2: The SBass, designed by Curtis Bahn.

Figure 2.3: The Rolky Asproyd: (a) the full controller housed in a wooden case; (b) two examples of interaction with the device.

Figure 2.4: The Rolky Asproyd's schematics.

Figure 2.5: The MTC Express Pad, by Tactex Controls.

Figure 2.6: The Lemur, by Jazz Mutant. A prototype at the SPCL.

Figure 2.7: Interacting with the Lemur.

Figure 2.8: The PebbleBox, by Sile O'Modhrain and Georg Essl.

Figure 2.9: The GyroTyre, an alternate controller built to exploit the physical behavior of a spinning wheel.

Figure 2.10: The Radio Baton, by Max Mathews and Bob Boie.

Figure 2.11: The Buchla Lightning II, by Don Buchla.

Figure 2.12: The third generation of the meta-instrument, by Serge de Laubier.

Figure 2.13: Detail of the Hall effect sensor and magnet on the MIDI flute.

Figure 2.14: The first prototype (top instrument) and the final version (bottom) of the MIDI flute.

Figure 2.15: Note the cabling on the first prototype of the MIDI flute (a) and the curved printed circuit board on the final model (b).

Figure 2.16: The LMA flute by Sølvi Ystad and Thierry Voinier.

Figure 2.17: Detail of the LMA flute's Hall effect sensor and magnet.

Figure 2.18: Detail of the modified cork of the LMA flute featuring a microphone to sense pressure.

Figure 2.19: Cléo Palacio-Quintin playing the hyperflute. (Photo by Carl Valiquet)

Figure 2.20: Note the cables from the sensors of the hyper-flute and part of the Microlab sensor interface placed on the back of the performer. (Photo by Carl Valiquet)

Figure 2.21: Breath sensor and tubes to measure airflow in the mouthpiece of the flute.

Figure 2.22: The fingering scheme of the Bleauregard (12-cycle four-bit Gray code).

Figure 2.23: The original MIDI horn design.

Figure 2.24: The original MIDI horn design by John Talbert and Gary Lee Nelson.

Figure 2.25: The Hirn, a wind controller designed by Perry Cook.

Figure 2.26: The Pipe and its layout diagram: (a) top view; (b) bottom view; (c) diagram.

Figure 2.27: A dancer experimenting with a do-it-yourself sensitive floor developed at the Federal University of Paraná, Brazil.

Figure 2.28: CyberBoots Functions.

Figure 2.29: Eric Johnstone's Podoboard.

Figure 2.30: The Litefoot, by Griffith and Fernström.

Figure 2.31: The Z-tiles: (a) top view; (b) sensors.

Figure 2.32: The Mouthsizer uses video cameras to track the performer's mouth. (The performer in the photograph is Jordan Wynnchuk.)

Figure 2.33: Kia Ng's facial expression controller.

Figure 2.34: The Phantom Omni by SensAble Technologies.

Figure 2.35: A force-feedback key by ACROE.

Figure 2.36: A prototype of the modular force-feedback keyboard. The keyboard is composed of sixteen slice motors.

Figure 2.37: (a) The force-feedback transducer with twelve slice motors and the associate electronics; (b) Jean-Loup Florens controlling a model of a bowed string.

Figure 2.38: The 3D stick can be assembled into the TGR to provide a continuous movement in 3D with force feedback.

Figure 2.39: The MIKEY, by Roberto Oboe.

Figure 2.40: Detail of the MIKEY showing its voice-coil motors.

Figure 2.41: The degrees of freedom of Charles Nichol's vBow, version 2.2.

Figure 2.42: Vincent Verfaille playing the Yamaha WX5 controller.

Figure 2.43: Passive markers can also be placed on fingers to study keyboard performances.

Figure 2.44: The Tooka by Sidney Fels and colleagues.

Figure 2.45: The Jam-O-Drum by Tina Blaine and Tim Perkins.

Figure 2.46: Global String is a musical string that spans a large geographical distance through the Internet.

Figure 2.47: The Orb-3 system, with eight active speakers forming an "auditory sphere," angled to provide versatile software-controlled diffusion.

Figure 2.48: Laser alignment: triangulation.

Figure 2.49: A comparison of digital musical instruments based on expressivity, immersion, and feedback, by Jörg Piringer (2001).

Figure 2.50: A seven-axis diagram from Birnbaum and colleagues (2005).

Figure 2.51: Examples of applications from Birnbaum and colleagues (2005).

CHAPTER 3

Figure 3.1: Three FSR sensors.

Figure 3.2: A small round FSR sensor attached to the fingertip of a glove for sound control.

Figure 3.3: Four FSRs, a bend sensor attached to a finger, and an infrared sensor attached to the wrist of a glove for sound control.

Figure 3.4: Butch Rovan's data glove. Notice its use with an acoustic instrument (clarinet), instead of sensors being placed directly on the instrument. (Photo by Muratet.)

Figure 3.5: The Hyperbow, designed by Diana Young. (Photo by Yael G. Maguire.)

Figure 3.6: Detail of the Hyperbow showing two strain gauges.

Figure 3.7: A data glove using bend sensors.

Figure 3.8: Examples of bend sensors.

Figure 3.9: A pliable music controller using bend sensors.

Figure 3.10: Performing deformation gestures on Mark Zadel's controller.

Figure 3.11: Bend sensor in the Tooka.

Figure 3.12: The LuSense Standard CPS^2 155 linear potentiometer, assembled in a metal support.

Figure 3.13: Suguru Goto and his SuperPolm controller.

Figure 3.14: Tactile gloves designed by Pierre-Yves Fortier.

Figure 3.15: Two position sensors, by Infusion Systems and by Eowave.

Figure 3.16: Robert Moog's ribbon controller.

Figure 3.17: Part of the Cellophone designed by François Handfield.

Figure 3.18: An example of an interface using a piezo sensor to pick up the vibrations of a bowed piece of wood in the Cellophone.

Figure 3.19: A transmitter-receiver pair of piezoelectric ultrasound sensors, model no. 40TR16F, with center frequency equal to 40.0 ±1.0 kHz.

Figure 3.20: Electrostatic ultrasonic sensors for use in reflection mode.

Figure 3.21: A 3D ultrasonic sensing system using three ultrasonic receivers and one transmitter (Lima et al. 1996).

Figure 3.22: Measurement of ultrasound attenuation.

Figure 3.23: A spring between the hands is used to keep the two ultrasound sensors facing each other.

Figure 3.24: Sharp's infrared sensor GP2D12.

Figure 3.25: The interactive frame uses a grid of infrared sensors to calculate the position of an object inside the frame area.

Figure 3.26: The Dimension Beam music controller.

Figure 3.27: Saxophonist Brad Vines with active infrared markers during a motion capture session at McGill University's Motor Control Laboratory in Montreal.

Figure 3.28: The Augmented Violin by Emmanuel Fléty and colleagues.

Figure 3.29: Michel Waisvisz's Web system uses Hall devices to measure the tension of a web of strings. The sensors were designed by Bert Bongers.

Figure 3.30: Capacitive sensing modes by Joe Paradiso and Neil Gershenfeld.

Figure 3.31: A three-axis accelerometer can be made from one-axis devices (ADXL 105) by mounting them at angles of 90°.

Figure 3.32: Inclination sensors.

Figure 3.33: An example of a musical interface using discrete pressure keys by Pierre-Yves Fortier.

Figure 3.34: A voltage divider is composed of two resistors in series.

Figure 3.35: A voltage divider using an operational amplifier (μA741).

Figure 3.36: The Wheatstone bridge.

Figure 3.37: Noninverting amplifier.

Figure 3.38: Inverting amplifier.

Figure 3.39: Voltage protection, designed by Emmanuel Fléty.

Figure 3.40: A variation of the voltage protection circuit shown in Figure 3.39, by Eric Johnstone.

Figure 3.41: Examples of sensor interfaces.

Figure 3.42: Several homemade sensors and their conditioning circuits.

Figure 3.43: Resulting voltages obtained using LabView and a 16-channel, 16-bit PCMCIA National Instruments data acquisition card.

Figure 3.44: The Cheapstick, by Alexander Jensenius and Rodolphe Koehly.

CHAPTER 4

Figure 4.1: Finger electrodes for sensing GSR.

Figure 4.2: Some of the components that are used for interpretation of the ECG signal.

Figure 4.3: The vectors generated by the bipolar limb leads.

Figure 4.4: Placement of the precordial ECG leads.

Figure 4.5: Active surface EMG electrodes integrate a built-in preamplifier and a built-in filter.

Figure 4.6: The standard 10-20 electrode placement system, where the electrodes are placed at positions measured at 10% and 20% of the head circumference.

Figure 4.7: Examples of neighborhood for electrodes F3 and Pz in the 10-20 electrode placement system.

Figure 4.8: A classic MLP neural network with one hidden layer and a single output unit.

Figure 4.9: The block diagram of the Brain Soloist system whereby the brain plays variations of an imagined riff.

Figure 4.10: A rhythmic part is continuously played and a riff is played sporadically. Immediately after a riff is played, the system checks the performer's EEG.

Figure 4.11: The overall block diagram for the Brain Conductor system whereby the performer steers the faders of a mixer with the brain.

Figure 4.12: Subjects will listen to blocks of tones containing a random inter-stimulus interval of between three and nine seconds.

Figure 4.13: Placement of the sensors in the conductor's jacket.

Figure 4.14: The sensors and approximate positioning that were used in one of the final forms of the conductor's jacket.

Figure 4.15: BCMI-piano is composed of four modules.

Figure 4.16: Spectral information is used to activate generative music rules to compose music on the fly, and the signal complexity is used to control the tempo of the music.

Figure 4.17: Each bar of a composition is produced by one of four possible generative rules according to the subject's EEG rhythm.

Figure 4.18: Example of a musical section mixing elements in the styles of Robert Schumann and Ludwig van Beethoven.

CHAPTER 5

Figure 5.1: A performed sequence and a score sequence.

Figure 5.2: Data structure for the dynamic programming approach to matching.

Figure 5.3: Calculating an element of the array.

Figure 5.4: Complete evaluation of the array.

Figure 5.5: Complete evaluation of the array with matches underlined.

Figure 5.6: The sequence of actions of a typical GA.

Figure 5.7: Binary string coding.

Figure 5.8: Stochastic sampling selection mechanism.

Figure 5.9: Ring, two-dimensional, and three-dimensional neighborhood schemes.

Figure 5.10: The basic architecture of GenJam.

Figure 5.11: A phrase embedded in the measure and phrase populations.

Figure 5.12: Swarm separation behavior.

Figure 5.13: Swarm alignment behavior.

Figure 5.14: Swarm cohesion behavior.

Figure 5.15: An event in Swarmusic's music space.

Foreword

At the beginning of the 21st century we stand at a fascinating point in the evolution of contemporary electronic music. The current availability of prodigious processing power not only in the form conventional and ubiquitous personal computers, but also in non-conventional processor designs, where signal-processing algorithms are mapped directly onto gate-array technologies has opened up new opportunities for designers and musicians alike.

The issues are not just technological—they are also philosophical in the broadest sense. Using *current* technologies, we can now involve the performer in the conceptualization as well as the performance of acoustic (and visual) art.

There has long been a debate whether this is necessarily a good thing. Many an audience member (and some composers) may have regarded a performer's less-than-perfect rendition of a score as an undesirable, distorting filter between the immaculate conception of the composer and the final realisation of the piece in the auditorium. Yet others have regarded the performer's interpretation or improvisation of a piece as an essential element of what is meant by art.

The state of technological development through much of the 20th century has meant that whatever we might have thought in relation to this debate, the reality was that the performer's art could make little and in many cases, no contribution to the realisation of a piece. The technology simply was not good enough. For example, an electro-acoustic composition had, in many cases, to be created as an output of a computer program (the "Music n" languages, Csound, and so on), possibly involving many hours of processing and further manipulation in the studio. In this case, a concept of real-time "performance" was simply out of the question in any realistic sense.

Of course, performers have been able to make a contribution to the realisation of electronic music through perhaps limited, but still useful means. A classic example is the use of MIDI-based systems since the mid-1980s. However, there is a danger that we regard such systems as "the" natural way to communicate electronic-acoustic art. MIDI was, perhaps, a good place to start, given the state of available technology in the latter part of the 20th century. Nevertheless, many (especially string and wind players) have argued that its basis in the keyboard player's technique has limited its usefulness in the future evolution of the performer's contribution. It is also perhaps an example of the developmental distortions, which may arise if we let engineers and commercial interests excessively influence the agenda in the evolution of contemporary music. (I speak as an engineer, as well as a wind player!)

The new technologies mean that we can start with a blank sheet of paper in the design of musical instruments and potentially, the music performed through them. This gives us great freedom, but also, great challenges. This stems from the fact that perhaps uniquely in the history of the performance of music, we are able to separate entirely the production of sound from the means used to control it. In computer parlance, we use different algorithms for the generation of sound from those used to perform it, and maybe (arguably) there is no particular reason for these two classes of algorithm to be inexorably linked in any direct sense.

This is in marked contrast to the history of the evolution of conventional acoustic instruments. We bow a string, blow a pipe, strike an acoustic resonator, and we know what nature of sound to expect and have some inkling of the means we should use to control it. The physical characteristics of the instrument dictate both points of view to a considerable extent. We also have the benefit of the experience of millennia in the way we have learnt to make these instruments.

At a fundamental level, we have few of these benefits (comfortable restrictions?) in the design of new instruments. We have few constraints, apart from the limits of our imaginations, but we also have the tyranny of the blank page. How should we proceed?

We are inspired by the nature of conventional instruments, but should we limit our thinking to their "good" characteristics? Many of them have unstable and non-linear acoustic behavior—something which the beginner rapidly becomes aware of, but which may be overlooked by the competent performer with years of practice and study. Should we listen to the engineer's view that an instrument should be "easy to use" or be "user friendly," especially when we are aware that these very acoustic imperfections give *skilled* performers the freedom of expression found in extended playing techniques for example? Alternatively, should we deliberately design such complexities and imperfections into new instruments?

We can produce these new designs in maybe a few days, and change them radically a few days after that. How are we to assess the effectiveness of our work, given that the history of performance points to the need of a lifetime's study even to start to be an acceptably good performer with existing instruments?

Conventional instruments have an essentially passive, although possibly complex, nature in the hands of the performer. How are we to (should we) use the capability of modern designs to adapt these behaviors and their response to performers' gesture through techniques related to artificial intelligence? What does this behaviour offer in terms of new musical approaches and responsibilities?

It is rare in art that such philosophical debate underpins the creative process, certainly in my own discipline. This makes instrument design a fascinating field to work in.

This book provides a timely and comprehensive primer for anyone working in the field. The authors have a thorough understanding of the current state of research in electronic instrument design, and their book brings together into one place a summary of some of the best current practice in this research. It deals with basic "bricks and mortar" issues such as sensor technologies and protocols so that this information is available in one place, at the designer's fingertips. At the same time it also provides a look over the horizon at those technologies, which have the potential to radically influence our view of what a musical instrument is in the electronic age. Go create!

Ross Kirk
York, April 2006.

Preface

With very few exceptions, electronic musical synthesizers have been designed since the earliest models to be played with a piano-like keyboard. Even when electronics technology became more advanced and miniaturized, the industry maintained the keyboard as the standard interface between musicians and synthesizers. Astonishingly, the appearance of the digital synthesizer and the definition of the musical instrument digital interface (MIDI) protocol did not change this trend. On the contrary, they consolidated it. It is not by chance that in pop music parlance, performers who played the synthesizers were often referred to as "keyboard players."

With the emergence of software synthesizers and the availability of faster and more affordable personal computers, musicians started to use the computer as a musical instrument. Software synthesis allowed for much more flexibility and programmability. An increasing number of musicians and researchers have begun to implement their own digital musical instruments and create a demand for controllers other than the keyboard. Programming tools such as Max/MSP and PD have greatly contributed to this trend.

The industry made a few attempts at providing new musical controllers, notably wind controllers. But these were still very much inspired by the functioning of existing acoustic instruments. In commercial terms, these controllers were not as successful as their keyboard counterparts, probably because by then those potential clients were no longer interested in simulating existing acoustic instruments. Rather, they were most likely interested in creating new types of instruments that required forms of control not fully achievable with devices that merely mimicked standard instruments.

The art of new digital instrument design therefore involves more than engineering clever synthesis algorithms. It also requires careful thinking about how such algorithms will be controlled by the performers. Because of the role organology plays in the formation of musical vocabularies, those musicians interested in musical innovation are increasingly choosing to design their own new digital musical instruments as part of their quest for new musical composition and performance practices.

There have been various interesting developments in the last few decades in a community that remained largely marginalized by academia and industry for a number of years. Apart from various papers scattered throughout conferences and journals and in the proceedings of the relatively new NIME (New Interfaces for Musical Expression) international conference series, there is no concise introduction to this fascinating topic.

This book is an attempt at introducing such developments with a view to informing researchers and musicians interested in designing new digital musical instruments with control and interaction beyond the keyboard paradigm. Our approach is to provide an overview of various developments on the design of novel gestural controllers and digital musical instruments, with various references to the literature on the subject. By following this approach, we hope to provide readers with a context to help them understand and compare the advantages and drawbacks of these interfaces, as well as tips to their design.

The book is divided into five chapters. In chapter 1 we discuss the notion of musical gestures, their acquisition, and their mapping onto the variables of a synthesizer. It serves as a general introduction to the other four chapters.

In chapter 2 we focus on gestural controllers. We review various examples of controllers and compare implementations of similar ideas. For didactical purposes, we classify gestural controllers into four groups according to their degree of similarity to existing instruments. Whereas the first class comprises acoustic instruments that were augmented by the use of various sensors, the second class includes gestural controllers that were modeled after the control surfaces of acoustic instruments, with the goal of completely reproducing their initial features. Then comes the class of gestural controllers inspired by existing instruments or intended to overcome some intrinsic limitation of the original models, but that do not attempt to reproduce them exactly. Finally, there are alternate controllers, which do not bear any strong resemblance to existing instruments. We then present various case studies on specific controller implementations, on issues of controller classifications, and on controller design evolution. The chapter ends with a discussion of advanced controller issues such tactile and force-feedback devices, high-end movement trackers, collaborative and Web-based devices, and adaptive controllers.

Chapter 3 follows with an introduction to sensors and sensor-to-computer interfaces. Here we present more than 20 different sensors and review their application in the design of various digital musical instruments. We then discuss methods for converting the sensor signals into data that can be used to control software sound synthesizers. Various sensor-to-computer interfaces are presented, including models that use the new Open Sound Control (OSC) protocol, which is emerging as an advantageous alternative to the MIDI protocol.

Chapter 4 introduces the notion of biosignal interfaces—that is, the use of electrical signals produced in the body, such as nerves, muscles, and brain signals, to control music. We present different types of biosignals and introduce basic techniques to render these signals useful for musical control. We focus on our own research into the design of brain-computer interfaces for musical control using the electroencephalogram (EEG).

Finally, in chapter 5 we discuss an interesting route to the design of new instruments that involves the provision of artificial intelligence in order to render such instruments interactive. Here, the notion of musical instruments as devices that produce sound in response to body gestures is enriched by the idea of musical instruments that generate music interactively. A great number of generative music systems exist, some of which take into account real-time interaction. But research into the mapping of gestures into generative music systems is still incipient in the sense that for most existing interactive systems it does not matter which type of gestural controller is being used.

Chapters 1, 2, and 3 were written largely by Marcelo Wanderley. Chapters 4 and 5 were written largely by Eduardo Miranda, the main editor for the text. The video examples of sensors were provided by David Birnbaum, Paul Kosek, Joseph Malloch, and Elliot Sinyor, graduate students at the Input Devices and Music Interaction Laboratory, McGill University.

The authors would like to thank James L. Zychowicz, the editor of this series, for the opportunity to publish this pioneering book. Our thanks to all contributors who kindly provided materials such as illustrations (including photos of their controllers), movies, and fresh information about their research work. We would also like to express our gratitude to Ross Kirk at the University of York's Music Technology Group for his comments on the manuscript and for writing the foreword.

Our warmest thanks to various colleagues as well as graduate students at McGill University and the University of Plymouth for their help and criticism, including Frederic Bevilacqua, David Birnbaum, Julien Boissinot, Bert Bongers, Bram Boskamp, Andrew Brouse, Darryl Cameron, Emmanuel Fléty, Pierre-Yves Fortier, Avrum Hollinger, Alexander Refsum Jensenius, Eric Johnstone, Rodolphe Koehly, Paul Kolesnik, Paul Kosek, Joseph Malloch, Mark Marshall, Richard Mckenzie, Axel Mulder, Gary Scavone, Elliot Sinyor, Atau Tanaka, and Mark Zadel. Marcelo Wanderley's research has been funded by grants from the Natural Sciences and Engineering Council of Canada, the Canadian Foundation for Innovation, and the Fonds Québecois de Recherche sur la Nature et les Technologies. Eduardo Miranda's research has been funded by grants from the John Simon Guggenheim Memorial Foundation, the Leverhulme Trust, and the European Union.

Eduardo would like to thank Alexandra and Fabio, and Marcelo would like to thank Anna and Martha for their patience and support during the writing of this book.

ONE

Musical Gestures: Acquisition and Mapping

The main focus of this book is on musical instruments that use digital sound synthesis methods to generate sounds. An instrument that uses computer-generated sound can be called a digital musical instrument (DMI) and consists of a control surface or gestural controller, which drives the musical parameters of a sound synthesizer in real time.

Both hardware and software (computer-based) sound synthesizers are widely available. In fact, sound synthesis is a broad research field in which there have been a number of important developments since the 1950s (Dodge and Jerse 1997; Miranda 2002). Several synthesis techniques have been proposed that are able to reproduce acoustic sounds with high fidelity or to create new sounds impossible to produce with existing acoustic instruments.

Gestural controllers can take any form, from that of an acoustic instrument (instrument-like or instrument-inspired controllers) to alternate controllers that do not resemble known acoustic musical instruments. Conversely, the addition of sensors to existing acoustic instruments can increase their control possibilities. Such modified instruments are known as extended or augmented instruments and represent a compromise between the use of a known, but somewhat limited, control surface of an acoustic instrument and development of completely new performance abilities using an alternate controller.

The number of possibilities for designing DMIs is vast. Moreover, apart from the obvious reproduction and extrapolation of the functionalities of acoustic musical instruments, DMIs may be designed for various other contexts: for nonexperts or for experts in other forms of art (such as dance, where a dancer can control the music being generated), for use by multiple performers, as distributed entities in local or distant facilities, and so on. Therefore, the design of a DMI is not a trivial issue; many questions must be answered before we can decide which approach may best suit our musical aims: Why copy or be inspired by acoustic instruments, with their inherent limitations, if any movement can be used as a control variable? What can augmented instruments offer to performers? Why design musical instruments only for experts? Why be limited to a one-person-one-device configuration when networking capabilities are available for virtually all computers nowadays? What new possibilities are offered by digital musical instruments with respect to other artistic contexts?

In this book, we review various examples of DMIs, focusing on the various examples of gestural controllers proposed in the literature. We suggest ways to make sense of the wide variety of existing controllers, explore the most common sensor techniques used in their design, and analyze DMIs that make use of biological signals. Finally, we comment on extended techniques to extrapolate the DMI concept to systems that include artificial intelligence and other advanced techniques.

■ 1.1 INTRODUCTION

Until the end of the 19th century, the design of musical instruments relied upon mechanical systems and the acoustic properties of tubes, strings, and membranes. With the advent of electricity, instrument designers started to experiment with the new possibilities offered by electrical and later by electronic means.

Examples of early electrical and electronic instruments are various (Chadabe 1997; Paradiso 1999), such as, for instance, the theremin (built in 1920 by Lev Termen), the ondes martenot, (built in 1928 by Maurice Martenot), and the trautonium (built in 1930 by Friedrich Trautwein). These instruments were just the first in a whole new range of possibilities offered to instrument designers, including new ways to generate sound and new ways to design control surfaces of any arbitrary shape. Today, the two most common ways to generate sound are through the use of a synthesizer and by means of a general-purpose computer. With the easy digital interconnection possibilities afforded by data communication protocols, anyone can connect different types of control surfaces to synthesizers and computers.

Here we review and discuss examples of DMIs, focusing specifically on their control surfaces. We will start by presenting a simple model of a DMI directly derived from traditional acoustic musical instruments.

1.2 A DIGITAL MUSICAL INSTRUMENT MODEL

For the purposes of this book we adopted the term digital musical instrument (DMI) to denote an instrument that contains a control surface (also referred to as a gestural or performance controller, an input device, or a hardware interface) and a sound generation unit. Both units are independent modules related to each other by mapping strategies (Figure 1.1).

The gestural controller (or control surface) is the device that provides the inputs to the DMI. It is where physical interactions between the performer and the instrument take place. The sound generation unit involves the synthesis algorithm and its controls. The mapping layer refers to the liaison strategies between the outputs of the gestural controller and the input controls of the sound generation unit.

Figure 1.1 A possible approach to the representation of a digital musical instrument.

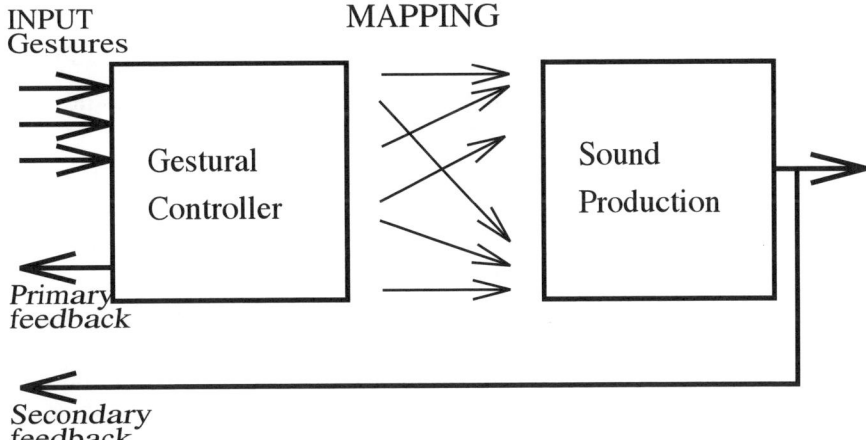

This separation between gestural controller and sound generation unit is impossible with traditional acoustic instruments, where the gestural interface is generally also part of the sound production unit. Take, for example, the clarinet: its reed, keys, and holes are at the same time both the gestural interface (where the performer interacts with the instrument) and the elements responsible for sound production.

The idea behind our approach to DMIs is analogous to breaking apart an acoustic instrument so that one could separate the two functionalities of gestural interface and sound generator and combine them in any desired way. Therefore, the notion of a fixed causality between an action and a sound in a DMI does not necessarily apply. The same gesture (cause) can lead to the production of completely different sounds.

Clearly, this separation of a DMI into two independent units is potentially capable of extrapolating the functionalities of a conventional musical instrument because it would no longer be tied to the physical constraints of the latter. Conversely, some fundamental characteristics of conventional instruments may be lost and/or difficult to reproduce. For instance, it is very difficult to emulate the tactile feedback inherent to vibrating mechanisms, since the vibration in a DMI is produced at the loudspeakers, which are usually decoupled from the gestural controller.

Let us now describe these parts of a DMI in detail, as one possible way to approach its design.

In order to design a new digital musical instrument, one typically needs to:

a. Decide on the gestures that will be used to control the system.

b. Define gesture capture strategies that will best translate these movements into electrical signals. This is typically done using a variety of sensors to measure hand, arm, lip, or other body movement, velocity of movement, pressure, or any other variable of interest.

c. Define sound synthesis algorithms that will create the sounds to be played; or, define the music software to be used for control of prerecorded musical processes.

d. Map the sensor outputs to the synthesis and music-control inputs. This mapping can be arbitrary, so any unusual combination would be as feasible to instantiate as any coupling of gesture to sound known in acoustic instruments.

e. Decide on the feedback modalities available (apart from the sound generated by the system): visual, tactile and/or kinesthetic.

1.3 PHYSICAL GESTURES

In order to devise new DMIs, it is important to start by analyzing the characteristics of the actions that will be captured. In computer music parlance, such actions are commonly referred to as *gestures*.

The study of gesture is a vast and complex field of research. Various communities explore gestures in different contexts, and, not surprisingly, the definition of what a gesture is may vary greatly across these communities.

Gesture may be considered the opposite of postures: gestures are dynamic, and postures are static (Mulder 2000). Other authors may only consider gestures to be hand movements that contain information (Kurtenbach and Hulteen 1990), or, more generally, movements that convey meaning to oneself or to a partner in communication (Hummels, Smets, and Overbeeke 1998).

In fact, the term gesture may be used to refer to a number of things such as empty-handed movements (together with speech or not), movements that involve the manipulation of an object, general body movements (movements of the hand or head, posture, and facial expressions), dynamic contours in music perception and performance, and even the sensations of touch, taste, and smell. This diversity has been well described by Pierre Feyereisen and Jacques-Dominique de Lannoy (1991): "To some extent, any movement or change in position of a body segment may be considered a gesture. Accordingly, the very notion of gesture refers to a great variety of phenomena. In an extended sense, the term gesture encompasses technical gestures that are used in various professions and that often involve tool use. From such a perspective, gestures are mainly actions before becoming means of communication."

In this book, the term gesture is used in a broad sense to mean any human action used to generate sounds. The term refers to actions such as grasping, manipulation, and noncontact movements, as well as to general voluntary body movements. We will start by discussing ways in which the various different types of gestures can be classified. Depending on the point of view and on the research area, different approaches have been adopted for classifying gestures.

1.3.1 Empty-handed versus Manipulation

One simple way to distinguish between gestures is to organize them based upon whether or not they involve contact with a device. This approach yields two groups:

a. Gestures for which no physical contact with a device or instrument is involved. These can be referred to as empty-handed, free, semiotic, or naked gestures.

b. Gestures where some kind of physical contact with a device or instrument takes place. These can be referred to as manipulative, ergotic, haptic, or instrumental gestures.

A substantial amount of research has been dedicated to the analysis of empty-handed gestures, mostly to their relation to speech (Feyereisen and Lannoy 1991; McNeill 1992; Quek et al. 2002; Goldin-Meadow 2003; Kendon 2004). Research on empty-handed gesture and speech produced a number of interesting discoveries, such as:

- The relationship between different gestures and speech (Kendon's Continuum)
- Types of gestures (for instance, iconic, deictic, metaphoric, and beats)
- Temporal structure of natural gestures
- Catchments and handedness, and their relationship to speech

Catchments are recognized when gesture features recur in two or more—not necessarily consecutive—gestures.

Manipulative gestures can be classified according to physical characteristics of the object or device being manipulated (Mulder 2000):

- Object type: solid, fluid, or gaseous
- Change effectuated: position, orientation, or shape
- Number of hands involved
- Indirection level: direct manipulation or manipulation through another object or tool

Another classification of manipulative gestures is based on their functions: prehensile or nonprehensile. Prehensile gestures may be classified according to the duration of the grasp and also to the type of grasp, for example, the level of precision, the number of fingers involved, and so on.

1.3.2 Manipulation versus Semaphores

Francis Quek and colleagues (2002) follow the line of reasoning presented above by opposing contact and noncontact gestures. They suggest that research efforts on the comprehension of human gestures are clustered around two kinds of gestures: manipulative and semaphoric.

Manipulative gestures are defined as those gestures whose purpose is to control some entity by applying a tight relationship between the actual movements of the gesturing hand or arm with the entity being manipulated. Semaphoric gestures in turn are defined as any gesturing system that employs a stylized dictionary of static or dynamic hand or arm gestures. These two groups differ in several ways: visibility of salient features of the hand, dynamics of hand movement, and availability of visual, tactile, and force feedback.

1.3.3 Descriptive, Functional, and Intrinsic Approaches

Christoph Ramstein (1991) presents an analysis of gestures using three distinct approaches: *descriptive*, *functional*, and *intrinsic*.

The descriptive (or phenomenological) approach is based on three criteria:

a. *Cinematic* criterion, consisting of an analysis of movement speed

b. *Spatial* criterion, involving the size of the space where the gesture takes place—for instance, large (e.g., arm movement) or small (e.g., finger movement)

c. *Frequency range* criterion, taking into account the decomposition of a movement with respect to its frequency content, approximately between several tenths of a Hertz (Hz) to 10 Hz

The functional approach refers to the possible functions a gesture may perform in a specific situation. For instance, instrumental gestures can transmit energy to a device or modify certain of its characteristics: a performer may bow a violin in order to put the strings into vibration (an excitation gesture) or change the length of the string to change the note's fundamental frequency (a parametric modification gesture).

Finally, the intrinsic approach focuses on the performer's conditions of gesture production. For example, the hand is suitable for fine motor action and perception owing to its dexterity and the density of nervous receptors at the fingertips. The feet are more suited to the performance of slower movements.

1.3.4 Expressive Content Approach

Yet another way of classifying gestures is by considering the subtle variations of a basic manipulative or empty-handed gesture that communicate expressive content. The main idea is to separate basic gestures that are part of a vocabulary of preestablished actions from variations of those basic gestures. A few people have used this approach to distinguish between symbolic and parametric gestures (Modler and Zannos 1997) or between gestures and gesture nuances (Orio 1999). Nicola Orio (1999) used the expressive content of a movement to study the gestures of an acoustic guitarist. He considered the position of the left-hand fingers on the strings (defining pitch) and the picking pressure of the right-hand fingers on the strings (defining loudness) as gestures belonging to defined classes: pitch and loudness, the basic levels of information conveyed to an audience. The way musicians perform these two actions produces a second level of information, that of the expressive content of these gestures, or gesture nuances. Nicola Orio related this second level of information with the information contained in the timbre of the instrument itself.

1.4 GESTURES IN MUSIC

In music, the term gesture may refer variously to musical gesture, performance gesture, or instrumental gesture.

In music, gestures made with the hands empty are mostly associated with the conductor's technique, although these are not always strictly empty-handed, since conductors usually hold a baton with the right hand. Several exceptions exist; for instance, Pierre Boulez conducts with no baton. Conductor's gestures are well defined, and each hand has its own musical roles, primarily tempo keeping with the right hand and loudness control and other expressive cues with the left (Rudolph 1950). In practice, this is not always obvious because the two hands frequently mirror each other.

The study of gesture in music is an important area of research that raises many issues about perception, performance, and emotional communication. According to François Delalande, "The question of gesture is . . . crucial in music. It lies in the intersection of two axes: one that binds together an observable action (the gesture of the instrumentalist) and a mental representation (the fictive movements evoked by sound forms), and another one that establishes a link between the interpreter (that produces the gestures) and the listener (who guesses, symbolizes and transforms them on an imaginary plane). The latter is established through a recording of the music" (1988; authors' translation). Delalande developed a study on the playing technique of Glenn Gould and suggested that gestures related to instrumental performance may be analyzed on at least three levels, from a purely functional level to a purely symbolic one:

a. *Effective gestures*: those gestures that actually produce the sound

b. *Accompanist gestures*: body movements such as shoulder or head movements

c. *Figurative gestures*: gestures that are perceived by the listener but do not necessarily correspond directly to a movement by the performer

Examples of figurative gestures are changes in note articulation, melodic variations, and so on. We focus on the portion of Delalande's gestural taxonomy that is related to instrumental performance. In this case, performer's gestures are related to the way in which an instrument is played—that is, to the instrumentalist's own technique.

1.4.1 The Gestural Channel

The basic starting point for studying performance gestures is effective movements, that is, those gestures that performers make in order to generate sounds. Claude Cadoz (1988) used the term "instrumental gestures" to define such movements. Instrumental gestures are considered to be a complementary mode of communication to empty-handed gestures. Therefore, they are unique in that they are a means of action on the physical world as well as communication means in a double sense: emission and reception of information. Cadoz proposed three different types of hand actions (or hand gesture functions):

a. *Ergotic*, in which there is an energy transfer between the hand and the object (the hand acts on an object)

b. *Epistemic*, which typically involves our capacity of touch and muscular/articulatory perception

c. *Semiotic*, that is, the function of meaning or of communicative intent

The semiotic function is the gestural function per se. It is the only function of gestures that are free or empty-handed and is exemplified by sign language, natural gesture, gesticulation, and pantomime.

It is important to note that these three functions are interdependent. Their interdependency is what characterizes the gestural channel, and particularly one of its possibilities: the instrumental gesture. In the instrumental situation, all communication channels can be required simultaneously, contrary to other situations involving communication.

1.4.2 The Instrumental Gesture

The instrumental gesture is defined as a modality specific to the gestural channel. It is complementary to empty-handed gestures, and it is characterized as follows (Cadoz and Wanderley 2000): it is applied to a concrete (material) object with which there is physical interaction, and specific (physical) phenomena are produced during a physical interaction whose forms and dynamics can be mastered by the subject. These phenomena may become the support for communicational messages and/or be the basis for the production of a material action.

1.4.3 The Ancillary Gestures

The terms ancillary and accompanist gestures have been used to designate those gestures that are part of a performance but are not produced in order to generate sound. These terms have a similar meaning to what Jane Davidson (1994) refers to as expressive movements (to be differentiated from expressive gestures in the sense discussed in section 1.3.4). In fact, ancillary movements are known to convey expressiveness in musical performance and therefore can be thought of as extra variables for sound generation and control (Wanderley 2002b; Wanderley and Depalle 2004; Wanderley et al. 2005).

Again, it is important to stress that any body movement or signal, not just the known actions of bowing, plucking, striking, blowing, and so on, can be used as a variable to control musical performance. Examples of actions not traditionally used to generate sounds include walking (Choi 2000), postural adjustments (McElligott, Dillon, and Dixon 2002), facial expressions (Lyons, Haehnel, and Tetsutani 2003; Ng 2004), dance movements (Camurri 1995), muscular tension (Lusted and Knapp 1996), and indeed nonmovement signals such as brainwaves (Miranda et al. 2003). All of these and many others may serve as effective means for sound control.

1.5 GESTURE AND FEEDBACK

One can approach the study of gestures by analyzing either the possible functions of a gesture during performance or the physical properties of a gesture. By identifying functional (in a specific context) or physiological gestural characteristics one can ultimately gain insight into the design of gesture acquisition systems. It is also important to be aware of the type of feedback that is available to the performer—visual, auditory, or tactile-kinesthetic.

Feedback can be studied according to its characteristics:

a. *Primary* versus *secondary*, where primary feedback encompasses visual, auditory (e.g., the noise of the clarinet key) and tactile-kinesthetic feedback, and secondary feedback relates to the sound produced by the instrument (Vertegaal, Ungvary, and Kieslinger 1996)

b. *Passive* versus *active*, where passive feedback relates to feedback provided through physical characteristics of the system (e.g., the noise of a switch) and active feedback is produced by the system in response to a certain user action (e.g., the sound produced by the instrument; Bongers 2000)

Tactile-kinesthetic feedback is also referred to as haptic or tactual (Bongers 1998b). It will be discussed in detail later in this book.

These feedback options are important in performing on acoustic instruments and are therefore necessary in gestural interfaces that aim at simulating the control surfaces of such instruments. In the case of a gesture that does not involve physical contact with a device (an empty-handed gesture), there is no imminent need to provide the user with tactile or force feedback. However, studies have suggested that feedback can improve the quality of open-air controllers (Rovan and Hayward 2000).

1.6 GESTURE ACQUISITION AND MAPPING

Once the gesture characteristics have been analyzed, the next step is devising an acquisition system that will capture these characteristics.

One of the main challenges of studying gestures to be used for playing a DMI is that the devices used to capture these gestures can vary substantially, since the design of the device depends on the gestures to be used. For example, consider the type of feedback available to the performer: in a manipulation gesture, the forces involved may vary significantly depending on the type of the grip (e.g., precision or force). A system that uses a grip gesture may provide the user with tactile and force feedback, which is common in several acoustic instruments, such as the force provided by the excitation mechanism in pianos or the tactile vibration on the lips of a saxophonist.

The design of the acquisition device for empty-handed gestures may also vary substantially depending on the specific gestures that will be used. For instance, consider the acquisition of two types of gestures related to speech: sign language and gesticulation. We know that sign languages have properties similar to those of spoken languages. Sign languages are regulated by commonly accepted rules and are not produced concurrently with vocal speech. Gesticulations that accompany spoken language have no explicit linguistic properties (vocabulary or grammar); they are normally idiosyncratic and have meaning only within the context of speech. Therefore, a system for understanding sign language would benefit from knowledge of these linguistic properties. The system would know beforehand the types of gestures to expect (vocabulary), how gestures would follow each other (grammar), possibly the handedness of the gestures, and so on. A system aimed at understanding gesticulation cannot rely on an established vocabulary and grammar. It would also have to use temporal features and other nonlinguistic cues. The system would also benefit from the analysis of the speech signal, because gesticulation and speech are intimately tied.

1.6.1 Gesture Acquisition Possibilities

In the well-known case of the interaction between performer and acoustic instruments, gesture can be captured in at least three different ways: *direct*, *indirect*, and *physiological* acquisition.

Direct acquisition. In direct acquisition, one or more sensors are used to monitor the actions of the performer. The signals from these sensors present individual basic physical features of a gesture such as pressure, linear or angular displacement, and acceleration. A different sensor is usually needed to capture each of the individual physical variables of the gesture. Depending on the type of sensors and on the combination of different technologies in various systems, different movements may be tracked. According to Bert Bongers (2000):

Sensors are the sense organs of a machine. Sensors convert physical energy (from the outside world) into electricity (into the machine world). There are sensors available for all known physical quantities, including the ones humans use and often with a greater range. For instance, ultrasound frequencies (typically 40 kHz used for motion tracking) or light waves in the ultraviolet frequency range.

Chapter 3 will discuss various sensing technologies and their musical applications in detail.

Indirect acquisition. Unlike direct acquisition, indirect acquisition provides information about performer actions from the evolution of structural properties of the sound being produced by an instrument. In this case, the only sensor is a microphone, that is, a sensor for measuring pressure or gradient of pressure. Due to the complexity of the information available in the instrument's sound captured by a microphone, different real-time signal processing techniques are used in order to distinguish the effect of a performer's action from environmental features, such as the influence of the room.

Generically, one can identify basic sound parameters to be extracted in real time. Wanderley and Depalle (2004) cite four parameters:

- *Short-time energy*, related to the dynamic profile of the signal, indicates the dynamic level of the sound but also possible differences in the position of the instrument in relation to the microphone. Therefore, in order to retrieve performer actions from the analysis of this parameter, one needs to consider the instrument's directivity and the fact that not all sounds produced by an instrument require the same effort.

- *Fundamental frequency*, related to the sound's melodic profile, gives information about fingering, for instance. The analysis of fundamental frequency may benefit from the information available from analysis of the short-time energy, as in the case of note octaviation with the increase of the energy supplied by the performer.

- *Spectral envelope*, representing the distribution of sound partial amplitudes, may give information about the resonating body of the instrument, for instance. It may also indicate the energy applied to the signal from the analysis of the decreasing slope of the envelope.

- *Amplitudes*, *frequencies*, and *phases of sound partials* can alone provide much of the information obtained by the previous parameters. They also allow the evaluation of sound enharmonicity, which is related to the position of a string pluck or of a strike of a membrane, for instance.

Examples of literature on indirect acquisition of performer actions include Barry Vercoe's work on score following (Vercoe 1984), Nicholas Bailey and colleagues' work on the phase vocoder in the control of sounds (1993), Eran Egozy's work on deriving musical features from the clarinet sound (1995), and Nicola Orio's (1999) and Caroline Traube and colleagues' (2003) work on the acoustic guitar.

Physiological signal acquisition. Finally, physiological signal acquisition includes signals such as the electromyogram (EMG), the electroencephalogram (EEG), the electrooculogram (EOG), and galvanic skin response (GSR), also referred to as biosignals. For instance, commercial systems, such as the BioMuse (Lusted and Knapp 1996; Tanaka 1993), have been developed to control music based on the analysis of muscle tension.

Chapter 4 will discuss biosignal interfaces in detail.

Compared to indirect acquisition, direct acquisition has the advantage of simplicity. The influence of different parameters on the resulting sound makes indirect acquisition difficult to handle. However, direct acquisition techniques may underestimate the interdependency of the various variables obtained owing to the independence of the captured variables. Physiological signal acquisition is potentially hard to master because signals are weak and highly contaminated with noise and spurious artifacts.

1.6.2 Mapping of Gestural Variables onto Synthesis Parameters

Once gesture variables are available, either directly from individual sensors or as a result of signal-processing techniques, one needs to relate these variables onto the parameters of the synthesizer(s) that will be used to produce the actual sounds. This relationship is commonly known in computer music as (parameter) mapping.

As mentioned above, unlike with acoustic musical instruments, where this relation is predefined, in DMIs one needs to establish it from scratch. The mapping of gestural variables onto the parameters of a synthesizer needs careful consideration because the relationship between them is far from obvious.

The number and characteristics of these input variables may vary enormously depending on the sound synthesis techniques in question. One may have amplitudes, frequencies, and phases of sinusoidal sound partials for additive synthesis; an excitation frequency plus the center frequency, bandwidth, amplitude, and skew of formants for formant synthesis; carrier and modulation coefficients (c:m ratio) for frequency modulation (FM) synthesis; and so forth (Dodge and Jerse 1997; Miranda 2002). How does one relate a gesture to a c:m ratio? In the case of physical models, the available variables are usually the input parameters of an instrument, such as blowing pressure, bow velocity, and so on. In a sense, the mapping of gestures to the synthesis parameters of a physical model could be considered more straightforward because the relation of these inputs to the synthesis algorithm already encompasses the multiple dependencies based on the physics of the particular model. But this simplicity comes at a price: it would be necessary to develop a highly skilled performance technique for playing with such controllers.

A first interesting point to consider is the role of mapping. In algorithmic composition, the mapping of gestures to sounds may be considered the composition itself: "Mapping in algorithmic composition is different from mapping in instrument design because composition is a process of planning and instruments are for realtime music production. The use of mapping which is integral to an instrument has both differences and similarities to the mapping that is an inherent part of algorithmic composition" (Doornbusch 2002).

In this text, we consider mapping to be an integral part of a DMI. In fact, it defines the DMI's essence (Hunt, Wanderley, and Paradiso 2003). Therefore, the mapping strategy chosen affects the way the instrument will be played and its effectiveness.

Considering mapping as part of an instrument, one can devise two main directions from the analysis of the existing literature:

a. The use of neural networks, feature extraction (e.g., principal component analysis [PCA]), or pattern recognition as tools to perform mapping (e.g., Lee and Wessel 1992; Fels 1994, Modler 2000)

b. The use of explicitly defined mapping strategies (Bowler et al. 1990; Rovan et al. 1997; Hunt and Kirk 2000; Goudeseune 2002; Van Nort, Wanderley, and Depalle 2004)

The main difference between these two directions consists in the chosen approach to mapping: either the use of a method that provides a mapping strategy by means of internal adaptations of the system through training or the selection of most important features among the set of signals, or the proposition of mapping strategies that explicitly define the relationships.

Explicit mapping strategies. The available literature generally considers mapping of performer actions to sound synthesis parameters as a few-to-many relationship. This is mostly true in the case of synthesis by signal models, such as source-filter or additive synthesis, where sometimes hundreds of variables represent the available synthesis inputs.

Three intuitive strategies relating the parameters of one set to the other can be devised:

a. *One-to-one*, where one synthesis parameter is driven by one gestural parameter

b. *One-to-many*, where one gestural parameter may influence various synthesis parameters at the same time

c. *Many-to-one*, where one synthesis parameter is driven by two or more gestural parameters

Obviously, a combination of these basic strategies is also possible; this is termed *many-to-many* (Iazzetta 2000).

The design of the chosen mapping strategy may then be chosen to reflect a specific interaction metaphor (Fels, Gadd, and Mulder 2002), may be devised as multiple layers (Fels 1994; Hunt and Wanderley 2002; Arfib et al. 2002), may be simple or complex, and so on. Indeed, complex mappings, although obviously not suitable for a beginner, may outperform simple mappings in some circumstances:

> Too often the instrument design will default to a single control device corresponding to a single musical (synthesis) parameter—a "one-to-one" mapping. It is also known that acoustic musical instruments have evolved over many hundreds of years into systems with greatly superior interaction capabilities than today's state-of-the-art real-time processors. Thus, the study of mapping strategies seems to be of paramount importance, since in many instruments the input variables are inter-related in both complex and non-linear relationships (Hunt, Wanderley, and Kirk 2000, p. 209).

In different real-life scenarios, similar situations occur (e.g., when driving a car). The problem in these situations is that there is not necessarily an obvious model of the mapping strategies that relate the input devices being manipulated by the user/performer to the system being controlled. Recent studies have shown that even in those situations that are not directly modeled on existing systems (i.e., acoustic instruments), complex mapping strategies can outperform one-to-one relationships. The question to be investigated in this case is the way in which these relationships should be set up (Hunt and Kirk 2000).

Independently from the strategy used, mapping is a very important research topic nowadays. Apart from an increasing number of papers on mapping in the International Conference on New Interfaces for Musical Expression (NIME) (Bencina 2005; Bevilacqua, Muller, and Schnell 2005; Steiner 2005), various papers in conferences and journals have recently discussed the role of mapping in instrument design, including its importance (Hunt, Wanderley, and Paradiso 2003) and limitations (Chadabe 2002). We refer the reader to the special issue of the journal *Organised Sound* 7(2), "Mapping Strategies in Realtime Computer Music" (Wanderley 2002a), for an overview of the various trends on the design of mapping strategies for digital musical instruments.

■ 1.7 FURTHER READING

Where to go from here?

For an overview of sound synthesis techniques, we recommend the textbooks by Dodge and Jerse (1985, 1997), Curtis Roads (1996), and Eduardo Miranda (1998, 2002).

There are various works on gestures, gesture capture, and mapping in the literature. Several examples are presented in the electronic publication *Trends in Gestural Control of Music* (Wanderley and Battier 2000).

Research on gestures is mostly based on empty-handed gestures that co-occur with speech. Several books address this topic, including David McNeill's *Hand and Mind: What Gestures Reveal about Thought* (1992), Susan Goldin-Meadow's *Hearing Gesture: How Our Hands Help Us Think* (2003), Adam Kendon's *Gesture: Visible Action as Utterance* (2004), and David McNeill's *Language and Gesture* (2000), which offers a good overview of various researches in this area.

Manipulative gestures have been somewhat less frequently discussed in the literature. Books on motor control and on virtual reality and robotics are good sources of information in this area. Very good examples of references are David Rosenbaum's *Human Motor Control* (1990) and Grigore Burdea and Philippe Coiffet's *Virtual Reality Technology*, 2nd ed. (2003).

Gesture capture has been discussed in various works, mostly in reference to the use of sensors and biosignals. An overview of various sources is presented in chapter 3 and 4, respectively.

Indirect gestural acquisition is a somewhat less developed area. Nevertheless, excellent works exist, for instance Eran Egozy's master's thesis on extracting control signals from the sound of a clarinet in real time (1995), as well as several works on score following (Vercoe 1984) and on the analysis of sounds from other acoustic instruments, such as the guitar (Orio 1999).

Finally, the study of mapping strategies has also drawn increasing attention from the computer music community. Excellent sources of information on mapping are the doctoral theses of Sidney Fels (1994), Axel Mulder (1998), Andy Hunt (1999), and Camille Goudeseune (2001). An overview of recent trends in mapping strategies is presented in *Organised Sound* 7(2), guest edited by Marcelo Wanderley (2002a).

TWO

Gestural Controllers

Although several examples of electronic musical instruments have been proposed in the past century, the number of interfaces for musical expression has increased dramatically since the 1980s (Piringer 2001). This fact is mostly due to the emergence of the MIDI protocol and the widespread availability of powerful, low-cost computers.

This chapter reviews various examples of gestural controllers. Our objective is to examine examples of controllers designed by researchers, engineers, and artists within the last few decades by loosely classifying controllers according to various factors, such as the degree of similarity to existing acoustic musical instruments or the number of performers using the controller at one time. We compare implementations of similar ideas and discuss case studies that present innovative solutions to prevent common interface shortcomings, such as the lack of haptic feedback.

The various existing gestural controllers can be studied from different points of view. Perhaps the most straightforward method would be to compare them in terms of their resemblance to existing acoustic instruments. By doing so, one can propose a range of possibilities (Manning 2004), from traditional acoustic instruments augmented by sensors and controllers imitating or inspired by existing acoustic instruments to totally new designs bearing little or no resemblance to existing instruments (Figure 2.1).

Atau Tanaka (2000) proposed to classify gestural controllers (or, more generally, DMIs) into physical or nonphysical based on their mode of interaction, and into mechanical or nonmechanical controllers. According to Tanaka, creating gestures to modulate light being picked up by a photocell, though it is a physical gesture, is not physical or mechanical from the point of view of the sensor. Conversely, a biosensor such as the BioMuse (Tanaka 1993) is not mechanical, but it is physical because it detects corporeal activity.

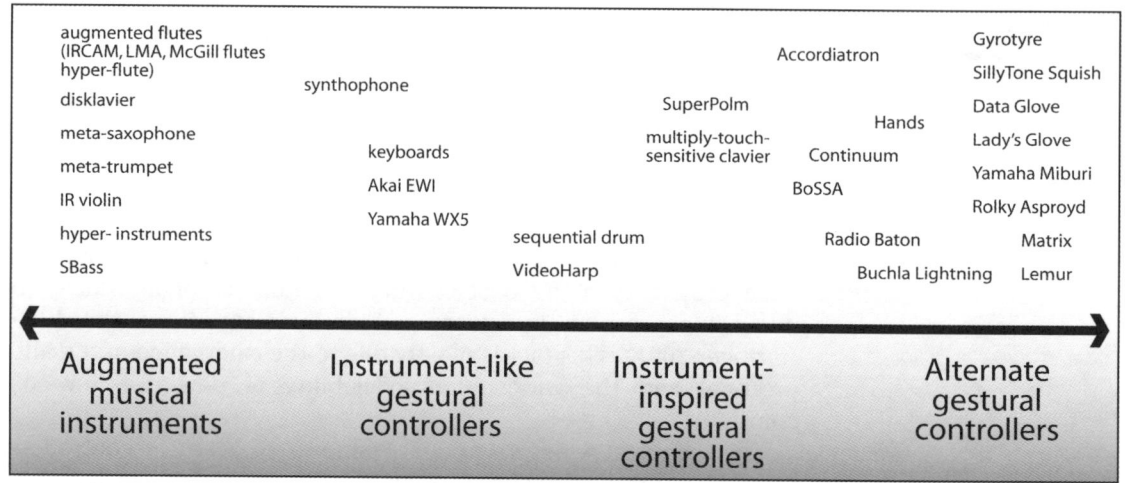

Figure 2.1 Comparing controllers with respect to their resemblance to existing acoustic instruments.

Other possible ways to compare controllers can include the number of people using a controller at one time (one or multiple performers, as in collaborative interfaces) and the spatial distribution of the music control system (local or remote, as in Internet-based systems), to cite but two. This chapter adopts a classification of new gestural controllers based on the degree of similarity to existing instruments:

- Acoustic instruments augmented by the use of various sensors
- Gestural controllers that are modeled after the control surfaces of acoustic instruments, with the goal of completely reproducing their initial features
- Gestural controllers inspired by existing instruments or that intend to overcome some intrinsic limitation of the original models, but that do not attempt to reproduce them exactly
- Alternate controllers that do not bear strong resemblance to existing instruments

As we shall see below, the last class of controllers is very broad in the sense that every controller that does not fit the first three classes may be considered an alternate controller. Before we proceed, please note that the computer music community tends to use the term "alternate controller" to mean "alternative controller." Although the latter term would be more correct, in this book we use the former because the community more commonly uses it.

Obviously, the above classification is not intended to be exhaustive or definitive, since boundaries may overlap and one controller may satisfy more than one criterion. However, such classifications can provide a means to make sense of the wide variety of developments in the area of gestural controller design. For instance, consider two modified saxophones: the synthophone, by Martin Hurni (Chadabe 1997), and the meta-saxophone, by Mathew Burtner (2002). Though the synthophone provided saxophone players with an interface that was the closest possible to that of the saxophone (it was built around a saxophone body), it did not produce acoustic sounds. Conversely, the meta-saxophone kept all the acoustic properties of the tenor saxophone and could therefore be played as a normal tenor saxophone and/or using the extra possibilities provided by the various sensors attached to it. In this case, the synthophone would be viewed as an instrument-like controller, the meta-saxophone as an augmented instrument.

Another example is the standard piano keyboard. An augmented piano can be created by adding Robert Moog and Don Buchla's Piano Bar to an acoustic piano (Moog 2005). Electronic keyboards offering piano keyboards and action mechanisms simulating those of acoustic pianos would be examples of instrument-like controllers, since they try to model accurately the original instrument's interface and feel. Finally, though keyboards such as Robert Moog's multiply-touch-sensitive clavier (Moog 1982) were inspired by the traditional piano keyboard, they extrapolate its functionalities to allow a multitude of sensing possibilities not available in the acoustic instrument.

■ 2.1 AUGMENTED INSTRUMENTS

Augmented instruments, also referred to as extended or hybrid instruments or hyperinstruments, are acoustic (sometimes electric) musical instruments extended by the addition of several sensors, providing performers the ability to control extra sound or musical parameters. The original instrument maintains all its default features in the sense that it continues to make the same sounds it would normally make, but with the addition of extra features that may tremendously increase its functionality.

The extensions to acoustic instruments may range from being very simple, such as including flexion sensors in drum brushes (Ng 2004), to highly developed sensor arrangements, such as those found in various hyperinstruments such as, for instance, the hyper-cello (Machover and Chung 1989; Machover 1992; Paradiso and Gershenfeld 1997).

Examples of instruments that have been augmented with sensors include flutes, trumpets, saxophones, guitars, pianos, double basses, violins, and trombones, among others. In fact, any existing acoustic instrument may be augmented to different degrees by the addition of sensors.

2.1.1 Examples of Augmented Instruments

Augmented pianos include the Disklavier piano, manufactured by Yamaha and used by composers such as Jean-Claude Risset (Risset and Duyne 1996) and David Jaffe and also widely used in music performance studies, as well as the Bösendorfer 290 SE piano (Moog and Rhea 1990).

String instrument examples include Peter Beyls's IR violin, developed in 1990 (Chadabe 1997); the "hyper" family of instruments developed at MIT by Tod Machover and collaborators (hyper-cello, hyper-viola, hyper-violin) (Machover 1992); and the augmented violin recently developed at IRCAM (Institut de Recherche et Coordination Acoustique/Musique) by Emmanuel Fléty and collaborators.

Curtis Bahn's SBass ("sensor bass") consisted of a five-string electric upright bass fitted with several sensors, including a touchpad mounted under the fingerboard, buttons, touch (position) sensors, force-sensing resistors (FSRs), rotary potentiometers, and a dual-axis accelerometer that senses slight movement and tilt (Bahn and Trueman 2001). Several pickups have also been added, such as a contact microphone placed under the hair of the tip of the bow (Figure 2.2).

An electric guitar example was developed by Bert Bongers for Gil Wasserman (Bongers 2000). Two augmented singing (or resonant) bowls have been developed, one by Atau Tanaka and Benjamin Knapp (2002) and used in Atau Tanaka's interactive piece *Tibet,* and the other, by Diana Young and Georg Essl (2003), using different sensor technologies (refer to section 2.4 for a discussion of the two singing bowl designs).

Figure 2.2 The SBass, designed by Curtis Bahn

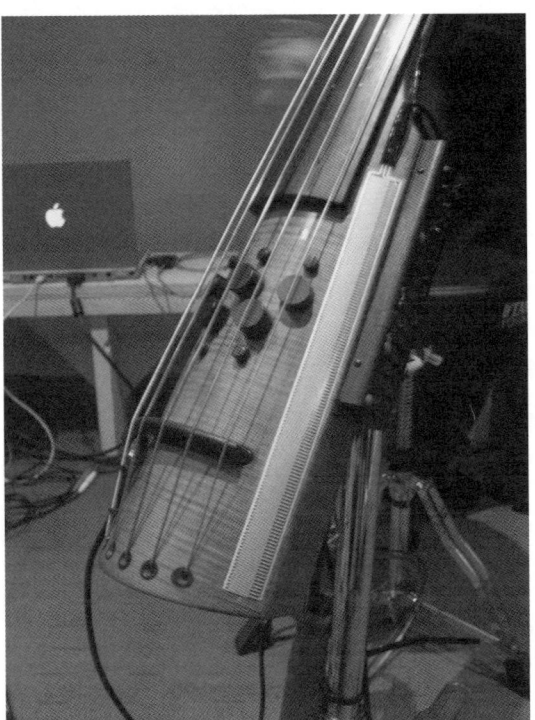

Matthew Burtner designed an instrument called the metasaxophone using FSRs (force-sensing resistors), triggers, and a dual-axis accelerometer (Burtner 2002). The FSRs were located on six keys (B, A, G, F, E, and D) and on two thumb rests. The triggers were located on the bell of the saxophone and below the thumb rests. The dual-axis accelerometer was located on the body of the instrument in order to sense the left–right and up–down tilts of the bell. Signals from the sensors were sent to a Basic Stamp microcontroller that sent out MIDI control messages.

Yoichi Nagashima and Tanami Tonu Ito (1999) developed an augmented sho, a traditional Japanese mouth organ that can be played using both directions of the breath stream. Sensors included touch switches used to detect finger position and an air pressure sensor placed in a tube that replaced one of the two decorative original bamboo tubes of the instrument.

Augmented trumpets. Perry Cook and Dexter Morrill (1989) built two augmented instruments based on the trumpet and the valve trombone. Pressure sensors (microphones) were placed on the mouthpiece of a trumpet and on the mute of a trombone for pitch detection, and on their horns for envelope following. Switches and linear potentiometers operated by the fingers or the thumb were mounted near the valves. Three switches mounted under the valves allowed for sensing of their positions (open or closed). These were actuated either by pressing the valves or pressing the switch actuator extensions below the valves. Foot pedals were also used as extra control variables.

Jonathan Impett and Bert Bongers created the meta-trumpet, an augmented trumpet using several sensors. Jonathan Impett proposed it as an instrument and composition environment built around a single instrument (Impett 1994). Several sensors were used to extend the acoustic trumpet:

- Ultrasound transmitters placed at the bell of the trumpet and receivers placed below and on the side of the performer in order to measure direction and speed of movement
- Two pressure sensors placed on the right of the third valve casing in order to measure finger pressure
- Two mercury switches to measure the angle of inclination of the instrument
- Magnetic field sensors to sense the position of magnets inserted in the bottom of the pistons
- Six switches used to change mappings or trigger musical events

Pitch and volume were obtained through analysis of the sound of the instrument using a pitch follower.

Augmented transverse flutes. The transverse flute is perhaps the most common acoustic instrument to be augmented with sensors. Different sensor technologies have been used depending on the goals of the various projects, allowing for the development of a variety of control strategies.

The most common additions to acoustic flutes are sensors on their keys to identify fingerings, such as in the MIDI flute, developed at IRCAM in the 1980s (Pousset 1992). However, fingering is just one of the possible control variables that can be obtained by augmenting a flute with sensors. Other variables can also be sensed, such as the inclination of the instrument, the rotation along its axis, its weight on the supporting fingers, and its distance to a reference

(Palacio-Quintin 2003), as well as information about the breath stream at the embouchure (da Silva, Wanderley, and Scavone 2005).

One may also note that since the flute is a monophonic instrument, pitch identification can be accomplished through indirect acquisition, that is, through analysis of the produced sound. However, one advantage of direct acquisition using sensors in the keys is that the fingering can be identified even when the flute is not being played (Ystad and Voinier 2001). Other control information that cannot be directly obtained from the analysis of sound, such as instrument inclination, can also be obtained with sensors. Problems with using sensors in this case include maintenance and obtrusiveness. Sensors and cabling may malfunction, and performers would need to learn how to play the sensors or adapt already learned performance techniques to control the desired variables. (Section 2.4.2 presents an overview of various segmented flutes.)

2.2 INSTRUMENT-LIKE AND INSTRUMENT-INSPIRED CONTROLLERS

Instrument-like controllers seek to model an existing acoustic instrument as closely as possible. Given the almost unlimited design possibilities offered by sensor technologies and electronics, why should one wish to design controllers that resemble existing acoustic instruments?

The obvious answer is that the great majority of performers play standard acoustic instruments. If the controller can be played like a standard instrument, then a large number of performers will be able to play the new controller without the need to develop new playing techniques. For instance, wind players are proficient at synchronizing tongue, breath stream, and finger muscles into a distinctive set of performance gestures that cannot be easily transposed to other control surfaces.

Another advantage is the potential use of an already learned playing technique to produce original sounds. Since gestural controllers can in theory play any sound imaginable in addition to those of their acoustic counterparts, performers can eventually play new sounds on an instrument-like controller using the playing techniques they have already mastered.

The problem is that it is no simple matter to play every sound perfectly using a specific gestural controller. As Michel Pascal (1999) suggests, "Instrumental gesture conditions the sound, and it is often not difficult to detect that a sound perfectly imitating a brass is in reality played from a keyboard." Control of articulation and sound modulation depends heavily on the characteristics of the control surface. Some controllers are simply not adapted to control certain sound events. For instance, with traditional MIDI keyboards, controlling the complex attacks typical of woodwinds often produces unsatisfactory results. Another potential problem with this approach is that instrument-like controllers will most probably inherit the limitations of the original instrument's design—for instance, ergonomic deficiencies, if any.

Despite the debate over whether it is worthwhile to make gestural controllers that are directly modeled on acoustic instruments, several instrument-like controllers exist and are available commercially. Also, they are used by a wide range of performers wanting to expand the musical possibilities of their instrumental technique.

2.2.1 Controllers That Model Acoustic Instruments

The keyboard type of instruments is prominently represented in the class of instrument-like controllers. Several controllers simulate the control surface of keyboard instruments by including weighted keys and the simulation of key mechanisms for realistic passive-force feedback simulation of the piano. Also, several wind instrument controllers are available commercially, indicating that wind instruments also seem to be a very popular model for instrument-like controllers.

Perhaps the controller that followed an existing wind instrument most closely was the synthophone, designed by Martin Hurni at Softwind Instruments in Switzerland. The synthophone was in fact an alto saxophone with the addition of several sensors. It cannot be considered an augmented instrument, like Matthew Burtner's metasaxophone, discussed earlier, because the synthophone did not produce acoustic sounds, just MIDI signals.

Considering controllers built from scratch to reproduce features of acoustic instruments, several wind instrument controllers exist, including commercial models by Akai and Yamaha. The Akai EWI (electronic woodwind instrument) line was based on Nyle Steiner's original EWI design. A wealth of information on the EWI and also on Steiner's EVIs (electronic valve instruments) can be found online at http://www.ewi-evi.com (accessed 1 July 2005) reference page for EWI and EVI players.

The Yamaha WX series, comprising the WX7, WX11, and, more recently, WX5 models, attempted to simulate the control surface of a saxophone by capturing the player's lower lip pressure using a plastic reed, breath pressure using a pressure sensor, and fingering with discrete keys; the plastic reed did not vibrate. In addition to saxophone-related features, several octave keys were available, allowing for a total range of seven octaves (in the WX5), as well as a pitch-bend wheel for continuous pitch variations. This range was much larger than that of an acoustic saxophone. The WX5 model also allowed for the simulation of the control surface of a recorder by changing the mouthpiece to a device without the reed.

2.2.2 Controllers Inspired by Acoustic Instruments

Slightly further from instrument-like controllers are devices that do not seek to reproduce exactly the control surfaces of existing acoustic instruments, yet their designs are directly derived from or inspired by the control surfaces of existing instruments. These controllers are referred to as instrument-inspired controllers.

The final form of an instrument-inspired controller can be substantially different from that of its original acoustic model. This can render the controller somewhat difficult to differentiate from alternate controllers; as can be seen later in this chapter, some controllers inspired by acoustic instruments can indeed be referred to as alternate controllers.

Instrument-inspired controllers require somewhat familiar gestural vocabularies inherited from the acoustic instruments by which they were inspired, therefore enabling access to performers who are familiar with such instruments. But unlike instrument-like controllers, these gestural vocabularies can be only partially transferred to the controllers. Indeed, one of the rationales for designing instrument-inspired controllers rather than instrument-like controllers is the possibility of overcoming the intrinsic limitations of the control surfaces of existing acoustic instruments.

Examples of instrument-inspired controllers. In the late 1970s, Max Mathews developed the sequential drum, a rectangular surface hit with the hands or a drumstick (Mathews and Abbott 1980). The strength of the strokes was measured with contact microphones (proportional to the amplitude of the signal) and the x and y positions, through grounding wires in a grid (29 x-sensing and 17 y-sensing wires). Four signals were obtained: a trigger pulse when the surface was hit, the amplitude of the stroke, and the x and y positions of the stroke, with a spatial resolution of approximately 2 cm in each direction.

The VideoHarp, by Dean Rubine and Paul McAvinney, is a well-known example of an instrument-inspired controller using neon light and light-sensitive memory cells to detect finger positions and other performance gestures (Rubine and McAvinney 1988). Yoichi Nagashima (1998) designed another harp-inspired controller, the harp sensor, using 13 vertical and 3 horizontal optical fibers placed on a wooden rectangular frame. The 13 vertical fibers (or "strings") were configured as in a classical harp, whereas the 3 horizontal ones were configured to allow for octave changes.

Another interesting example is the Accordiatron, designed by Michael Gurevich and Stephan von Muehlen (2001), its basic layout inspired by the squeezebox or the concertina.

With respect to wind instruments, one early example is the microprocessor-based digital flute (Yunik, Borys, and Swift 1983, 1985). Inspired by an acoustic transverse flute, this controller consisted of 10 switches and 2 control knobs mounted on a plastic tube, with a microphone located at the end of the tube sensing blow pressure. When the device was blown, the information obtained by the microphone controlled the attack, sustain, and decay of the tone produced. The blowing noise could be mixed with the synthesized tone to produce a breathy sound quality; the mixing could be adjusted by one of the control knobs.

Contrary to the normal fingering on a transverse flute, the microprocessor-based digital flute used an alternate fingering arrangement with notes on the staff directly related to the keys on the device. In order to play a note located on a line, the performer simply depressed the key corresponding to that line. In order to play a note located between two lines, the two keys corresponding to the lines above and below the note had to be depressed simultaneously. Any note could be sharped or flatted by simply depressing either the sharp key or the flat key in conjunction with the other keys. A maximum of three keys could be depressed at one time, and invalid fingerings—that is, fingerings not in a scale from middle C to the C two octaves above—were discarded (Yunik, Borys, and Swift 1985).

The question of alternate fingering arrangements in instrument-inspired controllers is a very interesting one. Unlike with acoustic instruments, no intrinsic acoustic properties constrain fingering in gestural controllers; the designer is free to implement any fingering imaginable. The choice of fingerings is therefore an open question, whose answer is highly dependent on the needs of the end user of the controller. Another example of alternate fingering for wind controllers is the one used by Gerald Beauregard in his Bleauregard, described later in this chapter.

Finally, it is interesting to mention two trombone-inspired controllers: Nicholas Collins's low brass (trombone-propelled electronics; Collins 1991) and Mark Bromwich's meta-trombone (Bromwich

1997). Both controllers were based on trombone bodies modified by the insertion of various sensors but were not designed to provide trombone players with an augmented trombone. Furthermore, unlike the synthophone, which provided saxophone players with a saxophone-like controller, both the trombone-propelled electronics and the meta-trombone were used as general gestural controllers.

2.2.3 Expanded Keyboard Controllers

As mentioned before, keyboard controllers are a very common commercial example of instrument-like controllers. But various developments have been proposed in order to improve the sensing possibilities of keyboard controllers, most notably by Hugh Le Caine (G. Young 1989), Robert Moog (1982), John Snell (1983), and Lippold Haken and colleagues (Haken, Abdullah, and Smart 1992; Haken, Tellman, and Wolfe 1998). Some of these developments are discussed below.

One early example of improved keyboard instrument is the electronic sackbut, by Hugh Le Caine. In its 1948 version, the edges of the keys were carved into rounded shapes to allow for the application of lateral finger pressure to move the keys to the left or to the right, therefore changing the pitch of the instrument (G. Young 1989). Other improvements in the electronic sackbut included sensitivity to vertical forces applied to the keys, allowing for volume control; the "glide strip," which allowed for glissandi between two notes; and a complex timbre control device to be operated by the performer's left hand. From 1953 to 1957, Hugh Le Caine also designed and built the touch-sensitive organ. Its keyboard was built with spring-mounted, electrostatic keys (capacitive sensing) whose vertical positions were continuously sensed.

More recently, the multiply-touch-sensitive clavier, devised by Robert Moog, was able to measure the vertical position of the key (from which the key velocity could be calculated), the aftertouch, and the continuous finger position on the key in two dimensions (side to side and front to back). By sensing the vertical position of a key, the device was able to detect a continuous variable that could be used as another control variable. This is rather different from the method used to calculate key velocity in most electronic keyboards, which measures the time it takes to move between two points a known distance apart.

In the original design of the multiply-touch-sensitive clavier (Moog 1982), an optical measurement of the vertical key position using a light-emitting diode (LED) and a phototransistor was used, with a graduated-density photographic film to control the amount of light shining on the phototransistor. A capacitive sensor replaced the LED-photodiode pair in a later version of the device (Moog and Rhea 1990).

As for the 2D fingering position on the key, an electrically resistive film with wires attached to its four corners was placed on each key for capacitive sensing of the position of the fingers. The pressure applied to the keys after they had been depressed was initially sensed with conductive rubber forming one plate of a variable capacitor. The other plate was an aluminum strip running across the keyboard. Pressing the key caused the contact area to increase and consequently increased the capacitance. A resistive film placed on top of a closely spaced conductive grid on a circuit board later replaced this sensor. An increase in finger pressure reduced the resistance across the grid.

John Snell (1983) suggested another improvement to the traditional keyboard whereby the rear part of each black key sloped down until it merged in height with the white keys. This resulted in a flat region behind the keys. With appropriate position sensors (John Snell suggested using a resistive strip similar to the one used in the multiply-touch-sensitive clavier), this design allowed for pitch slides normally impossible with traditional keyboards, as well for as a variable number of keys, avoiding the normal 12-key-per-octave limitation.

Another interesting development is the Continuum, designed by Lippold Haken and colleagues (Haken, Tellman, and Wolfe 1998). In its most recent incarnation, the Continuum features a sensitive surface with similar dimensions to that of the piano, but it allowed for continuous control in three dimensions: x and y (position) and z (force). We will discuss the Continuum in more detail in section 2.4.8 below.

A number of other developments have attempted to include the missing feel of the piano (and to some extent the organ and the harpsichord) keys by including actuators (or transducers) to provide force feedback to the performer (Cadoz, Lisowski, and Florens 1990; Gillespie 1992b; Oboe and De Poli 2002). These designs will be analyzed later in this chapter, in section 2.5.3.

■ 2.3 ALTERNATE CONTROLLERS

Alternate controllers are not directly modeled on or necessarily inspired by existing acoustic instruments. These may take various forms, from controllers that are modeled on or extend everyday objects, such as coffee mugs (Cook 2001), to controllers inspired by the sound-producing mechanisms of insects (Smyth and Smith 2003). This makes for a great variety of design possibilities.

Alternate controllers can be classified according to some of their features. Axel Mulder (2000) proposes the following classification:

a. *Touch controllers*: alternate controllers that still require the performer to touch a physical control surface. These control surfaces can be mobile or fixed in space. This class of controllers provides a haptic representation to the performer.

b. *Expanded-range controllers*: alternate controllers that may require physical contact in a limited form or that do not require physical contact but have a limited range of effective gestures; that is, the performer can always "escape" the control surface (make movements without musical consequence).

c. *Immersive controllers*: alternate controllers with few or no restrictions on performer movements. The performer is in the sensing field all the time; he or she cannot "escape" the control surface.

Immersive controllers can be grouped according to the visualization of the control surface into the following categories (Mulder 2000):

a. *Internal controllers*: the control surface visualization is the physical shape of the human body itself.

b. *External controllers*: the control surface is visualized as separate from the performer's body. It may even be impossible to visualize it as a physical shape.

c. *Symbolic controllers*: the control surface is not visible; it requires some sort of formalized gesture set (sign language, conducting) to be operated.

Note that the classification of immersive controllers into internal, external and symbolic controllers takes into account the visualization of the virtual control surface and the mapping strategies used, rather than the types of physical control surface (input devices) available. For instance, according to Axel Mulder, a bodysuit such as the one he designed himself is considered an internal controller, while another bodysuit such as Yamaha's Miburi is considered a symbolic controller (Mulder 2000). Similarly, data gloves could be considered external or symbolic controllers, depending on the application.

Jörg Piringer (2001) extended Axel Mulder's classification by grouping immersive controllers into partially immersive and totally immersive controllers. Partially immersive controllers include data gloves and other devices that respond to just part of the human body. Fully immersive controllers respond to the whole body. With fully immersive controllers, physical gestures without a musical signification are not possible.

2.3.1 Touch Controllers

There are several designs of touch controllers. Basically, any controller that uses manipulative gestures but does not resemble existing acoustic instruments can be considered a touch controller.

Some alternate touch controllers track finger positions and pressure on a surface, allowing for an intuitive control of musical processes. The Rolky Asproyd, designed by Eric Johnstone (1985), is a touch controller that identifies one or several fingers placed on a transparent surface illuminated from the side (Figure 2.3). The illuminating light is totally contained inside the glass for measuring reflection angles greater than a given threshold value, while it quickly dissipates through refraction for angles smaller than the threshold, a phenomenon known as total internal reflection. When a finger touches the glass, light illuminates it and is reflected in all directions.

The device consists of a Plexiglas surface, a 300-watt halogen lamp, and a camera positioned below the glass plate. The exact coordinates of the bright spots that appear at the positions of the fingers could be calculated from the video signals, along with other information such as elongation, angle, and size of contact area between the finger and the plate. A CRT display is placed face down above the plate and can be viewed through a half-silvered mirror (Figure 2.4). This allows for the display of information that is superimposed on the touch surface and on the fingers.

Other examples of touch controllers include the Continuum (Haken, Abdullah, and Smart 1992, described in section 2.4.8); the MTC Express Pad (Figure 2.5), by Tactex Controls; and the Lemur (Figures 2.6 and 2.7), by Jazz Mutant. By using fiber-optic technology, the MTC Express Pad can identify multiple pressure regions on its surface. The Lemur uses a touch-screen surface that allows for visual feedback. In both controllers, the positions of multiple fingers can be sensed (and also pressure, in the case of MTC Express), but only Lemur provides direct visual feedback on finger position.

Figure 2.3 The Rolky Asproyd: (a) the full controller housed in a wooden case; (b) two examples of interaction with the device.

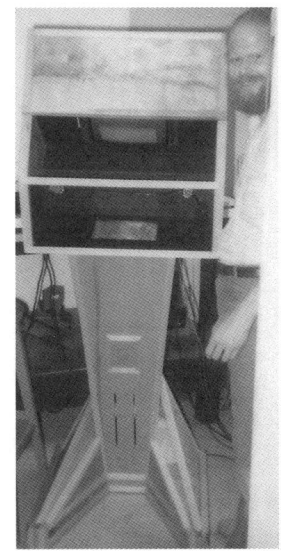

(a)

The Rolky Asproyd, view from below.

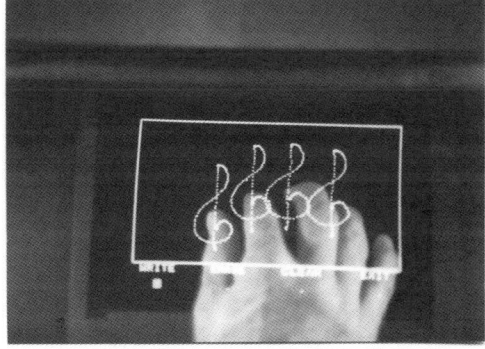

(b)

The Rolky Asproyd, operator's view as he draws with four fingers simultaneously.

Other finger-position-tracking controllers include the Buchla Thunder, with 36 pressure-sensitive elements; the Surface One, a prototype by Midiman; and the Stratifier, by Arie van Schutterhoef (2005). The later is able to output 16 continuous control variables using FSRs.

Another innovative touch controller design is the Matrix (an acronym for Multipurpose Array of Tactile Rods for Interactive eXpression), by Dan Overholt (2001), which consists of a matrix of 144 spring-mounted, vertically positioned acrylic rods in a 12 × 12 grid. The Matrix is a three-dimensional controller that allows for the control of fine details of timbre or other sound characteristics by the exertion of hand gestures and postures on the rods.

Figure 2.4   The Rolky Asproyd's schematics.

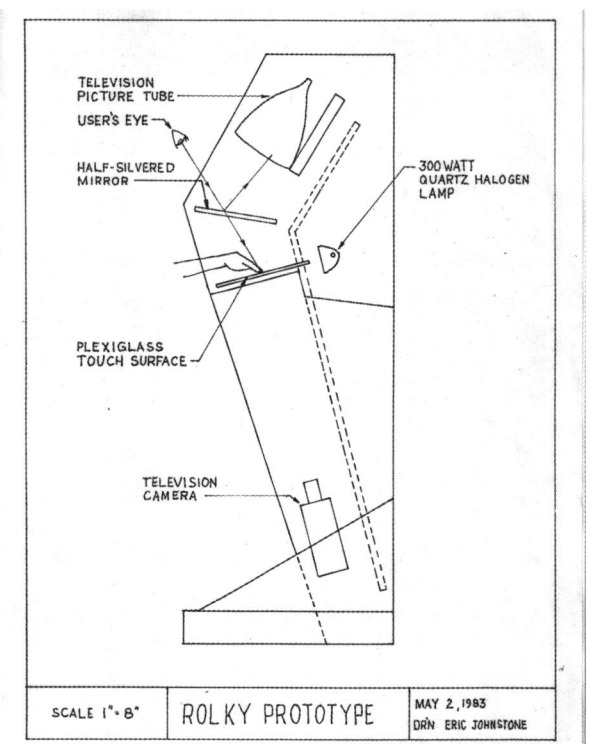

Figure 2.5   The MTC Express Pad, by Tactex Controls.

Figure 2.6 The Lemur, by Jazz Mutant. A prototype at the SPCL.

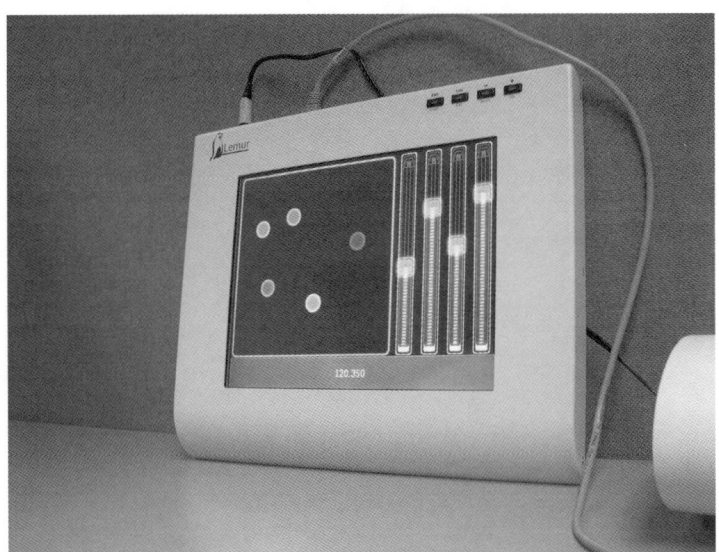

Figure 2.7 Interacting with the Lemur.

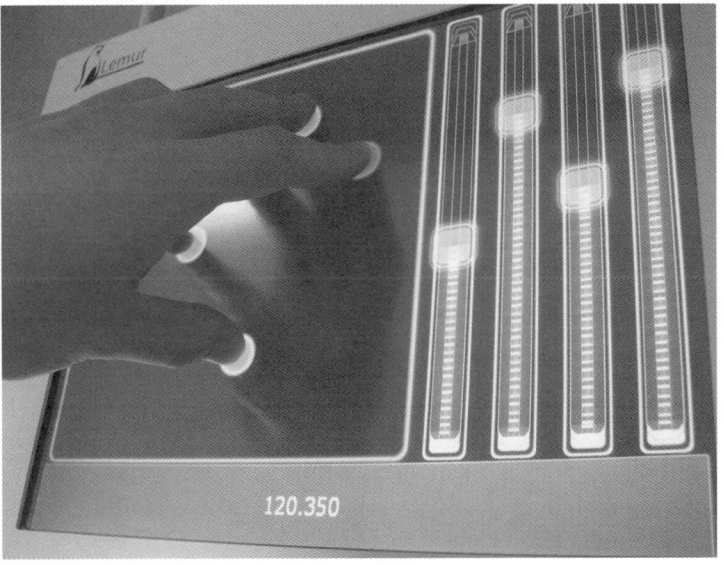

According to Axel Mulder's classification, touch controllers also include devices that allow for manipulation. There are various examples of such controllers. The Pacom, designed by Michel Starkier and Philippe Prevot (1986), can be considered a "control desk." Similar in shape to a mixing console, it houses various simple sensors and controllers such as linear and rotary potentiometers, shaft encoders, joysticks, and trackballs. In total, the Pacom has 24 sliders of various sizes, 2 multiturn potentiometers, two joysticks (with two and three degrees of freedom), 1 linear touch sensor, 6 shaft encoders (4 positioned vertically and 2 horizontally), 72 switches (of two different types), and 1 trackball. These amounted to 108 control devices, both discrete (on-off or step output) and continuous. The Pacom also had several LEDs, alphanumeric displays, and one alphanumeric liquid crystal display (LCD). The LEDs were associated to each control device and the alphanumeric displays to each of the shaft encoders, joysticks, and trackball, displaying their state.

In the mid-1990s, Roel Vertegaal and colleagues (1996) proposed a more flexible version of a control desk, in this case, a "musician's cockpit": the SensOrg Cyberinstrument. It uses several freely distributed sliders and knobs attached with magnets to various metal pad surfaces. All modules are mounted on gimbals attached to a rack with adjustable metal arms, allowing them to be placed in various positions or orientations. Other devices include a touch screen and the FingerprintR knob, which is a concave-shaped three-dimensional force sensor that conveys states of tension as exerted by changes in force by a finger. One interesting result of the SensOrg Cyberinstrument's inherent modularity is that it allows for the placement of sensors in positions that allow bimanual manipulation, where the dominant hand (usually the right hand) performs actions different from those performed by the nondominant hand.

More ecologically inspired touch controllers include the PebbleBox and the CrumbleBag, by Sile O'Modhrain and Georg Essl (2004). In the PebbleBox, real pebbles are placed inside a foam-padded box and the collisions between rocks are sensed using a microphone (Figure 2.8). A similar strategy is used in the CrumbleBag, where a flexible neoprene bag contains granular materials such as corn flakes, Styrofoam, or a metallic chain. In these cases, the control variables are derived from the analysis of the collision sound captured by the microphone. Basically, the sound is analyzed to obtain event detection in the temporal range of perception, amplitude, and spectral content measurements of the collision sounds. These variables are used to drive granular synthesis algorithms.

Both the PebbleBox and the CrumbleBag allow for direct haptic feedback inherent from the manipulation of real objects, but this feedback is obviously tied to the characteristics of the objects. It is also interesting to note that the interaction strategies are tied to the materials used. As the authors point out, each material suggests its own gestures: grabbing, dropping, tapping, crumbling, shuffling, rolling, and so forth.

As mentioned before, touch controllers can take any form. Brad Cariou's (1994) aXi0 Controller and Motohide Hatanaka's (2003) Bento-Box are based on industrial design and ergonomic considerations and do not resemble existing instruments. Other examples of alternate controllers include Michel Waizvisz's The Web, a groundbreaking design that responds with multiple, interdependent changes of parameters to single finger gestures (Waisvisz 2005); Walter Fabeck's Chromasone (Bongers 2000); Robert Huott's (2002) Ski; Laurel Pardue and Joe Paradiso's (2002) Musical Navigatrics; Mat Laibowitz's (2003) Basis (based on a DNA-like double helix shape); and Eric Singer's (2003) Sonic Banana, among many others.

Although not based on acoustic instruments, many of these controllers were inspired by or augment existing objects. An interesting exception is the SillyTone Squish Factory (Morris, Leitman, and Kassianidou 2004).

Figure 2.8   The PebbleBox, by Sile O'Modhrain and Georg Essl.

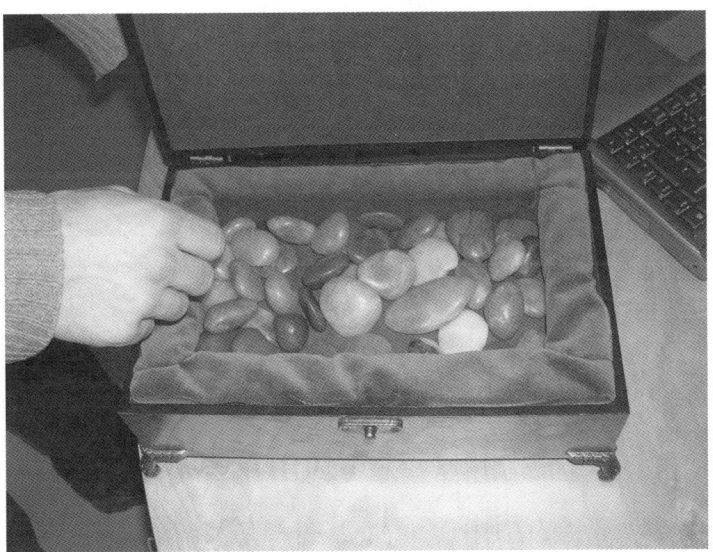

Another example of an existing object augmented by the use of sensors is the GyroTyre, a bicycle wheel mounted on a handle designed to take advantage of the precession effect (Sinyor and Wanderley 2005). The GyroTyre was built to exploit the physical behavior of a simple dynamic system: a spinning wheel (Figure 2.9). Several sensor technologies are used to measure the various possible movements. The phenomenon of gyroscopic precession causes the instrument to oscillate slowly when it is spun quickly, providing the performer with inherent proprioceptive feedback. Also, owing to the mass of the wheel and tire and the resulting rotational inertia, it maintains a relatively constant angular velocity once it is set in motion. The project also includes the implementation of a physical sequencer track, where the rotation of the wheel corresponds to one measure of music and sensors placed around the track can trigger repeating musical events, such as drum beats.

2.3.2 Expanded-range Controllers

The Radio Baton (also referred to as the Radio Drum), designed by Max Mathews and Bob Boie, consists of two batons (emitters), a receiving antenna board, and a control unit that tracked the three-dimensional movements of the two batons (Figure 2.10). Each baton

Figure 2.9 The GyroTyre, an alternate controller built to exploit the physical behavior of a spinning wheel

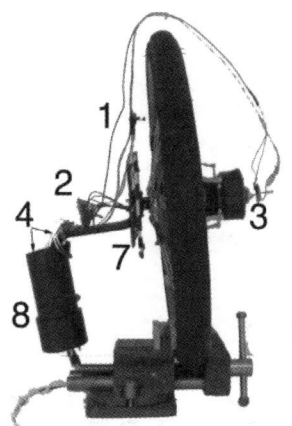

Figure 1: 1. Hall-effect sensor 2. Two-axis accelerometer 3. Gyroscope sensor 4. Force-sensing resistors 5. Magnet 6. Photodiode 7. Optical Sequencer Track 8. Handle

Figure 2.10 The Radio Baton, by Max Mathews and Bob Boie.

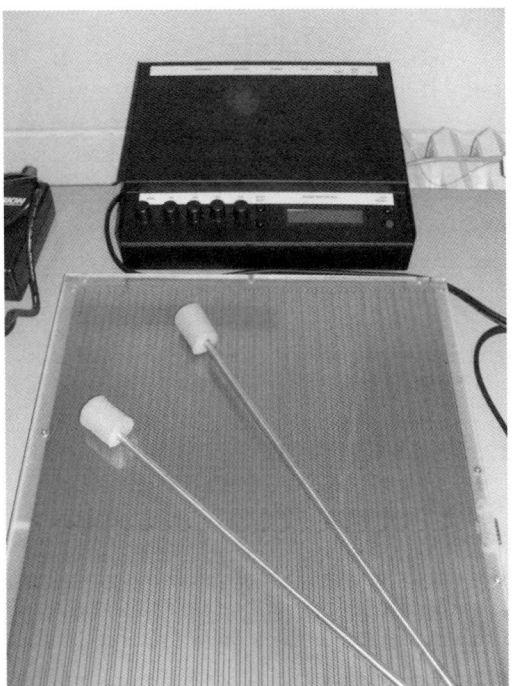

generates a signal with a specific frequency (50 kilohertz [kHz] and 55 kHz, respectively) so that it can be tracked individually by the receiving antennas (Mathews 2000). Apart from tracking the x, y, and z coordinates, the Radio Baton is also able to output trigger signals—for instance, when a baton generates a rapid down-up stroke. Two foot-pedal switches and four potentiometers can also be connected to the control unit.

The Radio Baton uses electric field sensing (capacitive sensing), where the baton acts as the first electrode and a receiving antenna as the second one. The distance between the electrodes influences the capacitance value (refer to chapter 3 for a discussion on electric field sensing and other sensing techniques). The Radio Baton has been widely used by various performers and composers to control prerecorded sequences of notes, to navigate in three-dimensional-parameter spaces, or as a percussion instrument. In the last case,

Andrew Schloss and Peter Driessen (2001) bypassed the control unit to increase the responsiveness of the controller: they relayed the raw analog signals from the antennas directly to a host computer, where digital signal-processing techniques were used to extract movement data.

The Buchla Lightning II, designed by Don Buchla, is based on two hand-held wands that emit infrared signals captured by a remote head placed in front of the performer (Figure 2.11). The horizontal and vertical positions of each wand can be individually tracked, allowing for four independent coordinates. Switches are also placed in the wands, allowing for extra control variables.

Apart from the different sensing technologies employed in the Radio Baton and in the Buchla Lightning II, one can see that the former provides three-dimensional position sensing and the latter is two-dimensional.

A more subtle difference is the frame of reference for the gestures employed: in the Radio Baton, the reference is the antenna board, usually placed horizontally on a table in front of the performer. In the Buchla Lightning II, the reference is the remote head in front of the performer, usually placed on a microphone stand. Placing the

Figure 2.11   The Buchla Lightning II, by Don Buchla.

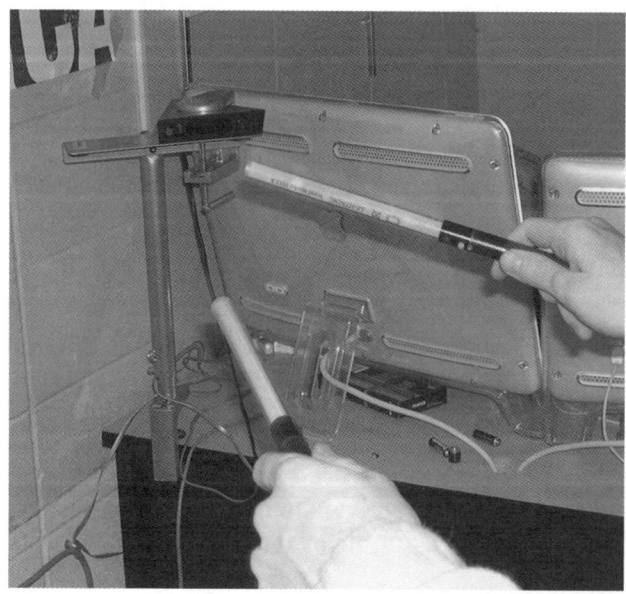

receiving antenna board on a wall allows for a similar reference, but the (wired) batons need to be close to the antenna for a strong enough signal to be obtained. In the Buchla Lightning II, the performer stands holding the wireless IR wands several meters away from the receiving head, making it less obtrusive. Depending on the use, one controller could be more adapted than the other.

A comparative summary is given below:

Controller	Radio Baton	Buchla Lightning II
Authors	Max Mathews and Bob Boie	Donald Buchla
Reference	Mathews 2000	http://www.buchla.com (accessed 1 July 2004)
Technology	Electric field sensing (capacitive sensing)	Infrared
Baton/wand	Wired batons	Wireless wands
Main output variables	Individual tracking of two batons in three dimensions	Individual tracking of two wands in two dimensions
Feedback	Auditory feedback (from host computer)	Auditory feedback (from internal synthesizer or host computer) and minimum visual feedback at the remote sensing head

Michel Waisvisz created Hands in the early 1980s to improve the use of hand and arm gestures and finger movements and pressures in sound control (Waisvisz 1985). The initial Hands prototype was based on two ergonomically shaped aluminum plates and provided sensing of the distance between the hands (through time-of-flight ultrasound sensing; see chapter 3), hand-tilt sensing using mercury switches, and various multifunctional switches and potentiometers. A second version was developed in the late 1980s in collaboration with Bert Bongers and was based on a single wooden frame for each hand. The Hands are worn by the performer on both hands, but unlike that of partially immersive controllers such as data gloves, the Hands' control surface consists of a device whose shape is not identical to the shape of the hands.

The MidiConductor is a modified version of Hands: one side is identical to the original Hands design, but the other was a handlebar device similar to bicycle handlebars. The MidiConductor was used by Edwin van der Heide to perform in the SensorBand (Bongers 1998a).

The meta-instrument, initially designed by Serge de Laubier and colleagues in the late 1980s (de Laubier 1998, 2000) allows for 32 simultaneous continuous control variables. Across three versions, designed in 1989, 1996, and 2005, respectively, the meta-instrument was a symmetrical structure for the left and right arms. Its second version employed ten pressure-sensitive keys forming two rows of five keys each on a handle. One finger could play four keys simultaneously with longitudinal and lateral movements. Two other keys were available for the thumbs. The handle was articulated around one axis and was itself connected to an elbow with two degrees of freedom. Counterweights behind the elbow were used to maintain the system in equilibrium (de Laubier 2000). The performer sat on a chair and laid his or her arms on the device, gripping the handle to access the keys. The third version of the meta-instrument uses wireless technology and is worn by the performer (so that it becomes a partially immersive controller), allowing for a much more flexible interface (Figure 2.12).

Figure 2.12 The third generation of the meta-instrument, by Serge de Laubier.

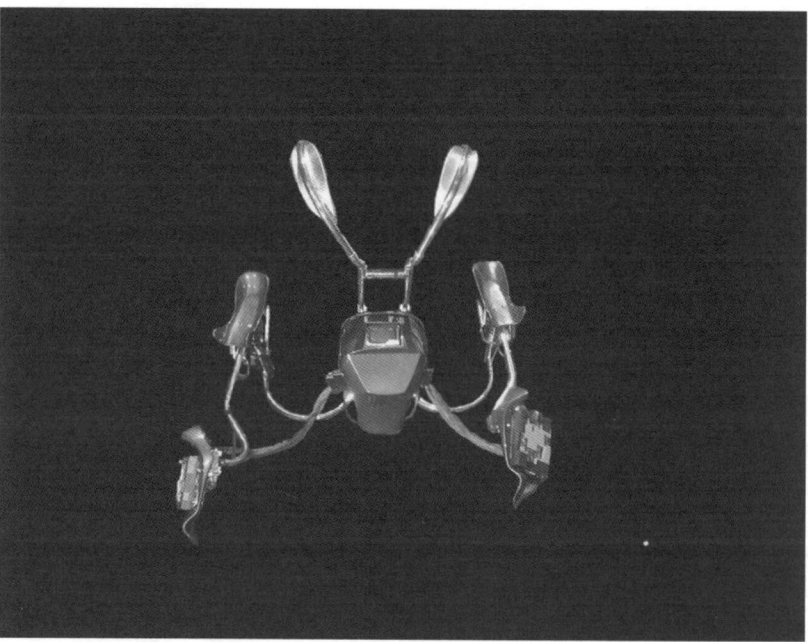

2.3.3 Immersive Controllers

As mentioned above, immersive controllers present few or no restrictions to performer movements—that is, the performer is always inside the sensing field.

Examples of partially immersive controllers include several data gloves—for instance, Laetitia Sonami's Lady's Glove, developed by Bert Bongers (Bongers 2000); Joseph "Butch" Rovan's FSR Glove; and commercial examples such as Mattel's Power Glove and Exo's Dexterous Hand Master, used by Tod Machover to perform his composition *Bug Mudra*. Another commercial product, the VPL Dataglove, was used by Axel Mulder in various experiments on mapping strategies (Mulder 2000).

Wayne Siegel and Jens Jacobsen's (1998) Digital Dance Interface, developed at DIEM (Danish Institute for Electronic Music), could also be considered a partially immersive controller, since it is worn by the dancer and allows for the measurement of joint angles in the elbows and knees. Another interesting musical application example is the Exoskeleton, described by Sergi Jordà (2002) and consisting mostly of potentiometers and mercury switches to measure limb position.

Fully immersive controllers include several body suits, such as Yamaha's Miburi, Mark Bromwich and Julie Wilson's Bodycoder (1998), and a body suit developed by Suguru Goto (2000). Body suits are also very common in motion tracking, such as for animation and virtual-reality applications (Burdea and Coiffet 2003).

■ 2.4. FOOD FOR THOUGHT: EXAMPLES AND DISCUSSION

In most cases, there are various options regarding the choice of sensor technologies to design a controller or perform a certain task. In this section we analyze a few case studies, highlighting the various possibilities for designing, classifying, and choosing from the various options of available gestural controllers.

2.4.1 Instrument-like, Instrument-inspired, or Alternate Controller?

The classifications discussed in this book should be thought of as pedagogical means to help one follow the developments in this fascinating area of computer music, rather than as a fixed labeling system.

In fact, the proposed classification of controllers introduced in this chapter has obvious limitations. Two examples are the BoSSa (introduced below) and the SuperPolm, controllers largely derived from the violin.

Dan Trueman and Perry Cook (1999) designed the BoSSA (Bowed-Sensor-Speaker-Array), a novel device inspired by the functioning of the violin. Its control surface consists of a modified violin bow, the R-Bow, augmented by the use of two FSRs mounted on soft foam in two locations between the bow stick and the hair. A dual-axis accelerometer is placed on the frog, allowing the measurement of relative position and motion in two dimensions and thus allowing the control of four continuous variables. The Fangerbored, a violin fingerboard, consists of a position sensor that can be played with the left hand, four FSRs that can be played with the right hand (which held the fingerboard), and another dual-axis accelerometer measuring tilt in two dimensions. In total, there are seven continuous data streams. Finally, there is the Bonge, a set of four foam-covered pieces of wood, each mounted in between two fixed FSRs. By bowing one of Bonge's "strings," data about the direction of the bow, pressure, and speed can be obtained. If bowed with the R-Bow, then a total of eight variables can be controlled: the four continuous Bonge parameters (one for each "string") and the four R-Bow variables.

Note that not all variables can be controlled simultaneously. For instance, one axis of the accelerometer in the Fangerbored cannot be used when the fingerboard is mounted on the BoSSA. Also, the four FSRs in the Fangerbored cannot be used when bowing the BoSSA because the right hand holds the bow.

Finally, it is important to mention BoSSA's complex sound-diffusion system. By using an array of 12 loudspeakers arranged on the surfaces of a dodecahedron, the authors are able to simulate the directivity characteristics of various acoustic instruments, such as the violin.

It is also worth noting that the authors built the BoSSA using only three types of commonly used sensors: FSRs, accelerometers, and a linear position sensor. This is an interesting lesson: it is not necessary to use the latest or most expensive sensor technology to obtain a sophisticated gestural controller.

The SuperPolm was created by Suguru Goto (2000) with the assistance of Patrice Pierrot and Alain Terrier at IRCAM. It is loosely based on a violin shape. In contrast to the violin, it does not have strings and is played with a hairless bow. Strings are replaced by four LuSense CPS^2 155 sensors (refer to chapter 3). These sensors are placed in pairs, forming a matrix that detects the position and pressure of a finger. It also contains an FSR in the chin rest, an accelerometer to measure tilt, and a numerical keyboard that allows the player to input numeric data.

Apart from the fact that the control surface is not exactly the same as that of a violin, Goto used the SuperPolm for very different purposes: to control granular synthesis and video sequences. This was a good example of a case where although the intention was to play the controller using violin-like gestures, the goal was not to create an electronic violin.

Considering the control surface of both controllers, the SuperPolm could be regarded as an instrument-inspired controller, while the BoSSA would be an alternate controller. With respect to the gestures used for performance, both still resemble the violin.

The same reasoning may be applied to the Radio Baton and the sequential drum. They can either be viewed as expanded-range alternate controllers (Mulder 2000) or as controllers inspired by acoustic drums.

2.4.2 Augmented Flutes

Four examples of augmented flutes are described in the literature. Perhaps the oldest example is the MIDI flute, designed at IRCAM. The initial version of the MIDI flute was built by Barry Vercoe and the flutist Lawrence Beauregard in the early 1980s using optical sensors installed on the keys of the flute and audio analysis to indicate the octave of the note played (Vercoe 1984).

The final prototype of IRCAM's MIDI flute was mainly designed by Michel Ducoureau, Michel Starkier, and Lawrence Beauregard (Pousset 1992). It consists of a transverse flute with threshold Hall effect sensors and magnets placed on rings around the keypads, so that fingerings can be identified and compared to fingerings stored in the control unit. No information is available on the absolute pitch of a note (Figure 2.13).

Figure 2.13 Detail of the Hall effect sensor and magnet on the MIDI flute. Note the black ring around the keypad holding the magnet.

IRCAM's MIDI flute was designed primarily to be used in the context of score-following systems, where a score was stored in the memory of a computer and the fingering information from the flute or other control variable indicated where the performer was in the score as the performance progressed. With this information, the computer could automatically adjust the performance of the accompaniment. The MIDI flute has been extensively used in various pieces, such as Pierre Boulez's . . . *explosante fixe* . . . and Philippe Manoury's *Jupiter*, among others. Having been used for several years, it is being gradually replaced by a commercial flute with indirect acquisition (i.e., audio signal processing) to identify the fingerings in order to avoid maintenance issues.

Perhaps the most interesting feature of the MIDI flute was that there were no cables connecting the sensors. A special flexible printed circuit board placed around the flute was created specifically for it. This printed circuit board allowed for a very elegant way to eliminate cabling in the instrument, which reduced the obtrusiveness of the sensor system (Figures 2.14 and 2.15).

Figure 2.14 The first prototype (top instrument) and the final version (bottom) of the MIDI flute. (The control unit where the fingerings are stored can be seen above the flutes.)

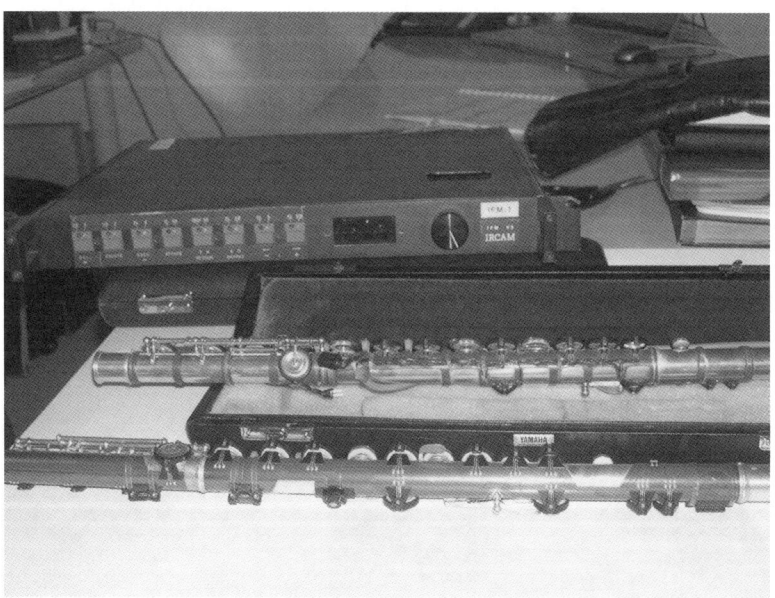

Figure 2.15 Note the cabling on the first prototype of the MIDI flute (a) and the curved printed circuit board on the final model (b).

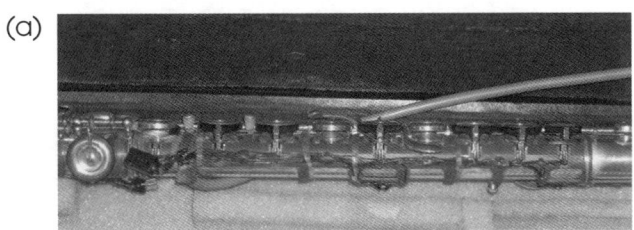

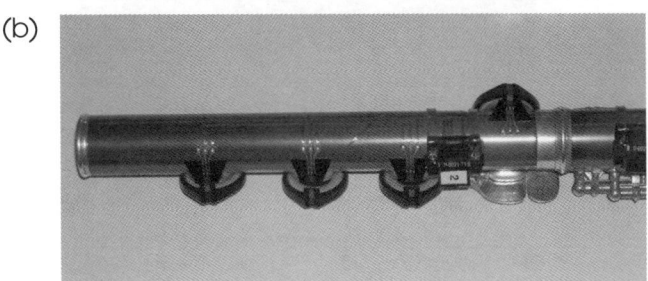

Sølvi Ystad and Thierry Voinier also developed an augmented flute called the LMA flute (Figure 2.16). They used linear Hall effect sensors and a microphone placed on a modified cork in order to measure acoustic pressure (Ystad and Voinier 1999). The pitch is determined by both the fingering information from the Hall effect sensors (Figure 2.17) and by the way in which the instrument is blown, sensed by the microphone on the modified cork (Figure 2.18).

The goal of this project was to use the augmented flute to control hybrid synthesis methods developed by Sølvi Ystad (1998). An interesting aspect of the LMA flute was the measurement of the speed with which a key was pressed or released. This information was used to control a synthesis algorithm simulating keypad noise.

Note in Figure 2.17 the different position of the magnet-sensor pair, compared to the MIDI flute shown in Figure 2.13. No rings are included on the keypads. Instead, a trail was placed with the Hall sensors on the backs of the keys.

Yet another approach to augmented flute design was proposed by Cléo Palacio-Quintin, who developed the hyper-flute using a large set of sensors (Palacio-Quintin 2003) (Figure 2.19). In contrast to the MIDI flute and the LMA flute, the hyper-flute does not output complete information on fingerings. Instead, it provides only the position of two keys (in 95 steps) and several other variables not taken into account by the other designs (Figure 2.20).

Figure 2.16 The LMA flute by Sølvi Ystad and Thierry Voinier.

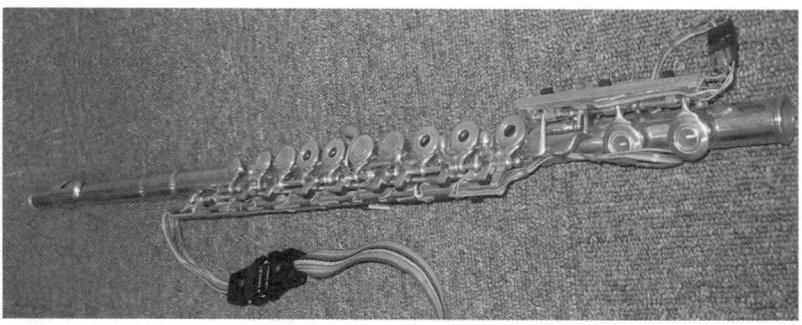

Figure 2.17 Detail of the LMA flute's Hall effect sensor and magnet.

Figure 2.18 Detail of the modified cork of the LMA flute featuring a microphone to sense pressure.

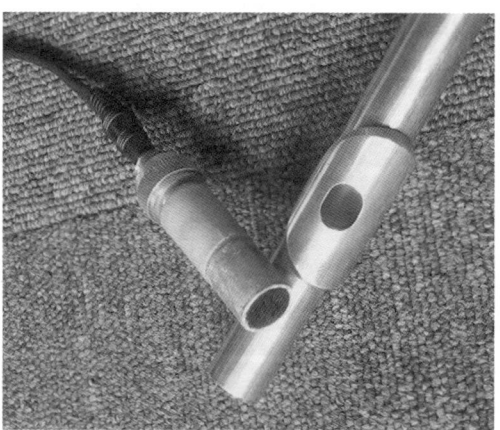

Figure 2.19 Cléo Palacio-Quintin playing the hyper-flute. (Photo by Carl Valiquet)

Figure 2.20 Note the cables from the sensors of the hyper-flute and part of the Microlab sensor interface placed on the back of the performer. (Photo by Carl Valiquet)

The main sensors used in the hyper-flute are:

- Magnetic field sensors (linear Hall effect) on two keys of the flute: G-sharp and low C-sharp
- Ultrasound sensors to measure the distance between the flute and the computer; the transmitter was placed on the computer monitor and the receiver on the flute
- Mercury tilt switches to measure tilt and rotation of the flute
- FSRs in contact points between the hand and the flute, under the left hand and both thumbs
- Several switches
- A light sensor to detect ambient light fluctuations

As mentioned before, it is important to note how the goal of the design will direct the choice of sensors to be used. One can identify several trends.

a. *Choice of Hall effect sensors*: Although the MIDI flute obtains fingering information using threshold sensors, therefore measuring only whether keys were open or closed, key position is continuously sensed with linear sensors in both the LMA flute and the hyper-flute.

b. *Number of keys sensed*: In the case of the hyper-flute, the strategy was not to obtain complete information about the fingering (as in the case of the MIDI flute and the LMA flute) but to provide two continuous control values for any musical purposes. The sensors were similar, but the goals were very different.

c. *Variety of sensors used*: A number of sensors are used in the hyper-flute, from mercury tilt switches to light-dependent resistors and ultrasound sensors. The previous two augmented flutes relied mostly on Hall effect sensors. The hyper-flute's approach allows for extra performance possibilities not directly related to classical flute techniques, but these require extensive learning.

d. *Cabling*: The MIDI flute used a flexible printed circuit board specially designed to be placed around the instrument to eliminate cabling from the sensors; minimum intrusiveness was a design goal in this case. In contrast to the MIDI flute, the cables are left visible on the other two flutes, and no attempt is made to hide them; in the hyper-flute cables are left unattached to the body of the device to avoid changing the flute's center of gravity owing to the weight of the cables toward the end of the instrument.

The unattached cables in the hyper-flute require that the performer adapt his or her playing technique to avoid disconnecting some of the sensors

One can also use sensors to obtain information on the flute's breath stream. Andrey da Silva and colleagues (da Silva, Wanderley, and Scavone 2005) built an augmented flute at McGill University with sensors to estimate the breath stream in the mouthpiece of a Boehm flute and used this information to control digital audio effects in real time. Because measuring the airflow at the embouchure of the flute is not a straightforward process, an alternate method for this measurement was found using a related parameter: the total air pressure close to the mouthpiece. This is obtained by using two probes mounted around the mouthpiece, as shown in Figure 2.21. The two probes are connected to a dual-input pressure sensor with sensitivity of approximately 0.02 volts per microbar (V/Pa). Because the sensor has two inputs, not only can the total pressure be sensed, but also the orientation of the breath stream with respect to the flute axis. This is calculated by taking the pressure difference between the two inputs.

Figure 2.21 Breath sensor and tubes to measure airflow in the mouthpiece of the flute.

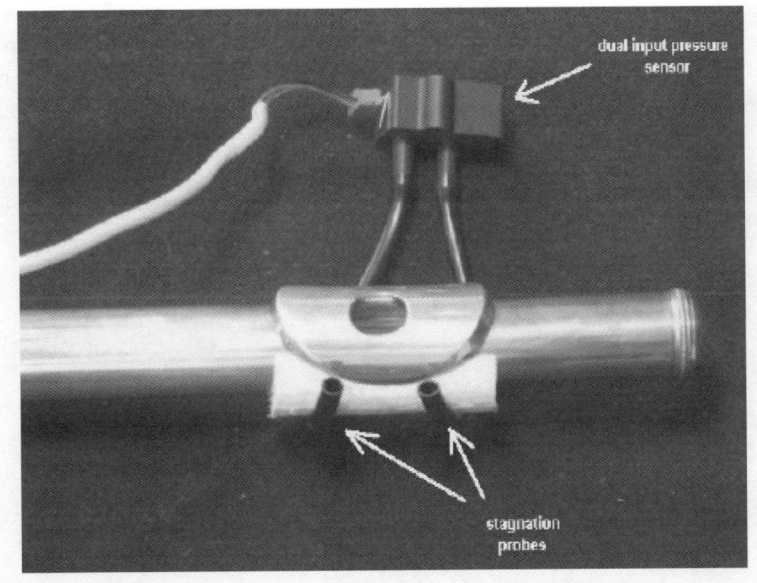

Another interesting feature of da Silva's design is the addition of an actuator attached to the neck of the performer to provide tactile feedback about the intensity of the breath stream being captured by the pressure sensor. The amplitude of the vibration of the actuator is proportional to the energy put into the pressure sensor; its frequency is fixed. In this case, the actuator was intended to aid the performer to learn how to control the sensors on the flute.

A comparative summary of the four augmented flutes discussed in this section is given as follows:

Augmented Flute	MIDI Flute	LMA Flute	Hyper-flute	Andrey da Silva's device
Authors	Michel Ducoureau, Michel Starkier, & Lawrence Beauregard	Sølvi Ystad and Thierry Voinier	Cléo Palacio-Quintin	Andrey da Silva, Marcelo M. Wanderley, and Gary Scavone
Reference	Pousset 1992	Ystad and Voinier 1999	Palacio-Quintin 2003	da Silva, Wanderley, and Scavone 2005
Variables	Key position (on-off)	Key position (continuous sensing) and sound amplitude	Key position (continuous sensing of only 2 keys), inclination, rotation of the flute, distance to the computer monitor	Total air pressure (around the mouthpiece) and the weight of the flute on the thumb
Sensors and actuators	Hall effect (on-off)	Hall effect (linear) and a microphone	Hall effect (linear), ultrasound, mercury switches, FSRs, LDR, switches and an external microphone	Air pressure (dual), FSR, and actuator to relay the intensity of vibration to the neck of the performer
Main purpose	Score-following control	Sound synthesis control	Interactive music control	Research

2.4.3 Augmented Singing Bowls

It is interesting to note that one can create controllers (or augmented instruments) that work similarly using very different sensing technologies. This section discusses two recent developments on augmenting Tibetan singing (resonant) bowls, one by Atau Tanaka and Benjamin Knapp, the other by Diana Young and Georg Essl.

Atau Tanaka and Benjamin Knapp (2002) used a gyroscope to sense the rotational velocity of the stick and the BioMuse EMG controller (Tanaka 1993). These two sensing technologies provide complementary means to sense gestural variables. In fact, the authors suggest that EMG sensors are superior at measuring isometric activity, where tension changes without altering the device's position (refer to chapter 4 for more information on EMGs). Localized motion sensors (also called inertial sensors), such as accelerometers and gyroscopes, are superior at measuring isotonic activity, where motion occurs without change in tension.

Diana Young and Georg Essl (2003) designed the hyper-puja, an augmented Tibetan singing bowl using dual-axis accelerometers, Hall effect sensors, and a pressure-sensitive (conductive) rubber in the puja (stick) to sense the pressure of the stick on the bowl. All sensor signals are sent to the host computer through wireless communication to avoid cabling.

An interesting aspect to consider in these two developments is the measurement of rotational velocity: the former measures this with a gyroscope, but the latter places magnets inside the singing bowl and uses two Hall effect sensors to detect the presence of magnetic fields. By counting the number of peaks in the sensor output over time (indicating a magnetic field), one can obtain the velocity of the stick.

2.4.4 Instrument-inspired Wind Controllers

Apart from Yunik, Borys, and Swift's microprocessor-based digital flute, described in section 2.2.2, several wind controllers inspired by existing acoustic instruments have been proposed in the literature. Gerald Beauregard (1991) designed the Bleauregard, a wind controller modeled on existing reed instruments (e.g., saxophones and clarinets), but it does not follow their original fingering schemes (which are based on the acoustics of columns of air in tubes). Instead, the Bleauregard uses a fingering scheme based on a modified Gray code, where only one bit of information changes from one state to the next. (Gray code is an ordering of 2^n binary numbers such that only one bit changes from one entry to the next. Gray codes for four or more bits are not unique, even allowing for permutation or inversion of bits.) This allows nonexpert performers to learn a more intuitive fingering arrangement, where notes close to each other have fingerings that do not differ greatly. Furthermore, only four right-hand fingers are used to select notes: the right thumb is left free to support the tube. Because four fingers give a total combination of 16 possible fingerings, Gerald Beauregard chose to include four extra notes besides the twelve notes in the scale. This fingering allows the performer to execute semitone trills by moving just one finger, with the exception of the starting note (Figure 2.22). Compare this fingering scheme with the one implemented in the microprocessor-based digital flute described in section 2.2.2.

Figure 2.22 The fingering scheme of the Bleauregard (12-cycle four-bit Gray code).

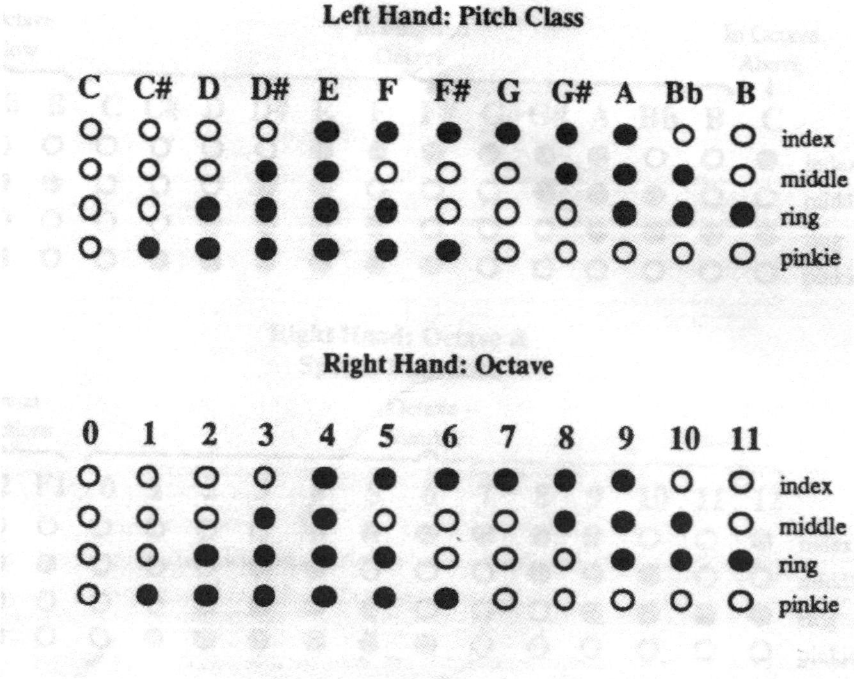

Another feature of the Bleauregard is its octave control: the four fingers of the left hand can control 16 variables; the left thumb is also free to support the device. A 12-octave range that extrapolates the MIDI note range was implemented. It offers more possibilities than other instrument-like woodwind controllers, such as the Yamaha WX5 controller discussed in section 2.2.1.

Finally, the Bleauregard features both drawing (inhaling) and blowing for breath control, a common performance practice with the harmonica. It was suggested, for example, that when the player draws a note, it could be stored in a queue and played together with blown notes, augmenting the possibilities of the instrument.

The MIDI horn was designed and built by John Talbert for Gary Lee Nelson in the 1980s (Chadabe 1997). It has been employed in a series of pieces and widely performed by Nelson. A brass instrument's mouthpiece can be attached to the breath controller to better capture the airflow, sensed by a pressure sensor (Figures 2.23 and 2.24).

Several pushbuttons are used in the MIDI horn: seven at the front side of the horn (placed in groups of four and three buttons) and one at the back. The first group of four keys simulates the four valves in some brass instruments (or three in trumpets). Each key lowers the pitch of the instrument by a different number of semitones: the first valve corresponds to two semitones, the second valve to one semitone, the third valve to three semitones, and the

Figure 2.23 The original MIDI horn design.

fourth valve to five semitones. The total combination of the four valves allows the performer to produce a chromatic scale of twelve different pitches.

Since the breath controller in the MIDI horn does not respond to the buzzing of the performer's lips to control register (as in acoustic brass instruments), three pushbuttons were added for this purpose. These three buttons allow for eight octaves of control. The fingering pattern is identical to that using the first three valves of an acoustic horn, but the subtracted interval is an octave instead of a semitone. The back button is operated by the thumb of the right hand and it controls several MIDI voice-change messages: when pressed, the front seven keys are interpreted as a seven-bit MIDI program number. Finally, a slider placed at the back of the horn allows for another continuous MIDI parameter—for instance, key velocity control.

Figure 2.24 The original MIDI horn design by John Talbert and Gary Lee Nelson.

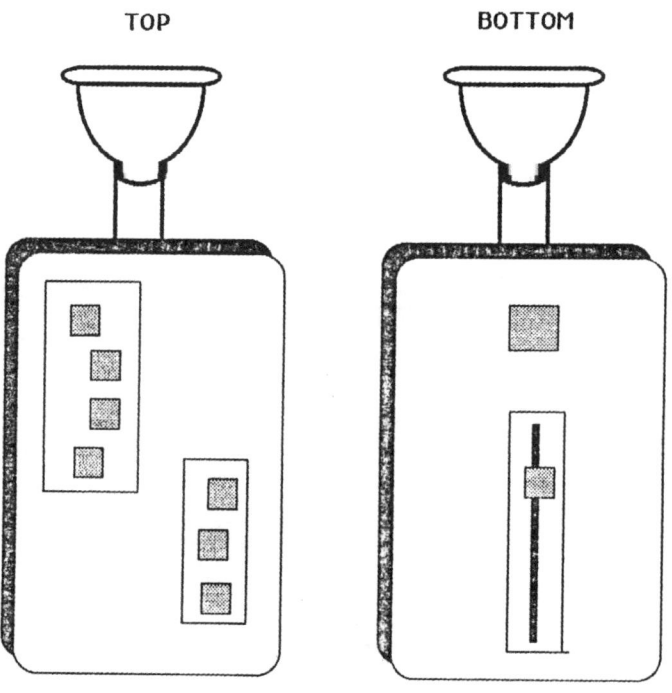

The main differences between the original MIDI Horn and its current version are:

- key velocity is sensed by changes of air pressure at the onset of notes;
- the 8th button (program change) was moved from the back to the front; and
- the back has eight more buttons that are mapped onto MIDI controls 84–91 and two joysticks mapped onto MIDI controllers 16–19.

Perry Cook (1992) developed another example: the Hirn, a MIDI-based controller. The Hirn was designed with the intention of allowing performers to effectively use the extra control bandwidth available in the mouth and hands. It extrapolates the capabilities of traditional wind instrument interfaces and was inspired by several acoustic wind instruments, providing linear slide control (as with the trombone), valve control (as with the trumpet), and fingering control (as with woodwinds), as well as control from the lip and breath pressure. The Hirn can sense rotation and translation in both hands, arm orientation, independent control with each finger, breath pressure, bite tension, and muscle tension of the upper lip using a myoelectric sensor (Cook 2001; Figure 2.25).

Figure 2.25 The Hirn, a wind controller designed by Perry Cook.

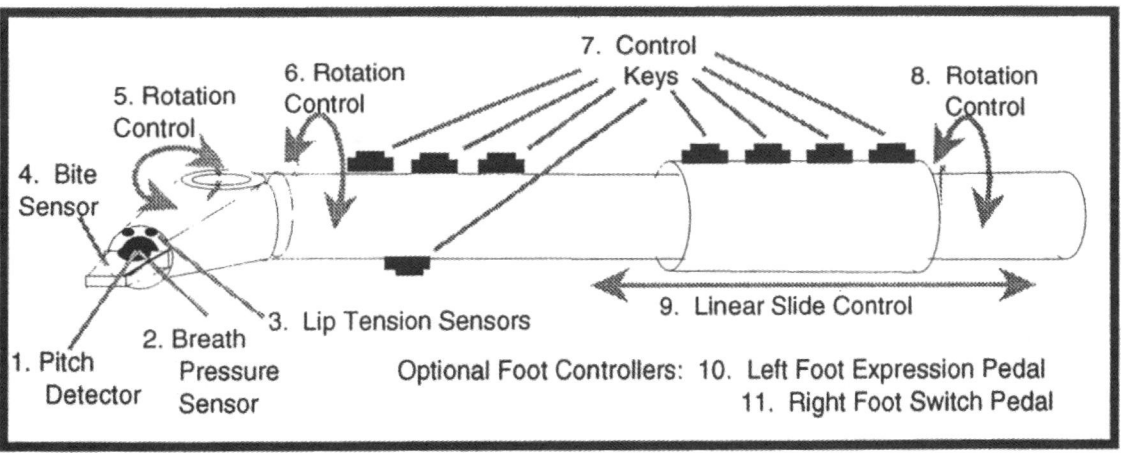

Finally, Gary Scavone (2003) designed the Pipe, a wind controller inspired by existing wind instruments, particularly the recorder, with several modifications, including the ability to use static-flow breath pressure and an alternate interface for breath pressure to allow device sharing (Figure 2.26). Static-flow breath pressure is obtained by closing the end of the tube opposite the mouthpiece, which is obviously not possible with acoustic wind instruments.

Figure 2.26 The Pipe and its layout diagram: (a) top view; (b) bottom view; (c) diagram.

(a)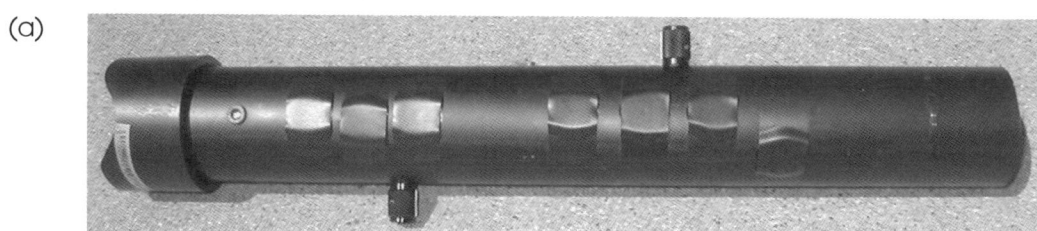

(b)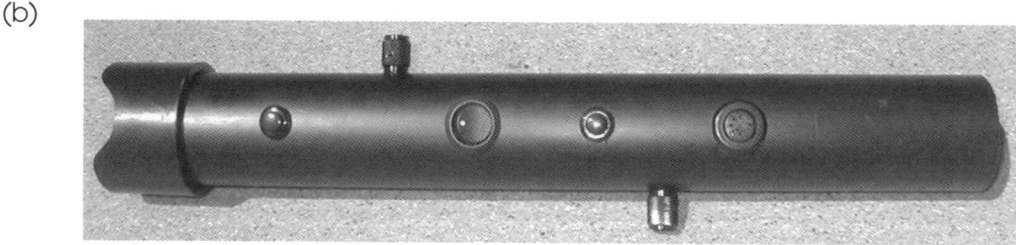

(c)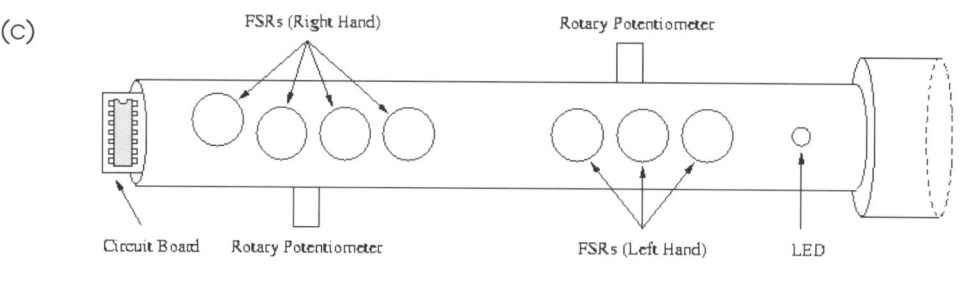

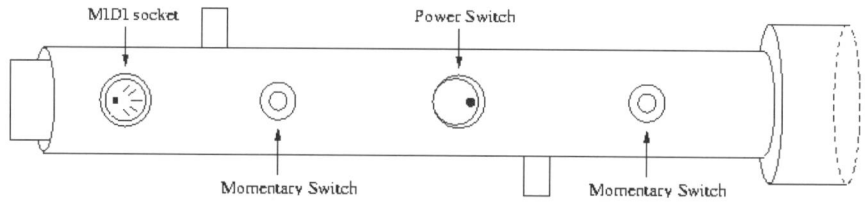

The Pipe basically consists of a compact tube, with seven FSRs placed on finger depressions drilled along its length. These are used for continuous sensing of fingering. The fingering scheme of the Pipe is similar to that of the recorder (the musical instrument). There is also a mouth cap that is positioned against the face of the performer, beyond the mouth and lips. This is intended to minimize hygienic concerns. The Pipe also features other sensors, such as dual-axis accelerometers, rotary potentiometers, and momentary switches.

Although inspired by the recorder, the Pipe was designed to overcome the limitations of this instrument, which in this case are airflow dynamics, discrete fingering, and the shape of the mouthpiece.

A comparative summary of the four instrument-inspired wind controllers discussed in this section is given as follows:

Controllers	MIDI Horn	Bleauregard	Hirn	Pipe
Authors	John Talbert and Gary Lee Nelson	Gerald Beauregard	Perry Cook	Gary Scavone
Reference	Chadabe 1997	Beauregard 1991	Cook 1992	Scavone 2003
Inspiration	The French horn	Wind instruments in general	Wind instruments in general	The recorder
Main features	A slider controlled by thumb and several switches; senses blow pressure with a horn type of mouthpiece	A new fingering scheme based on a modified Gray code, twelve octaves; senses both blowing and drawing	Translation and rotation of both hands, arm orientation; mouthpiece can be rotated to vary playing style (e.g., saxophone vs. flute)	Senses inclination, continuous fingering and static blow pressure; features a hygienic mouthpiece
Main purpose	To create a MIDI wind controller	To overcome the limitations of existing wind controllers	To provide extra control bandwidth	To explore various breath-control possibilities and physical models

2.4.5 Sensing Foot Movements

There are basically three options for sensing foot movements: the use of video cameras, either visible light cameras or infrared cameras and markers placed on the feet or shoes; the use of a sensing surface (or a sensitive floor); or the use of sensors on specially designed shoes or boots. We will not discuss camera-based systems in this text, but such systems are widely used for gait analysis in medical and physical rehabilitation tasks.

The other two options can be combined in one development, as in the PodoBoard, discussed below. The difference is related to the reference point: in the first case, the reference is the surface, while in the second the reference is the foot. A fourth option would be to employ indirect acquisition of the position and the force of the impact of the foot on the floor by analyzing the produced sound. Related techniques have been applied to detect the position of stick strikes on drum surfaces and to track knock positions on a large sheet of glass (Paradiso et al. 2002).

The design of a controller that uses foot movements depends on the types of movements that one wishes to sense. Important questions to be asked include: Does one want to sense only foot position or also strike energy? How many people will be acting simultaneously? How constrained should the movements be? (For instance, is the performer sitting or standing up?) Does the system need to identify each foot or different foot parts?

Sensing surfaces are not difficult to build, but do-it-yourself devices may not always be reliable. Nevertheless, there have been some successful cases. An example is the sensing surface developed by Marcus Lamar and collaborators. They created a sensitive floor using a matrix of contact points combined with a few other sensors for experiments with dancers (Lima et al. 1996). It consisted of sixteen sensitive regions (squares on a 4 × 4 matrix), with a grid of wires connected to the pins of the parallel interface of a computer. When the dancer stepped in one region, the wires would make contact, causing changes in voltage to be sent to the computer. Although extremely simple, this sensitive floor allowed for some interesting experiments, mostly with dancers who were not familiar with interactive systems for dance and music (Figure 2.27). The idea of grounding wires had previously been used in the sequential drum. One problem with this approach was the reliability of the wires, which tended to break.

Instrumental shoes can also be of very simple design. Insook Choi and Carlos Ricci (1997) created the CyberBoots, specially built boots with FSRs fitted beneath the soles of the shoes. CyberBoots identified walking patterns, referred to as "pattern-based gesture primitives," by analyzing the pressure signals from the FSRs under the toes and the heel in each boot. These data were then used to control sound and animation (Figure 2.28).

Figure 2.27 A dancer experimenting with a do-it-yourself sensitive floor developed at the Federal University of Paraná, Brazil.

Figure 2.28 CyberBoots Functions.

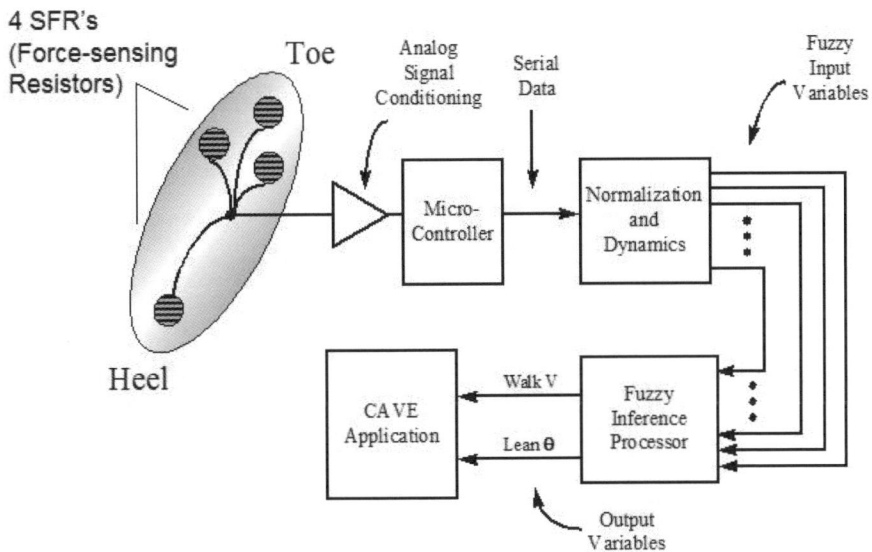

Eric Johnstone (1991) developed the PodoBoard, a MIDI sensitive floor, for Alain LaMontaigne, a clackage performer. (Clackage is a type of step dancing in which the performer is seated on a chair.) The PodoBoard consists of a surface measuring 91 × 102 cm, with a thickness measuring 2 cm and covered with an array of 1,440 square aluminum tiles (Figure 2.29). Metal plates and piezoelectric films are placed on the toes and heels of modified shoes. The metal plates are pulsed sequentially and allow the system to individually detect the toe and heel of each foot in two dimensions when it makes contact with the aluminum tiles. The piezoelectric films enable the measurement of the energy of the footboard impact, from which velocity information can be derived. Continuous movement of the feet can also be detected while they are in contact with the aluminum tiles.

Russell Pinkston and colleagues (Pinkston, Kerkhoff, and McQuilken 1995) developed the MIDI Dance Floor based on FSRs attached to four plastic sheets covered with polyethylene foam and placed beneath a standard dance floor. Each plastic sheet holds 32 FSRs. The foam is used to protect the FSRs from direct impact and to spread the force horizontally. The floor consists of a square grid

Figure 2.29 Eric Johnstone's Podoboard. Note the electronics on the sole of the shoe.

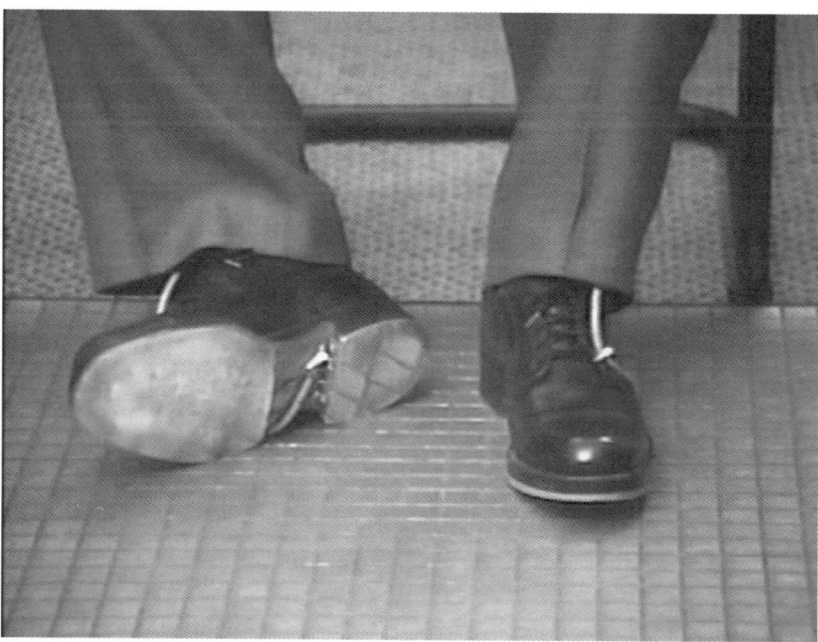

measuring 5 m^2 that forms 64 force-sensitive zones. Each zone is assigned to a separate MIDI note and a continuous controller number using a specially designed 64-channel voltage-to-MIDI interface. A total of 128 FSRs measuring 61 cm are used in pairs.

The LiteFoot, by Niall Griffith and Mikael Fernström (1998), relies on optical proximity sensors (Figure 2.30). Integrated infrared light-emitting diodes (IR LEDs) and photodiodes were configured at an angle of approximately 60°, distributed in a horizontal area measuring 1.76 m^2 and a surface 10 cm high. The floor was flooded with light and total of 1,936 sensors were scanned every 10 milliseconds. The LiteFoot could be used in two modes of operation: reflective mode and shadow mode. In the first, shoes with reflective soles caused light to reflect back to the sensor that emitted it. In the second, the shadows from the footsteps prevented light from reaching the sensors.

The Magic Carpet, developed by Joe Paradiso and collaborators (1997), senses foot pressure changes on its surface and also upper-body movements. It consists of a grid of piezoelectric shielded cables spaced roughly 10 cm apart under a carpet measuring approximately 15 × 25 cm. When submitted to footstep pressure, the piezoelectric cables produce a voltage with amplitude proportional to the dynamics of the footsteps. It is important to notice that, in contrast to the MIDI dance floor, the Magic Carpet does not provide information on continuous foot pressure. It provides only differences in pressure; that is, if a person stayed in the same position on the carpet, his or her weight could not be calculated.

The Magic Carpet also includes a pair of motion sensors using Doppler radar mounted on stands placed around the carpet to sense upper-body movements. A high-frequency signal of 2.4 gigahertz (GHz) emitted by an oscillator is received by an antenna after

Figure 2.30 The Litefoot, by Griffith and Fernström.

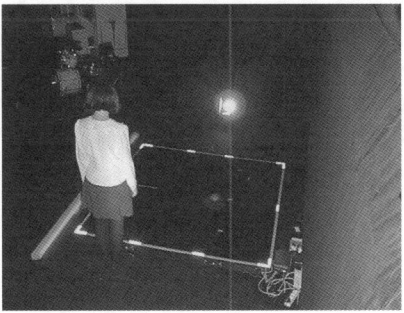

being reflected on a surface. When movement is performed within the range of the radar, the microwave signal reflecting back to the antenna has its frequency shifted up or down depending on the direction of the movements. Faster movements generate larger shifts. These frequency shifts are in the range of 0 hertz (Hz) to 100 Hz (Paradiso 1999).

The Z-Tiles (Richardson et al. 2004) are blocks that can be connected together in a network to form various sizes of pressure-sensing surfaces. Initially the authors developed their own FSR sensors using silicone rubber and carbon powder, but later they used standard Interlink FSRs. Each tile had 20 FSRs on its surface and 5 microcontrollers. One of them handled the pressure data from the FSRs (12-bit data scanned over 100 times per second), and the remaining 4 handled the communication with other tiles on the surface (Figure 2.31).

Figure 2.31 The Z-tiles: (a) top view; (b) sensors.

(a)

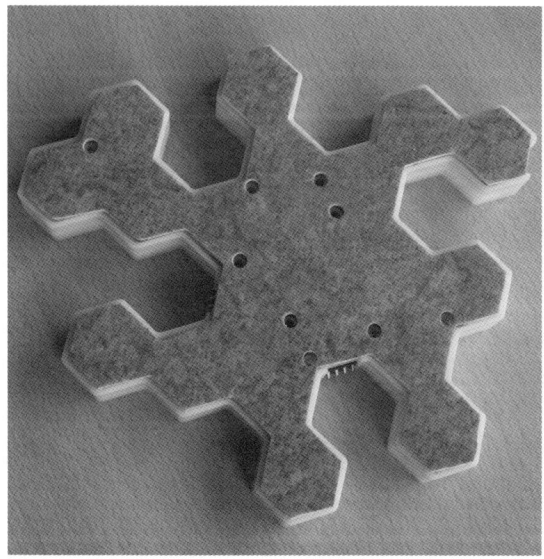

(b)

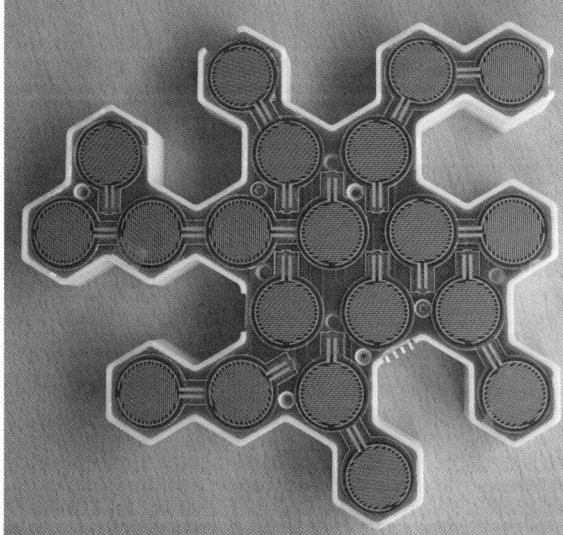

A comparative summary of the various sensing surfaces for sensing foot movements is given as follows:

	PodoBoard	MIDI Dance Floor	Magic Carpet	LiteFoot	Z-Tiles	CyberBoot	Instrumented dancing shoes
Reference	Johnstone 1991	Pinkston, Kerkhoff, and McQuilken 1995	Paradiso et al. 1997	Griffith and Fernström 1998	Richardson et al. 2004	Choi and Ricci 1997	Paradiso, Hsiao, and Hu 1999
Type	Sensitive floor and instrumented shoes	Sensitive floor	Sensitive floor and movement detector	Sensitive floor and movement detector	Sensitive floor	Instrumented shoes	Instrumented shoes
Sensing method	Piezoelectric films and matrix of contact points	Grid of FSRs	Grid of piezoelectric cables and Doppler radars	IR LED/diode pairs	Force-sensing resistors (FSRs) and other force-sensing components	Force-sensing resistors (FSRs)	Several
Main features	Position and pressure of each shoe; identifies tip and heel of each shoe; very fast response	Senses pressure and position of feet	Senses dynamic pressure, position of footsteps, and upper-body movement; very fast response time	Senses position using hundreds of IR diode pairs	Senses pressure and position; easily scalable	Measures force (FSR) at two points: under the toes and under the heel of each foot	Measure several parameters (16 in total); foot centered; measures position with ultrasound
Limitations	Needs specially prepared shoes; single seated performer; not easily scalable	Limited resolution and slow speed of response; not easily scalable	Does not measure pressure continuously; not easily scalable	Not easily scalable	Expensive and complex	Needs specially prepared shoes	Need specially prepared shoes
Purpose	To sense foot movements in clackage	To sense dance movements	General	To be used in Irish dance	General	To identify walking patterns	General; dance, posture analysis

2.4.6 Mouth Controllers

Examples of controllers developed to provide control variables using mouth movements include Nicola Orio's (1997) gesture interface controlled by the oral cavity, Michael Lyons and colleagues' (2003) Mouthsizer (Figure 2.32), Kia Ng's (2004) facial expression controller (Figure 2.33), and Thanasis Hapipis's (2005) ExoSinger. These controllers detect the shape of the mouth cavity, facial expressions, and position of the tongue, lips, and/or eyebrows.

Nicola Orio uses a small loudspeaker and a microphone, both placed inside the mouth. The loudspeaker sends a white noise signal that is filtered by the shape of the oral cavity and captured by the microphone. An analysis of the filtered signal indicates the shape of the oral cavity.

The Mouthsizer, the ExoSinger, and Kia Ng's devices are nonobtrusive controllers that use video cameras to track the position of the performer's lips and tongue (and eyebrows, in Kia Ng's system) through analysis of the video signal. The Mouthsizer and the ExoSinger use a small camera placed on a support on the performer's head; Kia Ng's controller uses a camera on a tripod.

The ExoSinger, developed by Thanasis Hapipis at the University of Plymouth, is a mouth controller that employs lip-reading technology to extract information from mouth movements to control a singing synthesizer. The controller consists of a mini-camera connected to a computer running the EyesWeb software to extract mouth movement parameters. These parameters are then sent via MIDI to another computer running a formant singing synthesizer.

Figure 2.32 The Mouthsizer uses video cameras to track the performer's mouth. (The performer in the photograph is Jordan Wynnchuk.)

Figure 2.33 Kia Ng's facial expression controller.

2.4.7 Conducting Gesture Systems

A number of systems for controlling music with conducting-like gestures have been proposed. Early systems related to conducting include the conductor program (Mathews 1976), the sequential drum (Mathews 1980), the microcomputer-based conducting system (Buxton, Dannenberg, and Vercoe 1980) and the conductor follower (Haflich and Burns 1983). There have been a number of other developments since then.

Conducting gesture systems can be approached from three main perspectives:

- Gesture acquisition using video cameras and/or existing devices (e.g., Buchla Lightning II)
- Design of novel control devices
- Software development for beat tracking and recognition of expressive gestures or to synchronize a score to gestural cues

Paul Kolesnik identified more than 20 conducting gesture systems (Kolesnik 2004), including:

- New baton-like devices (Keane and Gross 1989; Marrin and Paradiso 1997)
- Other sensor-based devices for gesture acquisition (Sawada, Ohkura, and Hashimoto 1995; Marrin 2000)
- Video analysis software to identify conductor movements (Bertini and Carosi 1992; Murphy, Andersen, and Jensen 2003), including techniques such as artificial neural networks (ANNs)

(Ilmonen and Takala 1999) and hidden Markov models (Usa and Mochida 1998; Kolesnik and Wanderley 2004)
- Software to control the performance of a prerecorded score (Mathews 1976; Dannenberg and Bookstein 1991)

Note the various approaches to the same problem: that is, to synchronize an already recorded score to the movements of a conductor. A comparative summary of a few developments is given in Table 2.1.

Table 2.1
A comparative summary of conducting gesture systems.

	Sequential drum	Microcomputer-based conducting system	MIDI baton system	Computer music system that follows a human conductor	MIDI conducting program	Light Baton
Reference	Mathews 1980	Buxton et al. 1980	Keane and Gross 1989	Morita, Hashimoto, Otheru 1989	Dannenberg and Bookstein 1991	Bertini and Carosi 1992
Input device(s)	Rectangular surface with wires making contact at strike point detected with a contact microphone	4-button cursor on a tablet, switches and sliders	Baton (a metal ball attached to spring wire inside a brass tube) and a footswitch	CCD camera, white glove (right hand) / baton marker	Keyboard or other MIDI device	CCD camera, baton containing a lamp
Tracked parameters	2D position of strike and force detected with a contact microphone	2D position of the cursor on the tablet	Acceleration of the baton controller and a footswitch signal to start and stop the score	Right hand: Arm / baton position in 2d space	Beats	Baton position in 2D space
Control variables	Tempo, loudness, and timbre or sound distribution	Pitch shift (octave) tempo, articulation, amplitude, richness (timbre) and cycle (loop)	Tempo	Tempo, dynamics	Tempo and score position	Tempo and score position
Software and hardware	4 CED programming language; PDP 11/34 computer controlling a 4C synthesizer	Microcomputer, synthesizer, and composition and performance control transducers	Garfield Time Commander (synchronization unit) and a MIDI synthesizer	Computer vision system, MIDI control unit	Special software; Commodore and Amiga hardware	Turbo Pascal 5.5 software and VISCA Vision Card

	Digital Baton	Multi-modal conducting simulator	Conductor's jacket*	Conductor following with artificial neural networks	Computer vision	Gesture recognition
Reference	Marrin and Paradiso 1997	Usa and Mochida 1998	Marrin and Picard 1998	Ilmomen and Takala 1999	Murphy, Andersen, and Jensen 2003	Kolesnik and Wanderley 2004
Input device(s)	Digital baton	Camera, two accelerometers, breath sensor	Jacket with four electromyogram (EMG) sensors, a respiration sensor, a heart rate sensor, a temperature sensor, and a galvanic skin response sensor	Datasuit with six-degrees-of-freedom sensors (replaced by accelerometers in demonstration version for cost reasons)	Video cameras	Video cameras
Tracked parameters	Pressure, acceleration, intensity, position sensors, and light captured by an external photodiode in 2D space	Right-hand acceleration and position, breath intensity, and direction of gaze	Muscle tension, breath intensity, heart rate, and skin response	3D positional information of the body	Position of right arm in 3D space	Position of right and left arms
Control variables	Tempo, dynamics, and effects	Tempo, dynamics, articulation effects, and phrasing (breath intensity)	Tempo, dynamics, articulation, accents, meter, pulse, vibrato, number of voices, and harmonic coloration	Tempo and articulation	Tempo	Expressive gestures
Software and hardware	LabView and Rogus McBogus MIDI library	Hidden Markov Model and movement recognition system	LabView, Visual Dev studio, Rogus MIDI library, and two networked computers	Neural network analysis system and FastTrak 6DoF sensor system	Computer vision system, EyesWeb, and Mixxx (an open source DJ tool)	EyesWeb, Max/MSP, OSC

*Teresa Marrin's conductor's jacket will be discussed in more detail in chapter 4.

2.4.8 Design Evolution: The Case of the Continuum

The Continuum, by Lippold Haken and colleagues (Haken, Tellman, and Wolfe 1998), is an interesting case study on the evolution of a controller's design. Though it has kept roughly the same final features, the Continuum's design has gone through three very different technological solutions.

The original Continuum used a finger tracking method where a playing surface was lit by a polarized light source from below. Note the similarity of this method to the one used in Eric Johnstone's Rolky Asproyd, described in section 2.3.1. Pressing a finger against the surface changed the light polarization, causing a ring pattern around the finger. A camera captured the image on the surface and an algorithm analyzed the rings in order to ascertain the position of each finger. Although it provided an accurate location of the fingers, this design had problems related to the amount of image processing needed to extract information from the ring patterns (remember that this was done in the 1980s). The overlapping of patterns when the fingers were close to each other jeopardized the individual position and finger pressure measurements. There were also problems related to excessive heating by the light source.

A subsequent version of the Continuum used a layer of conductive rubber (i.e., rubber with inserted carbon fibers) 1.25 cm thick to sense the pressure and the position of the fingers. A conductive sheet placed on top of the rubber supplied a constant voltage, and a board with an array of detecting pads at the bottom measured the current through the rubber. By applying pressure at a given point, the impedance was reduced locally, increasing the current passing through the rubber proportionally. Only those pads corresponding to the region under pressure could detect current change, allowing for the identification of the position of the finger. Because the rubber had high impedance horizontally, the effect was localized. Difficulties with this design included problems making the electronic connections to the rubber (high-quality conductive glue was used) and the lack of robustness of the rubber: after it had been used for some time, the fibers would break down and the rubber would became equally conductive in all directions (Haken, Abdullah, and Smart 1992).

The third version of the Continuum used rods with a section of roughly 3 × 3 mm and two rows of Hall effect sensors and magnets, one row on each side of the playing surface. By pressing a rod, magnets at each of its two ends moved with respect to the Hall effect sensors, and their positions could be measured. The x position was obtained by interpolating the pressure values on the rods under the finger. This was in fact a simplification over previous designs because the rods provided a physically discrete playing surface. The z position (pressure) was obtained by adding the values from the sensors at both ends of the rod under the finger and the y position by the ratio of the sensors at each end of the rod (Haken, Abdullah, and Smart 1992).

Another extraordinary example of design evolution is Serge de Laubier's meta-instrument, described in section 2.3.2, currently in its third generation.

■ 2.5 HAPTIC MUSIC CONTROLLERS: TACTILE AND FORCE FEEDBACK

Up to now this book has focused on controllers based on several sensing technologies that do not make use of actuators. The addition of actuators such as loudspeakers, tactile stimulators, or motors can provide tactile and/or force feedback to the performer. Force and tactile feedback together are called haptic feedback. (The term haptic refers to tactile and kinesthetic sensations.)

Tactile sensation is associated with discriminative touch such as the perception of surfaces. Receptors distributed unevenly on the skin and in subcutaneous tissues are sensitive to tactile information —for instance, thermal receptors and mechanoreceptors that are sensitive to mechanical vibration, skin stretching, and compression. Tactile sensation therefore comprises the sensations of vibration, pressure, texture, thermal properties, softness, wetness, and friction-induced phenomena, to cite but a few.

Kinesthetic sensation is related to the awareness of the state of our body. It includes information on position, velocity, and forces supplied by the muscles. Kinesthetic receptors are located mostly in the muscles and tendons.

Tactile feedback therefore aims to stimulate tactile receptors (basically, mechanoreceptors) distributed over the skin, while force feedback aims at creating forces to be sensed by the kinesthetic receptors in muscles and tendons.

In fact, all acoustic musical instruments have some form of acoustical and mechanical responses that are normally related to each other; both responses are important to performers (Gillespie 1999a, 1999b). When performing on acoustic instruments, performers also receive information related to the instrument's mechanical behavior, such as the vibrating strings and resonance of the body of the guitar, the vibrating reed and body of the saxophone, the forces produced by the action mechanism of the piano keys, and so forth. The mechanical behavior of acoustic instruments contributes to how performers feel their instruments.

Materials also exhibit inherent passive haptic feedback (mostly tactile) that may also be important in performance. For instance, the body of a controller built of plastic will feel different from a similar body made of wood in terms of temperature, texture, and possibly weight. In other words, part of the feel of a controller is provided by its intrinsic characteristics (materials, weight, etc.), which are constant for a given prototype. In this book, we are interested in devices in which haptic properties can be modified based on models of vibration and force patterns programmed in software and output by actuators.

When building controllers capable of active tactile and force-feedback response, the feel of the device becomes a design variable. In this book, we use the term haptic music controllers for controllers that exhibit active haptic feedback—in other words, controllers whose haptic feedback behavior can be modified according to software models. For instance, a keyboard in which each key is fitted with a motor and a motion sensor can realize programmable feel while a synthesizer offers programmable sound (Cadoz, Luciani, and Florens 1984; Gillespie 1999a). As with the relationship between gestures and sound using gestural controllers (i.e., mapping), arbitrary relationships between the feel and the sound can be explored.

Haptic music controllers can be of two main types:

- Tactile simulators that use mechanisms for skin sensation, vibrotactile devices that vibrate at a given frequency, and thermal devices
- Force-feedback devices

Force-feedback devices use mechanical systems with a wide bandwidth source of mechanical power, typically motors of several sizes. Tactile simulators use a matrix of pins, small vibrators, and loudspeakers. As Joseph Rovan and Vincent Hayward (2000) suggested, besides the difference in scale, tactile simulators reproduce the effect of the skin touching a source (e.g., vibration on a tactile ring), while force-feedback devices serve as mediating devices through which one explores or manipulates a virtual mechanical system.

Haptic interface technology is an important area of research in engineering, with applications to areas such as robotics and virtual reality. Several haptic devices have been proposed, and many are commercially available. They range from small tactile simulators to large exoskeletons to be worn by the user. An excellent source of information on haptic devices is the Haptics Community Web page at http://haptic.mech.northwestern.edu (accessed 15 February 2005).

Force-feedback input devices are common in general computer applications, mostly in games. Examples include force-feedback joysticks, gamepads, and driving wheels. One example of an affordable, generic, commercial force-feedback device is the Phantom Omni, by SensAble Technologies (Figure 2.34). This is a haptic device with six-degrees-of-freedom positional sensing and three-degrees-of-freedom force feedback, in which a user holds a stylus in order to touch and manipulate virtual objects displayed on a computer screen.

Figure 2.34 The Phantom Omni by SensAble Technologies.

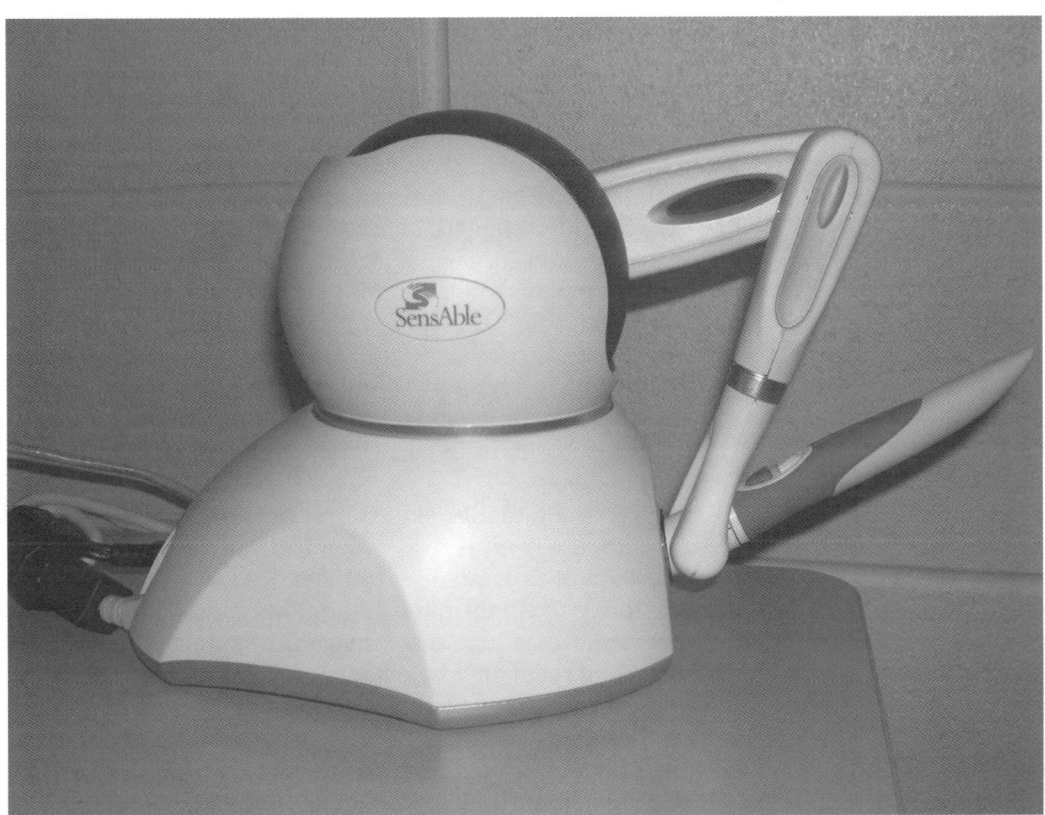

The application of haptic devices in music is an active research topic including:

- The design of new haptic music interfaces using commercially available sensors and actuators
- The design of new actuators to be used in new haptic music interfaces
- The development of models used to simulate the haptic behavior of these interfaces

Since the 1970s, various interfaces using haptic feedback have been designed simulating the feel of acoustic instruments (e.g., pianos, organs, harpsichords, and violins) or arbitrary devices such as tactile rings and floor pads, among other devices.

The following sections present a short survey of some of these developments, starting with haptic music devices that are not related to acoustic instruments.

2.5.1 General Haptic Music Devices

As with alternate controllers, general haptic music devices do not seek to reproduce the tactile and force-feedback behavior of existing acoustic instruments. They can be simple devices such as tactile rings (Bongers 1998b); haptic knobs used for sound editing, such as in TouchSound designed by Lonny Chu (Nichols 2003); and one-degree-of-freedom force-feedback devices, such as the one used in the Plank (Verplank, Sapp, and Mathews 2001). More complex interfaces include the Moose, a haptic mouse (O'Modhrain and Gillespie 1996).

Vibrotactile displays. Vibrotactile feedback system for music often use loudspeakers or small actuators mounted on rings or embedded in surfaces on which the performer can stand (Rovan and Hayward 2000).

Specially built tactile simulators were designed for the VR/TX ("virtual texture") project in order to transduce signals simulating the sensation of texture to performers. They were mounted on rings, on a custom glove controller, and on footpads. These tactile simulators consisted of a coil and a magnet of similar sizes and masses, with principal resonances well below the operating frequency range.

Temperature display. Homei Miyashita and Kazushi Nishimoto created an intriguing haptic controller using a thermodisplay keyboard capable of dynamically changing the temperature during the performance. They placed Peltier devices (thermoelectric coolers that work as heat pumps) between two ceramic plates placed on piano keys. Heat was transferred from one plate to another when current was applied. According to the authors, performers took about two seconds to perceive changes in temperature, with values up to 50°C, when contact became uncomfortable. Applications for such technology included systems for learning to play the piano and keyboard practice (Miyashita and Nishimoto 2004b).

Force feedback. These are controllers with force-feedback systems using motors. Many of the force-feedback devices proposed in the literature use voice-coil motors from surplus disk drives. Examples include the touchback keyboard (Gillespie 1992b), the Plank (Verplank, Sapp, and Mathews 2001), and the MIKEY (multi-instrument virtual keyboard) (Oboe and De Poli 2002). ACROE (Association pour la Création et la Recherche sur les Outils d'Expression) designed its own actuator, the slice motor used in their Modular Feedback Keyboard (Cadoz, Lisowski, and Florens 1990).

Also part of the hardware of tactile and force-feedback systems are amplifiers and electronic circuits to drive the actuators. They may range from audio amplifiers (as in the VR/TX system) and amplifiers obtained from personal computer hardware (as in the MIKEY) to specially built electronics (such as ACROE's modular feedback keyboard).

2.5.2 Models of Excitation

Once the actuators have been chosen, one still needs to define which signals will be used to drive them. The choice of haptic response in controllers is important because it affects the way in which the controller will be played.

Haptic feedback may be obtained by sending the audio produced by the computer to a small loudspeaker placed on the fingertips. This method provides performers with straightforward tactile information on the state of the sound. However, it may not always be an ideal solution because there are important differences between the haptic channels and the auditory channel. For instance, consider the perception of tactile events with varying frequencies. The frequency response that can be perceived by the sense of touch ranges from nearly 0 Hz to a few hundred Hz; but this is relatively poor when compared to the range of the auditory system, which can perceive frequencies up to 20 kHz. Joseph Rovan and Vincent Hayward (2000) reported that users of their tactile rings could perceive events ranging from 70 to 800 Hz, in eight to ten discrete frequency steps.

Using frequencies equivalent to note pitches is not the best strategy for displaying tactile information; one then needs to establish which tactile events to use (Gunther, Davenport, and O'Modhrain 2002). Chris Chafe has suggested that only certain musical events are useful as tactile events, such as timing, amplitude, and spectral weighting.

In their VR/TX system, Joseph Rovan and Vincent Hayward considered the use of large-scale "audio gestures," such as rapidly rising or descending pitch curves or correlating continuous pitch change to absolute position, to be more effective than sensing individual frequencies with the skin. They also considered spectral content (from pure sine waves to noise), amplitude envelopes of events (attack, sustain, and release) and the use of different sets of event repetitions as important perceivable tactile variables. The interesting feature of the VR/TX system was that it allowed performers of open-air controllers (or "expanded range controllers") to feel haptic cues related to their performance, including position in space.

Perhaps the most interesting effort to display tactile information to date was the development of the Cutaneous Grooves by Eric Gunther and collaborators (Gunther, Davenport, and O'Modhrain 2002). This system comprised twelve modified flat speakers and one low-frequency transducer (woofer) mounted on a plastic case, all sewn on a bodysuit. It was created in order to allow for "composing for the sense of touch." The most interesting part of the work was the definition of the dimensions of tactile stimuli that could be manipulated to form the elements of a basic vocabulary for a compositional language. These included frequencies (as a qualitative dimension, not an absolute indication), a continuum of intensities (from the threshold of detection to the limits of discomfort), various amplitude envelopes, the duration of events, the content of the waveforms, and the spatial location of events.

The definition of force-feedback models is also important, with implications for performance and learning. For instance, Sile O'Modhrain and Chris Chafe (2000) studied the time it takes to learn to perform short melodies on a virtual theremin using their Moose controller. The authors studied the influence of two force conditions: viscous dampers and springs. Subjects took longer to learn the viscous damper condition than the spring condition, although after sufficient training both conditions yielded similar performances.

Another example of research on models for driving haptic interfaces in music includes friction models for bowed strings (Serafin, Vergez, and Rodet 1999; Hayward and Armstrong 2000).

Attempting to simulate mechanical systems, Brent Gillespie designed a simplified model of the piano's hammers and keys, considering only movement from rest position to contact between hammer and string (Gillespie 1992a; Oboe and De Poli 2002). This model was improved by Roberto Oboe and Giovanni De Poli, who included hammer-string impact, key impacts, and the escapement effect.

In short, once the hardware to be used for the haptic interface has been defined, one needs to design the control system that will drive this hardware. In addition to the electronic circuits, one also needs to define software models for the stimulus and/or mechanisms that will be simulated. Obviously, this is a reversible process in the sense that one can start with the models and then define the hardware needed. Nevertheless, both tasks are important in the design of haptic music interfaces.

2.5.3 Simulating the Feel of Existing Instruments

Several projects have focused on the simulation of force-feedback effects in acoustic instruments, mostly on the feel of keyboard instruments (the piano, the organ, and the harpsichord) and of bowed strings.

ACROE's systems. The Transducteur Gestuel Rétroactif (TGR) designed by Jean-Loup Florens and colleagues at ACROE in France (Cadoz, Lisowski, and Florens 1990) comprises a series of force-feedback devices that have been developed over the last 25 years (Figure 2.35).

The bowing gesture transducer developed by Jean-Loup Florens (Florens 1978) is probably the first haptic device designed for musical application. This was the first version of the TGR, a force-feedback stick that could be manipulated in one dimension (horizontally). It featured force and displacement measurements, a feedback force of tens of newtons (N) in a distance of about 1 m and a response time of 1 ms. It was used in experiments involving the manipulation of simple virtual objects and sound synthesis (Cadoz et al. 2003).

Another force-feedback device developed by ACROE is La Touché, a piano key gesture transducer whose performance was reported as far superior than their first bowing TGR (Cadoz, Luciani, and Florens 1984). This transducer was used in ACROE's first real-time multisensory interaction experiments.

Yet another development was the modular force-feedback keyboard. One of the main difficulties of this development was to find

Figure 2.35 A force-feedback key by ACROE.

motors that were compact and powerful enough to allow the assembly of several modules side by side. The solution was to design their own actuator: the slice motor (Cadoz, Lisowski, and Florens 1990). The slice motor is a compact and powerful device with a maximum lateral dimension of 13.75 mm, which corresponded to the size of the back part of a piano key).

The idea behind the slice motor was that a common magnetic field was applied to all modules through a single magnetic polarization circuit. Each slice was composed of a magnet-coil pair, and forces were produced independently in each module, allowing for the modular assembly of the slices into a compact device (Figures 2.36 and 2.37). In each module, an LVDT (linear variable differential transformer) sensor measured linear displacements of up to 15 mm (with a resolution of approximately 3 µm). The slice motor supplied a force of several tens of newtons. In the first version of the slice motor, the maximum permanent force obtained in the magnet

Figure 2.36 A prototype of the modular force-feedback keyboard. The keyboard is composed of sixteen slice motors.

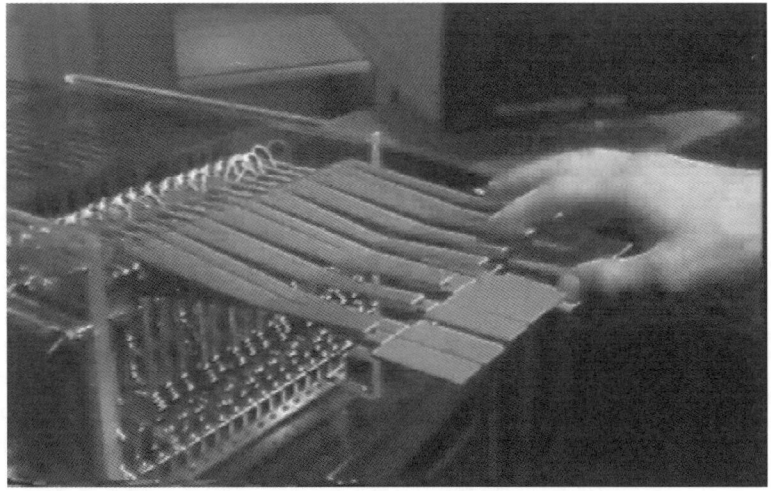

Figure 2.37 (a) The force-feedback transducer with twelve slice motors and the associate electronics; (b) Jean-Loup Florens controlling a model of a bowed string. With his left hand he controls the pitch of the note using one key (up-down movement). His right hand holds a stylus specially conceived to provide a three-dimensional movement using three force-feedback keys.

(a)　　　　　　　　　　　　(b)

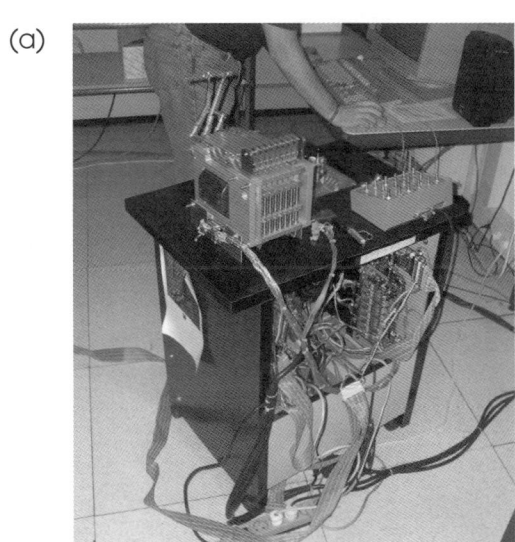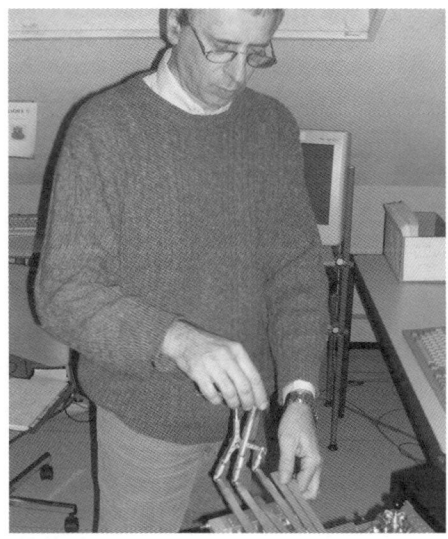

equaled 40 N, and the maximum transitory force was 80 N. The response delay to the input control was 0.2 ms, and the bandwidth was enough to sense or reproduce mechanical phenomena around 700 Hz to 800 Hz. ACROE's second generation of slice motors could reach a maximum force of 200 N per slice (Cadoz et al. 2003).

The sensor and motor modules could be "dressed" (from the French *habillé*) with various devices, providing systems with several degrees of freedom. This expanded the inherent one-dimensional movement (up-down) of the slices (Cadoz et al. 2003). These devices therefore took various forms (Figure 2.38): a classical piano-like keyboard, 2DoF (degrees of freedom) and 3DoF sticks, pliers, 6DoF stylus, and 6DoF platform or sphere (6DoF means three translations—x, y, and z—and three rotation variables—pitch, yaw, and roll—totaling six degrees of freedom).

Finally, one of the most important features of the modular feedback keyboard was that it drove physical modeling sound and image synthesis systems based on the CORDIS-ANIMA paradigm (Cadoz, Luciani, and Florens 1984). According to Claude Cadoz and collaborators, the TGR and the physical modeling (or simulation of physical objects) were two nonseparable components of a single approach

Figure 2.38 The 3D stick can be assembled into the TGR to provide a continuous movement in 3D with force feedback.

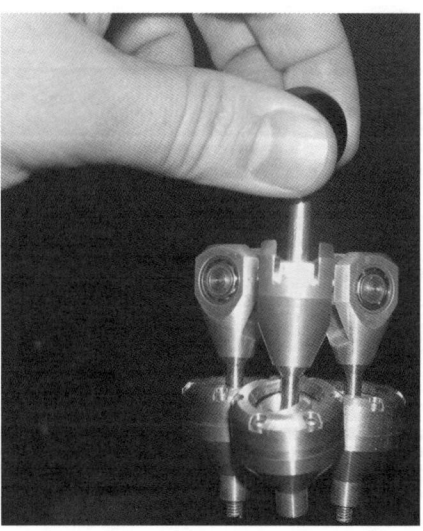

to control. Each of them gave their best when conceived and implemented within the context of the other. They considered these two concepts as nonseparable from the beginning of their work in 1976.

Touchback keyboard and the MIKEY. Brent Gillespie built the touchback keyboard using voice-coil type linear motors from disk drives. The initial prototype was built using motors originally designed for large disk drives, which had rather high inertia. Because of their size and inertia, they could not be used for the simulation of a piano keyboard consisting of multiple keys. Instead, they were used in the construction of a carillon keyboard. Optical encoders, tachometers, and strain gauges were used to measure the position (or velocity) of the keys and the force applied by the performer. A later version of the keyboard consisted of six keys the size of the piano's (Gillespie 1999b).

In a similar vein to the touchback keyboard, Roberto Oboe constructed the MIKEY also using voice-coil motors from disk drives (Figures 2.39 and 2.40). The authors reported to have achieved low friction and inertia with their device (Oboe and De Poli 2002). Apart from a more complete modeling of the piano action, the authors also simulated the mechanism of the harpsichord and of the Hammond organ. The position of the keys was measured with reflective sensors placed under the keys. The force applied to a key was derived from the current applied to the motor, without the need for special sensors.

Figure 2.39 The MIKEY, by Roberto Oboe.

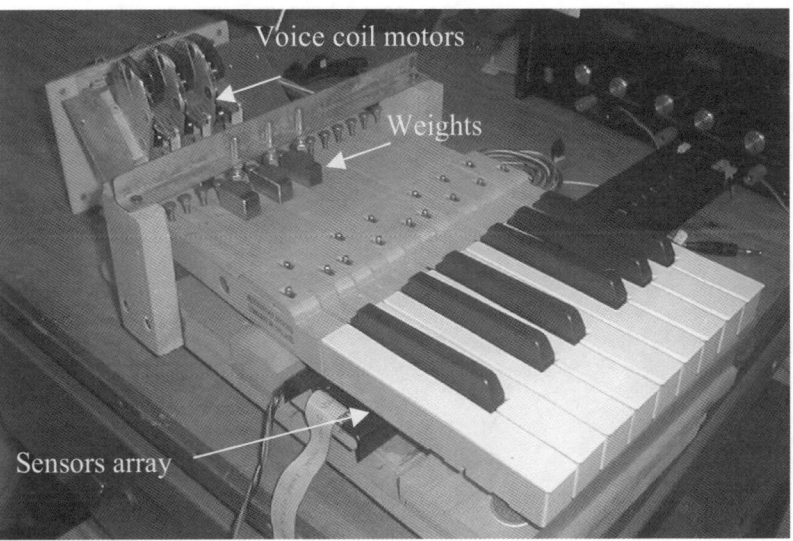

Figure 2.40 Detail of the MIKEY showing its voice-coil motors.

Weights were added to the backs of the keys to simulate gravity and therefore limit the range of forces to be generated by the voice-coil motors. Key regulators prevented the keys from "popping up" in fortissimo action, which also simulated the natural stop provided in acoustic pianos.

One interesting design aspect of the MIKEY was its low cost: the cost of each key was less than $10.00 (USD). It used motors and amplifiers taken from surplus hard disk drives, low-cost A/D and D/A converters (the same as those used in the sound boards of personal computers), low-cost digital signal processing (DSP) circuits, and inexpensive sensors.

Bowed string instruments. A number of researchers have addressed the development of the haptic control of bowed string instruments. For instance, Jean-Loup Florens and colleagues (Florens et al. 1986) developed a simulation of bowed strings using pressure and displacement sensors built onto a device that replaced the bow, although no force feedback was implemented at the time. Later, however, they implemented a bowed string simulation using ACROE's modular feedback keyboard, "dressed" with a stylus replacing the bow (Cadoz et al. 2003). This device was subsequently improved by Jean-Loup Florens and Cyrille Henry (2001).

Sile O'Modhrain used the Moose to test the playability of bowed-string physical models developed using the Synthesis ToolKit Library (STK) (O'Modhrain and Gillespie 1996; Cook and Scavone 1999). The lateral motion of the violin bow across a string was simulated with the x-axis of the Moose, while the bow's vertical motion on the string was simulated with its y-axis. Charles Nichols's (2003) vBow was designed as a force-feedback violin controller with four degrees of freedom (Figure 2.41).

The initial vBow prototype consisted of a single servomotor with a digital encoder allowing for one-degree-of-freedom force feedback in lateral motion (the first degree of freedom of the version shown in Figure 2.41). The second version of the vBow incorporated three more degrees of freedom: rotational motion across, vertical motion above, and longitudinal motion along the (virtual) string (Nichols 2002). The vBow was used for experiments on the expressivity of bowed-string physical models and on the efficacy of haptic feedback in music interfaces.

Figure 2.41 The degrees of freedom of Charles Nichol's vBow, version 2.2.

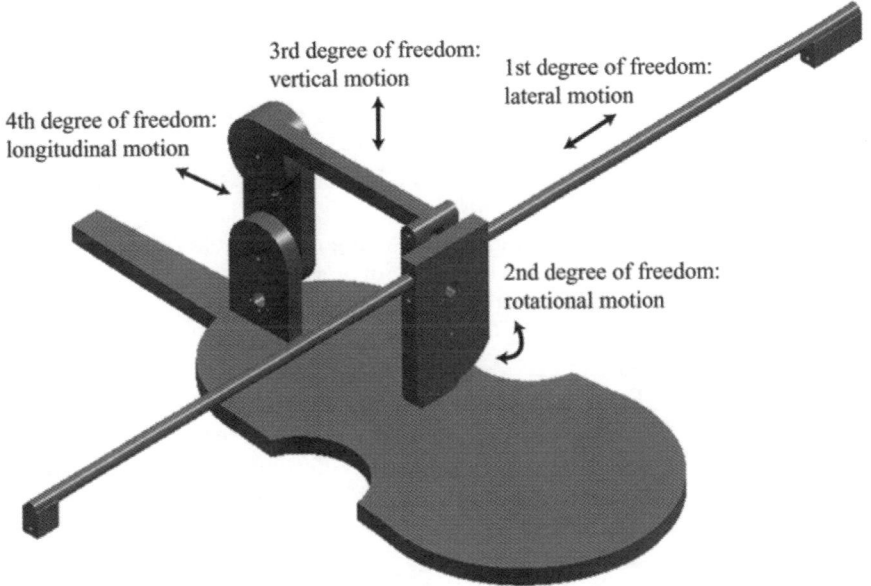

2.6 HIGH-END MOTION TRACKERS

High-end motion tracking systems can use several technologies for detecting the position of markers and/or sensors placed in the human body or in objects. The most common technologies currently available are magnetic and optical, but mechanical, ultrasound, and hybrid inertial trackers also exist. High-end motion trackers typically give three degrees of freedom per marker or six degrees of freedom per sensor, with up to several hundred markers or dozens of sensors per unit.

Real-time data analysis and output capabilities are available in several high-end trackers, making them usable in artistic contexts. The main limitations on the use of high-end trackers in music are portability and cost. Some optical systems using multiple cameras are not portable and often are complicated to set up. Moreover, high-end trackers may cost from thousands to hundreds of thousands of dollars (U.S.), depending on the technology and options used.

2.6.1 Magnetic Trackers

Magnetic trackers usually use two sets of three coils positioned orthogonally: one as a transmitter and one or more as receivers (Fuchs 1999). Each receiver (a sensor) can give accurate information on its position (x, y, z) and its orientation (pitch, yaw, roll) with respect to the transmitter.

One of the advantages of magnetic trackers is that they do not require a line of sight, as optical or ultrasound trackers do. In fact, a receiver can be tracked even if it is not "seen" by the magnetic source.

On the other hand, magnetic trackers have some limitations, most notably the need for cables for the sensors and sensitivity to metal parts in the environment, depending on the tracker used (Burdea and Coiffet 2003). Note that active optical trackers usually also need cables.

Examples of musical applications of magnetic trackers include the use of a Polhemus Fastrak to measure absolute position in the conductor's jacket (Marrin 2000) and in Virtual Bodhrán or Vodhrán (Marshall, Moynihan, and Rath 2002), and Ascension Technology's Flock of Birds in Pointing Fingers (Couturier and Arfib 2003).

2.6.2 Optical Systems

Optical movement acquisition systems basically come in two types: active and passive. Both use infrared light and cameras, reducing the interference of ambient light.

Markers in optical systems can only provide three degrees of freedom because they are viewed by the cameras as points in space. In order to get orientation information from optical markers, three markers need to be placed on the object whose orientation is to be measured.

Active trackers use LEDs and cameras to track the position of a marker in space (x, y, z); the LED converts electricity into infrared light. Because they use active markers, these systems need cables to convey energy to the LEDs so that they can send infrared signals to the cameras. There are wireless options where control modules using infrared or radio frequency (RF) allow for operation with various markers.

There are a number of optical systems available, most notably the Northern Digital Optotrak 3020 and the PhoeniX Technologies Visualeyez. Several markers can be used simultaneously (up to 256 or 512, depending on the device), as well as a variable number of cameras. Both systems use sets of three cameras prepositioned in bars, referred to as trackers. These systems allow for multiple trackers; standard configurations range from two to four trackers. Since the cameras are factory calibrated, the preplacement of the cameras in the trackers allows for great flexibility, speeding up the acquisition process.

Perhaps the biggest advantage of active optical trackers is their insensitivity to marker swapping. Since each marker is identifiable from its own ID (identity code), the system does not need to calculate trajectories of markers from frame to frame in order to identify them. This advantage is most notable when a large number of markers are placed close to each other. Another advantage of active over passive infrared trackers is their lower sensitivity to shiny objects in the room. This can be important when measuring the position of markers in shiny metal instruments, such as the saxophone, where reflections from the body of the instrument may show up as spurious markers in the measurement.

In passive systems, rings of IR LEDs on the cameras flood the capture space with infrared light, and markers reflect infrared light back to the cameras. Because markers are passive (i.e., no energy is needed), no cabling is involved, and they can be fixed to any object or body part.

Several markers can be used simultaneously, but the increase in the number of markers and the crowded placement of markers will invariably make extra demands on system processing. In contrast to active systems, in this case individual markers cannot be easily identified. In fact, in passive systems, markers are tracked from frame to frame by following their trajectories. If markers are not seen by some of the cameras during several frames and then reappear, it is difficult for the system to identify them as the same markers since no extra information is available apart from their x, y, and z coordinates.

Passive systems can typically use up to 24 cameras, with frame rates varying from 120 to 1,000 or more frames per second. More recent systems are able to use many more cameras, but the cost is usually high. Commercial examples include systems from Vicon Motion System, Motion Analysis, and BTS SpA (Elite and Smart systems).

An inexpensive recent option is the OptiTrack (http://www.naturalpoint.com/optitrack/, accessed 28 November 2005), by NaturalPoint, consisting of up to four USB cameras at 120 frames per second equipped with infrared light rings. Passive markers are used in the object of interest.

Musical applications. Christopher Dobrian and Frederic Bevilacqua (2003) used a Vicon System 8 to control sound synthesis. They developed a system called MCM (Motion Capture Music) in Java, C++, and Max/MSP (MCMMax). Information derived from the position of the markers (x, y, and z coordinates), such as velocity, acceleration, distance, and the angle between markers, was mapped in real time to synthesis parameters using linear, reversed, exponential, and logarithmic functions, as well as other functions stored in lookup tables.

Both an Optotrak 3020 and a Vicon System 460 have been used to study the body movements of performers of acoustic instruments (Wanderley 2002b). A database of performances is being assembled at McGill University's Input Devices and Music Interaction Laboratory (IDMIL) to allow the comparison of performances in terms of movement. These systems can also be used for the evaluation of performances using new gestural controllers (Figures 2.42 and 2.43).

■ 2.7 COLLABORATIVE AND WEB-BASED CONTROLLERS

In spite of the wide variety of existing gestural controllers more or less modeled on existing instruments, controllers do not need to be limited to the traditional musical instrument model consisting of

Figure 2.42 Vincent Verfaille playing the Yamaha WX5 controller. Note the passive markers on his body and on the controller, as well as two of the six M2 cameras of the Vicon System 460 at the Input Devices and Music Interaction Laboratory (IDMIL), McGill University.

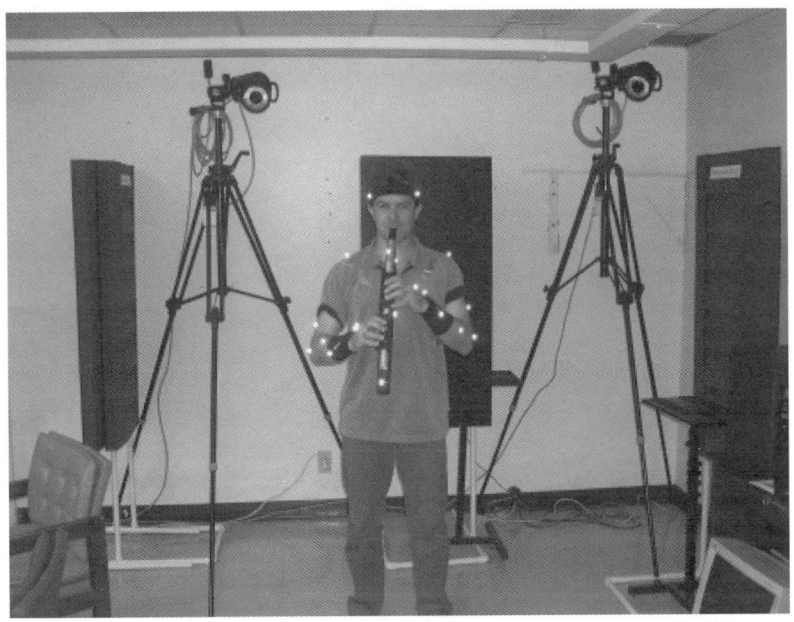

Figure 2.43 Passive markers can also be placed on fingers to study keyboard performances.

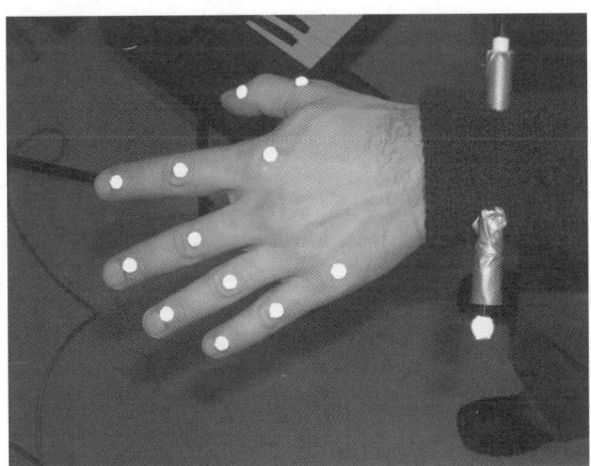

one performer playing one instrument (Jordà 2005). It is possible to design controllers where collaboration between performers is expected as the main control strategy, either locally (collaborative controllers) or in distributed instruments scattered through the World Wide Web (Web-based controllers).

Collaborative controllers, or collaborative interfaces, allow for more than one person to interact in a musical context. Unlike single-player controllers that could eventually be played by more than one person at the same time, collaborative controllers are made primarily for more than one player. They are designed to explore the communication and expression between players through music.

Collaborative controllers may address issues related to acoustic instruments such as the potential for expert performance through practice, as for instance, in the case of the Tooka (Fels et al. 2004) (Figure 2.44). They may also be created with highly limited control ability, allowing novices to participate in the musical interaction, as in the case of the Jam-O-Drum (Blaine and Perkins 2000) (Figure 2.45). In the former case, collaborative controllers can be considered multiperson instruments, with a history going back to pieces such as *Mikrophonie I* and *II*, by Karlheinz Stockhausen. In the latter case, collaborative controllers may be closer to interactive installations, where traditional notions of instrumental virtuosity and expressive performance capabilities may be of lesser importance. In contrast to the Western post-Renaissance focus on musical expression through virtuosity, collaborative musical experiences can enable the media of sound and music to enhance the communication opportunities and intimacy between novice players. In this case, instead of expert performance, the focus may be on allowing novices to increase their skills over a short period of time. The devices used in such collaborative systems may vary from a single controller played by various people at the same time to several controllers played by various people; these may or may not be identical.

The roles of the performers may be identical or differentiated. For instance, they would be identical if all performers can freely create musical material. Conversely, they would be differentiated when one or various performers create musical material that is further transformed by other performers. David Wessel and Matt Wright (2002) referred to this type of musical interaction as the catch-and-throw interaction.

In the case of multiple performers, turn-taking behavior may be introduced. The interaction is directed by one leader in order to avoid anarchy; an example of this can be found in Beatbugs (Weinberg, Aimi, and Jennings 2002).

Figure 2.44　The Tooka by Sidney Fels and colleagues.

Figure 2.45　The Jam-O-Drum by Tina Blaine and Tim Perkins.

An important issue to be considered when designing new controllers, especially collaborative ones, is the trade-off between ease of use for novices and control power for expert performance. David Wessel and Matt Wright (2002) advocate interfaces that are easy for novices to handle but have no ceiling on virtuosity. Gideon D'Arcangelo (2001) also supports the notion that the amount of time it takes to learn a controller in collaborative musical experiences must be minimized for first-time players (e.g., in installations in public spaces).

Ideally, a balance between virtuosity and simplicity should be achieved, but in practice, such a balance is difficult to obtain. In a review of various designs of collaborative controllers for novices, Tina Blaine and Sidney Fels (2003) have shown that the majority of these interfaces do not allow for expert performance because of the various design constraints implemented in order to make the interfaces accessible to nonmusicians. Furthermore, these authors suggested that the demographic for most multiplayer instruments is nonmusicians, and that it is unlikely that most of them have expectations of becoming expert performers on any musical instrument. In this case, designers of such controllers would not need to provide a high ceiling for virtuosity. One possible way to alleviate this problem is to design a controller that adapts to the user (Wessel 1991); adaptive controllers will be discussed in the next section.

As for Web-based controllers, we cite Global String. This was a multisite network music installation created by Atau Tanaka and Bert Bongers in collaboration with Kasper Toeplitz. The idea behind this project was to create a musical string (like the string of a violin or guitar) that spans a large geographical distance (Tanaka and Bongers 2001).

The installation consisted of a steel cable 12 mm in diameter and 15 m long connected to a "virtual string" on the network. The real part of the string stretched from the floor diagonally up to the ceiling of the space (Figure 2.46). Vibration sensors translated the physical vibrations to network data. These vibrations were transmitted to the other endpoint of the string, an identical steel cable. Striking the string on one side made it vibrate on the other side. Global String was designed as a musical instrument in which the network is supposed to act as its resonating body.

Sound was synthesized in real time by a software algorithm implementing a physical model of a string of unreal proportions. Audio, video, and sensor data were streamed between the sites, providing a live connection between the players.

Figure 2.46 Global String is a musical string that spans a large geographical distance through the Internet.

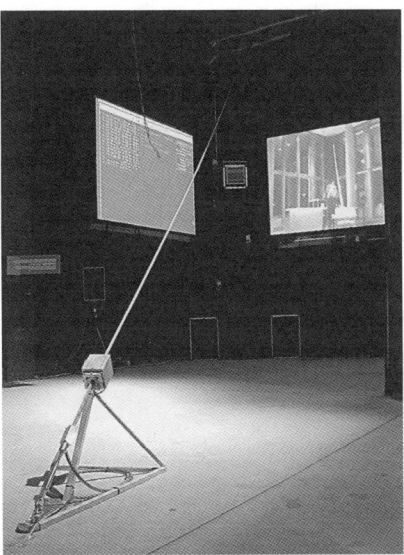

Global String implemented two sensor systems, one detecting rapid action on the string and the other following slower gross movements. These reflected two distinct modes of player interaction with the string. The high-frequency information was derived from a piezo transducer mounted on an aluminum block attached to the string. This signal was used as an audio rate control signal and for excitation of the audio synthesis engine. Low-frequency data were obtained from Hall effect sensors. Two small neodymium magnets were attached to the string, mounted in the aluminum block on the string, facing Hall effect detectors mounted orthogonally on a housing around the string. Two sensors were used, one for each degree of freedom of the string: movements on the horizontal and vertical axes. These voltages entered a sensor interface and captured movements of the string from 0 Hz to a software-limited maximum of 250 Hz.

An actuator translated electrical signals into perceivable physical events. Global String used an electromagnet to generate tactile cues to the player touching the string, creating a relationship to actions performed at the remote end. The electromagnet was excited in pulse mode with a high DC voltage. This pulled the string by an iron plate mounted on an aluminum block, generating a palpable pulse in the string and resulting in a haptic sense of telepresence.

Control data from the piezo sensor was multiplexed with local audio and video. The video image received from the remote site was projected and served to visualize the far end of the string. Received audio data was treated in two ways: it entered the local audio amplification system and was processed for peak detection analysis.

A second video projector alongside the string image projected audio signal visualization. The analysis consisted of a real time amplitude envelope and frequency spectrum of the sound from the two sites.

2.8 ADAPTIVE CONTROLLERS

Adaptive controllers are not straightforward to design. One alternative is to let the controller alter the mapping between sensors and sound, so that the essence of the instrument changes according to a given criterion (Hunt and Wanderley 2002). Joseph Rovan and colleagues (1997) proposed an example of an adaptive musical instrument, where a woodwind instrument-like controller (Yamaha's WX7 controller) was used to control additive synthesis simulation of wind instruments. By changing the mapping layer, the resulting instrument could behave in a simplified or in a more complex way. In the simplified way, the control parameters were all independent, making the instrument easier to play by novices. In the more sophisticated way, the blowing pressure and embouchure were tightly coupled, as in an acoustic reed instrument. In the first, simplified way, the instrument was easier to play, but the subtle control possibilities involving simultaneous blow and embouchure control were lost.

An example of an attempt at the design of adaptive controllers is the Orb-3 system, by Dan Livingstone and colleagues (Livingstone and Miranda 2004, 2005) at the University of Plymouth's Interdisciplinary Centre for Computer Music Research (ICCMR). It consists of robotic spheres, referred to as Orbs, housing a cluster of analog sensors, including LEDs, thermistors, and vibration and tilt switches, for measuring ambient light, ambient heat, general motion, and orientation. The system comprises four Orbs, which can be placed and relocated to generate and vary the data used to synthesize sound material for 7.1 sound diffusion, controlled by a gesture and motion-based video tracking system. The Orbs can move and reposition themselves autonomously or in collaboration, by integrating positional tracking and proximity triggers. This dynamic motion provides a visual element that reveals the compositional potential of the system while demonstrating some of the synthesis and diffusion properties that are influenced by the interaction between or within each sphere (Figure 2.47).

Each Orb sends data via a 2.4 GHz wireless interface to a laptop running Max/MSP. The software is designed to correlate different data against previous interactions, a form of compositional memory where environmental parameters of previous sessions are compared with current ones to identify repeated behaviors of the system and actions of participants. Previously unrecorded or new data configurations are identified and used to compose new sound events or

Figure 2.47 The Orb-3 system, with eight active speakers forming an "auditory sphere," angled to provide versatile software-controlled diffusion. Diffusion and synthesis generated from environment and interaction data collected by each Orb (spheres on the floor).

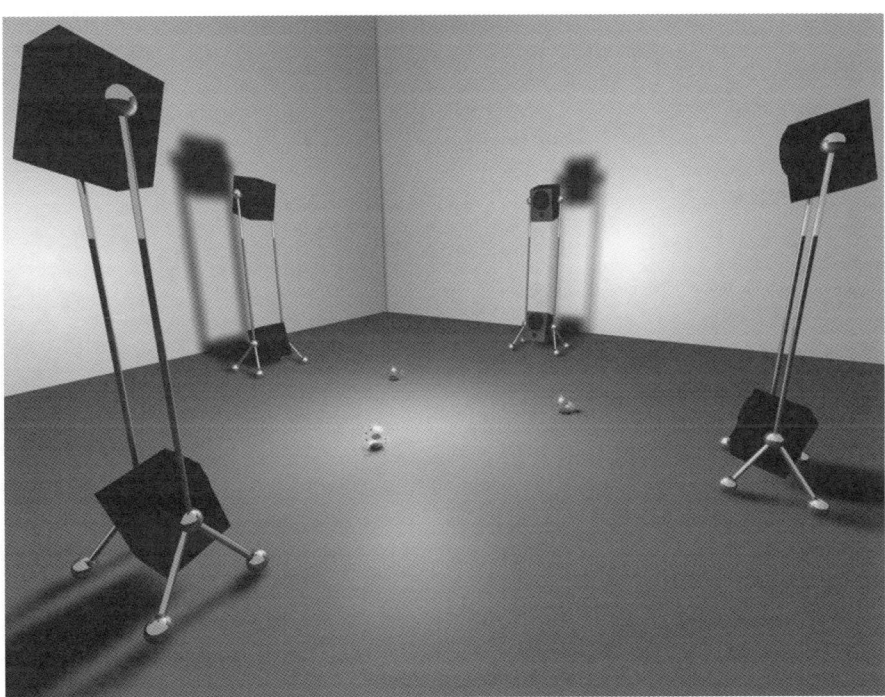

objects. The software sends data to each Orb to indicate its state and trigger visual or tactile feedback—for example, activating laser/proximity sensing for positioning, status LED, and force feedback. Each Orb has two modes: absorb and adapt. In absorb mode an Orb is autonomous and is located on the floor. Its sensors are calibrated to collect environmental data, ambient light, ambient temperature, relative position, and orientation. The adapt mode is activated when the alignment of Orbs is disturbed, either by walking between them, interrupting the laser tracking, or picking them up, which also activates vibration sensors and initiates orientation mapping. The angle and orientation of each Orb in this state directly influences the panning and diffusion rates of synthesized sounds (Figure 2.48).

As an adaptive system, the Orb-3 environment creates an opportunity for observing and recording forms of emergent behavior in relation to spatial sound interaction. This provides a structured framework to inform the design of mobile and autonomous interfaces, such as musical robots or adaptive social composition systems.

Figure 2.48 Laser alignment: triangulation. Lasers are activated; two Orbs are shown in listening absorb mode after calibration; one (lower right) is about to move out of alignment in response to parameter changes. It may move or rotate to attract participants; the system responds by panning a sound in relation to its movement.

2.9 COMPARING GESTURAL CONTROLLERS

As can be seen in this chapter and in the following ones, there are literally hundreds of examples of gestural controllers and digital musical instruments proposed in the literature. The question for someone thinking about performing with existing gestural controllers is: How to choose one controller instead of another for a specific musical task?

The comparison of controllers with DMIs has been proposed in various ways: from a human-computer interaction perspective (Wanderley and Orio 2002), where tools from that domain were adapted to the context of musical performance with new instruments, to a comparison of instrument features such as expressivity, immersion, and feedback (Piringer 2001; see Figure 2.49), and to the study of the efficiency of musical instruments (Jordà 2004).

Figure 2.49 A comparison of digital musical instruments based on expressivity, immersion, and feedback, by Jörg Piringer (2001). "Expressivity" appears on the y axis, with the categories very good, good, middle, and little (top to bottom). "Immersion" appears on the x-axis, with the categories Touch-controller, Extended-range, Partially Immersive, and Fully Immersive, an adaptation from Mulder 2000. Each shape represents an instrument; the size indicates the amount of feedback and the color indicates feedback modality.

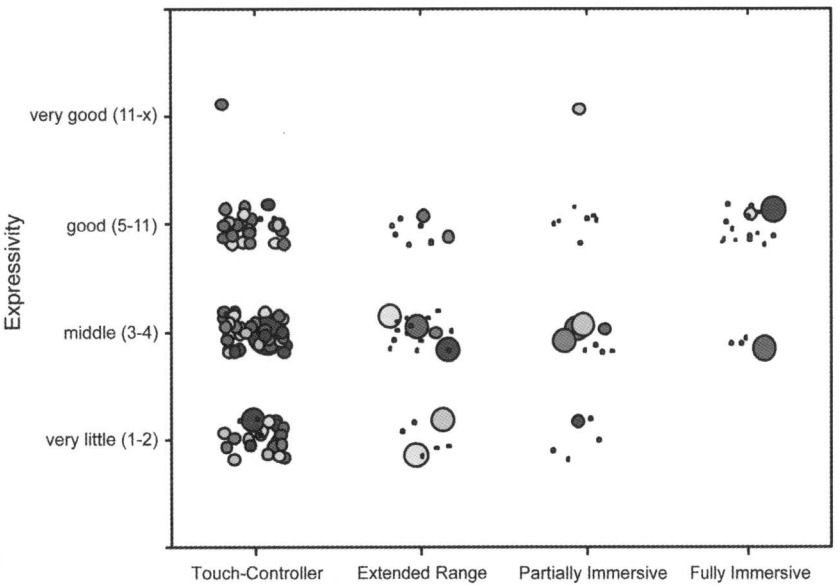

One can also compare devices from a purely technological perspective by looking at the sensor technologies involved, the feedback modalities available, the chosen mapping strategies and synthesis algorithms (Wanderley and Depalle 2004).

Yet another possibility is to consider features of the instrument and their roles, what could be named "interaction" perspective. For instance, in multimedia instruments, sound can be the secondary means of communication, after video, while in most musical instruments it is the primary communication channel. Some instruments may require (or allow building of) expertise from performers, while others have a low entry fee (Wessel and Wright 2002).

Interaction perspective. A possible collection of features to be compared in the interaction perspective include:

- The final goal of the interaction: expression of an idea, communication, or the exploration of an environment
- The level of expertise required from the user for the expected interaction to take place; a feature closely related to the final goal of the interaction
- Primary communication (perception) channel: auditory, visual, or haptic;
- Number of participants
- Location in space (close together or distant)
- The physical approach the user has to the system: contact or noncontact actions

Other related features could include:

- Body parts involved in the interaction: hand manipulation, hand gestures, other limb movements, whole-body movements, postures, etc.
- Number of degrees of freedom involved in each action
- Types of variables controlled (discrete or continuous) (Pressing 1990)

Figure 2.50 shows a seven-axis diagram designed to represent seven features of digital musical instruments and of interactive sound installations (Birnbaum et al. 2005). By plotting the equivalent characteristics of a chosen musical instrument in the diagram, one can easily derive possible applications (Figure 2.51).

Figure 2.50 A seven-axis diagram from Birnbaum and colleagues (2005).

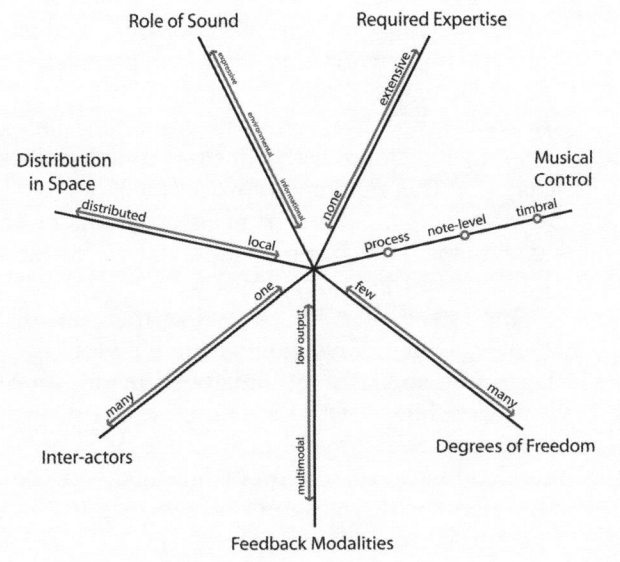

Figure 2.51 Examples of applications from Birnbaum and colleagues (2005).

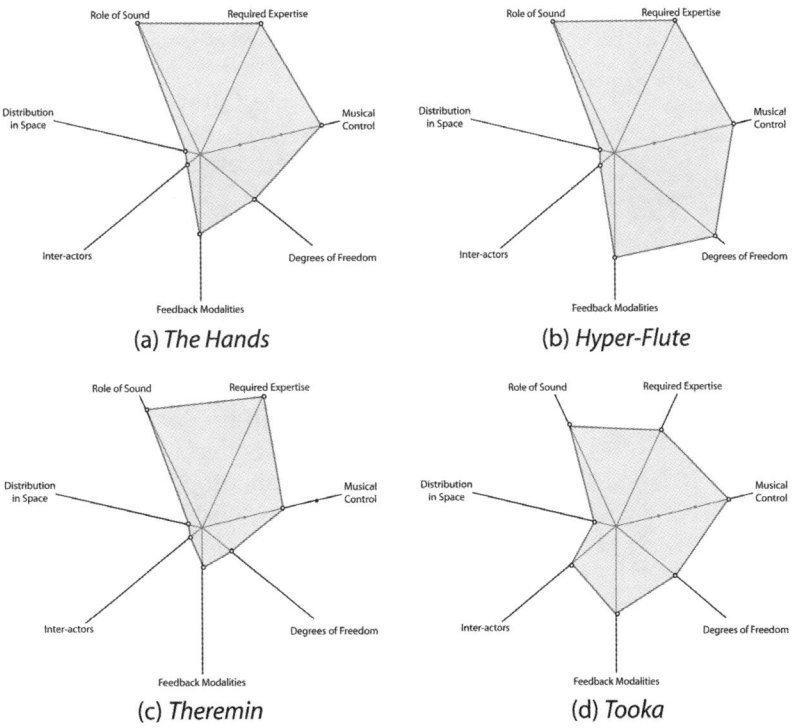

2.10 REMARKS ON DMI DESIGN

When studying the various controller designs available, one may have the impression that the job is complete once a design strategy has been chosen and a prototype controller built. This may not always be true. Very often several adjustments need to be made in order to fully obtain the desired functionalities. Furthermore, it is likely that this refinement process will be extensive and span a number of years, yielding various generations of controllers sharing the same name and basic functionalities, as seen in the discussion above about the Continuum.

This is the case for several of the controllers discussed in this chapter, which have gone through various refinements. Some of these refinements may have been made in order to solve inherent design problems. Others may be made owing to the availability of newer components and technology or in order to make controllers more robust. A typical procedure involves the replacement of original sensors with higher-performance and/or lower-cost ones.

Another reason for implementing improvements is that the designer may realize that extra functionalities could be added to the original device after a period of practice. Conversely, initial functionalities may have to be removed from the controller if they do not fulfill design expectations when put in practice. In short, the design of a controller may involve a lengthy trial-and-error process before a stable version is achieved.

One very useful set of practical principles for the design of novel control surfaces is given by Perry Cook (2001). Remarks such as "Smart instruments are often not smart," "Some players have spare bandwidth, some do not," and "Wires are not that bad (compared to wireless)" are clever observations on the design of new digital musical instruments.

Finally, it is important to stress that music controllers need to be used in performance in order to be fully evaluated! Only when playing a controller can the designer ultimately feel its flexibility and limitations. But we insist that complementary approaches, sometimes derived from other domains, may enlighten the design of novel instruments (Wanderley and Orio 2002). In fact, without a common basis for evaluation, differentiation between input devices turns out to be hazardous and is more likely to reveal personal tastes than to provide useful information for potential users.

2.11 FURTHER READING

Where to go from here?

The electronic publication (on CD-ROM) *Trends in Gestural Control of Music* (Wanderley and Battier 2000) addresses several of the concerns in this area. It consists of a selection of articles from pioneers in DMI use and design, including 24 tutorials, research articles and case studies on new interfaces, mapping, and gestural control of music, as well as an extensive bibliography and a list of resources. This publication also includes several videos and sound examples illustrating the articles, which are specially formatted for screen reading and printing.

Currently there is no scientific journal completely devoted to the design of DMIs or new controllers. However, existing computer music and music technology journals have devoted some special issues to these topics and are generally open to the publication of research articles, development reports, or aesthetic considerations related to new controllers. The three main journals specifically devoted to computer music and music technology research are *Journal of New Music Research* (formerly called *Interface*) published by Routledge, *Computer Music Journal*, published by MIT Press, and *Organised Sound*, published by Cambridge University Press. Special issues of these journals dedicated to interaction and new musical instruments include (since 1990 only):

- *Interface* 22(3), a special issue devoted to a workshop called "Man-machine Interaction in Live Performance," organized by Leonello Tarabella, that took place in Pisa in 1991
- *Journal of New Music Research* 32(4), a special issue devoted to the NIME conference, edited by the organizers of NIME 02, and including papers from both NIME 02 and NIME 03
- *Computer Music Journal* 14(1) and 14(2), on new performance interfaces, with the state of the art in 1990, and more recently issues 22(1) and 26(3), the later on the first NIME workshop in Seattle, 2001. The interest of *Computer Music Journal* in the topic can be inferred from the editorial of issue 16(3)
- *Organised Sound*, special issue 7(2) on mapping strategies for real-time computer music and issue 7(3) on interactivity
- *Leonardo Music Journal* and *Leonardo*, also published by MIT Press, often feature papers on the topic

Another source of information is conference proceedings, such as:

- The International Computer Music Conference (ICMC), established in the 1970s, a rich source of information. It does not address controllers specifically, but throughout the years various interfaces have been presented at this event.
- The International Conference on New Interfaces for Musical Expression (NIME), established in 2001 and dedicated entirely to new controllers. The proceedings of the various NIME conferences so far are freely available online at http://www.nime.org (accessed 1 May 2005).

Curtis Roads's book *Computer Music Tutorial* (1996) dedicates an entire chapter to new interfaces, with several examples of controllers and a number of photographs.

Grigore Burdea and Philippe Coiffet's book *Virtual Reality Technology* (2003) is a great source of information about motion trackers, data gloves, and tactile and force-feedback devices used in virtual reality. Burdea's *Force and Touch Feedback for Virtual Reality* (1996) is also a very good reference on those topics.

Two general works on computer music are worth mentioning:

- Peter Manning's *Electronic and Computer Music* (2004), now in its third edition
- Joel Chadabe's *Electric Sound: The Past and Promise of Electronic Music* (1997)

Neither book is directly related to new controllers, but both present very useful information on various developments in this area. Chadabe's book has an excellent chapter on new instruments and interfaces.

Finally, several Web sites present useful information:

- The Interactive Systems and Instrument Design in Music Web site (ISIDM) at http://www.igmusic.org (accessed 1 May 2005) presents information on interface design, mapping, and other topics, including substantial bibliographical resources.
- The ConGAS (Controlled Gesture Audio Systems) Project Web site at http://www.cost287.org (accessed 20 December 2005) has up-to-date information on controllers and devices.
- Michel Waisvisz's Archive at http://www.crackle.org (accessed 11 October 2005) is an excellent list of information from one of the most important controller designers and a virtuoso performer.

- Jörg Piringer's list of electronic instruments at http://joerg.piringer.net (accessed 11 October 2005) is a comprehensive list of controllers and other electronic musical instruments, available as an html or Excel file.
- Bill Buxton's directory of sources for input technologies at http://www.billbuxton.com/InputSources.html (accessed 11 October 2005), although not directly related to musical applications, is a comprehensive list of devices.

THREE

Sensors and Sensor-to-Computer Interfaces

This chapter introduces a number of sensor technologies and interfacing systems for creating gestural controllers. It reviews the applications of these sensors in the design of various musical systems and discusses methods for converting the sensor signals into data that can be used to control software sound synthesizers.

The main topic of interest in this chapter is data acquisition—that is, ways to measure physical phenomena and obtain signals suitable for use as input to control a computer or a music system.

The design of a gestural controller usually requires the measurement of a physical body action. The variables to be measured can consist of movements of the fingers, hands, arms, feet, legs, head, and/or eyes. Also, body postures, force applied to an object, and a number of other body-related phenomena may be measured. The data to be acquired may therefore be of various forms: position in space, velocity (or acceleration), inclination, temperature, and so on. These data then need to be transduced into electrical signals, usually in the form of a voltage or current, which is transformed into the digital signals of a communication protocol such as the well-known MIDI or the relatively new OSC (Wright and Freed 1997) so that they may be taken into account by software for musical performance.

■ 3.1 TRANSDUCERS, SENSORS, AND ACTUATORS

As mentioned above, in order to acquire information about body movements, forces, and so on, one usually needs to use devices that capture the phenomena of interest in terms of electrical signals. Such devices are commonly called sensors and transducers.

Sensors and transducers. Occasionally, the terms sensors and transducers are used interchangeably, but they are not exact synonyms. Technically, a transducer is an energy converter, a device that converts one type of energy into another. It implies that the nature of the input and the nature of the output are dissimilar (Pallàs-Areny and Webster 2001). For instance, a loudspeaker is a transducer because it converts electrical signals into acoustic waves (i.e., sound).

A sensor is a device that responds to stimuli by producing electrical signals. Technically, it is a "device that converts any type of energy into electrical energy" (Fraden 2004).

Note that not all authors agree on these definitions. For instance, David Nyce (2004) defines a sensor as "an input device that provides a usable output in response to a specific physical quantity input." He states that the output of many modern sensors is an electrical signal, but, alternatively, it could be motion, pressure, flow, or some other usable type of output. In this case, a pressure-sensing diaphragm that converts fluid pressure into force or position change is an example of a sensor.

A sensor may also modify an electrical signal; that is, it can be considered a modifier. In some contexts sensors can also be referred to as input transducers or detectors, for example, when used for measuring radiation.

Most, but not all, sensors are transducers, employing one or more transduction mechanisms to produce an electrical output signal (Smith 1993). For instance, a microphone is a sensor because it converts acoustic waves into electrical signals. Therefore, a loudspeaker, which vibrates when sound is produced by another source, could be considered a sensor. This is basically what happens with piezoelectric crystals used for measuring ultrasound waves (see section 3.3.8), where both the microphone and the loudspeaker are used interchangeably—in fact, the two devices are mechanically identical.

Transducers and actuators. An actuator is a device that converts electrical energy into other types of energy. It is therefore a transducer and can be considered the opposite of a sensor. An example is a motor that converts electrical energy into mechanical action. Other examples of actuators were introduced in chapter 2 where we discussed haptic and tactile feedback devices.

Actuators are sometimes referred to as effectors or output transducers, depending on the context of their application.

3.1.1 Types of Sensors

There are a great variety of sensors available for industrial applications, and many of them can be used for the design of gestural controllers. Sensors can be classified according to some of their most distinctive features. For instance, sensors can be direct or complex, passive or active, absolute or relative, contact or noncontact, and analog or digital.

A direct sensor directly converts the energy from an input into electrical signals, for instance, converting pressure into electric voltage. In contrast, a complex sensor is composed of a chain of transducers. It uses transducers that convert an input stimulus into other types of energy as well as transducers that convert this energy into electrical signals. The last transducer in this chain will invariably be a direct sensor, since its output is an electrical signal.

A passive sensor, also referred to as a self-generating sensor, generates electrical signals at its output without the need for an additional energy source. In simpler terms, a passive sensor either provides its own energy or derives it from the phenomenon being measured (Carr 1993). An example of a passive sensor is a piezoelectric sensor that converts mechanical vibrations into electrical signals without the need for an additional energy source. These sensors normally have only two wires, as no connection to a power supply is necessary.

Conversely, an active sensor needs energy from an external source (independent of the stimulus) in order to operate. An example of an active sensor is the GP2D12 IR position sensor by Sharp (see section 3.3.9), which needs electrical current from an external source to output a voltage proportional to the change of position of the object in front of it.

It is important not to confuse the notion of the active and passive sensors just described with the more common definition of active and passive electronic devices, such as electronic filters. A passive filter is typically composed of resistors, capacitors, and inductors. An active filter is typically composed of resistors, capacitors, and active components (usually operational amplifiers, but also transistors and diodes; Daryanani 1976).

An absolute sensor detects a stimulus in reference to an absolute physical scale, that is, independent of the measurement conditions. A relative sensor produces a signal that relates to some special case.

When a sensor does not need to be in physical contact with the source of the energy to be converted into electrical signals, it is referred to as a noncontact sensor. Otherwise it is referred to as a contact sensor. And whereas an analog sensor outputs a continuous electrical signal, a digital sensor outputs a signal in the form of discrete steps or states.

Jacob Fraden (2004) proposes other sensor classification schemes considering such attributes as the type of stimulus that is measured and its specification, types of conversion used, the materials they are made of, and the field of their application.

3.1.2 Sensor Specification

Once the variable to be measured is established, one needs to choose a suitable sensor from among the various options available. This may not be so trivial, because there are often several different types of sensors that can be used to measure the same variable. (See, for example, section 2.4.3.) One way to approach this problem is to consider the classification discussed in the previous section. For example, for specific applications it might be better to use a passive analog sensor rather than an active digital sensor. But if there are several options for passive analog sensors, then additional criteria must be used to aid the choice.

Several engineering textbooks propose schemes for the specification of sensors based on a number of characteristics. Some authors consider the most important sensor characteristics to be sensitivity, stability, and repeatability (Smith 1993). Other important characteristics relate to the linearity and selectivity of the sensor's output, its sensitivity to ambient conditions, and so forth.

Patrick Garrett (1994) considers six descriptive parameters applicable to sensors:

- *Accuracy*: the closeness with which a measurement approaches the true value of a measurand

- *Error*: the difference between a measurement and the true value of a measurand

- *Precision*: a measurement over some span described by the number of significant figures available (a precise sensor provides repeatable significant figures)

- *Resolution*: the smallest quantity that can be determined; the minimum change in the input necessary to produce a detectable change in the output

- *Span or full-scale input* (FSI): the extent of a measurement between any two limits; corresponds to the dynamic range of stimuli that may be converted by a sensor

- *Range*: the total extent of possible measurement values

Joseph Carr (1993) cites other characteristics, such as:

- *Offset*: the difference between the actual output and the specified output value under some particular set of conditions
- *Linearity*: the expression of the extent to which the actual measured curve of a sensor departs from an ideal curve
- *Monotonicity*: where the output always either increases or decreases with an increase of the input
- *Hysteresis error*: the deviation of the sensor's output at a specific point of the input signal when it is approached from opposite directions

Ramon Pallàs-Areny and John Webster (2001) consider precision to be the quality that best characterizes the capability of a measuring instrument. A precise instrument should give the same reading when repeated measures are taken of the same measurand under identical conditions, disregarding any coincidence or discrepancy between the result and the true value. This is a necessary but insufficient condition for accuracy.

The same authors also prefer to separate the characteristics of measurement systems into two main groups: *static* and *dynamic*.

Static characteristics are those that describe the behavior of a measurement system under slowly varying input signals, that is, signals that can be considered to be static. They include accuracy, error, precision, resolution, and linearity, as proposed by Patrick Garrett and Joseph Carr above, along with:

- *Repeatability*: the closeness of short-term successive results obtained using the same method and conditions
- *Reproducibility*: similar to repeatability, but for long-term measurements by different people and under different conditions
- *Sensitivity*: also referred to as scale factor; the slope of the calibration curve, where high slopes indicate high sensitivity

Dynamic characteristics describe the behavior of measurement systems under variable input signals. They include:

- *Dynamic error*: the difference between the measurement and the measurand when the static errors are zero
- *Speed of response*: the speed with which a measurement system reacts to changes in the measurand

3.2 SENSORS IN MUSICAL APPLICATIONS

Typically, gestural controllers use sensors that are commercially available, many of which have been designed for nonmusical applications, such as the automotive or biomedical industry. One can also develop one's own sensors, as mentioned in section 3.8.1 below about force-sensitive resistors and position sensors. Although not very common, there are cases where sensors that were developed for a musical application have been adapted for a different industrial application (Paradiso 2003).

A fair number of commercially available sensors can be used in musical applications. In most cases these are sensors for measuring variables produced by human actions, such as force, position, velocity, acceleration, and so on. In certain systems, including interactive audio installations, other sensors such as those for ambient light, magnetic detection, or even pollution may be of interest (Gaye, Mazé, and Holmquist 2003).

In general instrumentation circuits for industrial and medical applications, sensors typically need to be both precise and accurate and to present a reasonable resolution. In the musical domain, it is interesting to stress that the choice of sensor technology to match a specific musical characteristic relates to human performance and perception. In other words, musical applications do not necessarily share the same requirements as industrial or medical applications, and sometimes sensors with inferior characteristics can still be useful. For example, in some cases the output of a sensor that is not very accurate can be satisfactorily used to control timbre, but if it is used to control pitch, its inaccuracy will probably be more noticeable.

The resolution of an actuator used to generate tactile information might be one of the most important factors. Suppose that one wants to excite part of the skin of the hand and the leg of a subject in order to provide the person with information related to the position of a virtual object: the resolution of the transducer used in the hand will probably need to be much higher than that used in the leg because it is known that the hand has a larger number of tactile receptors. Cutaneous Grooves (Gunther, Davenport, and O'Modhrain 2002) was a good example of a musical application that uses various actuators to simulate tactile sensations.

3.3 REVIEW OF COMMONLY USED SENSORS IN MUSICAL APPLICATIONS

This section introduces a number of sensors used in musical applications. It presents the basic technical characteristics of these sensors, discusses their potential for the design of gestural controllers, and indicates examples of systems in which they have been employed.

Sensors can be classified according to the input variable that is sensed. This approach is used by Jacob Fraden (2004) and by Ramon Pallàs-Areny and John Webster (2001). Other authors present a specific set of sensors (e.g., only linear position sensors) according to their physical sensing mechanism (Nyce 2004).

Designers of gestural controllers often prefer to sort sensors according to the type of body actions they can sense, such as movement or pressure. But, as we have already seen, there are many other ways to classify these sensors: contact versus noncontact sensors, continuous versus discrete sensors, and so forth.

Sorting sensors by the type of variable sensed would require the introduction of the same sensor several times, which would generate unnecessary redundancy in our discussion; for example, the ultrasonic sensor can be used to sense position, velocity, and flow rate. In this book we will classify the various sensors according to their inherent technologies.

The sensors discussed in this section are as follows, presented in this order:

- Force-sensitive resistors (FSRs)
- Strain gauges
- Bend sensors
- Standard CPS2 155 and 1642 LinPots
- Linear and rotary potentiometers
- Tactile linear position sensors
- Piezoelectric sensors
- Ultrasound sensors
- IR sensors
- Visible light–sensing devices
- Hall effect sensors

- Magnetic tags
- Magnetoresistive sensors (or digital compasses)
- Capacitive sensors
- Accelerometers
- Gyroscopes
- Tilt sensors and mercury switches
- Air pressure sensors
- Other sensor types: vision-based systems, temperature sensors, humidity sensors, discrete keys, rotary encoders, LVDTs, galvanic skin response sensors, Doppler radars, and microphones.

The following sections briefly introduce these sensors.

3.3.1 Force-sensitive Resistors

A force-sensitive (or force-sensing) resistor (FSR) can be considered a tactile sensor, a special class of force or pressure transducer, which is characterized by its slimness. This is probably the most common sensor used in the design of new musical interfaces. FSRs are widely available, easy to use, and relatively inexpensive.

A force-sensitive resistor typically consists of a conductive-polymer film sensor whose conductance is proportional to the applied force. In other words, electrical resistance will decrease with the increase of force applied to the device; conductance is the inverse of resistance. This relationship is nonlinear because there is a switch type of response for low forces.

The Interlink FSR consists of two polymer films: one with a conductive surface and the other with printed electrodes facing the first one. Contact between the two surfaces causes the conductive layer to short the printed electrodes and therefore reduce the electric resistance of the device. Typically, its resistance will drop from greater than 100 kiloohms (kΩ) to about 100 ohms. Two other commercial examples are manufactured by LuSense and by Tekscan. LuSense force-sensitive resistors use a technology similar to that of Interlink FSRs, while Tekscan Flexiforce sensors use two layers of substrate composed of silver over polyester, followed by a layer of pressure-sensitive ink (Vecchi et al. 2000).

Fabricio Vecchi and colleagues (2000) have experimentally evaluated both the Interlink FSR and the Tekscan Flexiforce through a series of measurements. They concluded that the Flexiforce sensors present better response in terms of linearity, repeatability, time drift, and dynamic accuracy, while the Interlink FSRs are more robust.

It is not difficult, however, to make force- or pressure-sensitive resistor units at home. For example, Bert Bongers (2000) suggested a technique for making FSR units using two copper connectors and a conductive foam. According to Bongers, a cheap way of building pressure sensors such as this is with the black packaging foam used for transporting integrated circuits (ICs). This foam conducts electricity (to avoid static charges), and its resistance changes when it is compressed. Copper foil attached to both sides of the foam can be used to make the electrical connectors. (See section 3.8.1. for more information on homemade force and pressure sensors.)

Musical applications. Force-sensitive resistors have been extensively used in several designs, including controllers such as the force-sensitive floor (Pinkston, Kerkhoff, and McQuilken 1995), tactile gloves (Figures 3.2 and 3.3), CyberBoots (Choi 2000), Java MUG (Cook 2001), and the extended Wacom tablet (Wanderley et al. 2000). They have been used to extend the capabilities of acoustic instruments such as in the meta-trumpet (Impett 1994), the meta-saxophone (Burtner 2002), and the hyper-flute (Palacio-Quintin 2003). FSRs were also cleverly used to sense pulling force in alternate controllers, such as in the SillyTone Squish Factory (Morris, Leitman, and Kassianidou 2004).

Figures 3.1, 3.2, 3.3, and 3.4 show how Interlink FSR sensors were used in various projects. Figure 3.1 shows Interlink, LuSense, and Tekscan force sensors.

Figure 3.1   Three FSR sensors.

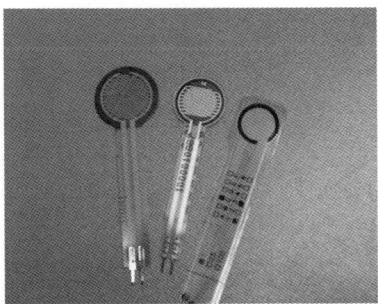

Figures 3.2 and 3.3 show the small round FSR of Figure 3.1 attached to the fingertip of a glove in order to create a tactile glove for sound control. Pierre-Yves Fortier designed this glove at McGill University, inspired by previous developments by Butch Rovan (Depalle, Tassart, and Wanderley 1997) and by the tactile gloves produced by Infusion Systems. Note in Figure 3.3 the appearance of two other sensors: a bend sensor on the finger and an IR sensor on the wrist. These sensors will be discussed below.

Figure 3.2 A small round FSR sensor attached to the fingertip of a glove for sound control.

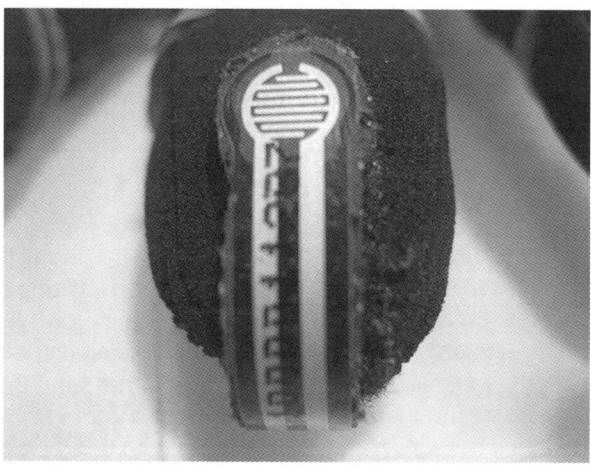

Figure 3.3 Four FSRs, a bend sensor attached to a finger, and an infrared sensor attached to the wrist of a glove for sound control.

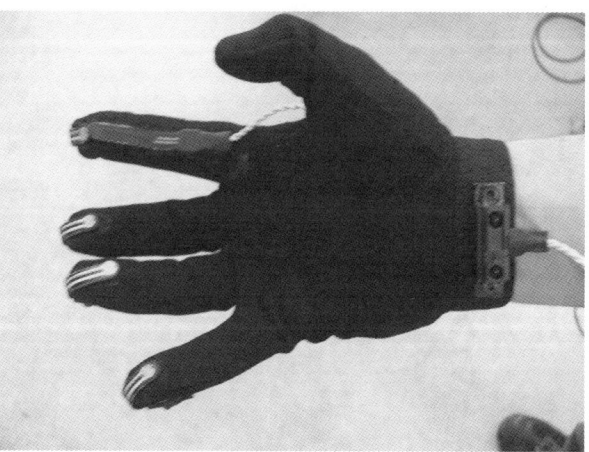

Figure 3.4 Butch Rovan's data glove. Notice its use with an acoustic instrument (clarinet), instead of sensors being placed directly on the instrument. (Photo by Muratet.)

Figure 3.4 shows Butch Rovan using his data glove while performing on a clarinet. His gloves use FSR sensors attached to the fingertips, bend sensors, and an accelerometer attached to the wrist.

As mentioned before, the advantages of FSR sensors are that they are easy to use and widely available commercially at affordable prices. One of the main disadvantages is that these sensors are fragile: they can easily break if bent excessively. Also, their measurements are nonlinear and qualitative since their resistance may drift if they are subject to prolonged pressure. Therefore, FSR sensors are not recommended for applications where absolute, quantitative measurements of force are required.

3.3.2 Strain Gauges

Strain gauges are resistive elastic sensors whose resistance is a function of applied strain due to mechanical stress. Their resistance decreases with compression and increases with tension (Fraden 2004). The change with applied force in the resistance of a material is called the piezoresistive effect (not to be confused with the piezoelectric effect, described below).

Strain gauges are more accurate than FSRs and provide a quantitative measurement of force; they are usually used in pairs in order to measure both tension and compression. In contrast to FSR sensors, there is no direct contact between an object (e.g., a finger) and the sensing element in strain gauges. The strain gauge measures changes in the properties of an object (tension or compression) to which the gauges are attached.

One of the main limitations of strain gauges is their restricted elastic range, which is less than 4% of the gauge length; this yields a much narrower force measurement range than the range of an FSR. Another limitation is that temperature interferes with its response.

In practice, another difference between the FSR sensor and the strain gauge is that the force to be measured in the former is applied directly to the sensor and perpendicularly to its surface, whereas in the latter the force is applied to the material under stress to which the gauge is bonded and in the same plane as the surface of the gauge.

Strain gauges are often used for sensing weight. An example is the system for center-of-gravity sensing used in a motion interface by Jun Yokono and Shuji Hashimoto (1998). In this system, the authors used strain gauges bonded under each side of a plate on top of which a user may stand or sit. Depending on the weight distribution of the body, the strain gauges changed their resistance, indicating the direction of motion of the interface.

Musical applications. The hyper-bow, designed by Diana Young (2002), is a good example of a music controller that employs strain gauges (Figure 3.5). Young used two pairs of strain gauges in order to measure tension and compression on a bow while playing a string instrument (Figure 3.6).

A more recent interface using strain gauges is the Celloboard, created by Joseph Malloch (http://www.music.mcgill.ca/musictech/idmil/projects/celloboard/celloboard.html [accessed 29 November 2005]). In the Celloboard, a strain gauge is used to measure the tension in the instrument's wooden neck. The strain gauge is a good choice to measure the small degree of flexibility of the wood.

3.3.3 Bend Sensors

As its name suggests, some of the properties of a bend sensor are affected when it is bent. A strain gauge can be considered a bend sensor because its resistance is affected when the material to which it is attached is bent.

A typical example is Flexpoint's bend sensor, consisting of a strip of plastic with conductive ink. Bending the sensor causes its resistance to increase. Initially designed for the Mattel Power Glove, it

Figure 3.5 The Hyperbow, designed by Diana Young. (Photo by Yael G. Maguire.)

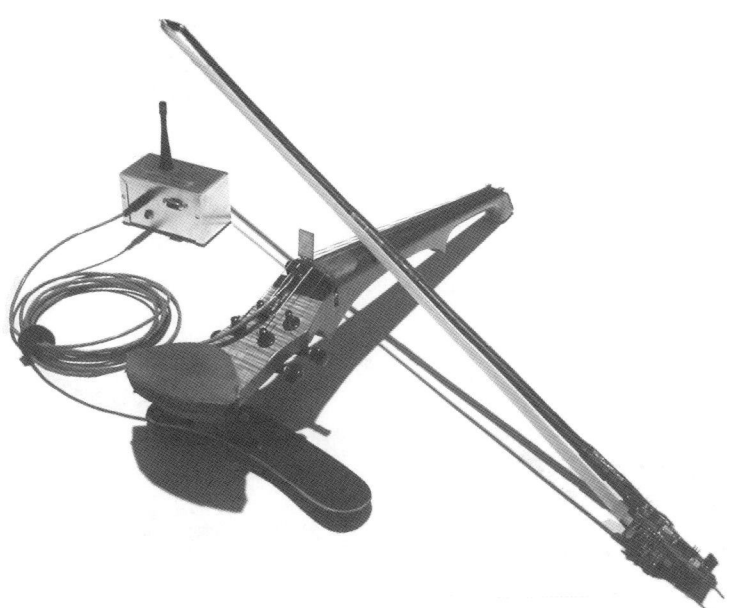

Figure 3.6 Detail of the Hyperbow showing two strain gauges.

has been used in several gestural controllers such as the Lady's Glove by Laetitia Sonami (Bongers 2000).

In 1994, Axel Mulder published an interesting paper on how to build a homemade data glove using flex sensors (1994a). Marcelo Wanderley, Patrice Pierrot, and Alain Terrier have also built data gloves by removing the flex sensors from secondhand Mattel Power Gloves (Figure 3.7). The interesting thing about the Mattel Power

Glove flex sensors is that the thumb sensor has a special format rather than being made in a straight line.

Bend sensors can be found in several sizes, such as BendMicro, BendMini, and BendShort, supplied by Infusion Systems (Figure 3.8). Their resistance changes with bending, from 6 kΩ (flat) to 500 kΩ (bent to 180°).

Another example of a bend sensor is the Shapetape sensor from Measurand. This sensor uses fiber-optic technology to measure both bend and twist. It is supplied with an interface allowing its connection to a computer, with a sampling rate of 189 Hz. The Shapetape sensor was used as an interface for creating and manipulating

Figure 3.7 A data glove using bend sensors.

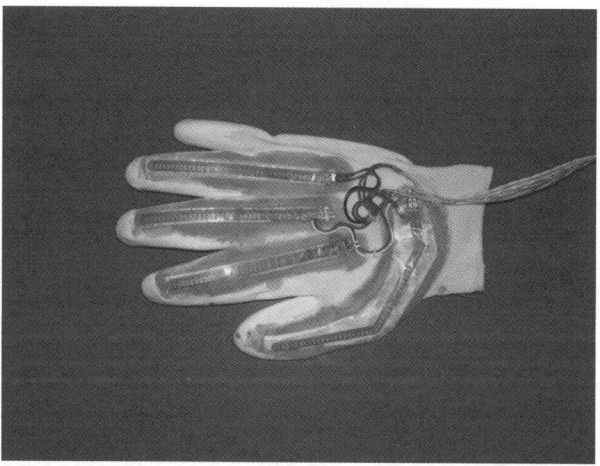

Figure 3.8 Examples of bend sensors.

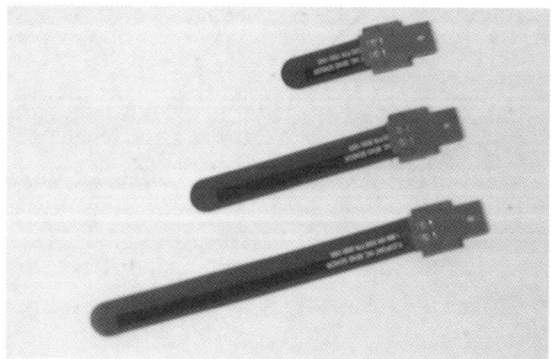

curves in graphics displays by Ravin Balakrishnan and colleagues (Balakrishnan et al. 1999).

Musical applications. Bend sensors are very useful because they can be easily attached to body parts or textiles. They have been used in several glove controllers (Mulder 1994a; Bongers 2000) and in dance-music interfaces, such as the Digital Dance Interface developed at the Danish Institute of Electronic Music (DIEM) by Wayne Siegel and colleagues (Siegel and Jacobsen 1998). Bend sensors may also be used back-to-back to measure bending in both directions. A music controller made with foam and with several sewn-on bend sensors designed by Mark Zadel is shown in Figures 3.9 and 3.10.

Bend sensors are also used in the Tooka (Fels et al. 2004), as seen in Figure 3.11.

Figure 3.9 A pliable music controller using bend sensors.

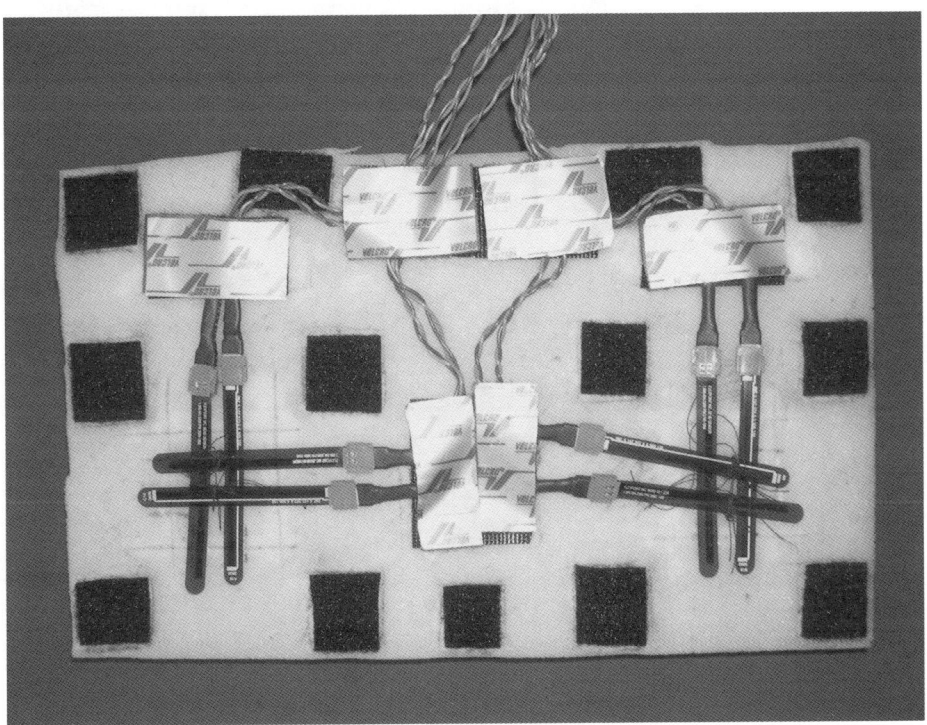

Figure 3.10 Performing deformation gestures on Mark Zadel's controller.

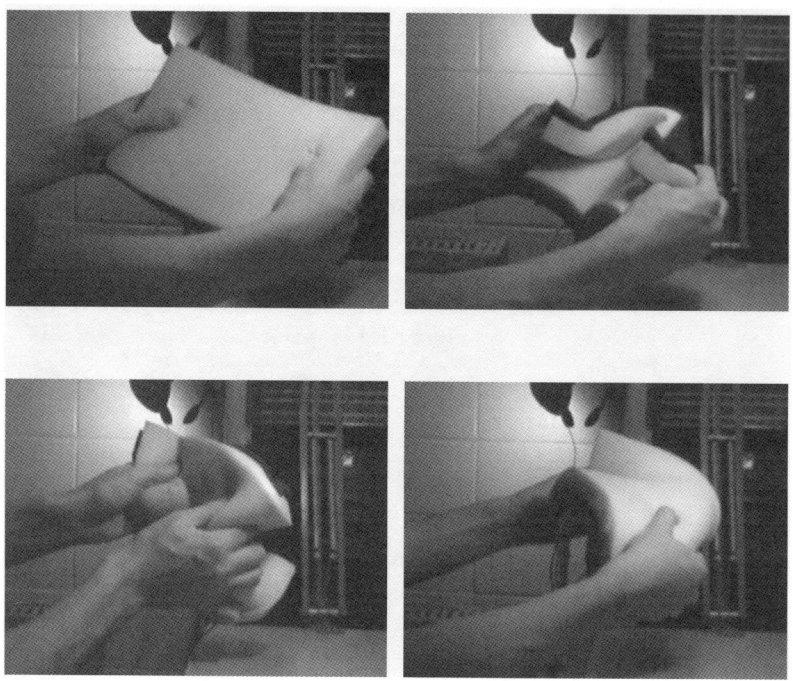

Figure 3.11 Bend sensor in the Tooka.

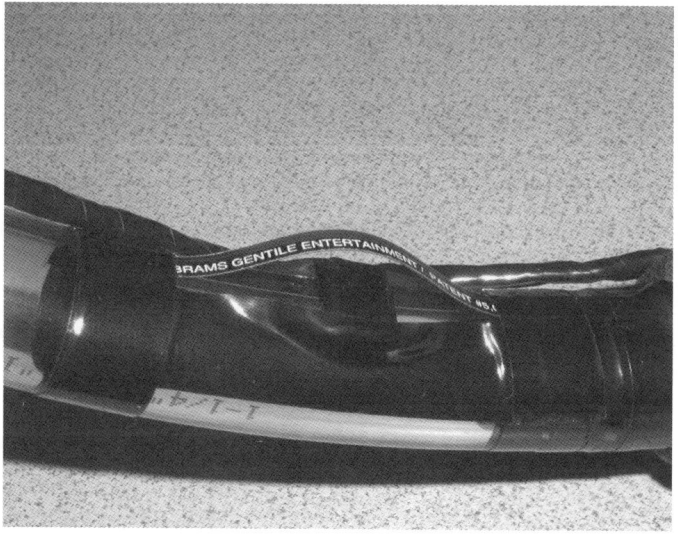

The Shapetape Model S1280C sensor has been used by Brian Sheehan (2004) to control a scanned-synthesis model as part of a controller called Squiggle.

3.3.4 LuSense Standard CPS² 155 and 1642 LinPots

The IEE (International Electronics and Engineering) LuSense Standard CPS² 155 FSR linear potentiometer, or LinPot, is a sensor that provides simultaneous measurements of both force and position of an object that is in contact with it.

It is important not to mistake position with displacement. These are not equivalent quantities. Whereas position refers to a measurement with respect to a constant reference value, displacement is a relative measurement whose reference is a previous value (Nyce 2004).

The CPS² 155 detection area is 105 mm × 15 mm (Figure 3.12). For pressures ranging from 0.5 to 100 N/cm², the resistance of the sensor changes from 1 MΩ to 5 kΩ. According to the IEE Specification Datasheet for the CPS² family of sensors, its resolution is smaller than 0.1 mm, and its typical response time is around 2 to 3 ms. This sensor requires a special conditioning circuit to separate the force and position signals that are output through the same wire. The CPS² 1642 sensor has the same operating principle as the CPS² 155, but its detection area is smaller: 65 × 15 mm.

Musical applications. The CPS² 155 sensor has been used in a number of interesting controllers, such as the SuperPolm, a violin-inspired controller designed by Suguru Goto, Patrice Pierrot, and Alain Terrier (Goto 2000). The SuperPolm uses four CPS² 155 units acting as if they were the strings of a violin (Figure 3.13).

Figure 3.12 The LuSense Standard CPS² 155 linear potentiometer, assembled in a metal support.

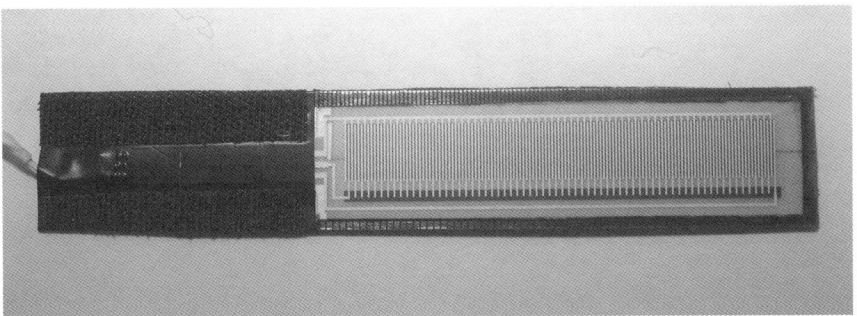

The CPS² 155 sensor has also been used together with two round FSR sensors in the extended Wacom tablet in order to provide four extra continuous control variables (Wanderley et al. 2000). Another interesting example is by Pierre-Yves Fortier as part of his tactile glove controller (Figure 3.14). He sewed a CPS² 155 onto the upper portion of a T-shirt, allowing him to control two extra continuous variables.

Figure 3.13 Suguru Goto and his SuperPolm controller.

Figure 3.14 Tactile gloves designed by Pierre-Yves Fortier.

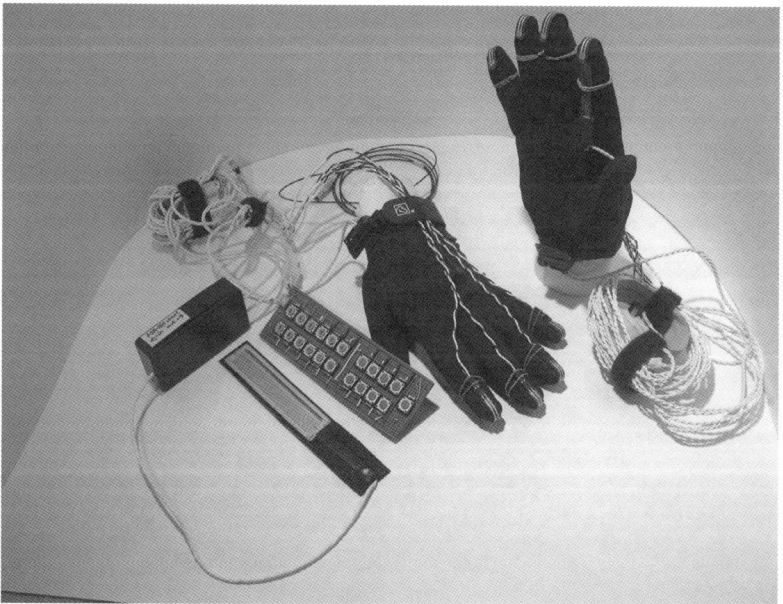

3.3.5 Sliders and Potentiometers

Sliders are linear position sensors, typically consisting of a resistive element and a conductive wiper that slides along the element, making electrical contact with it. The voltage at the wiper indicates the wiper position along the resistive element. Rotary pots (or rotation sensors) are rotary versions of sliders.

Potentiometers are often preferred for their low cost, availability, and simplicity of use. Their downside is that they can wear out easily, and oxidation between the wiper and the resistive element may develop rapidly.

Musical applications. Sliders are well known for their use in mixing desks. As music controllers, several generic slider banks have been developed to output MIDI signals, such as the Peavey 1600X, with 16 sliders.

Rotary potentiometers are also very common in musical interfaces. They had their days of glory in analog synthesizers, where dozens were used to control sound synthesis parameters.

3.3.6 Tactile Linear Position

Tactile linear position sensors can also be used to sense position in one or more dimensions. The resistance of the sensor varies according to the position of an object placed on top of its active area.

Infusion Systems has commercialized Slide, a one-dimensional linear position sensor that allows the measurement of the position of an object along its length. With an active area of 16.5×4.4 cm, its resistance varies from 0 to 3 kΩ when a finger is moved from one end of the sensor to the other. In contrast to the LuSense CPS^2 155, introduced earlier, this sensor does not measure the pressure applied to its surface. Eowave commercializes another touch sensor in sizes of 10, 30, and 50 cm (Figure 3.15).

Figure 3.15 Two position sensors, by Infusion Systems and by Eowave.

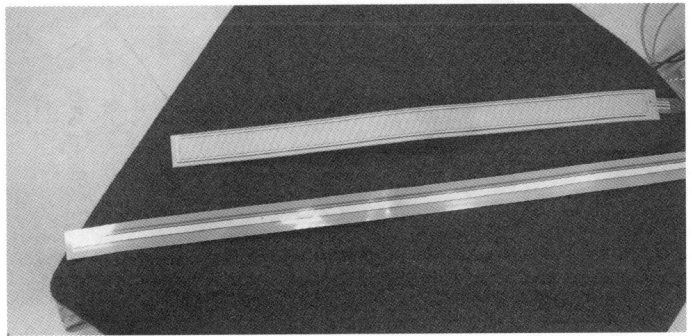

Another well-known example is the Moog ribbon controller (Figure 3.16), used in conjunction with the Moog modular synthesizer by musicians such as Keith Emerson.

Musical applications. Musical applications of linear tactile sensors are numerous and varied. One example is the touch (position) sensor used along the strings of the SBass, the augmented electric upright bass developed and performed by Curtis Bahn (Bahn and Trueman 2001) described in chapter 2.

It is possible to build a homemade tactile linear position sensor using video or audio tape or other materials such as conductive fabric. A strip of videotape is placed over a conductive surface of plastic or metal. The point where both make contact indicates a resistance value.

Some examples of simple homemade ribbon controllers are available on the World Wide Web at http://www.angelfire.com/music2/theanalogcottage/ribcont.htm, http://www.electronicpeasant.com/projects/ribbon/controller.html, and http://www.geocities.com/tpe123/folkurban/synthstick/synthstick.html (all accessed 1 March 2005).

François Handfield developed such a touch sensor for his Cellophone at McGill University (Figure 3.17) using conductive fabric available in antistatic bracelets for use during the manipulation of electronic components.

Figure 3.16 Robert Moog's ribbon controller.

Figure 3.17 Part of the Cellophone designed by François Handfield. One can see a position sensor (Infusion Systems) placed on top of an FSR (upper part of figure) and the homemade position sensor (lower part).

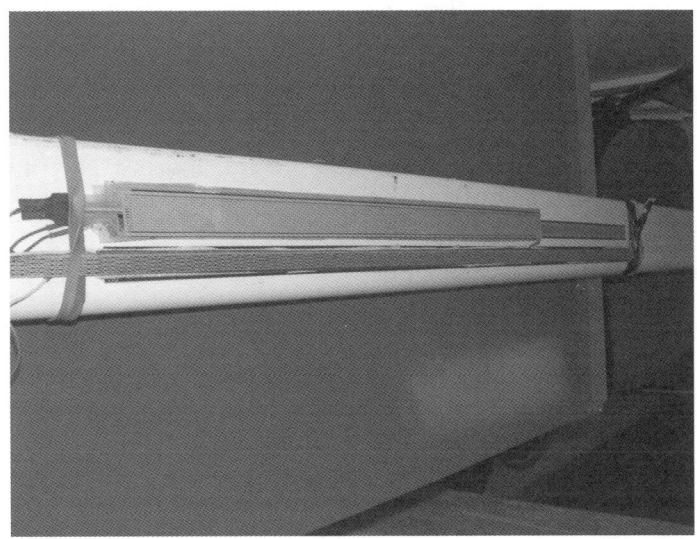

3.3.7 Piezoelectric Sensors

The piezoelectric effect is caused by the appearance of electric polarization in a material that strains under stress. Piezoelectricity is therefore a reversible effect: if a voltage is applied to a piezoelectric device, it will strain.

This effect exists in natural crystals (e.g., quartz), artificially polarized ceramics, and in some polymers. Piezoelectric devices are used in a number of sensors, such as ultrasound sensors and accelerometers. They provide a simple way to transduce force, shock, and vibration into an electric voltage, and they are relatively inexpensive and easy to obtain. Piezoelectric sensors, or piezos, are also very useful for measuring sound vibrations and have been used in microphones and contact pick-ups for string instruments.

Piezoelectric films are made of semicrystalline polymers such as the polyvinylidene fluoride (PVDF) piezo film, widely used in loudspeakers and headphones. When compared to crystal piezos, PVDF offers wide dynamic and frequency range and higher sensitivity and is mechanically tougher.

Musical applications. Piezos have been widely used to manufacture pick-ups for various acoustic instruments. They have also been used for picking up the sound of plastic keys scraping the corrugated surface of the Mutha Rubboard (Wilkerson, Ng, and Serafin 2002), for sensing slaps in the Beatbugs (Weinberg, Aimi, and Jennings 2002), and as one of the sensors in the Trible (Paradiso 2003).

Kynar piezo films have been used by Eric Johnstone in the shoes used to play PodoBard (Johnstone 1991) (see Figure 2.29), a MIDI foot controller designed to replace the maple plywood board in the step dance style called clackage. Kynar piezo films were used to indicate the velocity of the contact between each shoe and the board, proportional to the energy of the impact.

A PVDF piezoelectric foil has been used to sense the dynamic pressure of the heel in the instrumented shoes designed by Paradiso, Hsiao, and Hu (1999).

In Figure 3.18, one can see the use of a piezoelectric sensor for picking up vibration in François Handfield's Cellophone. A piezo attached to a piece of wood vibrates when bowed by an adapted plastic cleaning device. The vibration is transduced into electricity by the piezo.

Piezo crystals and PVDF films are also used in respiratory effort sensors, for instance, by Grass-Telefactor. For more information see http://www.grass-telefactor.com/products/transducers/effort1.html (accessed 1 March 2005).

3.3.8 Ultrasound Sensors

Ultrasound sensors are based on the measurement of the properties of acoustic waves with frequencies above the human audible range; that is, higher than 20 kHz. Typical techniques used with ultrasound sensors include:

Figure 3.18 An example of an interface using a piezo sensor to pick up the vibrations of a bowed piece of wood in the Cellophone.

- *Transit time* (or *time-of-flight*): measurement of the time of arrival of a pulse
- *Attenuation*: measurement of the intensity of a continuous signal
- *Frequency (Doppler effect) or phase shift*: when the source moves with respect to the receiver (or vice versa) or a moving object that reflects the ultrasound signal in reflection mode.
- *Velocity of the wave*: measurement of the speed of the wave or of the fluid flow

Piezoelectric ceramic or polymer transducers are used to generate the ultrasound signal (transmitters) and detect the arriving ultrasound signal (receivers). The same device may be used either as a transmitter (loudspeaker) or as a receiver (microphone).

Ultrasonic sensors are typically very directional; that is, maximum power is radiated perpendicularly to the transducer face. Also, they are normally tuned to a specific frequency (e.g., 40 kHz); therefore, for better efficiency, the frequency of the driving oscillator must be tuned to the resonant frequency of the piezoelectric ceramic.

In transit time, the measurement of the elapsed time between transmission and reception of an ultrasonic burst is performed. Transit time sensors yield highly linear and accurate outputs when measuring distance (Pallàs-Areny and Webster 2001).

Transit time measurement can be in reflection mode or in direct measurement mode:

- *Reflection mode* (or *echo ranging*): the ultrasound signal is reflected by a surface, with both transmitter and receiver in fixed positions. The distance between the sensor and the reflective surface is equal to half of the distance traveled; that is, the elapsed time multiplied by the speed of sound.
- *Direct measurement*: the transmitter and receiver are two separate devices, one moving in relation to the other.

In reflection mode (Figure 3.20), both transmitter and receiver can be placed at a certain angle or side by side. Another option is when the same device acts alternately as a transmitter and as a receiver (pulsed mode); an example of this is the Polaroid sensor, available from Acroname, Infusion Systems, or the York Electronics Centre at the University of York.

Figure 3.19 shows a transceiver-receiver pair, and Figure 3.20 shows ultrasound sensors that performs both actions.

Figure 3.19 A transmitter-receiver pair of piezoelectric ultrasound sensors, model no. 40TR16F, with center frequency equal to 40.0 ± 1.0 kHz.

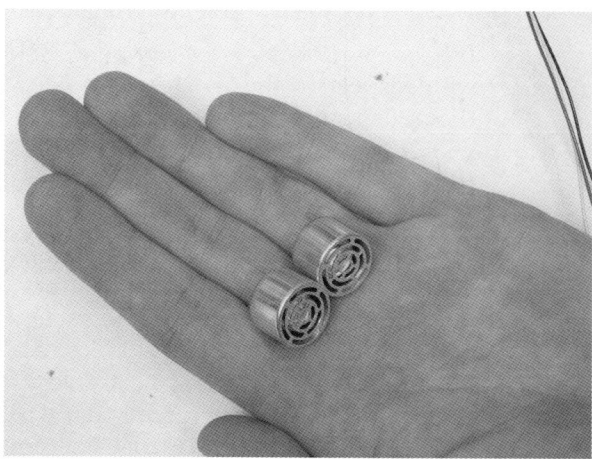

Figure 3.20 Electrostatic ultrasonic sensors for use in reflection mode.

In three-dimensional direct position measurement, three receivers at known distances receive a pulse sent by a moving transmitter, and a processing unit calculates the corresponding distances via triangulation (Figure 3.21). This method could use several transmitters placed at the same point whose distance to the receivers is to be measured to overcome directivity limitations of the ultrasonic devices. One can also use several receivers placed together for the

Figure 3.21 A 3D ultrasonic sensing system using three ultrasonic receivers and one transmitter (Lima et al. 1996).

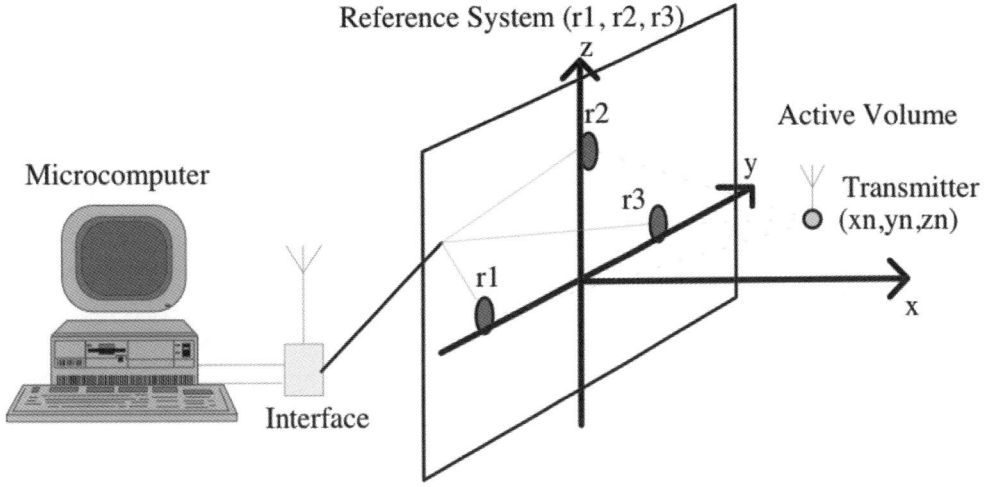

same reason. This is the principle behind an ultrasound triangulation device created at IRCAM in Paris (Auzet 2000; Fléty 2000).

Another option is to have a moving receiver and have the transmitters in fixed locations. The advantage of this option is that stronger ultrasound signals can be sent through the transmitters since there is no limitation on the size of the batteries used to supply the power. The disadvantage is that each transmitter would need to send pulses at different times in order to be individually received by the moving receiver. In other words, the system would be slower. This option has been adopted in GAMS, a media controller designed by Will Bauer and Bruce Foss (1992).

The measurement of transit time needs to be very accurate: for a speed of sound equal to 340 m/s, the ultrasound wave takes less than 3 ms to travel 1 m. This level of measurement usually requires the use of microcontrollers to send the pulse and accurately calculate its time of arrival. Ultrasound position measurements using frequency shift or signal attenuation may be easier to attain.

The frequency shift of an ultrasound sine wave sent by a transmitter and reflected back to a receiver by a moving surface depends on the speed of both the moving surface and the sound at a given temperature. For a 40 kHz sine wave in an environment where the speed of air is equal to 340 m/s (with the transmitter and the receiver at very close locations), a reflecting surface moving at 5 m/s will cause a frequency shift of ±1176.5 Hz.

Soundcards nowadays come with sampling frequencies of 96 kHz or 192 kHz, so it is feasible to send an ultrasound signal (e.g., 40 kHz) through one audio channel of the soundcard, receive it back in another channel, and then measure its frequency (or its attenuation). Note that not all soundcards with sampling frequencies of 96 kHz or higher are capable of sending or receiving ultrasound signals, because of their frequency response. In fact, some low-cost soundcards will not present suitable frequency response at frequencies over 20 kHz and may just filter out frequencies over the audio range.

Johannes Taelman (2002) used a piezo ceramic transmitter and an electret microphone as the receiver on two different channels of a soundcard, with minimal additional electronic development. With frequency shift measurement, both the transmitter and receiver can be placed in fixed positions (reflection mode) so that movements can be detected without the need for any device to be attached to the body. This system detects only the motion of an object; its absolute position is not measured.

Musical applications. Geof Holbrook, inspired by Michel Waisvisz's Hands (Waisvisz 1985), designed and implemented a hand-held controller that measures the relative distance of the performer's hands. But unlike Waisvisz's Hands, which used time-of-flight of ultrasonic pulses, this controller measured the attenuation of the ultrasound signal. Two ultrasound sensors were connected to two channels of a MOTU 828 mkII interface, and a 40 kHz sine wave was generated in Max/MSP and sent through the transmitter. The intensity of the sine wave at the receiver was then measured.

Figure 3.22 illustrates this principle. A signal generator was connected to an ultrasound sensor fed with a sine wave signal at 40 kHz, and the intensity of the signal sensed by the receiver was analyzed by an oscilloscope.

Although the intensity of sound did not vary linearly with distance, this method works well for short distances. Another limitation is related to the high directivity of the ultrasound sensors. To solve the directivity problem in his design, Holbrook included a spring between the hands as a way to keep his two ultrasound sensors facing each other all the time (Figure 3.23), with the added benefit of creating passive force-feedback proportional to the distance between the hands.

Figure 3.22 Measurement of ultrasound attenuation. Because of the strong directivity of the sensors used, even a slight angle change can attenuate the signal.

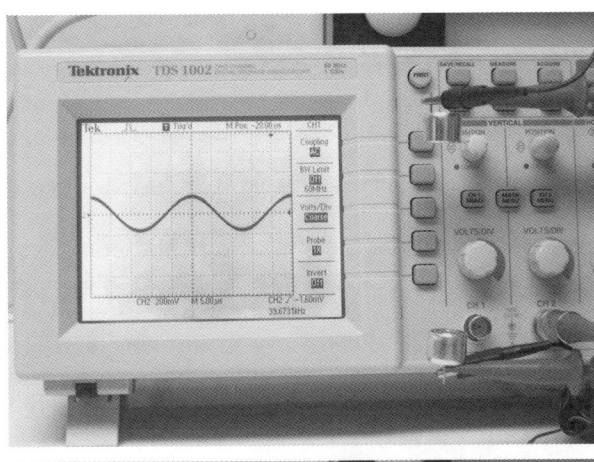

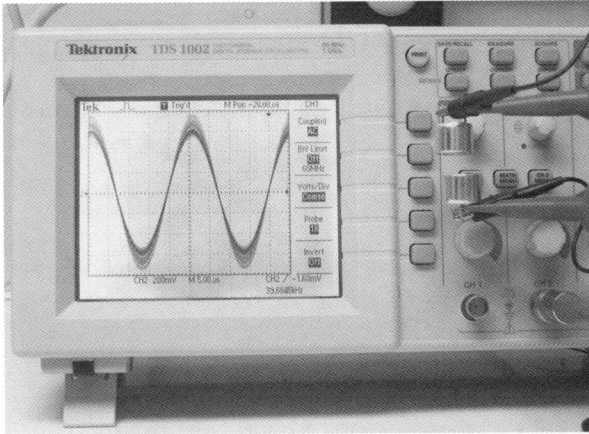

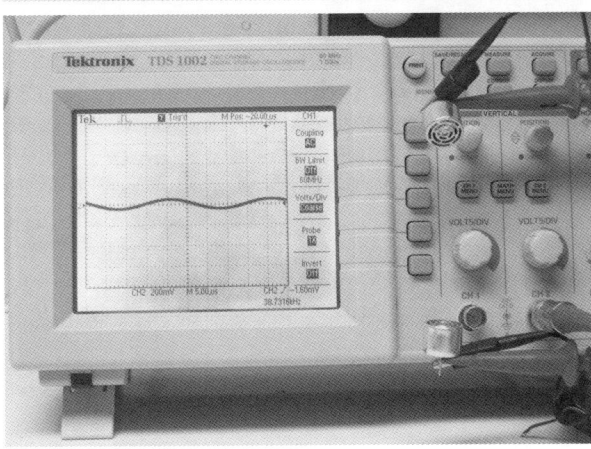

Figure 3.23 A spring between the hands is used to keep the two ultrasound sensors facing each other.

Transit time measurement has been used in the Hands (Waisvisz 1985), in the MIDIConductor, and in several developments using the SensorLab or the MicroLab interfaces, such as the Gesticulator (Bongers and Harris 2002). Transit time is also the operating principle behind distance measurement in Sonami's Lady's Glove (Bongers 2000) and in Impett's meta-trumpet (Impett 1994). Both SensorLab and MicroLab have an ultrasound distance measurement signal, but with different resolutions: 14 bits in the SensorLab, 7 bits in the MicroLab.

The hyper-flute uses ultrasound transit time measurement with the MicroLab in order to measure the distance of the flute from a computer screen (Palacio-Quintin 2003). A popular example of the use of transit time ultrasound measurement in the computer games industry is the distance measurement provided with the Mattel Power Glove.

Tsutomu Kanamori and colleagues (Kanamori et al. 1993) designed an interface using eight pairs of ultrasound transmitters and receivers. The transmitters were placed on the hands and body of a performer, and the receivers were arranged around the performer. Each channel was transmitted individually and received simultaneously by the receivers. The authors report that these sensors could detect their position within a 3 m cube with 9 mm accuracy.

GAMS uses four ultrasonic loudspeakers (50 kHz tweeters) and up to four microphones attached to the performer's body to measure the time-of-flight of ultrasonic pulses at frequencies between 20 kHz and 30 kHz (Bauer and Foss 1992).

Reflection-mode transit time has been used in many sound installations, mostly based on the original Polaroid electrostatic device. Examples of commercially available devices using this principle include the Far Reach sensor by Infusion Systems and the gesture sensor designed at the University of York, both in pulsed mode. An early example of a system for the detection of large gestures was proposed by Philippe Prevot (1986).

Finally, frequency shift has been used by Johannes Taelman (2002) to implement an airdrum.

Ultrasound sensors have also been used as part of dance-music interfaces. The V-scope (Ronen and Lipman 1991)—employing ultrasound sensing of several wireless transmitters (called "buttons") using three receivers—was used at the University of Genoa's Department of Communications, Computer and System Science (DIST) (Camurri 1995).

Another way of using ultrasonic signals in musical applications is by means of a medical ultrasound scanner with a probe placed under the subject's jaw (Vogt et al. 2002). The resulting 2D image of the tongue profile is input to an optical flow algorithm that calculates the degree of motion and uses this information to control musical parameters.

3.3.9 Infrared Sensors

IR sensors are based on the measurement of properties of light signals with frequencies below that of visible red. Since light travels much faster than sound, measurement of the time-of-flight with infrared is not commonly performed in musical applications: it would require time measurements in the range of nanoseconds instead of milliseconds as is the case with ultrasound. Instead, the amplitude or angle of arrival of a signal is measured. As in the case of ultrasound, IR sensors may also be used in direct measurement mode (a pair of IR devices) or in reflection mode (both emitter and receiver in the same device). IR sensors may also be used as motion detectors (on-off), without providing a continuous distance measurement. As Jacob Fraden (2004) points out, optoelectronic motion detectors rely on electromagnetic radiation in the optical range, specifically having wavelengths from 0.4 to 20 µm. These sensors are basically the same as those used in house alarms for detecting intruders.

One popular type of infrared continuous distance measurement sensor working in reflection mode is Sharp's GP2D12 sensor (Figure 3.24), where both the IR emitter and the receiver are packaged together in the same device. It includes all the electronics needed to make it a self-contained device that can be directly plugged into a sensor-to-MIDI or OSC interface. The GP2D12 receiver determines the angle of incidence of an infrared pulse sent by the emitter and reflected back by an object, approximately every 32 milliseconds. Then it outputs an analog voltage signal corresponding to the measured distance. The receiver transmits the IR signal to a specific region of a linear CCD (charge-coupled device) array depending on

Figure 3.24 Sharp's infrared sensor GP2D12.

the angle of incidence: the further the object, the smaller the angle (Hurbain 2004).

Different lenses change the usable range of detection. For instance, although the Sharp GP2D12 has a range of detection of 10 cm to 80 cm, the GP2D120 has a range of detections of 3 cm to 30 cm. Another model of reflective IR sensor is the Honeywell HOA1397 (Bongers 2000).

Infusion Systems commercializes two IR proximity sensors: Close, with a range of measurement of 2.5 cm to 17.5 cm, and ReachClose, with a range of 20 cm to 150 cm. Although both are IR proximity sensors, their technologies are slightly different. Close uses unmodulated diffuse infrared reflection, whereas ReachClose is a sensor from Sharp, which uses modulated infrared reflection. Infusion systems also provides MoveOn, an IR motion sensor that detects movement on a cone with a range of 2.5 m within an angle of 60° to 5.0 m within an angle of 10°.

Advantages of ultrasound sensing include its simplicity and low cost. Main disadvantages include the need for line of sight (the transmitter and receiver must "see" each other), lower resolution compared to other systems, and the sensitivity to multiple signal reflections from objects that are not part of the measurement system, which may cause false measurements.

Difficulties with IR sensors include the need for line of sight and sensitivity to visible light. In fact, low-cost infrared technology is generally "near-infrared technology" and shares a few characteristics with visible sensors: the technology is basically the same, and the applications are similar. For example, many photodetectors have sensitivities in both the visible and the infrared range. Generally all silicon-based photodetectors are sensitive to a wavelength of approximately 1,000 nm, (750 nm is the upper limit of visible light). Filters are usually added to limit the range of sensitivities. For example, a black-and-white camera can be used as an IR sensor by removing the filter put in front of the CCD.

Musical applications. IR motion detectors are often used in interactive sound installations. Pairs of infrared devices, an IR LED and a photodetector, were used by Emmanuel Fléty (2001) to implement an interactive frame, a device consisting of an aluminum frame 2 × 1.5 m in diameter inside which the position of a person was detected (Figure 3.25). The detection area inside the frame had a grid of infrared beams spaced 10 cm apart on both coordinates,

Figure 3.25 The interactive frame uses a grid of infrared sensors to calculate the position of an object inside the frame area.

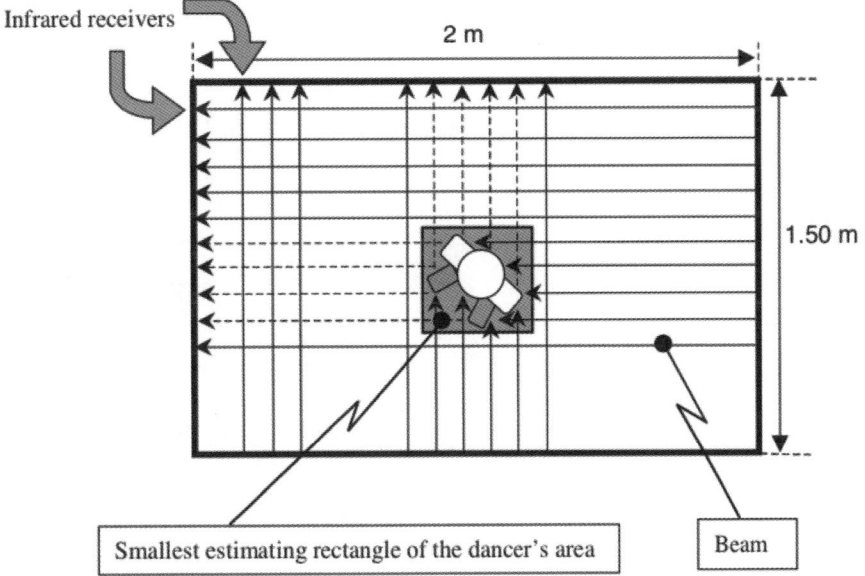

each emitted by an IR LED and sensed by its respective photodetector. Whenever an object was inserted in the frame, the corresponding beams were intersected and the infrared light was obstructed. The position of the object could be calculated from this information with respect to the frame.

Other projects using a pair of IR devices (an IR emitter and a photodiode sensor) include the Rollerblade Wheel Encoder and the Rings of Light, designed at Stanford University's Center for Computer Research in Music and Acoustics (CCRMA; Wilson et al. 2003), and the GyroTyre, by Elliot Sinyor at McGill University (Sinyor and Wanderley 2005).

Reflective IR sensors such as the Sharp GP2D12 sensor have been used in a number of different projects. For instance, Pierre-Yves Fortier attached such a sensor to the wrist of the performer in order to sense the distance between the performer's hand and body. These sensors have also been employed in the E-Mic (Extended Mic-stand Interface Controller) project to measure the microphone stand's distance from a performer (Hewitt and Stevenson 2003).

Commercial developments include the Dimension Beam, which senses infrared light by reflection (Figure 3.26). This technology was later licensed to Roland for use in the HPD15 HandSonic Percussion Controller.

Figure 3.26 The Dimension Beam music controller.

Another commercial product using infrared sensing is the Buchla Lightning II, where two sticks generate infrared signals that are sensed by a receiver placed a few meters in front of the performer. The system is capable of detecting the 2D movements of each stick separately and uses this information to generate musical signals in various ways.

High-quality 3D movement trackers such as the Optotrak 3020 or the newer Optotrak Certus, both by Northern Digital, use cameras to track the position of active infrared markers placed on the body of a person or on an object (Figure 3.27). With accuracy of approximately 1 mm in 3D and with high sampling rates, they allow for very accurate tracking of multiple points within a given space range (see the section on high-end movement trackers in chapter 2, section 2.6.2).

As seen in the Sharp IR sensors described above, infrared light can also be modulated at a specific frequency and detected by a receiver tuned to that specific frequency. This allows the use of IR sensors without having the problem of interference from background light. This technique is being employed in the Augmented Violin, currently in development at IRCAM, where modulated infrared light is used to detect string vibration (Figure 3.28). The

Figure 3.27 Saxophonist Brad Vines with active infrared markers during a motion capture session at McGill University's Motor Control Laboratory in Montreal.

Figure 3.28 The Augmented Violin by Emmanuel Fléty and colleagues.

Overtone Violin, developed by Dan Overholt (2005), is another example of the use of IR sensors on a violin controller. It uses IR LEDs above and a pair of IR photodiodes below each string. Infrared light is directed across each string in order to cast a moving shadow on the photodiodes, allowing for the measurement of string vibration without the need for a resonating body.

3.3.10 Visible Light-sensing Devices

Visible light-sensing devices can be of several types, such as photoresistors, photodiodes, or phototransistors. In general, photo devices can be tuned to be sensitive to different light wavelengths, including infrared.

The LDR (light-dependent resistor, also known as photocell) is a device whose resistance changes with light intensity. Depending on the device, its resistance may drop from several MΩ to a few kΩ when light strikes its surface. Photoresistors are used in simple circuits for illumination control, such as systems that automatically switch the lights on in the evening and off at dawn. They are popular in art installations.

Photodiodes and phototransistors convert photons into charge carriers. A phototransistor is a combination of a photodiode and a transistor. Variable light intensity on the base of the transistor allows for a variable current gain output of the device. These sensors are often paired with LEDs.

The main difficulty with using light-sensing devices in a music controller is that they are very sensitive to ambient conditions. Because our eyes are quick to adapt to varying light conditions, we tend to assume that the light conditions of different environments are similar when in reality this might not be the case. LDR sensors will sense changes in light conditions, even those we cannot perceive with our own eyes. This requires careful and constant sensor calibration. For instance, suppose that a certain voltage level is set for triggering a MIDI note. If light sensors are calibrated for a piece to be performed in the morning, this calibration may not be ideal for a performance in the afternoon, because the light conditions of the venue will probably have changed.

As mentioned above, visible light variations may also be an issue for IR sensors, but, conversely, infrared signals may influence visible light sensors—for instance, when using devices that radiate infrared light, such as stage lights.

Musical applications. LDRs can be very useful in interactive sound installations for sensing light variations or shadows. But LDRs can also be used as part of instruments, such as in the LDR Controller (Favilla 1994).

One early application of photocells for controlling synthesizers was a device called Interactif Spatio-musical, designed in 1984 by Jacques Serrano. It consisted of 48 panels, each containing 64 photocells (3,072 cells total), placed together on a wall measuring 6×2 m. Movements and gestures of users passing in front of the wall, which was illuminated by light projectors, created shadow areas that were sensed by the photocells. Analog signals from the cells were multiplexed, converted into digital signals, and processed by a computer that controlled six different synthesizers. One interesting aspect of this development was that the same movement would not necessarily produce identical sounds, but this was a conscious decision of the designer. The size of the wall allowed several people to interact with the system at the same time.

In general, optical sensors—both infrared and visible light—are commonly used because of their low cost, high accuracy, and simplicity.

In John Cage's *Variations V* (1965; choreography by Merce Cunningham), photocells designed by Billy Klüver were used to sense the movements of dancers and to trigger sounds. More information is available at http://www.johncage.info/workscage/variations5.html (accessed 1 March 2005).

In the 1970s, Hugh LeCaine used a light bulb, a teardrop-shaped shutter, and a photocell to measure the vertical position of keys in his Polyphone (G. Young 1989).

LED-phototransistor pairs were used by several designers to measure keyboard key position or velocity. The key-sensing mechanism for the Bösendorfer 290 SE recording piano was designed with two LED-phototransistor pairs with shutters, one below the key and the other near the base of the hammer (Moog and Rhea 1990). This system was based on an on-off operation: the shutter either blocked the light or allowed it to shine on the phototransistor. The time difference between when the key was fully depressed and when the hammer struck the string was inversely proportional to the hammer velocity.

Robert Moog (1982) developed a key-sensing mechanism using a phototransistor pair and a shutter, with the addition of a photographic film with graduated density, which regulated the amount of light in the phototransistor. This allowed for continuous sensing of the vertical position of keyboard keys.

Other examples of interfaces using optical sensors include the VideoHarp (Rubine and McAvinney 1988) and the LiteFoot (Griffith and Fernström 1998). The latter used IR sensors.

3.3.11 Hall Effect Sensors

Hall effect sensors are devices that are sensitive to a magnetic field. A magnet that provides a magnetic field source is attached to a moving part whose distance to the Hall device is to be measured. The Hall effect sensor produces an electrical output that varies with the position of the magnet, the sensor being sensitive to the polarity of the magnet.

There are two types of Hall effect sensors, linear and threshold (or digital). Linear sensors produce an output voltage that changes continuously with respect to the position of the magnet. Threshold (or digital) sensors switch between two voltage levels according to the position of the magnet; the sensors use a built-in hysteresis function that prevents multiple switches. In both types of Hall effect sensors, the relationship between the distance from the magnet to the Hall device and the output voltage is nonlinear because the strength of the magnetic field varies inversely with the square of the distance between the magnet and the device.

The range of the measurement depends on the magnet used, but in general it is on the order of a few centimeters.

Musical applications. Hall effect devices have been used in several gestural controllers where accurate short-distance measurement is important.

Examples include the measurement of the position of flute keys (Ystad and Voinier 2001; Palacio-Quintin 2003), the position of trumpet valves in Jonathan Impett's meta-trumpet (Impett 1994), and the position of the thumb with respect to other fingers, as in Laetitia Sonami's Lady's Glove (Bongers 2000), where one magnet is attached to the thumb and four sensors to the fingertips.

Other gestural controllers using Hall effect devices include the hyper-puja by Diana Young and Georg Essl (2003), in which Hall effect sensors measured the speed of rotation of a stick, and the Plank (Verplank, Sapp, and Mathews 2001), in which Hall devices measured rotary position. Also, Michel Waisvisz's Web uses Hall-effect devices to measure the tension of a Web string (Bongers 2000) (Figure 3.29).

3.3.12 Magnetic Tags

Another type of magnetic field sensing device is the magnetic tag. Basically, the technology behind magnetic tags is the same as that used in antitheft alarm systems in shops, where a fixed search coil excites simple inductor-capacitor circuits or magnetostrictive strips. Magnetostriction is the change in the dimension of a material when it is subjected to an external magnetic field.

The tags have specific frequencies (the "ID" of each tag) determined by their design characteristics; therefore several tags of various frequencies can be detected individually when sweeping the frequency of the coil. Whenever the sweeping frequency of the reader

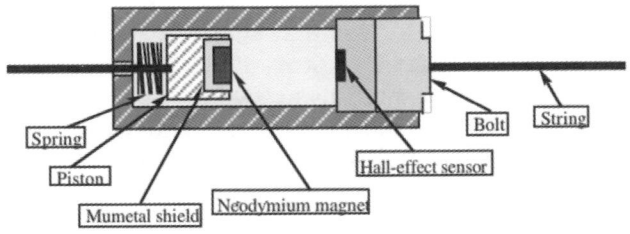

Figure 3.29 Michael Waisvisz's Web system uses Hall devices to measure the tension of a web of strings. The sensors were designed by Bert Bongers. © 2000. Reprinted with the permission of IRCAM–Centre Pompidou, Paris, France.

coil equals the center frequency of a specific tag, this tag will resonate; that is, it will be remotely excited by the coil, and the reader can identify its presence.

The main advantages of magnetic coupled tags include the fact that they do not require line of sight; that is, the tag does not need to be "seen" by the reader coil. Some nonmetal materials may be part of the interface without influencing the measurement. Another interesting feature is that each tag can be uniquely determined, such as its presence in the system as well as its position and its orientation, depending on the tag design and complexity. Limitations include the maximum number of tags that can be identified by a system (which is dependent on the sweeping frequency range and resonance width of the tags) and the limited speed of reading.

Musical applications. Kai-yuh Hsiao and Joe Paradiso (1999) measured three tag characteristics: center frequency (ID), resonance width, and integrated coupling amplitude in order to generate sounds and musical sequences. In their system, these characteristics were read 30 times per second for up to 30 different tags. More interestingly, the authors made some of these characteristics dependent on external variables such as touch (e.g., pressure of a finger) or temperature, providing extra degrees of freedom in their interface. Hsiao and Paradiso also used several inductor-capacitor (LC) tags in 13 objects whose positions (and orientation, in one case) were tracked. The tag parameters were associated to musical attributes such as harmony, melody, embellishments, and additional sound. The same group proposed a similar application of resonant tags in a system called Musical Trinkets (Pardue and Paradiso 2002).

3.3.13 Magnetoresistive Sensors

Magnetoresistive sensors, or electronic compasses, are devices that are sensitive to the magnetic field of the Earth. Like ordinary magnetic compasses, electronic compasses indicate the user's orientation with respect to the geomagnetic field of the Earth. In a typical compass, a magnetic needle aligns itself with Earth's magnetic north, and orientation can be determined from this alignment.

Magnetoresistive sensors are devices that sense weak magnetic fields when compared to magnetic fields provided by magnets. Electronic compasses can be implemented using two magnetoresistive sensors that are placed in the same plane at a 90° angle to one another, each measuring the x- and y-components of the magnetic field of the Earth. The direction heading is obtained from the two sensor signals.

Electronic compasses are typically used in combination with microcontrollers, allowing for a more accurate orientation measurement. The magnetoresistive effect is the change in the electrical resistance of a material when it is subjected to an external magnetic field.

One commercial example of a magnetoresistive sensor is Honeywell's HMC1023 sensor, configured with three magnetoresistive elements in three orthogonal axes, with a field range of ±6 gauss and a minimum detectable field of 85 µgauss. (The Earth's field is equal to 0.5 gauss.) Other commercial examples include the Philips Semiconductor KMZ51 and KMZ52 devices. Compasses ready for musical applications are also available—for instance, the MIDICompass (from the University of York) and Orient (from Infusion Systems), to cite but two.

At this point it is important to clarify the difference between Hall effect sensors (introduced earlier) and magnetoresistive sensors. A magnetic field applied to a current-carrying conductor will exert a force on the electrons that will cause some of them to deviate from their path. If the relaxation time owing to lattice collisions is relatively short, then the drift of electrons to one side of the conductor yields a transverse electric field (i.e., the Hall voltage) that opposes further electron drifts. If that relaxation time is relatively large, then there is a noticeable increase in electric resistance, termed the magnetoresistive effect (Pallàs-Areny and Webster 2001).

Musical applications. One example of musical applications of magnetoresistive sensors is the MIT Media Lab's Instrumented Shoes, which use a three-axis magnetometer giving orientation with respect to geomagnetic field of the Earth (Paradiso, Hsiao, and Hu 1999).

3.3.14 Capacitive Sensors

Capacitive sensors offer a flexible and accurate way to measure distance. The capacitance value of a parallel plate capacitor will be directly proportional to the effective areas of the plates (A) and the properties of the material between them (k, the relative permittivity of the dielectric, or dielectric constant of the material between the plates), and inversely proportional to the distance between the plates (d), as follows:

$$C = \frac{k\varepsilon_0 A}{d}$$

where ε_0 is the permittivity of free space (this is a constant value).

Changing any of the three variables (k, A, or d) will change the value of the capacitance. For instance, decreasing the distance between the plates or inserting a material with higher permittivity between them will increase the capacitance. Decreasing the effective area of the plates by, for example, moving them longitudinally with respect to each other, will decrease the capacitance.

Capacitive sensing can be considered as part of a broad class of techniques called electric field sensing. Joe Paradiso and Neil Gershenfeld (1997) consider three modes in electric field sensing: load, shunt, and transmit (Figure 3.30). In load mode, the distance between an object (e.g., the body of a performer) and a single electrode is measured through a change in the capacitance of the electrode to ground. The proximity of the body will increase the effective capacitance to the ground of the antennas, due to the dielectric constant of the body. This is the position-sensing mechanism used in the theremin, where the capacitive coupling between the hands of a performer and each of the two antennas control the characteristics of the output signal: the vertical antenna controls the frequency, and the horizontal one controls the amplitude of the sound.

In shunt mode, an electric field is already in place between two (or more) electrodes. The presence of all or part of the performer's body between the electrodes changes the (originally known) field strength between them, owing to the large capacitance of the body to ground.

Comparing both shunt and load modes, the boundary conditions of the electric field in the former are known—they are set by the transmit-receive electrode geometry—while the boundary conditions in the latter are unknown. Thus, whereas using N electrodes in shunt mode will allow for $N(N-1)$ independent shunt measurements, only N measurements will be allowed in loading mode (Paradiso and Gershenfeld 1997).

Finally, in transmit mode, the performer should be very close to the transmit electrode, for example, standing or sitting on it. The transmitter electrode sends the electric field to the receiver electrode through the body of the performer. As Paradiso and Gershenfeld (1997) observed, unlike the other two modes (loading and shunting), in transmit mode it is possible to uniquely detect one individual out of many by listening for the frequency being emitted from the body of the connected person.

Examples of commercially available capacitive sensors include the Motorola 33794 evaluation kit, with continuous proximity sensing of up to nine electrode inputs, and the family of touch sensors from Quantum Research Group, including on-off keys (QTouch) and linear (QSlide) and rotary slides (QWheel). Well-known examples of capacitive sensors are those used in laptop trackpads and in Apple's iPod.

Musical applications. As mentioned before, perhaps the best-known example of a capacitive-sensing musical interface is the theremin. Another early use of this sensing technique was made by Hugh Le Caine, who used capacitive sensing in the left-hand timbre control device of his electronic sackbut (G. Young 1984).

Robert Moog (1982) used capacitive sensing to measure two-dimensional finger position in the keys of his multiply touch-sensitive clavier. A resistive film placed on the surface of the key formed one plate of a capacitor, while the finger of a performer formed the other plate, grounded through the body (Moog and Rhea 1990). The resistive films were connected with wires on each of their four corners, where high-frequency AC voltages were applied. By calculating the differences between the corner currents due to finger position on the key and dividing by the total current, two signals were available, one proportional to the left-to-right position and the other to the front-to-back position of the finger.

The original multiply touch-sensitive clavier also included a capacitive sensor made of a conductive rubber and a strip of anodized aluminum running along the keyboard frame. Finger pressure caused the rubber to touch the strip. Greater pressure increased the contact area between the rubber (the first capacitor plate) and the strip (the second plate), therefore increasing its capacitance.

Robert Moog later used another capacitive sensor to continuously measure the vertical position of the clavier's key, replacing the original LED, phototransistor, and shutter sensor.

Several interfaces made at the MIT Media Laboratory use capacitive sensing, including the Spirit Chair (using transmit mode), the Gesture Frame, and the Sensor Mannequin (Paradiso and Gershenfeld 1997). Other applications include the Radio Baton (Mathews 1991), the Mutha Rubboard (Wilkerson, Ng, and Serafin 2002), the Termenova (Hasan, Paradiso, and Yu 2002) and the EpipE (Cannon, Hughes, and O'Modhrain 2003; Hughes, Cannon, and O'Modhrain 2004).

3.3.15 Accelerometers

Accelerometers are very popular sensors in new musical controller design. They measure linear (or translation) acceleration in one or more axes, and most of them can also sense inclination, depending on their sensitivity. They are also useful for measuring shock.

Figure 3.30 Capacitive sensing modes by Joe Paradiso and Neil Gershenfeld. Reprinted with permission by the authors and from *Computer Music Journal* 21:2.

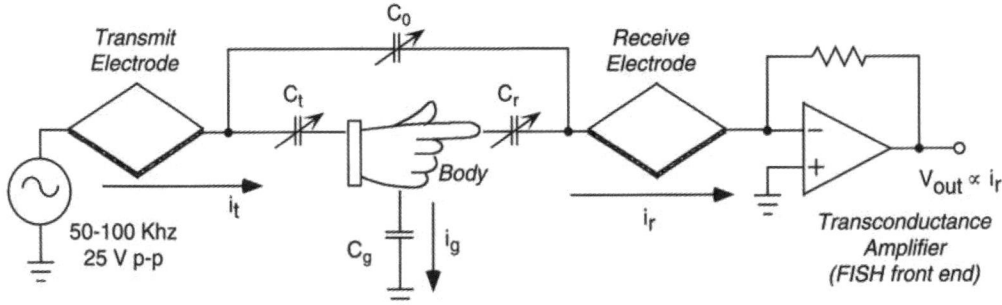

Equivalent circuit for all modes of electric field sensing

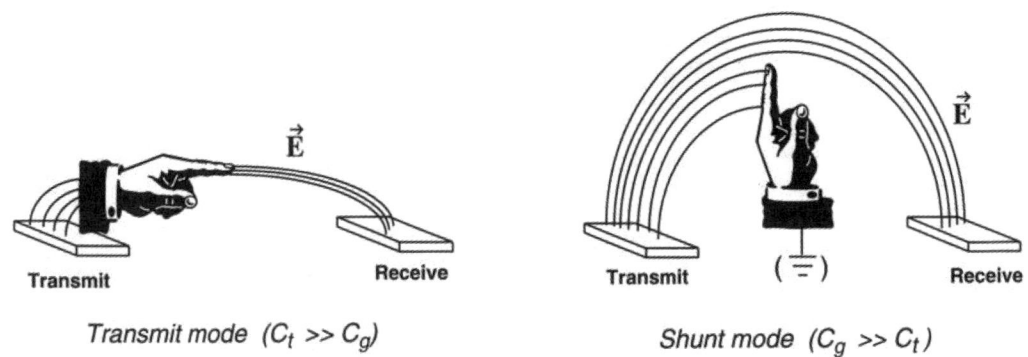

Transmit mode $(C_t \gg C_g)$ Shunt mode $(C_g \gg C_t)$

The principle behind measuring acceleration can be understood by looking at a mass-spring system. According to Jacob Fraden (2004), an accelerometer can be specified as a device with a single degree of freedom with an inertial mass (also referred to as proof mass), a spring-like supporting system, and a frame structure with damping properties. Force, such as that resulting from Earth's gravity, applied to the mass will tend to cause it to move with a given acceleration. The resulting displacement can be measured either by capacitive, piezoelectric, or piezoresistive sensors.

Currently, the most common accelerometers used in musical interface design are micromachined integrated circuits (ICs), where the inertial mass and the equivalent of a spring are embedded in a single silicon chip. One example is the one-axis ADXL105 sensor by

Analog Devices. It can sense positive or negative dynamic accelerations, such as shock and vibration, and static accelerations, such as inertial forces, gravity, or tilt. According to the specification given by Analog Devices, the ADXL105 sensor is a surface micromachined polysilicon structure built on top of the silicon wafer. Polysilicon springs suspend the structure over the surface of the wafer and provide a resistance against acceleration-induced forces. Deflection of the structure is measured with a differential capacitor consisting of two independent fixed plates and a central plate attached to the moving mass.

Another technology used to implement accelerometers is thermal convection. Thermal convection accelerometers have a bubble of heated air sealed inside the sensor package cavity as the only moving element. When an external force such as motion, inclination, or vibration is applied, the bubble moves, creating an output signal proportional to the movement (Bugnacki, Pyle, and Emerald 2001). The Memsic 2125GL dual-axis thermal accelerometer is capable of measuring both dynamic acceleration and static vibration within a range of ± 2 g and is electrically compatible with other commercial dual-axis accelerometers.

Other multiple-axis devices include the ADXL202 sensor, a dual-axis accelerometer with duty cycle output (± 2 g) by Analog Devices, or Measurement Specialties' ACH-04-08-05, a three-axis accelerometer with piezoelectric sensing (± 250 g).

In order to build a three-axis accelerometer from a one-axis model, it is necessary to mount three single-axis accelerometers at 90° to one another (Figure 3.31). If dual-axis accelerometers are available, then two of them can be mounted at 90° to obtain a three-axis acceleration measurement.

Accelerometers can have very different characteristics in terms of sensitivity, acceleration range, frequency response, output noise, and price. The choice of an accelerometer for a specific project will depend on the type of analysis of the movements one wants to sense.

Different authors disagree on the range of accelerations produced by the human body; they may range from around 0.04 g to 10 g, with frequencies of less than 12 Hz (Verplaetse 1996), to over 20 g in common hand movements (Sawada, Ohkura, and Hashimoto 1995; Sawada, Onoe, and Hashimoto 1997).

Independent of the absolute values of acceleration to be measured, micromachined accelerators are reasonably priced and easily available. They are also easy to interface with other devices

Figure 3.31 A three-axis accelerometer can be made from one axis devices (ADXL 105) by mounting them at angles of 90°. Note the gyroscope evaluation board at the left side of the photograph.

because they often come with the necessary electronic circuitry for signal conditioning.

Infusion Systems currently offers two accelerometer options: GForce2D and Tilt2D (a two-axis inclination/acceleration device) and GForce3D (a three-axis acceleration device).

Different types of accelerometers can be used in the same interface to measure various parameters. For example, Tsutomu Kanamori and colleagues (1993) have used two types of accelerometers in a controller that they have designed for interactive digital art applications:

- *Narrow-range type*: sensing from -1.5 g to $+1.5$ g with frequency ranging from 0 Hz to 10 Hz
- *Wide-range type*: sensing from -20 g to $+20$ g with frequency ranging from 1 Hz to 1000 Hz

The two types of sensors are complementary. Narrow-range sensors are used to detect inclination (performer posture angles in slow movements) and wide-range ones to detect impact, such as performer jumps.

Finally, accelerometers usually present one of two types of output signals: pulse-width modulation (PWM) or analog voltage signals. PWM output accelerometers are very useful with microcontrollers with PWM inputs. Accelerometers outputting analog voltages would be the choice when using analog-to-MIDI or OSC interfaces or the analog inputs of microcontrollers.

Musical applications. As mentioned above, accelerometers have been widely used in the design of new music controllers. A few examples include the meta-trumpet (Impett 1994), Laetitia Sonami's Lady's Glove (Bongers 2000), the BoSSA (Trueman and Cook 1999), and the Instrumented Dancing Shoes (Paradiso 1999), among several others. In fact, almost every controller that uses tilt and inclination measurements employs accelerometers for doing so, with the notable exception of the Hands (Waisvisz 1985), which employs mercury switches. The resolution of the inclination measurement may not be high with accelerometers, but it is higher than that of on-off tilt sensors.

Accelerometers can also be improvised from existing components. Bert Bongers (2000) describes a technique for building homemade accelerometers using needles and coils taken from electronic panel meters. An acceleration applied to the device will cause a voltage in the coil due to the inertia of the needle-coil system. Bongers reported the use of such a device in Air Drums, by Palm Tree Productions.

The raw signals obtained with accelerometers (i.e., vibration, shock, inclination, and acceleration) can be used to control musical events directly. For instance, shocks above a certain threshold can be used as triggers, and vibration can be used to control the vibrato of a sound or produce a tremolo effect. But such signals can also be analyzed in order to extract meaningful information for specific applications.

Hydeyuki Sawada and colleagues (Sawada, Ohkura, and Hashimoto 1995; Sawada, Onoe, and Hashimoto 1997) implemented a conducting system using three-axis accelerometers. They devised analysis methods to extract kinetic features from acceleration data for both the left and right hands of a conductor. These features were used as inputs to a neural network for gesture recognition. With the accelerometer system, they obtained results for tempo detection from hand gestures similar to results obtained previously using a video camera (Morita, Otheru, and Hashimoto 1989).

3.3.16 Gyroscopes

Gyroscopes, or gyros, are sensors that measure angular velocity. Traditionally, they have been used in navigation systems (e.g., in airplanes), but more recently they have been extensively used to detect rotation in video and photo cameras.

Traditional gyroscopes are mechanical devices that comprise rotating parts. They function based on the principle of the conservation of angular momentum. In musical interfaces, gyros are typically micromachined devices based on Coriolis acceleration, where rotating parts have been replaced by vibrating elements. The Coriolis acceleration of a body appears whenever that body moves linearly in a frame of reference that rotates on an axis perpendicular to that of the linear motion (Fraden 2004). The resulting acceleration, which is directly proportional to the rate of rotation, comes from a third axis perpendicular to the plane containing the two other axes.

The sensing of Coriolis acceleration in vibrating gyroscopes is accomplished by an oscillatory motion orthogonal to the input axis of a sensing element inside the gyro (Verplaetse 1996). If the sensor is rotated on its input axis, the vibrating element undergoes Coriolis forces in a direction that is tangential to the rotation (i.e., orthogonal to the vibratory and rotating axis). Optical gyroscopes also exist.

In comparison to digital compasses, which indicate direction with reference to the magnetic field of the Earth, gyroscopes have the advantage that they do not need an external reference. This is an important aspect to consider in applications where a reference may not be available (e.g., in space) or where electromagnetic interference may affect the measurement.

As with the case of accelerometers, gyroscopes can be mounted at angles of 90° to obtain measurements of angular velocity in multiple axes.

Examples of commercially available micromachined gyroscopes include the ENC-03M by Murata and the ADXRS300 by Analog Devices, both with an angular velocity of ±300° per second.

Accelerometers and gyroscopes are often regarded as inertial devices, because neither require an external reference (Verplaetse 1996). Also, it is important to bear in mind that neither an accelerometer nor a gyroscope is suitable for absolute position measurement, and that the two can be combined in order to provide multiple-axis sensing.

Musical applications. Tsutomu Kanamori and colleagues have used three gyroscopes attached to the headband of a shakuhachi performer to continuously measure angular velocity of the head in three axes (Kanamori et al. 1993). Atau Tanaka and Benjamin Knapp

(2002) used a gyroscope to measure the relative position of a stick around a resonating bowl. As a different approach to measuring velocity, a stick moving on the edges of a bowl was proposed by Diana Young and Georg Essl (2003), using Hall effect sensors and magnets, as discussed in chapter 2. A gyroscope was used in the MIT Media Lab's instrumented shoes in order to sense twists and spins (Paradiso, Hsiao, and Hu 1999), together with several other sensors. Sile O'Modhrain and colleagues used gyros, accelerometers, and compasses in the M.E.S.H., an instrumented personal digital assistant that is able to sense its position in space, as well as to provide vibrations through a high-fidelity vibrotactile display or audiological actuators (Hughes, Cannon, and O'Modhrain 2004).

3.3.17 Tilt Sensors and Mercury Switches

Tilt sensors, also called inclinometers or gravitational sensors, are devices that measure their angle in relation to the center of gravity of the Earth (Figure 3.32).

Depending on the type of the sensor, it can produce discrete or continuous output signals. Discrete (on-off) sensors will give one of two output values depending on their inclination. This is the case with the commonly used mercury switches. By rotating the switch with respect to the ground, the mercury element will move inside the sensor, turning an electrical switch on or off.

One commercial example is the TiltOn, a mercury switch–based single-axis inclination sensor supplied by Infusion Systems.

Figure 3.32   Inclination sensors.

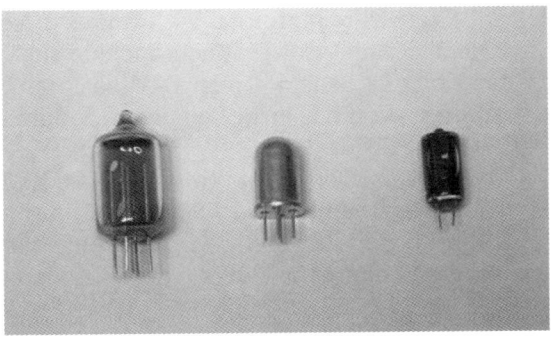

More sophisticated devices are needed, however, if one wishes to obtain continuous inclination measurements. Examples of sensors to measure continuous inclination include electrolytic tilt sensors, such as those provided by the Fredericks Company, with ranges between $\pm 1°$ and $\pm 80°$, and also arrays of photodetectors (Fraden 2004).

As discussed before, some accelerometers can also be used as continuous inclination sensors in one or more axes. For instance, the ADXL202 can measure inclination in two axes with respect to the ground.

Musical applications. Mercury switches have been used in various musical interfaces, most notably in the Hands (Waisvisz 1985). The Hands uses four mercury switches at the four cardinal points, allowing for eight different measurements of hand position with respect to the ground, analogous to a compass giving the directions north, south, east, west, northeast, northwest, southeast, and southwest. Mercury switches have also been used in the hyper-flute (Palacio-Quintin 2003) and in Sergi Jordà's Exoskeleton (Jordà 2002).

3.3.18 Air Pressure Sensors

Sensors that measure air pressure, especially breath pressure, are very useful for musical controllers inspired by existing acoustic wind instruments. Also, they can be employed to give performers additional continuous control variables; for instance, keyboard players already using their hands and feet may wish to use a breath pressure sensor to control additional expressive parameters.

Typically, air pressure sensors for musical applications are composed of a diaphragm (a membrane or a plate) and a strain gauge. The diaphragm will deform with pressure, and this deformation is mechanically sensed by the strain gauge, causing a change in its resistance.

Examples of air pressure sensors for musical applications include MPXV5010 by Motorola, with a pressure range of 0 psi to 1.45 psi. Other commercial products include the XFGN-6 series by Fujikura, and the All Sensor 1-inch D4V dual-input pressure sensor used by Andrey da Silva in his augmented flute (da Silva, Wanderley, and Scavone 2005).

Musical applications. Motorola MPXV5010 air pressure sensors have been used in Gary Scavone's Pipe (Scavone 2003) to measure blowing pressure. Air pressure controllers have also been used in several commercial MIDI controllers, such as Yamaha's WX5 and WX7, and in breath controllers for use with keyboard synthesizers.

Sidney Fels and colleagues have used pressure sensors in the Tooka, a two-person instrument controlled by breath (Fels et al. 2004; Fels and Vogt 2002; see Figure 2.45). Another interesting example is the GraspMIDI, designed by Hydeyuki Sawada and colleagues (Sawada, Onoe, and Hashimoto 1997). The GraspMIDI is composed of four units, each consisting of a pressure sensor inserted in a small balloon with a diameter of about 3 cm. The sensors measure the internal pressure of the balloon when it is deformed. These units are packed into a spherical silicone ball.

3.3.19 Other Sensors

A number of other types of sensors exist in addition to the ones introduced above. Because it would be impractical to cover all existing sensors in this book, this section ends with a brief introduction to a few other sensors that may be useful for building gestural controllers.

Camera-based systems (sometimes referred as *computer vision systems*) are very commonly used in interactive systems. Several systems exist, with varying degrees of complexity and flexibility. One early example is the Oculus Ranae (Collinge and Parkinson 1988), which could detect portions of an image that changed in brightness. The name of the system was a reference to the eyes of the frog, which can see only moving objects. In the Oculus Ranae the image was divided into regions, and the system was able to identify the amount of movement in each region. Strictly speaking, it was not a computer vision system since it did not allow the identification of image characteristics (e.g., objects), but only changes in pixels from one frame to another. It has been used in interactive installations and music improvisation systems.

Several camera-based systems have been used in systems to identify conductor movements, as discussed in chapter 2. Examples include the Vision System (Morita, Otheru, and Hashimoto 1989) and the Light Baton (Bertini and Carosi 1992). Basically, these systems use CCD (charge-coupled device) cameras and devices attached to the baton: a white marker and a small lamp, respectively. A camera-based system that identifies the baton to which no devices are attached to was proposed by Declan Murphy and colleagues (Murphy, Andersen, and Jensen 2003).

General computer vision systems for artistic applications include the Very Nervous System (VNS), by David Rokeby, BigEye from STEIM, EyeCon from Palindrome, Eyesweb from DIST (http://www.eyesweb.org, accessed 29 November 30, 2005) and Jitter, from

Cycling '74, among many others. These systems are widely used in interactive installations, dance-music systems, expressive gesture analysis, and many other applications. A recent application of Jitter to create gesture analysis tools has been proposed by Alexander Jensenius (Jensenius, Godøy, and Wanderley 2005).

Temperature sensors can be useful for interactive installations. One common temperature sensor is the thermistor, a temperature-sensitive resistor. Infusion Systems commercializes Hot, a thermistor that measures temperatures in the range of −40°C to +100°C. Application of temperature sensors in music controllers includes a system called Sonic City (Gaye, Mazé, and Holmquist 2003) and the use of a thermistor in Sound Kitchen (Shiraiwa, Segnini, and Woo 2003).

Humidity sensors (or *moisture sensors*) detect changes in the humidity of the air or of an object. Moisture sensors have been used on the human body to detect finger contact at the holes of the shakuhachi (Kanamori et al. 1993). They are also potentially useful in interactive installations.

A dual temperature and humidity sensor commercialized by Infusion Systems is the Hot&Humid. It measures temperatures from 0°C to 60°C and a relative humidity of 10% to 95%.

Discrete pressure keys or *on-off pressure sensors* (Figure 3.33) have been used in various interfaces, such as the Hands, mentioned earlier.

Figure 3.33 An example of a musical interface using discrete pressure keys by Pierre-Yves Fortier.

Rotary encoders are useful for measuring rotary movement: they continuously output a sequence of pulses when turned. One application of rotary encoders is Pacom, an interface developed in the 1980s at IRCAM in Paris to control the 4X synthesis machine (Starkier and Prevot 1986).

Linear variable differential transformers (LVDTs) are very accurate position sensors. They comprise three or more moving coils within which a magnetically permeable core moves to provide variable coupling between the primary and one or more secondary coils (Nyce 2004). They are very accurate and linear, with high resolution. LVDTs were used to measure key positions in the ACROE's TGR (Cadoz, Luciani, and Florens 1984).

Galvanic skin response sensors (GSRs), described in section 4.2.2, measure skin conductivity.

Doppler radars have been used to detect motion in the Magic Carpet (Paradiso et al. 1997), as described in section 2.4.5.

Finally, various types of *microphones*, some of which are made with piezoelectric materials, can also be used in the design of alternative music controllers. Examples of the use of microphones in gestural interfaces include a system developed by Joe Paradiso and colleagues (2002) that located the position of knocks and taps on a large sheet of glass. PebbleBox and CrumbleBag, by Sile O'Modhrain and Georg Essl (2004), are also good examples using microphones, where the manipulation of physical grains of arbitrary material was used for interacting with a granular sound synthesizer.

3.4 SIGNAL CONDITIONING

Signal conditioning is a vast topic with a number of different possibilities and techniques. The following paragraphs introduce a few basic signal-conditioning techniques that can be used to condition the signals produced by many of the sensors described above. A lengthy discussion on conditioning techniques is beyond the scope of this book. See also chapter 4 for techniques for conditioning biosignals.

3.4.1 Voltage Divider

The voltage divider is a simple yet useful circuit for conditioning the signal from various types of sensors. Sensors that use voltage dividers include FSR, bend, and LDR sensors, to cite but three examples.

Basically, a voltage divider is composed of two resistors in series, one connected to the voltage supplier (e.g., +5V) and the other to the ground (Figure 3.34).

Measuring the voltage at the connection between the two resistors yields:

$$V_{out} = \frac{Rb}{Ra + Rb} \cdot V$$

Consider, for instance, that the resistor Ra is replaced by an FSR. In order to understand the effect of the force applied to the FSR on the output voltage, consider substituting Ra with 10 different resistors, one at a time, with values of 100 kΩ, 90 kΩ, 80 kΩ, ... 10 kΩ. For Rb equal to 50 kΩ, the output voltages will be as shown in Table 3.1:

Table 3.1: Output voltages for different values of Ra and Rb equal to 50kΩ.

Ra (kΩ)	Vout (V)
100	1.67
90	1.79
80	1.92
70	2.08
60	2.27
50	2.5
40	2.78
30	3.125
20	3.57
10	4.17

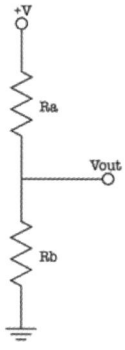

Figure 3.34 A voltage divider is composed of two resistors in series.

In practice, an operational amplifier is also used as part of the conditioning circuit in order to isolate the voltage output from loads in the measurement (Figure 3.35). A voltage follower, also referred to as a unity gain noninverting amplifier or impedance adapter, is then used to relay the voltage at the connection between *Ra* and *Rb* to its output.

One of the limitations of the simple voltage divider presented above is that the output voltage will not be zero when the applied stimulus is zero, unless the sensor resistance is close to zero (Carr 1997).

3.4.2 Wheatstone Bridge Circuit

A Wheatstone Bridge is a circuit composed of four resistors (Figure 3.36).

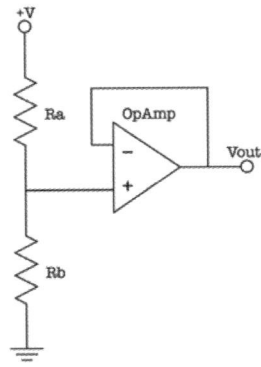

Figure 3.35 A voltage divider using an operational amplifier (μA741).

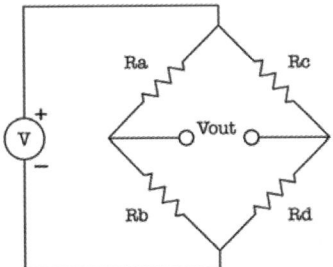

Figure 3.36 The Wheatstone bridge.

When a voltage is applied across the voltage dividers, an output voltage appears across the opposite nodes. Compared to the simple voltage divider discussed earlier, the Wheatstone Bridge allows for zero output under zero stimuli, provided the correct resistor values are selected.

This circuit is widely used with highly sensitive sensors such as strain gauges (Yokono and Hashimoto 1998; D. Young 2002).

3.4.3 Amplifier

Sometimes it may be important to amplify the voltage output level of the sensor to a level compatible with the 0–5 V inputs of most interfaces (or analog-to-digital converters). This can be easily implemented using operational amplifiers and a couple of resistors.

The gain is proportional to the ratio of the two resistor values, with the final gain depending on the amplifier configuration (see Figures 3.37 and 3.38):

- Noninverting amplifier: $Vout = (1 + Rb/Ra) \times V$
- Inverting amplifier: $Vout = -(Rb/Ra) \times V$

Figure 3.37 Noninverting amplifier.

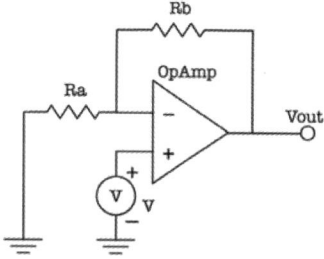

Figure 3.38 Inverting amplifier.

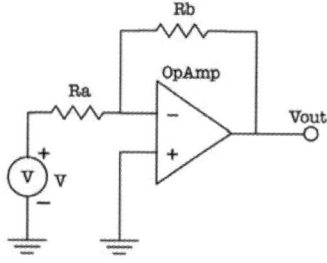

3.4.4 Voltage Protection

A voltage limiter is sometimes employed in signal conditioning to avoid voltages higher than 5 V or lower than 0 V that might damage the interface (Fléty 2000). It uses two diodes (with voltage drops of 0.7 V), forcing the voltage swing at the output of the sensor to between −0.7 V and +5.7 V. The resistor is used to limit the current flowing into the interface (Figure 3.39).

A variation of the circuit shown in Figure 3.39 is presented in Figure 3.40, where the resistors $R1$ is placed between the operational amplifier and the diodes D1 and D2, to better control the current supplied by the operational amplifier (or op amp).

3.4.5 Filters

A low-pass filter (LPF), also called an integrator, removes signals above a given threshold frequency, technically called cut-off frequency. Conversely, a high-pass filter (HPF, also called a differentiator) removes signals below the cut-off frequency.

LPFs and HPFs can vary substantially in design and can have diverse characteristics. For example, they can be passive or active, analog or digital.

Figure 3.39 Voltage protection, designed by Emmanuel Fléty.

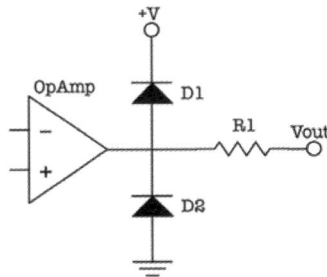

Figure 3.40 A variation of the voltage protection circuit shown in Figure 3.39, by Eric Johnstone.

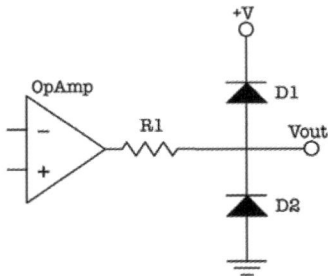

Useful practical circuits implementing active LPFs and HPFs are presented in the first volume on sensors of Joseph Carr's *Electronic Circuit Guidebook* (1997). Another source of information for the design of active low-pass and high-pass filters is the FilterPro software by Texas Instruments.

Other useful filters include band rejection filters, which may be used to remove an unwanted frequency band from an input signal.

■ 3.5 SENSOR INTERFACES

The user has to deal with two different issues in the design of a new controller. The first is to choose a physical effect or sensor, which detects the gesture to be interfaced to the computer. The second is to adapt that sensor to the practical and musical needs of the equipment you wish to control i.e. your computer software or MIDI instrument (STEIM, at http://www.steim.org/steim/sensor.html, accessed 1 March 2005).

As seen from the various sensors described above, the signal obtained at the output of a sensor is often an analog signal, that is, voltage or current. In order for it to be processed by a computer, it is necessary to convert this analog signal into digital codes. This conversion is usually accomplished using sensor interfaces.

Although there may be a tendency in the market to present some of the commercially available sensor interfaces as innovative devices, the electronics behind most of them are standard and well known to electronic engineers. The basic architecture of a sensor-to-MIDI interface consists of:

- A multiplexer (MUX) allowing the use of multiple signal inputs
- An analog-to-digital converter (ADC) that converts the analog signals into digital codes
- A universal asynchronous receiver/transmitter (UART) for serial transmission of the digital codes (often in the MIDI format)

Nowadays, the ADC and the UART (and sometimes also the MUX) are found as part of a single microcontroller, such as those provided by Microchip or Atmel. The advantage of such microcontrollers is that they feature in-chip memory space for implementing basic low-level routines for management of input, data manipulation, and output routing. This is useful for implementing systems that use multiple outputs in multiple MIDI channels, as in the case of IRCAM's AtoMIC Pro interface.

3.5.1 Sampling Rate and Resolution

Two important issues to be considered when designing sensor interfaces are the input sampling rate and the sampling resolution.

The input sampling rate needs to be higher than double the maximum frequency of the actions of the performer, so that the system accurately describes these actions. This rule is known as the sampling theorem, also referred to as the Nyquist or Shannon theorem.

Although one could reasonably consider that the actions of a performer generate a range from a few Hertz to a few tens of Hertz, fast actions can certainly be at higher frequencies. The sampling rate that is typically used for acquisition of musical control gestures is 200 Hz (Mathews and Bennett 1978). Some systems may even use higher values, ranging from 300 Hz to 1 kHz, depending on the application. Although higher sampling rates may be needed in special circumstances, 1 kHz is considered enough for most interface applications.

Various sampling rates may be used in the same system, depending on the nature of the actions to be sampled. One example is the Bösendorfer 290 SE recording piano, which uses three different sampling rates: 50 Hz for the sostenuto pedal, 100 Hz for the sustain pedal, and 800 Hz for the key sensors (Moog and Rhea 1990).

One sensor interface that allows for multirate sampling is the AtoMIC Pro interface manufactured at IRCAM. Each input can be sampled at different rates, up to 128 times slower than its reference rate. This allows for optimization of the operation of the interface, since sensors that do not require fast acquisition rates (e.g., ambient light or temperature sensors) can be sampled at much slower rates. This scheme optimizes the available bandwidth of the interface for sensors that require faster rates.

The sampling resolution may vary from 7 to 16 or more bits. The more bits allocated to represent a signal, the smaller the quantization error. That is, the closer the resulting signal will be to the original analog one, provided that the sampling rate is correctly chosen. But higher resolutions imply higher bandwidths, as well as the need for larger storage space. The sampling resolution of a system should be set as a function of the nature of the performance actions to be sensed.

The sampling resolution is a harder parameter to change in most commercial sensor interfaces because this is fixed by the analog-to-digital converter (ADC) of the interface. Sometimes an option is available, for instance in the I-Cube, where both 7-bit and 12-bit resolutions are possible.

3.5.2 Digital Protocols

Until recently, MIDI has been the main protocol for digital message exchanges between synthesizers and computers. MIDI was proposed in the early 1980s by several synthesizer manufactures in order to allow for communication between devices of different brands. The MIDI protocol was designed with the keyboard paradigm in mind, which limited its resolution and its ability to handle continuous parameter changes. Other limitations of MIDI include speed of communication (31,250 bits per second), rigid addressing options, and the need for specific hardware. It must be noted, however, that a fair number of music systems have used communications protocols other than MIDI in order to avoid such limitations. One example is TGR (Transducteur Gestuel Rétroactif), built at ACROE (Cadoz, Lisowski, and Florens 1990) described in chapter 2.

Considering that MIDI was created more than 20 years ago, it is astonishing that it is still much used in digital musical instrument design. To appreciate the longevity of MIDI, just compare the personal computers available at the time when MIDI was proposed, in the beginning of the 1980s, with current computers. Despite its several limitations, MIDI still remains popular and useful.

Concerning the various discussions and the advantages and disadvantages of the MIDI protocol (Moore 1987), strictly speaking, non-MIDI users face the need for appropriate communication drivers for the various platforms. Sometimes they have to implement these drivers themselves. But these problems are becoming increasingly irrelevant today because more flexible communication protocols, such as OSC, are becoming the de facto choices for data exchange between music devices.

OSC is a relatively new protocol for communication among computers, sound synthesizers, and other multimedia devices (Wright 1998; Wright et al. 2003). Developed by Matt Wright and colleagues at the Center for New Music and Audio Technology (CNMAT), at the University of California, Berkeley, it is optimized for networking technology and overcomes several of the limitations of MIDI. OSC is a more general protocol than MIDI in the sense that it does not favor keyboard-based controllers and does not rely on specific hardware.

According to its developers, OSC is an open, efficient, transport-independent, message-based protocol (Wright and Freed 1997). It is designed with client-server architectures in mind. Its message addressing is based on a URL-style symbolic scheme. Each OSC server is defined with an address, and this may be changed dynamically. Because of OSC's addressing scheme and pattern-matching abilities, the current address of a server can be discovered through its query system. Queries here are messages from clients requesting information from the server. OSC messages consist of an address pattern, a string that specifies:

- Which entity (or entities) the message is addressed to
- A type tag
- The kind of message
- The arguments
- The data contained in the message in various formats, including ASCII strings, 32-bit floating point, integer numbers, and chunks of binary data

OSC's flexibility is its main feature. In fact, an OSC application consists of a dynamically changing set of objects arranged hierarchically, and each of these objects has a set of messages that can be sent to control its behavior.

OSC implementations in various programs may differ, but all are based on the original CNMAT code.

3.6 EXAMPLES OF SENSOR INTERFACES

This section introduces a number of sensor interfaces proposed in the literature or available at the time of the writing of this book. Some examples are shown in Figure 3.41.

3.6.1 Analog-to-MIDI Interfaces

Various analog-to-MIDI interfaces have been built. Examples of interfaces include:

- SensorLab, made by STEIM (Netherlands)
- MicroLab, a system based on the SensorLab
- Digitizer/I-Cube, manufactured by Infusion Systems (Canada)
- MiniDig, a new, small version of the Digitizer from Infusion Systems
- Wi-miniDig, a Bluetooth version of the MiniDig

Figure 3.41 Examples of sensor interfaces.

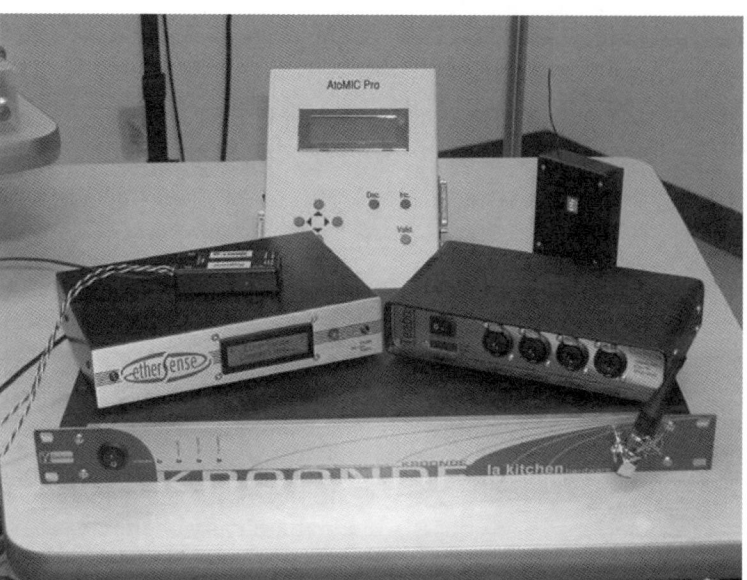

- AtoMIC Pro, made by IRCAM (France)
- EoBody, a system derived from AtoMIC Pro, manufactured by Eowave (France)
- MIDICreator, from the University of York (UK)
- Kit PAiA, made by PAiA Electronics (USA)
- MidiBox, from Notam (Norway)
- MidiTron, by Eroktronix (USA)
- Pocket Electronics, by Doepfer Musikelektronik (Germany)

Some of the main features of the above analog-to-MIDI interfaces include:

- Maximum number of analog inputs, usually ranging from 8 to 32 inputs
- Availability of digital inputs (allowing for the configuration of the interface or for on-off inputs from switches, for instance) and digital outputs
- Maximum sampling frequency varying up to 1 kHz. The maximum sampling frequency per input is dependent on the number of active inputs and a function of the limited speed of the MIDI protocol

- Resolution of 7, 10, 12 or 14 bits
- Available outputs include MIDI and other formats, such as parallel digital outputs
- Availability of multiple independent MIDI outputs, increasing the effective data conversion rate of the interface
- Configuration software for setting up operational features

It is important to stress that the speed and resolution of these interfaces are limited by the specifications of the MIDI protocol and not necessarily by the capabilities of their electronic circuits.

3.6.2 Analog-to-OSC Interfaces

Analog-to-OSC interfaces are recent developments. Examples available at the time of writing this book include:

- Toaster, from La Kitchen (France)
- Kroonde, a wireless interface from La Kitchen
- Ethersense, from IRCAM (France)

These recent interfaces generally offer a more powerful list of options apart from the protocol itself—for instance, increased resolution. Also, wireless signal transmission is becoming commonplace in analog-to-OSC interfaces.

3.6.3 Do-it-yourself Interfaces

An alternative to using commercial products is to build one's own interface using microcontrollers or Teleo modules provided by Making Things at http://www.makingthings.com (accessed 18 March 2005).

The advantage of using microcontrollers is their flexibility: in such cases one is free to design the interface with any imaginable feature. However, one needs appropriate knowledge of electronics and programming.

Various researchers have developed their own sensor-to-MIDI/OSC interfaces. Most notably, Bill Verplank and colleagues at CCRMA have extensively used microcontrollers, first the Basic Stamp, then the Atmel, to develop their own systems (Verplank, Sapp, and Mathews 2001; Wilson et al. 2003).

The HID interface developed by Mark Marshall is a recent example of a DIY interface using the Atmel microcontroller. HID design specifications and code are available at http://www.music.mcgill.ca/musictech/idmil/projects.htm (accessed 11 October 2005).

3.7 USING AUDIO INTERFACES TO TRANSMIT CONTROL SIGNALS

In some cases it is possible to connect sensors to the standard audio input of the computer. Since almost every computer nowadays comes with a stereo minijack socket for audio input, this option can be very economical. If gesture data can be sent as audio signals, no additional interface is needed.

The initial problem is the frequency range of both types of signals: audio signals range roughly from 20 Hz to 20 kHz, while human gestures are basically limited to a few Hz. It is therefore not usually possible to send gesture signals through an audio interface without further preprocessing. A straightforward procedure is to amplitude-modulate the low-frequency gesture signal with a carrier of higher frequency (in the audio range), input the modulated signal through the available audio input, and then demodulate the received signal in order to handle it. This is basically what Andrew Schloss and Peter Driessen (2001) have done to use the inner analog signals from the Radio Baton (or Radio Drum) to control a software sound synthesizer. By not using MIDI, they were able to capture the full complexity of the data output by the capacitive sensors of the Radio Drum. These were analog signals band-limited to 700 Hz in three channels, each corresponding to one of the three coordinates representing spatial 3D positions of the drum sticks. The problem with this scheme was the identification of meaningful gestures from the raw analog signals. In order to identify the strikes, the authors filtered the signal using filters tuned to the pulse shape of percussive strikes and a peak detector to find points with zero vertical velocity and negative acceleration. The signal processing was programmed in Max/MSP, and it was able to detect repetitive strikes at intervals of 39 ms even for gestures with low amplitudes.

It is also possible to convert the low frequency signals from the sensors onto the audio range. Another example is the SensorBox, designed by Jesse Allison and Timothy Place (2003). The SensorBox converts the analog voltages of up to 10 sensors onto signals in the upper frequency range of audio. Allison and Place considered that frequencies above 17 kHz would not be used in interactive systems.

Therefore, they filtered the audio signal using a low-pass filter with a cut-off frequency of about 17 kHz. Voltages from the sensors controlled oscillators in the range of 18 to 20 kHz. These signals were then mixed with the 17 kHz band-limited audio signals and entered the computer through a standard audio input. A recent version of this interface, called Teabox, is now commercialized by Electrotap: see http://www.electrotap.com/teabox/ (accessed 18 March 2005).

3.8 FOOD FOR THOUGHT

Let us finally discuss two new approaches to building flexible, low-cost devices.

3.8.1 Homemade Pressure and Position Sensors

As mentioned earlier in this chapter, most sensors used in the design of gestural controllers are commercially available. Specifically, many technologies have been developed to deal with force and tactile position-sensing devices. However, these devices have common drawbacks: they only exist as products with predefined sizes, shapes, and electrical characteristics. Musical instrument designers thus need to adapt the dimensions and characteristics of their interfaces to these existing sensors. In most cases this limited choice is not necessarily a problem; but in some cases, the existing shapes and sizes of commercial sensors are not adapted to the designer's needs.

Exceptions to this rule include capacitive sensing devices (Paradiso 2003), homemade touch (position) sensors using videotape or conductive fabric, force sensors using antistatic foam or carbon particles inserted in silicone—the Plubber, by Mikael Fernström—and accelerometers using needles and coils taken from electronic panel meters (Bongers 2000), as seen earlier. But can one systematically design one's own sensors? Which types of sensors can be developed at home effectively?

Rodolphe Koehly and Marcelo Wanderley have conducted a systematic study on various possibilities for developing force or pressure and tactile position sensors (Koehly 2005; Wanderley and Koehly n.d.). The aim of this work was to study existing conductive material technologies and consider how to create "homemade" sensors—or, at least, "computer music laboratory–made" sensors—

using these technologies. The goal was not to compete with industrial sensors but rather to find inexpensive conductive materials sensitive to mechanical stress that could be molded into various shapes and sizes.

They classified conductive materials into three main categories. All three categories use metallic or other conductive pigments, usually in the form of conductive inks or glues, the difference being how they are mixed and the method of application.

- *Complex materials*: A nonconductive material covered with a conductive ink layer enabling surface conductivity, or uniform conductive junction between two conductive materials (with the use of glue)
- *Composite materials*: A polymer used as an elastic matrix with conductive pigments uniformly distributed inside it
- *Porous materials*: Conductive foam, electret polymers and paper; compressing such a material decreases the air volume inside it, increasing its conductance

Using several variations of these materials, they built prototypes of force and position sensors and measured their electrical characteristics. Figures 3.42 and 3.43 show force sensor prototypes and their voltage outputs, respectively. Results were comparable to

Figure 3.42 Several homemade sensors and their conditioning circuits.

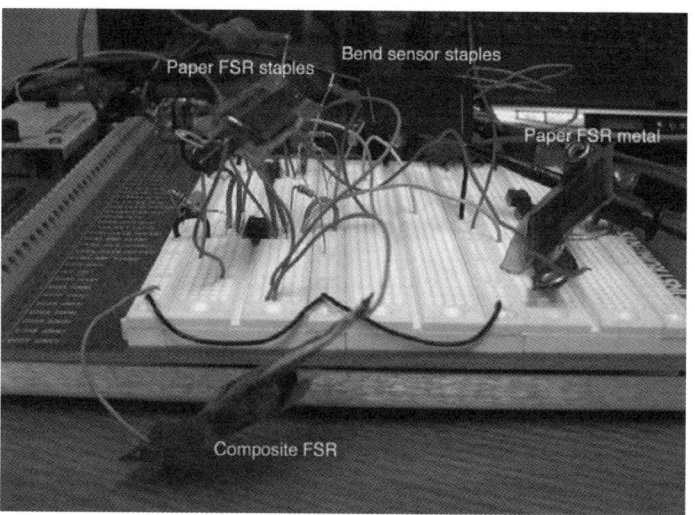

Figure 3.43 Resulting voltages obtained using LabView and a 16-channel, 16-bit PCMCIA National Instruments data acquisition card.

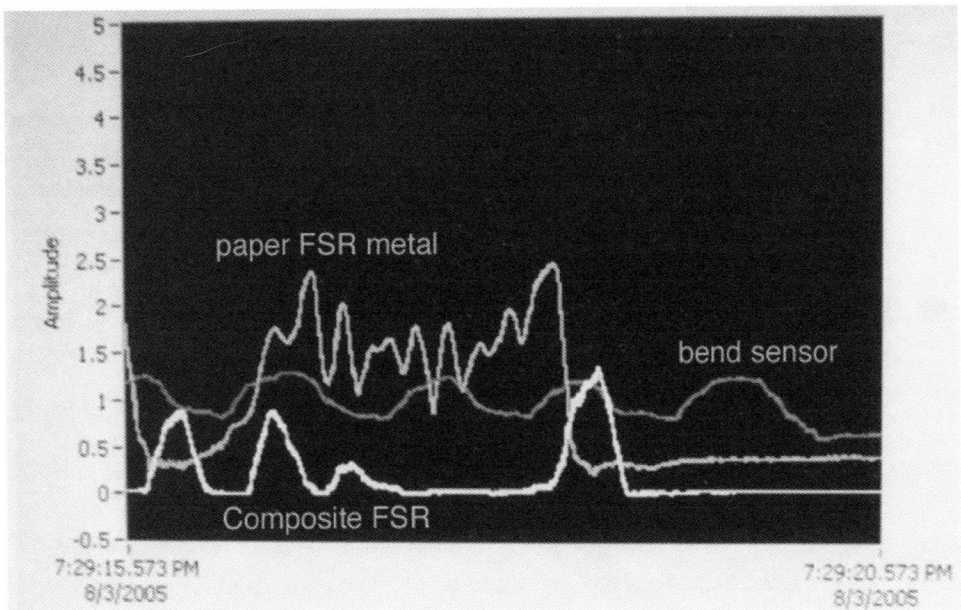

those obtained using commercially available industrial sensors, showing that it is possible to develop low-cost sensors with various shapes and sizes. Applications of this work are far reaching, including musical interface design, augmented instruments, and robotics.

3.8.2 Inexpensive Controllers

One direct application of homemade sensors is the design of low-cost musical controllers. In fact, the use of various commercial sensors in one controller can result in substantial costs, even if rather inexpensive sensors such as FSRs are used. Moreover, the use of commercial sensor-to-computer interfaces can boost the price of an instrument to several hundred U.S. dollars.

Another potential problem is the need for multiple copies of the same controller. Suppose a device whose sensor, electronics, and interface cost amounts to US$50, a reasonable value. Now imagine using it in an undergraduate class of 20 students, another very reasonable number. The cost could easily amount to US$1,000.

To circumvent these issues, Alexander Jensenius and Rodolphe Koehly (Jensenius, Koehly, and Wanderley 2005) at the Input Devices and Music Interaction Laborarory at McGill University developed the Cheapstick, a low-cost controller using sensors developed by Koehly (described above) and electronics obtained from commercial gamepads (Figure 3.44).

Obviously, the simplicity of the Cheapstick's design does not allow for the same level of sophistication found in some controllers, but it has proven very useful in simple, pedagogical applications.

■ 3.9 FURTHER READING

The Sensors and Actuators pages of the International Computer Music Association's Interactive Systems and Instrument Design Working Group Web site at http://www.igmusic.org (accessed 11 Sep-

Figure 3.44 The Cheapstick, by Alexander Jensenius and Rodolphe Koehly.

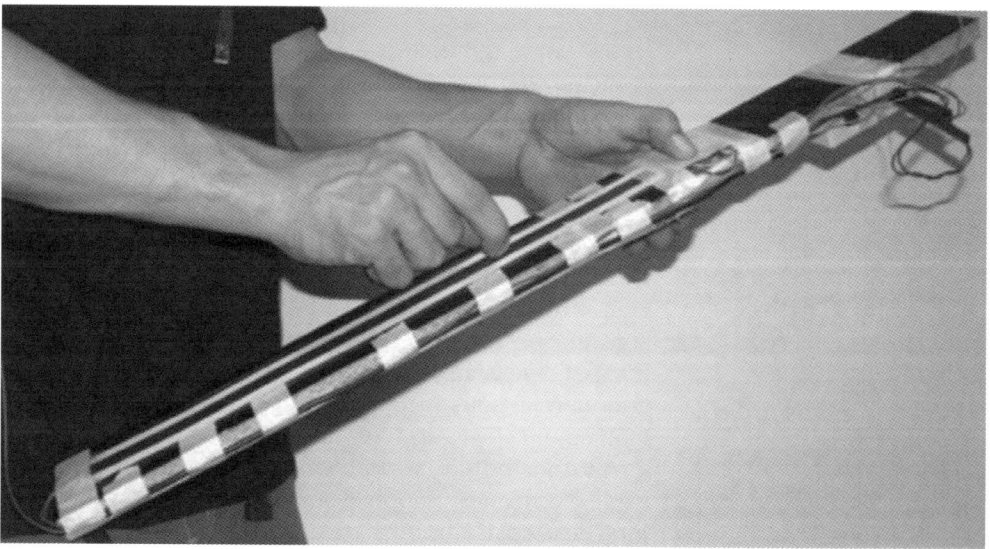

tember 2004) presents articles related to sensors and applications, and links to manufacturers and distributors of sensors.

One good source of technical information on selected sensors is the Web site of Infusion Systems (http://www.infusionsystems.com, accessed 1 March 2005), the manufacturers of the I-Cube system, where they present technical details on the sensors they commercialize. But for obvious reasons they do not give the part numbers and manufacturers of their sensors. Similar to Infusion Systems, but with less detail, is the Web site of La Kitchen (http://www.la-kitchen.fr/index.html, accessed 1 March 2005), featuring various sensors for musical applications. Other companies that offer varied sensors for artistic applications include Electrotap (http://www.electrotap.com, accessed 1 March 2005), Eowave (http://www.eowave.com, accessed 1 March 2005), and the University of York's Electronics Centre (http://www.midicreator.com, accessed 1 March 2005), to cite but three.

There are several articles, journals, and textbooks available on sensors. Starting with sensors for use in computer music, the following publications constitute excellent sources of information:

- B. Bongers (2000), "Physical Interfaces in the Electronic Arts Interaction Theory and Interfacing Techniques for Real-time Performance," in M. Wanderley and M. Battier (Eds.), *Trends in Gestural Control of Music* (Paris: IRCAM—Centre Pompidou), pp. 41–70. This essay presents a comprehensive survey of the numerous designs in which the author has been involved and clearly explains the choice of sensors he made in each one.

- W. Putnam and R. B. Knapp (1996), "Input/Data Acquisition System Design for Human Computer Interfacing," course notes available at http://ccrma.stanford.edu/CCRMA/Courses/252/sensors/sensors.html (accessed 27 February 2005). This paper presents a few sensors (piezos, FSRs, accelerometers, biopotential sensors, and microphones) and describes the electronic circuits necessary for signal conditioning as well as examples of how to use these sensors.

- J. Paradiso (1999), "The Brain Opera Technology: New Instruments and Gestural Sensors for Musical Interaction and Performance," *Journal of New Music Research,* 28(2):130–149. This paper describes the various sensor technologies and devices used in the MIT MediaLab's *Brain Opera* project.

The following articles are more specialized on specific sensor technologies:

- C. Verplaetse (1996), "Inertial Proprioceptive Devices: Self-motion-sensing Toys and Tools," *IBM Systems Journal,* 35(3–4): 639–650. This article focuses on inertial sensing devices such as accelerometers and gyroscopes.
- J. Paradiso and N. Gershenfeld (1997), "Musical Applications of Electric Field Sensing," *Computer Music Journal* 21(2):69–89. This article focuses on the various uses of electric field sensing.
- E. Fléty (2000), "3D Gesture Acquisition Using Ultrasonic Sensors," in M. Wanderley and M. Battier (Eds.), *Trends in Gestural Control of Music* (Paris: IRCAM—Centre Pompidou), pp. 193–207. This essay focuses on 3D gesture acquisition using ultrasonic sensors.
- J. Paradiso, K.-y. Hsiao, and E. Hu (1999), "Interactive Music for Instrumented Dancing Shoes," *Proceedings of the 1999 International Computer Music Conference* (ICMC99), Beijing, China, pp. 453–456. This paper focuses on magnetic tags.

A number of papers, journals, conference proceedings, and books are available on industrial sensors that can be used in computer music applications, such as most of those we have reviewed in this chapter. Recently, the IEEE (Institute of Electrical and Electronic Engineers) launched *Sensors Journal,* a technical journal dedicated to all aspects of sensors. Although the information in this journal may be unnecessarily technical for most readers interested in computer music, they often present surveys on selected sensor themes that may be of interest. Another excellent source of information on sensors is *Sensors Magazine* (http://www.sensorsmag.com, accessed March 1, 2005).

We recommend the following books on sensors:

- J. Fraden (2004), *Handbook of Modern Sensors: Physics, Design and Applications*, 3rd ed. (London: Springer-Verlag). This book presents a wealth of information on a wide variety of sensors, with clear explanations and drawings of many devices. A good starting point is the excellent chapter "Physical Principles of Sensing," which gives the reader a broad view of several sensing possibilities.
- R. Pallàs-Areny and J. G. Webster (2001), *Sensors and Signal Conditioning*, 2nd ed. (New York: Wiley Interscience). This book also presents much information on several industrial sensors, but we

find it slightly more technical than the book cited above. One of the strong points of this book is that each chapter on a specific sensing variable is followed by another chapter on related conditioning circuits.

- D. S. Nyce (2004), *Linear Position Sensors: Theory and Application* (Hoboken, NJ: John Wiley and Sons). Although this book has a much smaller range of coverage owing to the choice of topic, we find it very accessible and complete. For instance, seeing the historical perspective behind each sensing principle (also present in less detail in the books above) provides interesting background. The explanations of the sensing principles are very clear and well written.

Additionally, two books by Joseph Carr are excellent sources of information, mostly for beginners:

- J. J. Carr (1993), *Sensors and Circuits: Sensors, Transducers, and Supporting Circuits for Electronic Instrumentation, Measurement, and Control* (Upper Saddle River, NJ: Prentice-Hall). In this book the author presents a comprehensive review of several sensor technologies grouped according to the sensed variable—for example, resistive, capacitive, and inductive sensors; temperature sensors; position and displacement sensors; and so on.

- J. J. Carr (1997), *Electronic Circuit Guidebook*, vol. 1, *Sensors* (Indianapolis: Prompt Publications, Howard W. Sams). This book also discusses several sensors, but its strength is the practical examples of signal conditioning circuits presented and clearly explained. The book gives several practical implementations useful for musical projects and is a must for beginners starting to build their own interfaces.

Dan Sullivan and Tom Igoe's *Physical Computing* (Boston, MA: Muska & Lipman 2004) is an excellent practical resource for people interested in sensors, mainly those using the Basic Stamp microcontroller. This book provides practical information on electronics, circuitry, sensors, and code examples for the Basic Stamp.

Very good references for more experienced readers include the following handbooks:

- John Webster, ed. (1998), *The Measurement, Instrumentation and Sensors Handbook* (Boca Raton, FL: CRC Press), is an impressive collection of information on all aspects related to sensors and measurement. Although it may be very useful for musical and artistic applications, it is targeted toward industrial applications.

- Jon Winson, ed. (2005), *Sensor Technology Handbook* (Burlington, MA: Newnes Publications), is another very recent book with extensive coverage of various industrial sensing technologies.

FOUR

Biosignal Interfaces

In this book we use the term biosignal to refer to electrical signals produced in the body, such as nerve, muscle, and brain signals.

The electrical nature of the human body has been recognized for more than a century. In the 1840s, the physiologist Emil Heinrich du Bois-Reymond reported the detection of electrical discharges created by the contraction of the muscles of his arms (Lusted and Knapp 1996). Du Bois-Reymond made these observations using a galvanometer, a device for measuring voltage. He attached the wires of the galvanometer to his body using pieces of blotting paper soaked in saline. Du Bois-Reymond's method for detecting muscle contraction still forms the basis of current practice in electrophysiology, albeit using more sophisticated electrodes and amplifiers.

The measurement and analysis of biosignals requires sophisticated sensor technology. These signals are normally sensed using electrodes attached to the body, and they normally need to be amplified by a factor as high as 10,000 in order to be useful. Moreover, these signals must be harnessed by means of numerical methods in order to infer their meaning. Only then can the behavior of the biosignals be used to operate a musical system.

■ 4.1 BRIEF INTRODUCTION TO ELECTRODES AND ELECTRICAL SAFETY ISSUES

Biosignals are normally produced by action potentials in nerve fiber bundles or by extracellular potentials generated by the movement of ions in and out of cells during depolarization and repolarization. Because most biosignal sensing is extracellular and takes place at some distance from its origin, what is sensed is the combined voltage of the simultaneous activation of many components (nerves, muscle fibers, or neurons). The signals are conducted through the tissue of the body and detected by sensors, normally electrodes.

It is a common mistake to assume that the electrodes "pick up" electrical activity, which is then sent to a computer for processing. In fact, current flow is measured through a loop composed of the subject, electrodes, wires, and the recording equipment. The voltage fluctuations produced in the subject can be calculated because the resistance to current flow is taken as a reference.

Charge movement in the brain, muscles, or nerves generates the electrical activity. The charge moves into one electrode, goes through the circuitry of the amplifiers, and enters back into the subject through another electrode. Therefore, the subject and the amplifier form a complete circuit loop.

Standard surface electrodes are normally applied to the skin with a conductive gel, and the skin should normally be prepared with abrasion beforehand in order to remove oils and layers of dead skin that may interfere with the electrical conductivity. The conductive gel is essentially a malleable extension of the electrode: it maximizes skin contact and is required for low-resistance recording through the skin. However, electrode technology is rapidly evolving; more ergonomic sensors with built-in signal processing capability and wireless data transmission will soon be available on the market at an affordable price.

4.1.1 Electrical Safety

When working with biosignals, electrical safety should be carefully observed in order to prevent accidents. It is always preferable to use equipment that runs on disposable batteries (e.g., alkaline or lithium batteries) rather than mains AC. Should a mains connection be absolutely necessary, then it must be supplied by three wires: hot, neutral, and earth wire. Hot means that there is alternating voltage (e.g., ± 110 V); neutral is the reference for the hot line from the power company, and it is not necessarily at 0 V; the earth is the earth connection.

One of the main problems with biosignals is current leakage. This is mostly caused by faulty earth connection or inappropriately long power supply wires. This is manifested in the signal by the appearance of accentuated noise. A common cause of leakage is when the subject is attached to two pieces of electrical equipment but only one is properly earthed. If the subject is earthed to both devices, then the leak current may flow from the earth wire of one machine, through the subject, and into the earth of the other machine. All equipment attached to the subject should be connected to the same power strip and to a single earth.

People with a pacemaker must avoid anything involving electrodes. Leakage is particularly hazardous for the detection of the heartbeat (through electrocardiography, or ECG) in pacemaker wearers, especially when the electrodes are placed near the myocardium. Also, when detecting muscle activity (through electromyography, or EMG) it is important that the earth is on the same limb as the active electrode so that leakage currents do not flow through the heart.

Note that the recommendations in this section are not exhaustive, as different equipment requires different types of precaution. You should always seek professional advice before using them. Also, it is important that a professional electrician inspect all electrical connections on a regular basis. One must always carefully read the safety instructions that accompany the equipment.

■ 4.2 EXAMPLES OF BIOSIGNALS

This section introduces a number of biosignals that can and have been used to control computer systems, including musical systems.

4.2.1 Eye Movement: Electrooculogram

The electrooculogram, or EOG, is a measurement of eye movement and gaze. The retina and the cornea of the eye form what could be considered an electrical battery, owing to a difference in potential between them: the retina exhibits slightly more negative voltage than the cornea. As we move our eyes this difference varies, generating tiny voltage fluctuations over the face. This can be detected with electrodes placed near the eyes. With suitable electrode placement, it is possible to detect voltages that vary proportionally to eye movement. EOG has been used in a number of systems to move a computer cursor. For example, Lusted and Knapp (1996) reported a system for cursor control using a pair of electrodes to detect vertical eye displacement and another pair to detect horizontal eye movements. There have also been news reports on systems using a visual keyboard displayed on the computer screen where the user can type by selecting the keys using eye movement alone.

4.2.2 Skin Conductivity: Galvanic Skin Response

The galvanic skin response (GSR), also referred to as the electrodermal response (EDR), measures electrical skin conductivity normally taken from the palm or fingertips. GSR recordings are easily obtained using finger electrodes (Figure 4.1).

Easily measured and relatively reliable, GSR has been used in psychophysiological experiments as an index for measuring emotional state or arousal. However, there is no consensus as to exactly what the measurements mean. In physiological terms, GSR reflects sweat gland activity and changes in the sympathetic nervous system—that is, the system responsible for the provision of energy in emergency situations like hunger or fear (by raising blood pressure, heart rate, and so on). Such activity causes changes in the relative conductivity of a small electrical current between the electrodes. The activity of the sweat glands in response to sympathetic nervous stimulation results in an increase in the level of conductivity. A relationship seems to exist between sympathetic activity and emotional arousal, but it is difficult identify the specific emotion being elicited. Any stimulus capable of causing some form of arousal can evoke changes to the signal.

4.2.3 Heartbeat: Electrocardiogram

An electrocardiogram (ECG or EKG) is a recording of the small electrical waves generated by heart activity and is widely used to monitor the electrical workings of the heart. With each beat, an electrical

Figure 4.1 Finger electrodes for sensing GSR.

wave travels through the heart: this wave causes the muscle to squeeze and pump blood. ECG is perhaps the best known of the biosignals. Cardiologists are able to identify heart abnormalities thorough visual interpretation of ECG waveforms. Figure 4.2 shows some of the various components of the waveform that are used to interpret this biosignal. For instance, whereas the P wave represents the depolarization impulse across the atria, the Q, R, and S waves represent the ventricular depolarization. The downward stroke followed by an upward stroke is called the Q wave; the upward stroke is called the R wave, and any downward stroke preceded by an upward stroke is called S wave. The T wave represents the repolarization of the ventricles (the chambers which collect and pump blood out).

The following information can be determined from the ECG tracing, but only the first two are normally sought in a controller:

- Heart rate
- Heart rhythm
- Whether there are abnormalities in how the electrical impulse spreads across the heart
- Whether there has been a prior heart attack
- Whether there may be coronary artery disease
- Whether the heart muscle has become abnormally thickened

Figure 4.2 Some of the components that are used for interpretation of the ECG signal.

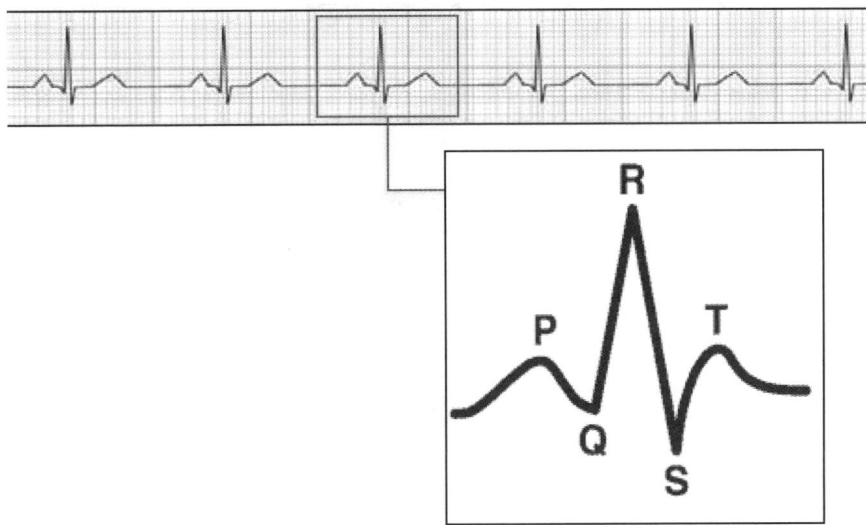

The electrical currents in the heart have been measured for more than 100 years. Willem Einthoven developed the basics of the ECG at the beginning of the 20th century; in the 1920s he was awarded a Nobel Prize for his discovery of the mechanism of the electrocardiogram.

A small pulse of electric current initiates a normal heartbeat. This tiny electric shock spreads rapidly through the heart and makes the heart muscle contract. If the whole heart muscle contracted at the same time, there would be no pumping effect. Therefore the electrical activity starts at the top of the heart and spreads downward, and then up again, causing the heart muscle to contract in an optimal way for pumping blood.

The electrical waves in the heart are recorded in terms of millivolts. For clinical purposes, ECG is typically recorded using 12 leads: 6 limb leads and 6 precordial leads.

Three of the limb leads are bipolar in the sense that each lead requires two electrodes placed on the skin. If one connects a line between two electrodes, one has a vector, with the positive end being at one electrode and the negative at the other. The positioning for the bipolar leads (referred to as leads I, II, and III, respectively) is called Einthoven's Triangle. Figure 4.3 illustrates the vectors generated by the limb leads. The lead marking indicates the positive pole of the lead.

Figure 4.3 The vectors generated by the bipolar limb leads.

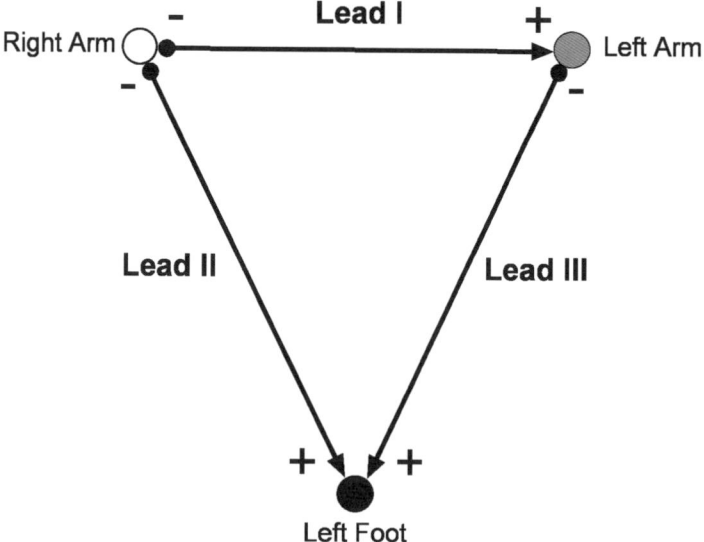

The other three limb leads are called augmented leads because two electrodes are required for a negative pole and one positive electrode to form the positive pole, as indicated in Table 4.1:

Table 4.1
The placement of the augmented limb leads.

Augmented Lead	Positive electrode	Negative electrodes
aVL	Left arm	Left foot + right arm
aVR	Right arm	Left foot + left arm
aVF	Left foot	Left arm + right arm

The precordial leads are referred to as V1, V2, . . . , V6, respectively. They are used to measure the amplitude of cardiac electrical current in an anterior-posterior fashion with respect to the heart (Figure 4.4).

The principles of ECG recording are as follows: when the overall electrical current of the heart goes toward a particular lead, it registers a positive deflection. Current that goes away from the lead registers a negative deflection. Current that is at 90° or perpendicular to the vector of the lead registers 0. When a current is not in the direction of the vector but slightly off (e.g., at 60° to the direction of the vector), then the amplitude of the deflection will be decreased.

Figure 4.4 Placement of the precordial ECG leads.

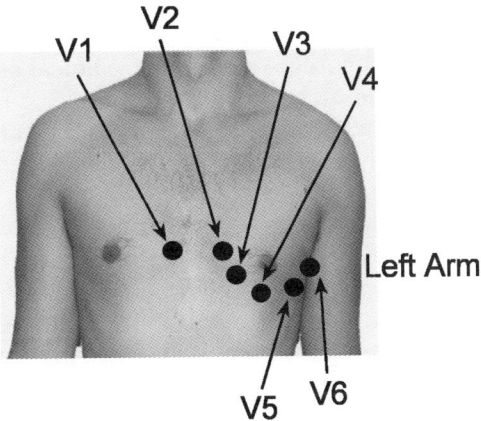

In the case of the 12-lead scheme, the ECG display consists of 12 views of the electrical impulse generated by the heart. Various cardiac abnormalities can be localized to specific areas of the heart based on these 12 views.

Note, however, that the 12-lead scheme is standard for clinical application. If one is only interested in sensing the heartbeat, it is possible to do so using much simpler schemes—for example, by means of the single earlobe sensor commonly supplied with exercise bicycles to measure the heart rate.

4.2.4 Muscle Sounds: Electromyogram and Mechanomyogram

The electromyogram (EMG) is a method for measuring muscular activity: it measures the depolarization of a muscle when it contracts. The coordination of a movement involves a great number of action potentials. The EMG corresponds to the contribution of all groups of neighboring muscles at the point of the recording.

The EMG effectively relates muscle activity and force, but this relationship is not linear. As with most biosignals, the EMG is relatively easy to qualify but rather difficult to quantify. A number of researchers are investigating the potential of EMG to control artificial limbs. The major difficulty with EMG is that it is hard to quantify the movement because the signal does not always represent the effort applied to make the movement.

There are a few different types of electrodes for EMG, ranging from monopolar needle electrodes to noninvasive active electrodes. The monopolar needle electrode consists of a fine needle that is fully insulated with the exception of a very small region at the tip. This electrode requires reference and ground electrodes: a superficial reference electrode is placed on the skin over the muscle being monitored and a superficial ground electrode is placed on the skin near the recording electrodes. Clinical studies and monitoring often use needle electrodes, for example, for nerve conducting studies (Misulis 1997). Since this requires the careful observation of medical and safety procedures, needle electrodes are impractical for a musical system.

At present, active EMG surface electrodes are the best option for musical systems. They are called active because they integrate a built-in preamplifier and a built-in filter. They are placed on the surface of the skin and require little skin preparation. These electrodes are differential units designed using parallel-bar contacts (Figure 4.5).

Figure 4.5 Active surface EMG electrodes integrate a built-in preamplifier and a built-in filter.

The mechanomyogram (MMG) is not an electrical signal, but it is discussed in this book due to its acoustic nature. Muscle fibers produce vibrations, many of which are audible and detectable on the surface of the body. The activity of contracting muscles can he heard through a stethoscope as a rumbling sound. Although muscle vibrations were first observed in the 16th century, they have been largely neglected in physiological research. Only recently has the scientific community rediscovered the potential of muscle vibrations for clinical use. The fact that muscles produce sounds is of great interest to musicians.

Recordings of muscle vibrations can be made with a sound or vibration detector (e.g., pressure microphone or accelerometer) on the skin over the contracting muscles. The signal reflects the mechanical performance of muscles, hence the name mechanomyogram. Once detected, MMG signals can then be analyzed and processed in the same way as electrical EMG signals.

Muscle sounds are the product of lateral movements, or oscillations, of muscle fibers. The frequency of these sounds seems to be determined by the stimulation rate. The dominant frequency of muscle sounds during voluntary contraction falls below 20 Hz. The nature and force of contraction produces frequency variations, and different muscles may produce different frequencies. For example, the frequency of the biceps branchii (a muscle on the upper arm that acts to flex the elbow) ranges from approximately 11 Hz to 19 Hz (Rhatigan et al. 1986) and that of the masseter (the quadrilateral muscle for chewing that covers most of the lateral side of the mandible) ranges from approximately 7 Hz to 15 Hz (L'Estrange, Rowell, and Stokes 1993).

Detecting muscle sounds is not an easy task. Our body produces a number of other acoustic signals, which impede the isolation of muscle sounds. Different sensors have been used in MMG, such as accelerometers, stethoscopes, and microphones. The most commonly used microphones are contact microphones because they capture the signal directly from the skin surface without its passing through the air. Important considerations when choosing an MMG sensor are its frequency response and its weight. The low-frequency cut-off needs to be about 1 Hz and the upper cut-off 100 Hz. Although the dominant frequency of muscle sounds is below 20 Hz, one should allow for higher components of the spectrum as well. Lightweight sensors are preferable because the weight of the sensor may distort the muscle surface. In addition one should pay attention to the pressure applied to the sensor for securing it to the skin, because this can influence the signal. Careful attention should be given so as to not jeopardize the movement of the muscle in question when attaching the sensors; elastic or rubber straps are often recommended for this. In order to detect signals from the deeper muscle fibers the sensors should be pressed firmly onto the skin, but excessive pressure may limit the movement of the muscle.

Owing to its mechanical nature, muscle sound needs less amplification than EMG. According to Maria Stokes and Max Blythe (2001), it is possible, however, to use the same amplifiers used for recording electrical biosignals such as EMG, but the frequency range and intensity settings should be appropriately adjusted.

Changes in the force of voluntary muscle contraction generally cause changes in the intensity and frequency of the signal, but the relationship between MMG and force is not always linear. It varies according to the muscle in question and may vary from individual to individual for the same muscle. Though the relationship is nonlinear, intensity and frequency are proportional to force. Frequency is detected less reliably than amplitude, but this will probably improve as MMG technology progresses.

More information on MMG, including references to ongoing research, can be found in the book *Muscle Sounds,* by Maria Stokes and Max Blythe (2001).

4.2.5 Brain Activity: Electroencephalogram

Neural activity generates electrical fields that can be recorded with electrodes attached to the scalp (Misulis 1997). Some of this activity is generated by action potentials of cortical neurons. The electroencephalogram, or EEG, is the visual plotting of this signal, but nowadays people normally use the initials to refer to the electric fields themselves. These electrical fields are extremely faint, with amplitudes on the order of only a few microvolts. In order to be displayed and/or processed, these signals must be greatly amplified.

The EEG is measured as the voltage difference between two or more electrodes on the surface of the scalp, one of which is taken as a reference. Normally, this reference is an electrode placed in a location that is assumed to lack brain activity, such as the ear lobe or the nose. It is also common practice to calculate the EEG of an electrode by averaging the signal from all electrodes and then subtracting it from the signal of each electrode.

The EEG expresses the overall activity of millions of neurons in the brain in terms of charge movement, but the electrodes can detect this only in the most superficial regions of the cerebral cortex. The source of the EEG has been a question of continuous scientific study, yet many questions remain unanswered. In humans, the thalamus seems to be the main source of EEG, because oscillations at the thalamic level activate cortical neurons. Individual frequencies probably depend on differing sites of generation with differing projections.

The EEG is a difficult signal to handle because it is filtered by the meninges (the membranes that separate the cortex from the skull), the skull, and the scalp before reaching the electrodes. Furthermore, the signals arriving at the electrodes are integrated sums of signals arising from many possible sources, including the heartbeat and eyeblinks. Although experts can diagnose brain malfunction from raw EEG plots, this signal needs to be further scrutinized with signal processing and analysis techniques in order to be of any use for a music system.

There are basically two conventions for positioning the electrodes on the scalp: the 10-20 electrode placement system (as recommended by the International Federation of Societies for EEG and Clinical Neurophysiology) and the geodesic sensor net (developed by Electric Geodesics). The 10-20 system uses 21 electrodes placed at positions that are measured at 10% and 20% of the head circumference (Figure 4.6). The terminology for referring to the position of the electrodes is based on a key letter that indicates a region on the scalp and a number that specifies the exact position: F = frontal, Fp = frontopolar, C = central, T = temporal, P = parietal, O = occipital, and A = auricular (the earlobe). Odd numbers are used for electrodes on the left

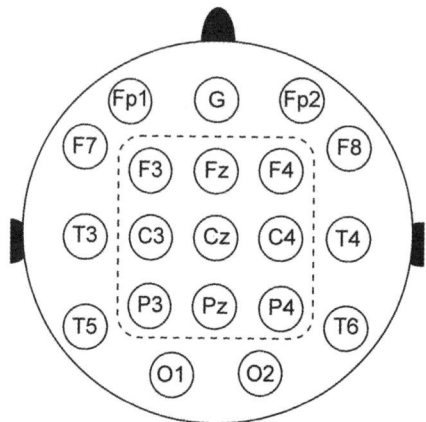

Figure 4.6 The standard 10-20 electrode placement system, where the electrodes are placed at positions measured at 10% and 20% of the head circumference. Reprinted with permission from *Leonardo* 38:4.

side of the head and even numbers for those on the right side. The geodesic sensor net is a configuration for dense arrays of 64, 128, or 256 electrodes, forming a geodesic pattern.

The sequence of electrodes being recorded at one time is called a montage. Generally speaking, montages fall into one of two categories: referential or bipolar. Referential means that the reference for each electrode is in common with other electrodes; for example, each electrode may be referenced to an electrode placed on the earlobe. An average reference means that each electrode is compared to the average potential of every electrode. Bipolar means that the reference for one channel is active for the next; for example, in the longitudinal bipolar montage, channel 1 is Fp1-F3. This means that Fp1 is the active electrode and F3 is the reference. Channel 2 is F3-C3, so that F3 is now the active electrode and C3 is the reference, and so forth.

■ 4.3 BIOSIGNAL CONDITIONING

A thorough introduction to biosignal conditioning (or processing) is beyond the scope of this book; this is a huge and evolving topic. The following paragraphs are intended to give only a glimpse of the great variety of signal conditioning methods that can be used in biosignal controllers.

Biosignal conditioning normally involves the pre-processing, feature analysis, machine learning, and mapping stages. For didactic reasons, these stages will be discussed below using simple signal processing techniques and examples biased toward an interface to control music using the EEG (Miranda et al. 2003).

4.3.1 Pre-processing

Biosignals often contain unwanted components, or noise. What is useful in a signal and what is an unwanted component depends on what is being measured. In some cases the signal-to-noise ratio is high, and the signal can be discerned from other electrical activity by means of a suitable filtering and/or noise rejection technique.

Two of the most important causes of electrical noise in biosignals are stray capacitance and stray inductance. The small amount of capacitance that exists among electrode wires, power lines, and tissue-electrode contact allows a charge gradient to be built up. This is called stray capacitance. The charge flows unpredictably into the amplifier and alters its response to the signal.

Stray inductance is the production of current in a wire by a surrounding magnetic field; the movement of current through the wires of an electrical device produces a magnetic field. This magnetic field is often very weak but can nevertheless induce electrons to flow through another wire, such as an electrode lead. The effect is negligible if electrode resistances are small and the signal current flow is large. However, if electrode resistances are high and the signal current flow is small, then induced current becomes a substantial fraction of the total current input to the amplifier. This is one of the reasons that power mains interference is more prominent when electrodes have high impedances. Broken wires or loose electrode leads increase this problem. Power mains interference can be reduced by:

- Ensuring proper grounding
- Keeping electrode impedances low and approximately equal
- Keeping power mains cables away from electrode leads
- Using shielded cables

Movement of the subject or the electrode wires may result in undesired components caused by a disturbance in the junction potentials between the electrode and skin and by movement of electrode leads. Junction potentials are stable only as long as the electrode system is stable. Moving electrode leads changes the amount of stray capacitance and the distribution of current caused by stray inductance. For instance, the EEG often contains unwanted components derived from muscle activity: eye movements, blinking, swallowing, and other spurious limb movements generate undesirable components that mask those components one is interested in analyzing. Even if a subject stands immobile and closes his or her eyes, involuntary minor eye movements still can produce undesirable components. These components can be detected and eliminated by comparing fast and slow running averages of the difference between signals from the electrodes that are placed near the eyes. An example of an algorithm provided by Alexander Duncan at the University of Glasgow (Duncan 2001) to remove such undesirable components is given as follows:

```
Fast = 0
Slow = average of difference of first 10 samples
FOR each sample DO:
    Diff = difference in voltage of eye channels
    Fast = (+ (* 0.8 Fast) (* 0.2 (- Diff Slow)))
    Slow = (+ (* 0.975 Slow) (*0.025 Diff))
    IF |Fast| > eye_blink_threshold THEN reject segment
```

The algorithm compares the deviation between fast and slow running averages of a pair of EEG channels with a threshold. An eye-blink is detected when the deviation exceeds the threshold level of 70 µV.

Also, one or more electrodes may be faulty or be misplaced. When this happens, the EEG from those electrodes should be excluded from further processing; these are technically referred to as bad channels.

A low-pass filter (LPF) can be applied to attenuate signals higher than, say, 40 Hz with the objective of reducing power mains hum noise and minimizing equipment interference. An eighth-order LPF Butterworth filter (Hamming 1989) can be applied to individual channels of EEG data for this purpose.

A Laplace spatial filter can be employed to boost the manifestation of individual channels by separating local EEG from larger global effects (Peters, Pfurtscheller, and Flyvberg 1997; Roberts and Penny 2000). This filter is very simple: it works by subtracting from the signal of each electrode the average of the signals of its nearest neighbors, as follows:

$$x'^{n,k}_c(t) = x^{n,k}_c(t) - \frac{1}{|\Omega_c|}\sum_{i \in \Omega_c} x^{i,k}_c(t)$$

where Ω_c is the neighborhood of channel c, for all channels, and $|\Omega_c|$ is the cardinality of Ω_c. Note that Ω_c can vary according to the location of different electrodes (Figure 4.7).

In the case of bipolar montage (refer to section 4.2.5), a bipolar reference is calculated simply by subtracting the secondary electrode j from the active electrode i:

$$Vbip(i) = V(i) - V(j)$$

Independent component analysis (ICA) is also a powerful technique for separating independent sources mixed into several sensors. This is particularly useful, for example, for teasing out artifacts embedded in the data. It is a technique aimed at recovering unobserved signals or sources from observed mixtures, exploiting only the assumption of mutual independence between the signals. The observed signals are obtained at the output of multiple sensors, and each of these sensors receives a different combination of the source signals. Several implementations of ICA algorithms exist; a well-known example is the ICA algorithm proposed by Jean-François Cardoso (1999).

4.3.2 Feature Analysis

Power spectrum analysis. Power spectrum analysis is one of the most popular techniques for analyzing biosignals. It consists of deconstructing the signal into partials and determining their individual frequencies and relative amplitudes within specified epochs, or windows.

Figure 4.7 Examples of neighborhood for electrodes F3 and Pz in the 10-20 electrode placement system. Reprinted with permission from *Computer Music Journal 27:2.*

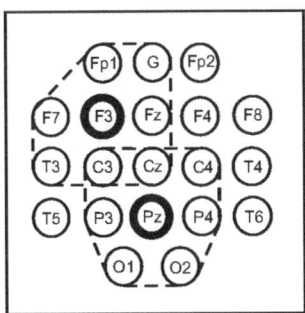

Power spectrum analysis is primarily based upon Fourier-based techniques, such as the discrete Fourier transform (DFT), all highly familiar to electronic musicians (Miranda 1998). In short, DFT analysis breaks the signal into different frequency bands and reveals the distribution of power between them. This is particularly useful for EEG because the distinct configurations of power distribution in the spectrum of the signal can indicate different "mental states." For example, an EEG spectrum with salient low-frequency components is associated with a state of drowsiness, whereas an EEG spectrum with salient high-frequency components is associated with a state of alertness. There are six recognized bands of EEG activity, also referred to as EEG rhythms, each of which is associated with specific mental states. Note, however, that there is controversy as to the exact frequency boundaries of these bands. Also, there is no agreement as to the mental states that are associated to these bands. Table 4.2 gives an indication of what is perceived to be consensual values and plausible associations, but bear in mind that these associations are tentative and might be controversial.

Table 4.2
Bands of EEG activity and associated mental states for a healthy young adult.

EEG rhythm	Frequency band	Mental association
Delta	$\delta \leq 4 Hz$	Sleep
Theta	$4\ Hz < \theta \leq 8\ Hz$	Drowsiness, trance, deep relaxation, deep meditation, hypnosis
Alpha	$8\ Hz < \alpha \leq 13\ Hz$	Relaxed wakefulness (normally generated with closed eyes)
Low beta	$13\ Hz < \beta(-) \leq 20\ Hz$	Wakefulness, alertness, moderate mental activity
Medium beta	$20\ Hz < \beta(m) \leq 30\ Hz$	High alertness, intense mental activity
Gamma (also referred to as high beta)	$\gamma > 30\ Hz$	Hyper-awareness, stress, anxiety

Hjorth analysis. Bo Hjorth introduced a method for clinical EEG analysis (Hjorth 1970) that may also be used to analyze other types of biosignals. The method is based on an amplitude-time analysis and uses three parameters: *activity*, *mobility*, and *complexity*.

Hjorth analysis is attractive because it represents each time step (or window) using only three variables. Moreover, this is done without conventional frequency domain description. There may be a lack of clarity if the input signal has more than one peak in the power spectrum. But this problem can be alleviated by band-pass filtering the signal beforehand.

The parameters of a signal are measured for successive epochs (or windows) of one to several seconds. Two of these parameters are obtained from the first and second time derivatives of the amplitude fluctuations in the signal. The first derivative is the rate of change of the signal's amplitude. At peaks and troughs the first derivative is zero. At other points it will be positive or negative depending on whether the amplitude is increasing or decreasing with time. The steeper the slope of the wave, the greater the amplitude of the first derivative. The second derivative is determined by taking the first derivative of the first derivative of the signal. Peaks and troughs in the first derivative, which correspond to points of greatest slope in the original signal, result in zero amplitude in the second derivative, and so forth.

Activity is the variance of the amplitude fluctuations in the epoch. Mobility is calculated by taking the square root of the variance of the first derivative divided by the variance of the primary signal. Complexity is the ratio of the mobility of the first derivative of the signal to the mobility of the signal itself. There is no clear agreement as to what these measurements mean in terms of mental states. It is common sense to assume that the longer a subject remains focused on a specific mental task, the more stable is the signal, and therefore the lower is the variance of the amplitude fluctuation.

Barlow analysis. Barlow analysis calculates three parameters: *mean amplitude*, *mean frequency*, and *spectral purity index* (or *spectral width*). Mean amplitude is the mean amplitude value of the window, and mean frequency shows the mean of all frequencies in the window. Spectral purity index (SPI) is a measure of the regularity of the signal. The maximum of the SPI is one for a sinewave. It will have values of less than one if a band of frequencies is present. Irina Goncharova and John Barlow (1990) demonstrated that if subjects close their eyes, the mean frequency stays almost unchanged, but the SPI decreases significantly. As with Hjorth analysis, the reliability of

Barlow analysis is dependent on the number of peaks in the power spectrum. A band-pass filter helps to alleviate this problem.

Data reduction. The objective of data reduction is to create a manageable and meaningful representation of a signal. It is also aimed at compressing the data in order to reduce the number of variables for further processing.

Linear auto-regression (AR) is a popular technique for representing signals in terms of estimations of its spectral density in time (Anderson and Sijercic 1996; Peters, Pfurtscheller, and Flyvberg 1997; Penny et al. 1999).

AR models a time series $u(t)$, $t = 1, \ldots, T$, as the linear combination of N_o earlier values in the series. N_o is referred to as the order of the auto-regression, as follows:

$$\hat{u}(t) = \sum_{i=1}^{N_o} \alpha(i) u(t - i)$$

where $\alpha(i)$, $i = 1, \ldots N_o$ are the auto-regression coefficients. It is the calculation of the coefficients $\alpha(i)$ that gives the estimation of the spectral density one would be interested in obtaining. These coefficients are normally calculated using the stepwise least squares algorithm (Kay 1988).

All features derived from the time series data should be calculated from nonoverlapping short segments (e.g., between 1 and 2 seconds' duration). The length of the window varies according to specific cases. A sixth-order AR model normally works perfectly well as a compromise to balance the trade-off between generalization and accuracy, an important balance to consider in data reduction optimization.

4.3.3 Machine Learning

Biosignal-based interfaces most frequently bypass the machine learning stage by mapping the results from the feature analysis stage directly onto musical or sound-processing algorithms. However, machine learning is needed in cases where the system is required to be adaptive. In the case of a brain-computer interface (BCI), for example, it may be necessary to train the computer to identify patterns of information automatically in the EEG that are associated with specific mental states, but whose nature may vary from subject to subject. Once the computer has been trained to identify such patterns then the system can be programmed to trigger musical processes when such patterns are identified in the incoming stream of EEG.

Machine learning is a major sub field of artificial intelligence (AI) research. It would be impractical to give a thorough introduction to machine learning in this book, so the reader is invited to refer to classic texts such as Tom Mitchell's book *Machine Learning* (1997). In short, machine learning is an area of AI dedicated to the development of techniques for programming machines to make classifications, identify patterns, and induce concepts. A well-known class of techniques for implementing machine learning systems is known as connectionism, or artificial neural networks (Gurney 1997). Artificial neural networks are inspired by the functioning of the brain and are particularly good for learning how to identify patterns of information. Other useful machine learning techniques include hidden Markov models (Rabiner 1989) and Bayesian networks (Neapolitan 2004).

In the following paragraphs we illustrate how a simple multi-layer perceptron (MLP) neural network (Figure 4.8) can be used to identify patterns of information in biosignals. Assume that the objective of the following example is to detect and classify variations in the spectral density of the EEG associated with different musical mental activities.

Figure 4.8 A classic MLP neural network with one hidden layer and a single output unit. Reprinted with permission from *Computer Music Journal* 27:2.

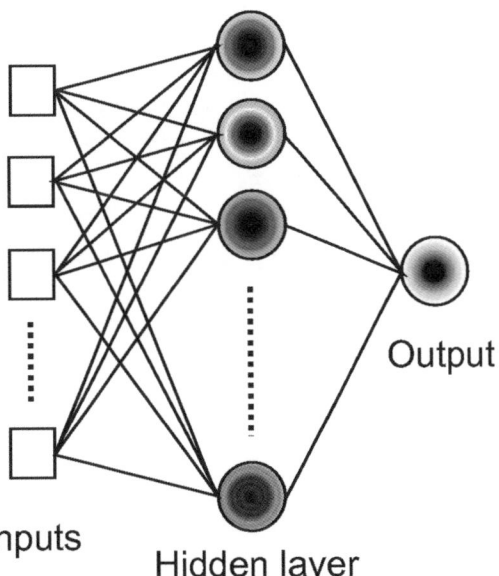

In this example, the training EEG data are obtained while subjects perform prescribed mental tasks; protocols of data collection will be discussed in section 4.4 below. The data is pre-processed, submitted to power spectrum analysis, and subsequently reduced using a sixth-order linear auto-regression algorithm; each training example given to the network is therefore represented by six auto-regression coefficients. This generates a corpus of training data that is divided into two sets: the training set proper and a test set. The latter is used to assess whether the network has learned to identify the various patterns correctly. The MLP network is trained using a scaled conjugate gradient algorithm, as described by Christopher Bishop (1995), and the following logistic sigmoid transfer function:

$$\varphi(v) = \frac{1}{1 + e^{-v}}$$

where $\varphi(v)$ is the neuron's output for input v.

After training, the contents of the test set are propagated forward through the network for assessment. They are awarded a score of 1 for a correct identification and 0 for an incorrect identification:

$$award\,(p) = \begin{cases} 1: f(y) = true \\ 0: f(y) = false \end{cases}$$

where $f(y)$ is a post-processing function that converts the continuous output of the sigmoid output units into a binary form comparable to the target vectors. The exact nature of $f(y)$ depends on the number of output units in the network and how the target vectors are constructed. When presented with an input pattern, the trained network produces a single valued output within the range [0,1]. In this case, a simple post-processing function is used as follows:

$$f(y) = \begin{cases} 1: y > 0.5 \\ 0: y \leq 0.5 \end{cases}$$

In the case of *n*-way identifications, these can be encoded as n-bit target vectors. For instance, three-class target vectors [1,0,0], [0,1,0] and [0,0,1] may represent class (1), class (2) and class (3), respectively. When presented with an input pattern, the trained network would produce three continuous outputs within the range [0,1]. In this case the post-processing function can be a competitive transfer function that returns a vector where the highest value is allocated 1 and the others 0.

BIOSIGNAL INTERFACES   193

4.3.4 Music Control

In order to give a good idea of how the output of the MLP network described above can be used to control musical devices, we briefly introduce two hypothetical brain-computer music interfacing (BMCI) systems: Brain Soloist and Brain Conductor.

The block diagram for the Brain Soloist system is illustrated in Figure 4.9. Firstly, the neural network is trained to identify when the incoming EEG corresponds to active or passive listening (see section 4.4.2). The performer who plays the music should be the same person whose EEG data was used to train the system. In this context, active listening happens when one replays the experience of hearing some music, or part of that music, in the "mind's ear." Conversely, passive listening happens when one listens to music without making any special mental effort. In daily life experience we are likely to be listening passively if we are relaxing to peaceful music or engaged in some other task while listening to music playing in the background.

Figure 4.9 The block diagram of the Brain Soloist system whereby the brain plays variations of an imagined riff. Reprinted with permission from *Computer Music Journal* 27:2.

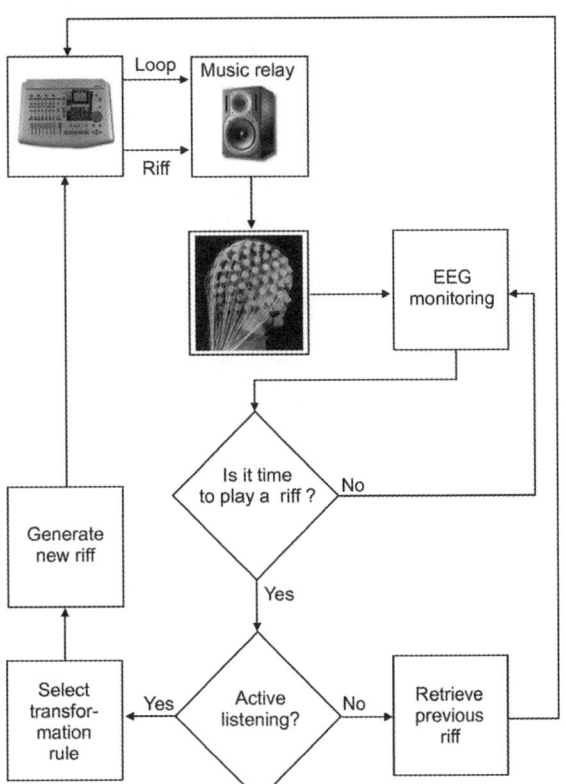

The system features transformational rules that generate slight variations on a given short musical riff (a short, catchy musical phrase that is usually repeated many times in the course of a piece of music). The system works as follows: a rhythmic part is continuously played and a riff is played sporadically (Figure 4.10). Immediately after a riff is played, the system checks the EEG of the performer. If it detects active listening behavior, then the system activates a transformation rule to generate a variation of the riff that has just been played. Otherwise it does not generate anything and waits for the subject's response to the next sporadic riff. Sporadic riffs are always a repetition of the last played riff; in other words, the riff does not change until the system detects active listening behavior. The initial riff is given by default.

The Brain Conductor system is inspired by the metaphor of the conductor who steers the orchestra's expressive performance of a musical score. In Brain Conductor, the EEG is used to steer a computer's performance of expressive aspects of a musical score. In this case, the score constitutes a number of tracks of recorded music. All tracks are recorded with equal loudness (volume) levels. The performer steers the loudness of two tracks by focusing on the parts that are being played on the left and on the right of the stereo field (Figure 4.11).

Figure 4.10 A rhythmic part is continuously played and a riff is played sporadically. Immediately after a riff is played, the system checks the performer's EEG. Reprinted with permission from *Computer Music Journal* 27:2.

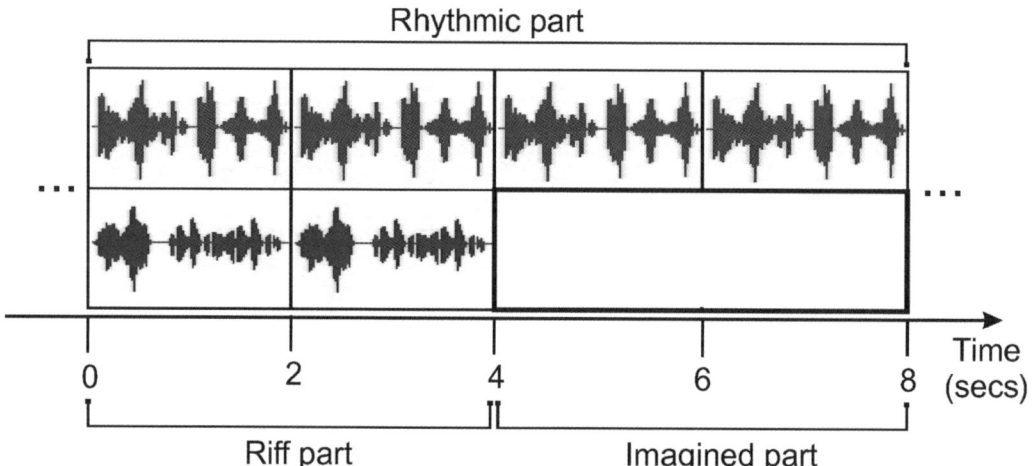

Figure 4.11 The overall block diagram for the Brain Conductor system whereby the performer steers the faders of a mixer with the brain. Reprinted with permission from *Computer Music Journal* 27:2.

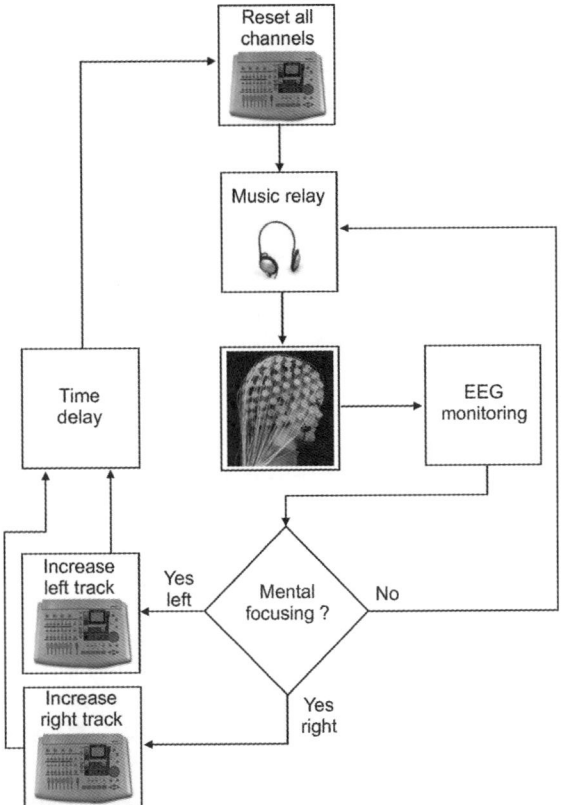

Firstly, the neural network is trained to identify whether the incoming EEG corresponds to focusing on the music panned to the left or to the right side of the stereo field over a pair of headphones. As with the previous example, the performer who plays the music should be the same one whose data are used to train the system. Then the music is played back and the system checks the EEG of the performer. If it detects a mental focus on the musical part that is panned to the left of the stereo field, then the system will increase the amplitude of the left channel track. Conversely, if it detects a mental focus on the part that is panned to the right, then the system will increase the amplitude of the right channel track. The system features a confidence measure whereby the degree of confidence determines the increase in loudness. After a few seconds, the loudness of the modified track returns to the initial default level.

■ 4.4 PROTOCOLS FOR COLLECTING TRAINING DATA

A protocol describes a procedure for collecting biosignals for analysis. The following paragraphs describe two examples of protocols for collecting EEG data devised by Alexander Duncan and referred to as auditory stimulus and active listening protocols, respectively (Miranda et al. 2003). For the sake of consistency with the previous examples, it is assumed that the data will be used to train the MLP network described in section 4.3.3.

4.4.1 The Auditory Stimulus Protocol

The objective of the auditory stimulus protocol is to produce data to train the MLP network to distinguish between segments recorded immediately preceding and immediately following a simple auditory stimulus heard over silence.

The identification task is to determine, on a segment-by-segment basis, the class of one-second multichannel EEG segments, where class (1) = pre-stimulus onset and class (2) = post-stimulus onset.

Subjects perform a single recognition task while listening to a continuous sequence of auditory stimulus trials, each consisting of one of four tones. The stimulus set consists of four blocks of 100 one-second trials, each with a random inter-stimulus interval between three and nine seconds (Figure 4.12). Each trial plays one of four sinusoidal tones at 300 Hz, 400 Hz, 420 Hz, and 600 Hz, respectively, from a pseudo-random playlist. There are 25 trials of each tone per block. Subjects are asked to listen to the tones and think about which of the four they have just heard. In order to maintain the subjects' interest in the trials, the four tones are presented in random order and with varying inter-stimulus intervals. A rest period of approximately one minute is allowed between the blocks.

The trials are segmented into pre-stimulus onset and post-stimulus onset segments of one second each, labeled class (1) and class (2), respectively. Each subject yields 200 trials, resulting in 400 segments (that is, assuming that there are no bad trials). The train-

Figure 4.12 Subjects will listen to blocks of tones containing a random interstimulus interval of between three and nine seconds. Reprinted with permission from *Computer Music Journal* 27:2.

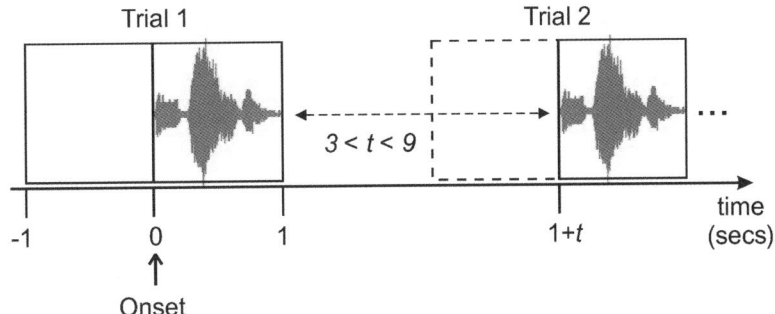

ing can be evaluated by sparing some of these segments to be used as data to test how well the network can recognize their classes.

4.4.2 The Active Listening Protocol

The objective of the active listening protocol is to produce data to train the network to identify whether a subject is engaged in one of two mental tasks: active listening or passive listening. In this context, the active listening task is defined as replaying the experience of hearing some music, or part of that music, in the "mind's ear." Conversely, the task of passive listening is defined as listening to music without making any special mental effort.

The stimulus set consists of six blocks of trials, giving the subject the chance to relax. Each trial lasts for eight seconds and consists of two parts: a rhythmic part, lasting for the entire trial, and a melodic riff part, lasting for the first half of the trial. It is during the second half of each trial that the mental task is performed. The rhythmic part comprises four repetitions of a one-bar rhythm loop. Two repetitions of a one-bar riff loop starting at the beginning of the trial and terminating halfway through are superimposed on the rhythmic part. In total, there are 15 unique riff loops: 5 played on a synthesized piano (acoustic grand piano MIDI timbre, GM = 1), 5 using a typical electronic timbre (synth voice MIDI timbre, GM = 55), and 5 on an electric guitar (a real instrument as opposed to a synthesized one). The music is in the style of a pop club-like dance tune at 120 beats per minute, 4 beats per bar. The background rhythm loops seamlessly for the entire duration of each trial block. Blocks are named after the task the subject is instructed to perform on that block, and they are ordered as shown in Table 4.3. Each of the 15 riff parts is presented four times in each block in random order.

Table 4.3
The stimulus set for the active listening protocol comprises six blocks of trials.

Block	Subject 1	Subject 2	Subject 3
1	Active	Passive	Counting
2	Passive	Counting	Active
3	Counting	Active	Passive
4	Active	Passive	Counting
5	Passive	Counting	Active
6	Counting	Active	Passive

Blocks are named after the mental task the subjects are instructed to perform. Subjects are instructed to perform one of three mental tasks while listening to a continuous sequence of trials:

a. *Active listening*: Listen to the looped riff that lasts for two bars, then immediately after it finishes, imagine that the riff continues for another two bars until the next trial begins.

b. *Passive listening*: Listen to the entire four-bar trial with no effort; just relax and focus on the continuing background part.

c. *Counting task*: Listen to the looped riff that lasts for two bars; then, immediately after it finishes, mentally count the following self-repeating sequence of numbers: 1, 10, 3, 8, 5, 6, 7, 4, 2, 1, 10, and so forth.

The identification task here is to determine the class of two-second multichannel EEG segments, where class (1) = active listening, class (2) = passive listening, and class (3) = counting task.

The rationale for including the counting task is as a control to determine whether the EEG features that might allow for differentiation between the imagery and relaxed listening tasks are not merely a function of a concentrating versus a nonconcentrating state of mind. The hypothesis here is obvious: the ability to classify musical materials into these three classes, two of which require mental effort, is an indication that effort-related tasks involving different mental faculties produce different EEG patterns.

Only the last four seconds (i.e., the second half of each trial) are considered for analysis. These four-second segments must be further divided into 2 two-second segments. Thus each trial yields 2 segments. There are 120 trials for each of the three conditions, and each subject produces a total of 720 segments: 240 segments for each condition. For evaluation purposes, the data can be randomly partitioned into training set and testing set, e.g., resulting in 650 training segments and 70 testing segments.

4.5 BIOFEEDBACK

Biofeedback is a means of monitoring, or becoming aware of, functions of the body that would normally be taken for granted, such as variations in our body temperature or pulse rate (Robbins 2000). Biofeedback devices produce information associated with physiological states that can be analyzed for scientific purposes or directly used for artistic means, among other things. As a simplistic example, consider a biofeedback system composed of a thermometer and drugs for lowering body temperature. The thermometer is used to read and analyze our body temperature. If the temperature is higher than a specific threshold, then we take the drugs to bring the temperature down; the effect of the drugs can be monitored by taking our temperature again. An important aspect of biofeedback is that the analysis of the information extracted from one's body can prompt one to take an action in order to achieve a certain physiological goal. Analysis and action thus feed information back to each other—hence the term biofeedback.

Biofeedback systems have become popular among those wishing to control their physiological functions more accurately for a number of purposes, including making music. Applications of this technology range from the treatment of migraine headaches to meditation.

Early work in the field of achieving specific mental states through biofeedback focused on learning to enhance alpha rhythms. As shown in Table 4.2, alpha rhythms refer to brainwave components occurring between the frequencies of 8 Hz and 13 Hz. They are found in the EEG spectrum when we daydream and are often associated with a state of meditation. When connected to a biofeedback device one can learn to recognize and eventually gain control of bursts of alpha rhythms, thus gaining the ability to enter a state of heightened awareness. The composer David Rosenboom (1990a) has conducted a number of experiments with alpha rhythms. He implemented a threshold detector to discriminate against any signal whose amplitude was less than a preset level, which could be raised or lowered for each subject. Initially the feedback was simply a 160 Hz tone triggered by the presence of alpha rhythms in the EEG signal. The threshold was set for each subject at the outset of training such that feedback was easily triggered by an alpha rhythm burst. Sessions varied in length from 30 minutes to 48 hours and took place in a darkened room. Amounts of increase in alpha rhythms, measured in the percentage of time spent emitting them, varied from no increase in the worst case to an increase from 10% at the onset of a session to 91% in the span of about 1 hour in the best case. Subjective reports of the experience by participants ranged from "no effect" to "extreme euphoria." In most cases, subjects whose lifestyle included rigorous mental and physical discipline, including musicians, Zen masters, gymnastic champions, and scientists, achieved the greatest successes.

Experiments such as those conducted by David Rosenboom provide reasonable evidence that humans can indeed learn to produce alpha rhythm activity. It remains to be seen, however, whether it would be possible to learn how to control the production of other EEG patterns as effectively, including EEG patterns associated with musical cognition. Researchers at ICCMR in Plymouth are addressing this question.

4.6 EXAMPLES OF BIOSIGNAL SYSTEMS FOR MUSIC

This section introduces two examples biosignal systems to control music: the conductor's jacket and BCMI-piano.

It should be mentioned at this point that there have been a few attempts at the design of multipurpose biosignal systems for music, such as BioMuse and WaveRider, to cite but two well-known examples.

BioMuse was developed at Stanford University's Centre for Computer Research in Music and Acoustics (CCRMA) in the late 1980s by Hugh Lusted and Benjamin Knapp. Featuring eight input channels for EOG, EMG, and/or EEG, it was originally designed to enable people with impaired movement and paralysis to operate a computer for recreational purposes. The system was introduced as a commercial product consisting of a rack-mountable device containing eight input channels, a programmable amplifier, an analog-to-digital converter, and a digital signal-processing (DSP) chip. The system was furnished with a library of DSP algorithms for processing the biosignals, and the output data was in the form of MIDI controller messages.

WaveRider was developed by MindPeak, a company based in California (http://www.mindpeak.com, accessed 28 February 2005). Its design is more modern than BioMuse and it is mostly marketed as an EEG system, but it can well be used with other biosignals such as EMG and GSR. The system allows for user-specified associations of different frequency bandwidths of the EEG spectrum with MIDI data. When a specific frequency component reaches a given threshold value, then the system triggers the actions that are associated with the bandwidth where the frequency falls. Different EEG bandwidths can be associated with different MIDI messages to playing notes on a synthesizer.

4.6.1 The Conductor's Jacket

The conductor's jacket was developed by Teresa Marrin for her doctoral dissertation at MIT Media Lab (Marrin 1999, 2002). The system comprises a wearable Lycra jacket furnished with electrodes to capture gesture activity and a software system (called Gesture Construction) that interprets these measurements and uses them to control a musical system.

Conducting is a gesture-based art form, a craft for skilled practitioners. Conducting resembles dance in many ways, but it is active rather than passive in relation to the music. Conducting involves a sophisticated system of gestures that has evolved over approximately 300 years. Although a huge variety of conducting techniques exists, there is a canon of literature on the subject that attempts to clarify and define the basic elements of the technique—for example, Max Rudolph's book *The Grammar of Conducting* (1950). Taking established basic elements of conducting practices as her point of departure, Teresa Marrin aimed at further developments in interactive music systems by means of biosignal interfaces. The rationale was that hybrid forms of musical performance, such as conducting, should be built on existing vocabularies of instrumental gestures.

The conductor's jacket project was distinctive because it explored musical phenomena in the continuum between actuating discrete notes and shaping their higher-level behaviors. Here a performer did not have to literally play every note directly. He or she behaves more as an orchestral conductor would. The system was aimed at shaping higher-level features in the music without controlling every discrete event.

Prototyping the system. The basic premise of the project was to build a device to sense as many potentially significant signals from a performing conductor as possible without interfering with their behavior. Before building the actual performance system, Marrin studied ways to sense conducting gestures effectively. A number of different jackets were prototyped for these studies. Sewn into each jacket were physiological sensors relating to muscle tension (4 EMG sensors), breathing (1 sensor), heartbeat (1 sensor), skin conductance (1 sensor), and temperature (1 sensor). In addition, one of the professional subjects wore a magnetic position-sensing device (Figure 4.13).

The main concern was to leave the conductor free to conduct rehearsals and concerts in the jacket without any disturbances or distractions for the audience or orchestra, while providing data on the conductor's gestures. The most important human factor in the design of the conductor's jacket was the need to provide a device that would not constrain or cause discomfort to a conductor during performance. Data should be gathered in a professional context, as opposed to a laboratory setting, in order to generate realistic results. A discussion on the design criteria issues, including the rationale for the selection of electrode placements, can be found in Marrin's dissertation (1999).

Conducting data were collected from six subjects (three professional orchestra conductors and three students) during a total of 12 hours of rehearsals and performances. Analysis of the data resulted in over 30 features reflecting intuitive and natural gesture tendencies in conducting.

The choice of which muscles to read the EMG from was particularly critical at this stage of the project. The initial pilot studies focused on the biceps, triceps, and lateral deltoid muscles in the upper arm. However the triceps measurement was replaced in a later stage by measurements of the extensor muscle in the forearm because the biceps and triceps seemed to provide redundant information.

The extensor muscle ended up being very important. Since it runs along the outside edge of the forearm, connecting the bone of the upper arm to the hand, its EMG provided information about the use of the wrist, particularly when it differed from the use of the upper arm.

The collected data were carefully catalogued with their associated videotape segments. A visual analysis of the videotapes produced a number of significant types of conducting information that

Figure 4.13 Placement of the sensors in the conductor's jacket. (Note: This is not the cut of the actual conductor's jacket, but a schematic to illustrate the placement of the sensors.)

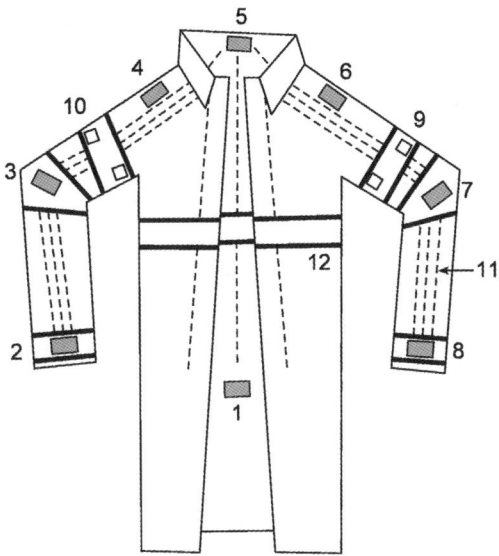

1 - 8	Motion-capture sensors
9 - 10	EMG sensors
11	Conduit channels for sensor cables
12	Band with heart rate, respiration, skin conductance and temperature sensors

were relatively consistent across individuals and contexts. For example:

- Use of left hand for expressive variation
- Direct, one-to-one correlation between muscle tension and dynamic intensity
- Division of labor between biceps, triceps, and forearm
- Link between respiration and phrasing
- Galvanic skin response (GSR) peaks at the beginning of every piece

Although the elaboration given in the dissertation does not contain exhaustive evidence for these different types of conducting information, Marrin provided coherent interpretation of the data and defined general frameworks within which the features have meaning. Cogent examples were used to elucidate the various phenomena with enough detail to be tested with more exhaustive research at a later stage. For instance, in the section at beginning of the Allegro non troppo movement of Piotr Ilyitch Tchaikovsky's Symphony No. 6, the conductor gave a large-scale crescendo and diminuendo over approximately nine measures. The relative scale between the softest and loudest portions appeared to retain its proportionality: the EMG scaled from pianissimo up to fortissimo and back down to pianissimo.

The final version of the jacket also used the hand's opponens pollicis muscle and the shoulder's trapezius muscle. The opponens pollicis muscle flexes and adducts the thumb, and the trapezius raises or draws back the shoulder. These were not used in the conductor study because they would have impeded the normal use of the baton.

The Gesture Construction software. The Gesture Construction software used the wearer's gestures to perform music in real time. A bank of filters extracted several of the features that were found in the conductor study, including beat intensity and the alternation between the arms. These features were used to generate expressive effects in a musical score, such as beat, tempo, articulation, and note lengths, to cite but four.

The software was a real-time musical system that used the conductor's jacket to control its musical behavior. The system had several components, including a range of real-time filters and schemes for mapping gesture-related data onto musical processes. The idea behind the Gesture Construction software was to detect expressive features from incoming data in real time and synthesize them into a range of musical effects. The rationale was that these effects should convey qualities that general audiences could recognize as being similar to the original, visually perceived gesture.

The performance version of the jacket included EMG measurements from the left and right biceps, the left and right forearm extensors, the left and right hands (the opponens pollicis muscle), and the shoulders (trapezius). All sensors were held in place on the surface of the skin by means of elastic bands, and the leads were sewn onto the outside of the jacket with loops of thread (Figure 4.14).

The system involved two separate computers: the first filtered and processed the data, and the second mapped the data onto algorithms that generate MIDI output. Various real-time filters extracted relevant features from the sensor data, mostly to do with informa-

Figure 4.14 The sensors and approximate positioning that were used in one of the final forms of the conductor's jacket.

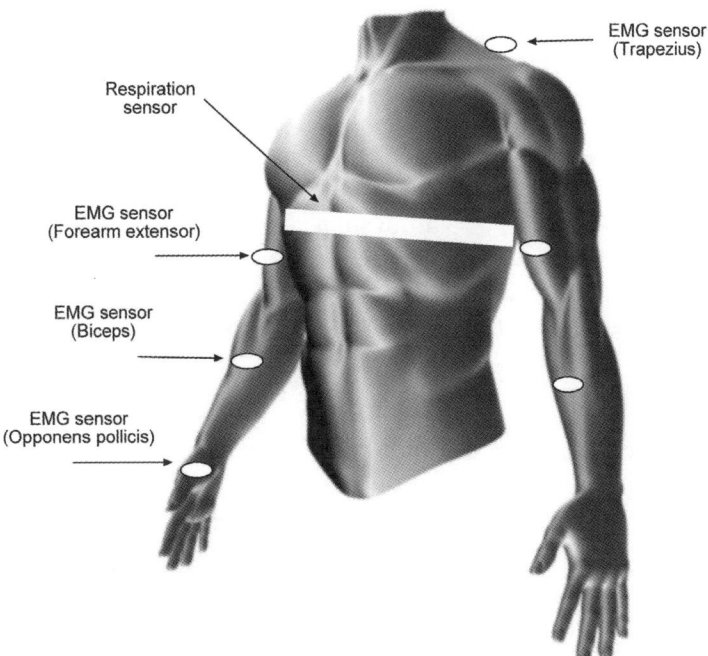

tion in the time domain such as beat detection, beat intensity, and envelope follower. Beat detection was extracted for both the left and right bicep signals, and beat intensity was extracted in order to measure the force of each beat. The envelope follower generated a smoother version of the EMG signals, closely following its contour.

Mapping conducting gestures onto musical processes. Perhaps the most important musical unit for conductors is the beat they produce with their gestures. A downward motion, called an ictus, indicates these beats; the ictus changes direction and appears to bounce upward. Marrin implemented a direct-drive paradigm whereby each beat was directly given by a specific gesture and the music stopped and started instantaneously. If no beats occurred, then no notes were played; if a beat occurred then one beat's worth of notes was played, and so on. The music was encoded in a fixed order and rhythm, reflecting the Western classical convention of the written score. Once started, the score could progress only in one direction until complete, but no notes would play unless first triggered by the beat of the performer. Tempo detection was used for determining the distances between consecutive notes, both within and across beats.

Cut-offs are another critical aspect of the gesture repertoire of conductors. Like beats, they are strong gestures that indicate the stop time of a held note or pause. The system was programmed such that if a cut-off were needed, it could be fulfilled with a beat. If a particular score had a fermata indicated, then the end of the fermata would be triggered by a beat. Thus beats and cut-offs were indicated by the same gestures, but the context provided by the score determined how the gestures were interpreted and used.

The system also controlled the volume of the notes. The algorithms used a weighted combination of a number of parameters, including the force with which the current beat was made and the previous volume, so as to smooth the contour. A number of other musical algorithms were implemented with which to control pitch, accents, timbre, morphing, balances, and voice numbers; interested readers are invited to refer to Marrin's dissertation for more information (Marrin 1999).

A proof-of-concept example orchestral piece was implemented, where the action of the right bicep muscle determined the beats, tempo, beat volumes, and cut-offs. The right forearm controlled articulations: sustained contraction of the muscle yielded longer notes and therefore a legato quality, whereas shorter contractions of the muscle yielded shorter notes with a staccato quality. The aggregate values of the left arm muscles versus the right arm muscles determined the panning of the instruments.

4.6.2 Brain-computer Music Interfaces

The Interdisciplinary Centre for Computer Music Research at the University of Plymouth is developing technology to interface the brain directly with music systems. This field of research is known as brain-computer interfacing (BCI), and a growing number of researchers worldwide are working in this field. What is unique about the work developed by the ICCMR team, however, is that it is devoted to the development of BCI systems for musical applications and pays special attention to the development of generative music techniques tailored for such systems. We can call such systems brain-computer music interfaces (BCMIs).

Hans Berger, an unknown German psychiatrist at the time, first measured human brainwaves in 1924. He termed these measured electrical signals in the brain the electroencephalogram, literally, "brain electricity writing." Berger first published his brainwave results in 1929 in an article entitled "Über das Elektroenkephalogramm des Menschen" (On the electroencephalogram of humans (Berger 1929). The English translation would not appear until 1969. Berger was a curious, complex, and enigmatic figure in the history of medical science. He had a lifelong obsession with finding scientific proof of a causal linkage between the psychic world of human consciousness and the physiological world of neurological electrical signals.

Today, the EEG has become one of the most useful tools in the diagnosis of epilepsy and other neurological disorders. Further, the fact that a machine can read signals from the brain has sparked the imaginations of scientists, artists, and other enthusiasts, and EEG has made its way into a number of other applications.

In the early 1970s, Jacques Vidal, a researcher at the University of California, Los Angeles, developed the first tentative work toward a BCI system. The results of this work were published in 1973 in a paper entitled "Toward Direct Brain-computer Communication" (Vidal 1973). To date, most BCI research efforts have been aimed at developing technology to help people with special needs communicate via computer systems and/or control mechanical tools, such as a wheelchair or a prosthetic limb. Comparatively little has been done to address the use of BCI technology for musical applications.

As early as 1934, a paper in the journal *Brain* had reported a method for listening to the EEG (Adrian and Mathews 1934). It is now generally accepted that it was the composer Alvin Lucier, in 1965, who composed the first musical piece using EEG: *Music for Solo Performer*, a piece for percussion instruments played by the resonance of the performer's EEG (Lucier 1976). Lucier placed electrodes on his own scalp, amplified the signals, and relayed them through loudspeakers that were "directly coupled to percussion instruments, including large gongs, cymbals, tympani, metal ash cans, cardboard boxes, bass and snare drums" (Lucier 1980). The low-frequency vibrations emitted by the loudspeakers set the surfaces and membranes of the percussion instruments into vibration.

Later in the 1960s, Richard Teitelbaum used various biological signals, including the EEG and ECG, to control electronic synthesizers. Over the next few years he continued to use EEG and other biological signals in his compositions and experiments as triggers for early versions of Robert Moog's electronic synthesizers (Teitelbaum 1976).

In the early 1970s David Rosenboom began systematic research into the potential of EEG to generate artworks, including music (Rosenboom 1990a). Drawing on concepts from cybernetics (Wiener

1948), he developed EEG-based musical interfaces associated with a number of compositional and performance environments that used the state-of-the-art EEG technology of the day. In particular, he explored the hypothesis that it might be possible to detect certain aspects of our musical experience in the EEG signal. For example, in an article that appeared in 1990 in *Computer Music Journal*, he introduced a musical system whose parameters were driven by EEG components believed to be associated with shifts of the performer's selective attention (Rosenboom 1990b).

Thirteen years later, a new article in *Computer Music Journal* (Miranda et al. 2003) reported experiments and techniques to enhance the EEG signal and train the computer to identify EEG patterns associated with different cognitive musical tasks.

Approaches to BCMI system design. Generally speaking, a BCMI is a system that allows one to interact with a musical device by means of signals emanating directly from the brain. Currently the most viable option for tapping the brain for BCMI is the EEG. There are basically two ways of tapping brain signals using the EEG: invasive and noninvasive. Whereas invasive methods require the placement of sensors connected to the brain inside the skull, noninvasive methods use sensors that can read brain signals from the outside the skull. Invasive technology is becoming increasingly sophisticated, but this is not a viable option for music because the health and safety risks are extremely high to even think about it.

It is possible to identify three categories of BCI systems in general:

a. *User-oriented*: These are BCI systems where the computer adapts to the user. Metaphorically speaking, these systems attempt to "read the mind" of the user to control a device. For example, Chuck Anderson and Zlatko Sijercic (1996) reported on the development of a BCI that learns how to associate specific EEG patterns from a subject to commands for navigating a wheelchair.

b. *Computer-oriented*: These are BCI systems where the user adapts to the computer. These systems rely on the capacity of the users to learn to control specific aspects of their EEG, affording them the ability to exert some control over events in their environments. Examples have been shown where subjects learn how to steer their EEG to select letters for writing words on the computer screen (Birbaumer et al. 1999).

c. *Mutually oriented*: These are BCI systems where the user and computer adapt to each other; they combine the functionalities of both categories. The combined use of mental task pattern classification and biofeedback-assisted online learning allows the computer and the user to adapt. Prototype systems to move a cursor on the computer screen have been developed in this fashion (Peters, Pfurtscheller, and Flyvberg 1997; Penny et al. 1999).

Those who have attempted to employ EEG as part of a music controller have done so by associating certain EEG characteristics, such as the power of the EEG alpha waveband (or rhythm) to specific musical actions. These are essentially computer-oriented systems, as they require the user to learn to control their EEG in certain ways. This is very difficult to achieve without appropriate training. An effective method for learning to achieve specific mental states is based upon the notion of biofeedback (see section 4.5).

BCMI-piano. The BCMI-piano system, developed at the University of Plymouth, falls into the category of computer-oriented systems. However, the motivation for this system departs from a slightly different angle compared to other BCI systems. It was intended as a system that would make music by "guessing" what might be going on in the mind of the subject rather than as a system for explicit control of music by the subject. Learning to steer the system by means of biofeedback would be possible, but this possibility has not been investigated.

It is acknowledged that the notion of "guessing" the mind here is extremely simplistic, but it is plausible: it is based on the assumption that physiological information can be associated with specific mental activities (Petsche and Etlinger 1998).

The system is programmed to look for information in the EEG signal and match the findings with assigned generative musical processes. For example, if the system detects prominent alpha rhythms in the EEG, then it generates musical passages associated with the alpha rhythms. These associations are arbitrary, and they determine the different types of music that are generated in association with different mental states.

The system comprises four main modules (Figure 4.15): braincap, analysis, music engine, and performance.

The brain signals are sensed with seven pairs of gold EEG electrodes on the scalp that form a rough circle around the head (bipolar montage): G-Fz, F7-F3, T3-C3, O1-P3, O2-P4, T4-C4, and F8-F4. A discussion on the rationale behind this configuration falls beyond the scope of this chapter. It suffices to say that the system is not looking for signals emanating from specific cortical sites; rather, the

Figure 4.15 BCMI-piano is composed of four modules. Reprinted with permission from *Leonardo* 34:4.

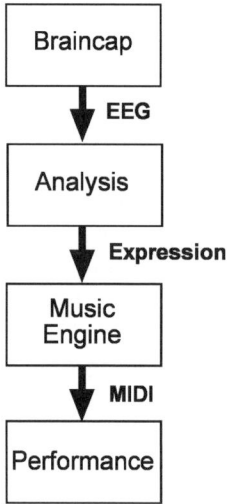

idea is to sense the EEG behavior over a wide surface of the cortex. The electrodes are plugged into a real-time biosignal acquisition system manufactured by Guger Technologies.

The analysis module generates two streams of control parameters. One stream contains information about the most prominent frequency band (power spectrum analysis) in the signal and is used by the music engine to compose the music. The other stream contains information about the complexity of the signal (Hjorth analysis) and is used by the music engine to control the tempo and dynamics of the music (Figure 4.16).

The core of the music engine module is a set of generative music rules, each of which produces a bar or measure of music. The system learns these rules based on given examples of musical pieces of different styles or from different composers. Three books by David Cope, also published by A-R Editions, give a good introduction to machine learning of musical styles (Cope 1991, 1996, 2000).

A composition is then constructed out of a sequence of musical bars (Figure 4.17). For each bar there are a number of generative rules, each of which is associated with different EEG rhythms and different musical styles or composers. Roughly speaking, every time the system has to produce a bar, it checks the power spectrum of the EEG at that moment and activates one of the generative rules.

Figure 4.16 Spectral information is used to activate generative music rules to compose music in real time, and the signal complexity is used to control the tempo and dynamics of the music. Reprinted with permission from *Leonardo* 34:4.

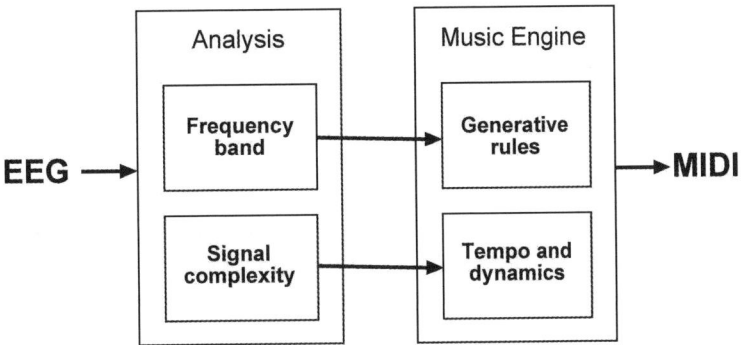

Figure 4.17 Each bar of a composition is produced by one of four possible generative rules according to the subject's EEG rhythm. Reprinted with permission from *Leonardo* 34:4.

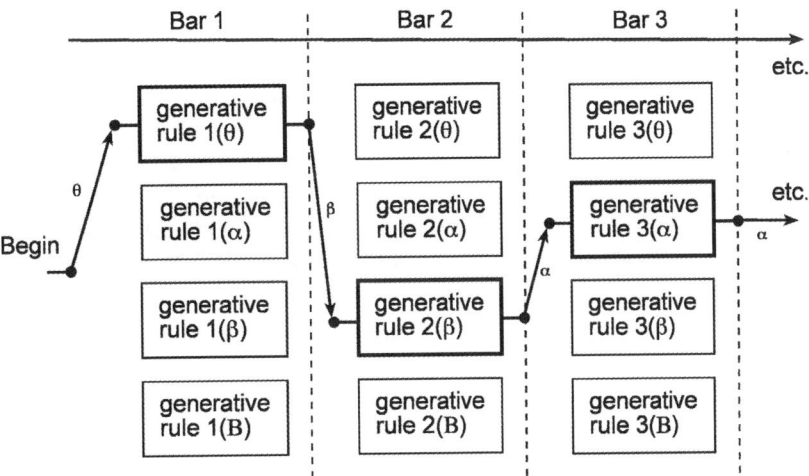

The system is initialized with a reference tempo (e.g., 120 beats per minute), which is constantly modulated by the signal complexity analysis.

The EEG (i.e., the power spectrum analysis) can influence the mixture of different style elements found in the different musical examples given to train the system. It can generate music that contains, for example, more Schumann-like stylistic elements when the spectrum of the subject's EEG contains salient low-frequency components (e.g., alpha rhythms), and more modern or jazzy elements when the subject's EEG contains salient high-frequency components (e.g., beta rhythms).

Example-based musical generation systems are often based on formalisms such as transition networks or Markov chains to recreate the transition logic of what follows what, either at the level of notes or at the level of similar "vertical slices" of music. For example, David Cope (1991, 1996, 2000) uses such example-based musical generation methods but adds phrase-structure rules, higher-level compositional structure rules, and well-placed signatures, earmarks, and unifications. The act of recombining the building blocks of music material together with some typical patterns and structural methods has proved to work satisfactorily. This type of self-learning predictor of musical elements based on previous musical elements can be used on any level or for any type of musical element, such as note, chord, bar, phrase, section, and so on. However, there must be logical relationships on all those levels.

BCMI-piano uses a statistical predictor devised at ICCMR by Bram Boskamp at the level of small vertical slices of music such as a bar or half bar, where the predictive characteristics are determined by the chord (harmonic set of pitches, or pitch class) and by the first melodic note following the melodic notes in those vertical slices of music (see example below). The system generates small musical phrases with a beginning and an ending that also allows for the real-time influence from a given EEG signal. It generates phrases of music by defining top-level structures of sentences and methods for generating similarity or contrast relationships between phrases. These look like this (LISP-like notation):

```
S →     (INC BAR BAR BAR BAR BAR
        HALF-CADENCE 8BAR-COPY)
```

From this top level, the system then generates rules to select a valid musical building block for each symbol, including rules that incorporate the EEG information. For example:

```
INC →   ((EQUAL 'MEASURE 1)
        (EQUAL 'COMPOSER EEG-SET-COMPOSER))
```

```
BAR →    ((CLOSE 'PITCH 'PREV-PITCH-LEADING)
         (CLOSE 'PITCH-CLASS 'PREV-PITCH-CLASS-LEADING)
         (EQUAL 'COMPOSER EEG-SET-COMPOSER))
```

This already defines a network that generates a valid musical measure with a beginning and an ending, including real-time EEG control through the variable EEG-SET-COMPOSER. The generative engine will find a musical element for each of the constraint sets generated above from INC and BAR by applying the list of constraints in left-to-right order to the set of all musical elements until there are no constraints left, or until there is only one musical element left. This selection process is illustrated below.

The database of all musical elements contains music from different composers, with elements tagged by their musical function, such as "measure 1" for the start of a phrase, "cadence" for the end, "composer" for the composer, and the special tags "pitch" and "pitch class" that are both used for correct melodic and harmonic progression or direction. Table 4.4 shows an example (SCHU = the composer Robert Schumann).

Table 4.4
An excerpt from the database of musical elements.
C = composer, P-CLASS = pitch class, P = pitch,
PCL = pitch-class leading, PL = pitch leading, TPE = type.

ID	CO	P-CLASS	P	PCL	PL	TPE
SCHU-1-1-CAD	SCHU	((0 2 7) (0 2 4 5 7 11))	74	((0 4 9) (0 2 4 5 7 9 11))	76	CAD
SCHU-1-1-MEA-6	SCHU	((5 9) (0 5 7 9))	81	((0 2 7) (0 2 4 5 7 11))	74	BAR
SCHU-1-1-MEA-5	SCHU	((0 4) (0 4 7))	76	((5 9) (0 5 7 9))	81	BAR
SCHU-1-1-MEA-4	SCHU	((0 4) (0 3 4 6 7 9))	83	((0 4) (0 4 7))	76	BAR
SCHU-1-1-MEA-3	SCHU	((0 4) (0 3 4 6 7 9))	76	((2 7 11) (2 5 7 9 11))	83	BAR
SCHU-1-1-MEA-2	SCHU	((2 7 11) (2 5 7 9 11))	83	((0 4) (0 3 4 6 7 9))	76	BAR
SCHU-1-1-MEA-1	SCHU	((0 4) (0 3 4 6 7 9))	76	((2 7 11) (2 5 7 9 11))	83	INC

Table 4.4 shows the main attributes that are used to recombine musical elements. P-CLASS (for pitch class) is a list of two elements. The first is the list of start notes, transposed to the range of 0–11. The second is the list of all notes in this element (also transposed to 0–11). P is the pitch of the first (and highest) melodic note in this element; by matching this with the melodic note that the previous element was leading up to we can generate a melodic flow that adheres in some way to the logic of where the melody wants to go. The PCL (for pitch-class leading) elements contain the same information about the original next bar; this is used to find a possible next bar in the recombination process. Then there are the INC, BAR, and CAD elements. These are used for establishing whether these elements can be used for phrase starts (incipients or cadences).

Simply by combining the musical elements with the constraint-based selection process that follows from the terminals of the phrase structure rewrite rules, the system ends up with a generative method that can take into account real-time EEG information. This generates musical phrases with a domino-game-like building-block connectivity:

```
((EQUAL 'MEASURE 1)
 (EQUAL 'COMPOSER EEG-SET-COMPOSER))
```

Assuming that there are also musical elements available from composers (or styles) other than SCHU, the first constraint will limit the options to all incipient measures from all musical elements of all composers. The second constraint will then limit the options according to the current EEG power spectrum analysis, limiting them to one composer (or style) associated with the current EEG activity, as follows:

```
((CLOSE 'PITCH 'PREV-PITCH-LEADING)
 (CLOSE 'PITCH-CLASS 'PREV-PITCH-CLASS-LEADING)
 (EQUAL 'COMPOSER EEG-SET-COMPOSER))
```

In the given phrase structure, the rule that follows from BAR then defines the constraints put upon a valid continuation of the music. This constraint will limit the available options one by one and will order them according to the defined-by-rule preferences. The CLOSE constraint will order the available options according to their closeness to the stored value. For example, after choosing:

```
(SCHU-1-1-MEA-1
    P-CLASS ((0 4) (0 3 4 6 7 9))
    P 76
    PCL ((2 7 11) (2 5 7 9 11))
    PL 83
    BAR INC
    CO SCHU)
```

as the beginning, `PREV-PITCH-LEADING` will have stored 83, and `PREV-PITCH-CLASS-LEADING` will have stored ((2 7 11) (2 5 7 9 11)). This will result in measures 2 and 4 being ranked highest according to both pitch and pitch class, and measure 6 and the closing section ranked close according to pitch class. Measure 6 is also close according to pitch. This weighted choice gives a degree of freedom in the decision. The music will not get stuck in repetitive loops, but it will find the closest possible continuation when no perfect match is available. The system can still find a close match in this way if the third constraint has eliminated all the obvious choices that are available—for example, because a jump is requested to the musical elements of another composer, who might not use the same pitch classes and pitches.

Figure 4.18 shows an example score that mixes elements from the musical style of Robert Schumann and Ludwig van Beethoven. In this example the EEG has jumped back and forth from bar to bar between the two styles, giving interesting contrasts. The harmonic and melodic distances are quite large from bar to bar, but they are still the optimal choices in the set of chosen elements from the two composers.

■ 4.7 FURTHER READING

There are not many references dedicated exclusively to the use of biosignals to control musical systems. The following book, edited by David Rosenboom back in the 1970s, is probably the only book ever published on this topic:

- D. Rosenboom, ed. (1976). *Biofeedback and the Arts: Results of Early Experiments.* Vancouver: Aesthetic Research Centre of Canada Publications.

Rosenboom published an interesting monograph on using the EEG to control music:

- D. Rosenboom (1990). *Extended Musical Interface with the Human Nervous System.* ISAST Leonardo Monograph Series. Berkeley, CA: International Society for the Arts, Sciences and Technology.

Rosenboom also published an interesting paper in 1990 in *Computer Music Journal* 14(1).

Figure 4.18 Example of a musical section mixing elements in the styles of Robert Schumann and Ludwig van Beethoven.

Andrew Brouse published a survey of EEG-based music systems entitled "A Young Person's Guide to Brainwave Music" in the on-line magazine *Horizon 0*(15), available at http://www.horizonzero.ca/ (accessed 3 January 2006).

Recommended references on biosignal processing for signal conditioning include:

- R. Weitkunat, ed. (1991). *Digital Biosignal Processing.* Oxford: Elsevier. This book provides a comprehensive and concise means of acquiring an understanding of some of the basic aspects of the application of DSP to biological signals. Some background on DSP is required to follow most of the chapters.

- E. N. Bruce (2001). *Biomedical Signal Processing and Signal Modelling.* Hoboken, NJ: Wiley. This book provides a framework for understanding signal processing of biomedical signals and what it tells us about signal sources and their behavior. Each chapter begins with a detailed biomedical example illustrating the methods under discussion and highlighting the interconnection between the theoretical concepts and applications. Although it is a biomedical engineering book, it is a useful text for those interested in learning more about biosignals.

There are a number of biomedical engineering publications, but their contents may be too specialized for the general reader. These journals are, however, good sources of information for researchers:

- *BioMedical Engineering OnLine*, published by BioMed Central, http://www.biomedical-engineering-online.com/ (accessed 3 January 2006)
- *Computer Methods in Biomechanics and Biomedical Engineering*, published by Taylor & Francis
- *IEEE Transactions on Biomedical Engineering*, published by IEEE

FIVE

Toward Intelligent Musical Instruments

■ 5.1 THE LEGACY OF ELECTROACOUSTIC MUSIC

Electroacoustic music is defined in *The New Grove Dictionary of Music and Musicians* as music in which electronic technology, now primarily computer based, is used to access, generate, explore, and configure sound materials, and in which a loudspeaker is the prime medium of transmission. There are two main genres of electroacoustic music: acousmatic and live electronics.

Acousmatic music is intended for listening exclusively through loudspeakers and exists only in recorded form (e.g., on tape, compact disc, or any other form of analog recording or digital storage). In live electronic music the technology is used to generate, transform, or trigger sounds (or a combination of these) in the act of a performance. This may include producing sounds with acoustic instruments and/or voice combined with electroacoustic devices and/or computer systems. The public often finds strictly acousmatic electroacoustic music concerts inaccessible because there is no performer on site playing the music, but, rather, audio equipment, loudspeakers, and cables.

Paradoxically, the beginning of the 20th century witnessed a wave of attempts to eliminate the human performer from music. A number of composers created pieces for mechanical piano with the intention of restricting to an absolute minimum the intervention of the performer's personality in their music. This musical trend coincided in many ways with the emergence of acousmatic electroacoustic music, which provided a perfect vehicle for eliminating the personality of performers from musical compositions. The composer, who in effect performs the work while entrusting it to a fixed realization, can painstakingly construct compositions realized for tape.

At first glance, eliminating performers entirely from music does not seem to make much sense today. One has to consider, however, a number of historical variables in order to understand the importance of electroacoustic music culturally and technically.

The emergence of electroacoustic music accompanied the quest of Western composers for new modes of expression and artistic exploration of the technology for recording and playing back music, which started to appear around the 1920s. Moreover, electroacoustic music certainly paved the way for a great number of new practices for live performance and even composition live with electronics and computing equipment. The practices of sampling, mixing, and remixing music live popularized by the DJ culture (Reighley 2000) and the live coding practices of laptop musicians (Collins 2003) are good examples. Another important legacy of electroacoustic music is that it has encouraged composers to think of space as an effective compositional parameter (Trochimczyk 2001). Composers performed electroacoustic pieces by distributing compositional elements onto different recording tracks and controlling the faders of a mixing console whose channels were patched to different arrangements of loudspeakers in a concert hall. In this sense we could say that in many ways the mixing console was for the electroacoustic composer what the violin was for a performer: it became a tool for performance, or, in electroacoustic music parlance, a tool for sound diffusion.

It is important to mention that a number of composers have not totally discarded the importance of performance, giving rise to electroacoustic music with live electronics. Though a number of devotees have concentrated their efforts on developing the art of acousmatic tape music (Bayle 1993; Windsor 1995), many composers have endeavored to include human performance in electroacoustic music since the early stages of its development by composing works combining performers and tape. *Transición II*, composed by Mauricio Kagel in 1959 for piano, percussion, and two tape recorders, is perhaps the first example of the use of a tape recorder as a live performance aid (Sutherland 1994). In it, the percussionist played on the soundboard and strings of the piano while the pianist played on the keyboard. One tape recorder played electroacoustic material prepared prior to the performance, and the other tape recorder was used to record the performance so it could be cut into loops and reproduced during the performance. Also, *Mikrophonie I*, composed by Karlheinz Stockhausen in 1964, can be cited a classic example of live electronic music, but from a different perspective (Maconie 1976). In this case, there was no tape component. The piece used a large tam-tam with two microphones held on either side of the instrument, each connected to an amplifier and loudspeaker via an adjustable bandpass filter. It required six performers: two for playing the tam-tam, two for varying the positioning of the microphones, and two for controlling the settings of the filters and associated amplifiers.

Another example is the piece *Hornpipe*, composed by Gordon Mumma in 1967 and described as an interactive work for solo horn, cybersonic console, and a performance space (Mumma 1975). The cybersonic console altered and created sounds based on data input by the performer. It used microphones for capturing the sound made by the horn and the acoustic resonance of the space. Then it analyzed these signals and used the results to control sound processors. During the course of the piece, the horn player freely selected pitches that affected the electronic processing in different ways.

In the mid-1960s, the introduction of voltage-controlled synthesizers opened the way for a number of interactive techniques. Essentially, a control voltage is an electrical signal that can be used to automate analog synthesizer processes. Almost anything that can be changed on an analog synthesizer module can be controlled with voltages. The amount and duration of voltages became an abstraction that could be applied to numerous parameters. The keys of the keyboard of a voltage-controlled synthesizer produced higher voltages for higher tones and lower voltages for lower tones. Envelope followers turned any kind of analog signal, even acoustic sounds played via a microphone, into voltages. In this way, changes in dynamic levels could be applied to various synthesis parameters. For instance, a number of composers have used voice to control sound synthesis by translating the amplitude of spoken utterances into voltages by means of an envelope follower. The microphone converted sound into an electrical signal that was subjected to real-time analysis, and the results of the analysis were used to control the synthesizer. There were a number of musical attributes that could be extracted for use as control signals, such as the start time (determined by a threshold detector), the amplitude envelope (extracted by means of an envelope follower), and the fundamental frequency (extracted by means of a pitch detector).

■ 5.2 THE EMERGENCE OF THE COMPUTER

Leaving aside important historical and political differences between several groups developing the art of electroacoustic music worldwide (Manning 2004), the increased use of the computer in musical practices was a natural progression for the great majority of electro-acoustic composers, and new styles and forms of computer-mediated musical performance soon emerged.

Most of the computer music research developed during the 1970s focused on sound synthesis and processing methods using mainframe computers to produce tape pieces. One notable exception was the Groove system. This is the result of pioneering work in real-time computer systems developed at Bell Labs. Groove featured the ability to control the tempo, dynamic level, and balance of synthesis algorithms in real time (Dodge and Jerse 1985). Another notable example appeared in 1980s: the 4X machine, developed at IRCAM (Di Giugno, Kott, and Gerzso 1981). The 4X machine took the concept of speed and power in the domain of real-time DSP to unprecedented levels.

Early interactive computer music systems built in the late 1970s and early 1980s often were digital-analog hybrid systems consisting of a digital computer sending voltages to one or more analog synthesizers. The rapid development of digital technology in the 1980s led to dramatically improved techniques for interactive composition. In the early 1990s, IRCAM produced the IRCAM Signal Processing Workstation (ISPW) to replace the 4X, and Di Giugno designed the Mars workstation at IRIS (Instituto di Ricerca per l'Industria dello Spettacolo) (de Cecco, Lindeman, and Puckette 1992; Di Giugno and Armand 1991). The development of powerful general purpose computers that were fast enough for real-time DSP had an immediate impact on the proliferation of portable interactive systems suitable for use on stage. The availability of small, affordable, and sophisticated personal computers has enabled numerous musicians and programmers to begin exploring interactive computer music on their own, without the need for support from large institutions.

MIDI controllers have provided a consistent way of inputting performance information and other physical gestures onto the computer. The limited amount of data transferred via MIDI has enabled standard personal computers to handle music processing in real time. However, these limitations mean that important musical information (e.g., timbre) and other constantly changing musical subtleties have not been well represented (Wiggins et al. 1993).

5.2.1 Approaches to Computer-mediated Performance

It is possible to identify the emergence of at least two major approaches to computer-mediated musical performance: the *active playback* approach and the *algorithmic* approach.

In the active playback approach a pre-established score is interpreted during playback. The computer is programmed to interpret and perform a given score, but the performer intervenes to influence the evolution of the performance. For instance, Max Mathews's Conductor system uses a three-dimensional joystick to control the relative amplitudes of the individual voices of played-back polyphonic music (Dodge and Jerse 1985). Raising the baton nearer to specific positions causes the voice assigned to that particular position to become louder. In a similar fashion, the sequential drum, also designed by Max Mathews, consists of a rectangular surface wired to exhibit four characteristic signals when struck: a trigger pulse, a voltage in proportion to the stroke, and two voltages that indicate the coordinates of the location of the stroke (Mathews 1989). The musical implementation of the sequential drum starts with entering the sequences of pitches to be played into the computer. The performer then controls the rhythm of the sequence (by timing the strokes), the amplitude of the notes (by the strength of the strokes), and their timbre (by the position of the stroke on the tablet).

Drawing on research into artificial intelligence, the computer music community developed a number of systems that compose musical material during the performance in response to some form of in-performance control: the algorithmic approach. Such types of systems have made a great impact, in the form of intelligent automatic music accompaniment. There can, however, be a number of sophisticated forms of interaction with the computer during performance, ranging from systems that generate suitable chord progressions to systems that can make compositional decisions during the performance (Dean 2003).

5.2.2 Interactive Music

Interactivity has become a major consideration in computer-mediated performance. Composers have applied a number of technologies in order to make music interactively, from artificial intelligence to haptic interfaces. The output of such systems often consists of either a collection of predefined material, triggered on the basis of distinct conditions, or generated algorithmically in real time, or a combination of both. Much of this work is called interactive.

The *Collins English Dictionary* definition of interaction outlines an action that involves reciprocal influence. In the field of physics, the term leads us to understand that an exchange of energy takes place. In the context of computer music, an interactive music system may be defined as one whose behavior changes in response to musical inputs.

In human conversation, the starting point of a dialogue is known by only one of the parties. Although some discussions have a preexisting agenda, in general the terrain of the conversation is not known in advance by the other party. It is a process of the exchange of ideas. This process of interaction is extremely dynamic, with each of the parties constantly monitoring the responses of the other and using their interpretations of the input from the other parties to make alterations to their own response strategy, picking up points of personal interest, expanding them, and negating points of contention. As in human dialogue, musical interaction requires musical understanding involving a huge number of shared assumptions and conventions based on years of collective experience.

However, the term interactive music has often been used in a much broader sense to describe systems that can be controlled live but do not necessarily display any form of musical understanding. A sensible compromise is to consider that a music system is interactive if it is programmed to interpret the actions of a performer in order to control musical parameters. The capability of the system to understand the music and react intelligently in response to the input signals defines its degree of sophistication. It is here that artificial intelligence can enhance the design of such systems.

An artificial intelligence–based interactive music system should promote the exploration and discovery of new outcomes. Ideally, the outcomes should be realistic to the extent that they confirm the cognitive schemes that the performer develops as their relationship with the system deepens. Designers of such systems are therefore concerned with the capabilities of our musical cognition and embed into their systems models able to emulate some of those capabilities. The system should be able to emulate intelligent behavior by modeling human hearing, understanding, and response. The response must be believable in the sense that it seems appropriate for the action taken and for the style of the music in question.

Performers can participate in the creation of an interactive musical piece depending on the amount of freedom they are granted to influence the material generated by the computer. For example, a fully notated, predetermined score could be made slightly interactive by allowing a performer to control a single parameter of the piece, such as tempo. In more sophisticated interactive pieces, performers may be able to control many significant musical parameters at once, and the composition can change dramatically during performance. Many types of musical processes can be represented in software to perform specific tasks. In the most extreme cases the computer can be furnished with the ability to respond to a great variety of performance variables, and therefore interactive compositions succeed by encouraging spontaneity while remaining within the boundaries of a dynamic context that seems whole and engaging.

Intelligent interactive systems can also be used by composers to experiment with ideas while creating a new piece. The immediacy of interactive techniques in generating and manipulating musical materials provides the composer with an interactive laboratory, where musical ideas and time-varying compositional processes are quickly realized and refined.

■ 5.3 COMPUTER MUSICIANSHIP

It would be impractical to implement a fully comprehensive model of musical listening in an interactive music system. A practical solution is to focus on modeling those aspects that are believed to be most important for delivering the tasks the system will be required to perform.

An approach to modeling musical understanding that naturally comes to mind would be to use computational techniques for the analysis of musical scores. However, this might not be the best approach, because these systems often have random access to the written score. That is, they can consult it in any order regardless of the temporal presentation of the piece. Conversely, an interactive music system has to scan the music sequentially, as people do when they listen to music. The groupings and relationships a human listener forms can only arise from cognitively available perceptual events and the interaction of these events with short-term and long-term memory. The machine should in some way have an ability to listen to ongoing music. The problem is that it is tricky to design models of musical listening, even very simplified ones.

Basically there are two strategies for furnishing interactive music systems with intelligence for listening to incoming musical input: *score-oriented* and *performance-oriented* strategies.

Score-oriented strategies use predetermined stored music events to match against music arriving at the input. Such systems often employ score-following techniques to accompany a performer by matching their realization of a particular score against a stored representation of that score. Much of the early research into interactive music systems was motivated by a desire to implement efficient score-following techniques. Score following assumes a fully notated, predetermined score, with the computer attempting to follow, linearly, the performer's note-by-note location during a performance. The computer then supplies an accompaniment by matching expected input from the performer to a similar score of a match list stored in memory.

A musical score is composed of an abstract set of symbols representing instructions for performers to interpret and execute a series of musical events. It specifies what will be played, how and when it will be played, and who will play it. The score specifies the timing, coordination, and interpretation of musical events during a performance. These events are often organized using the traditional categories of beat, meter, and tempo. Such categories allow the composer to preserve and employ familiar ways of thinking about temporal flow, such as specifying some events to occur on the downbeat of the next measure or at the end of the bar. Scores for interactive music systems may, however, have many different forms, not necessarily related to traditional musical scores. Such scores may comprise the structures, data, and mechanisms for timing computer events. For example, a score may contain a structure that organizes the data and the mechanisms required for a performance. Sometimes actions may be produced when specific incoming data are matched to the same data stored in memory. At other times actions may be produced based on a more general analysis of a performance. A score may include the actual data for producing a musical response, such as pitch information or sequences, and it may also include control messages that are not intended for musical output.

A number of sophisticated real-time pattern-matching techniques have been developed for applications in score following. Roger Dannenberg's score-following algorithm using the dynamic programming technique is a classic example (Buxton, Dannenberg, and Vercoe 1986).

Score following is, however, just one of many ways to organize an interactive work. Performance-oriented systems do not assume the realization of a predetermined score in the sense that these systems do not necessarily have a stored representation of the music they expect to find at the input. Performance-oriented systems do not necessarily employ traditional metric categories but often use more general parameters involving perceptual measures such as density and regularity to describe the temporal behavior.

The performance-oriented approach is suitable for implementing interactive systems for musical improvisation. Musical improvisation poses one of the greatest challenges for artificial intelligence because the computer is required to produce music in contexts that can be unstructured and unpredictable. The system must be programmed with the ability to rely on some kind of common musical sense in order to derive structure from what it hears and produce coherent responses. The musical material and its development are largely unknown in advance.

An important characteristic of performance-oriented systems is defined by the way in which they respond to the incoming music. Responses can be *generative, transformative,* or *sampled.* Generative responses use sets of rules to generate musical output from scratch driven by the incoming music—for example, rules that generate different pitch structures according to the distribution of specific pitches in the incoming musical stream. Transformative responses apply transformations to the incoming material in order to produce variants. Such transformations are applied to live input as it arrives. These variants may or may not be recognizably related to the original. Finally, sampled responses use prerecorded musical fragments in response to the input. Some aspects of these fragments may be varied in performance, such as the tempo of playback, dynamic shape, and rhythmic variations.

5.3.1 Dynamic Programming Primer

One thing that computers can do better than humans is to follow extremely detailed instructions quickly and accurately. This opens up new possibilities for music technology and indeed for interactive music systems. For instance, the computer can be programmed to produce complex harmonic textures according to the pitch of an incoming solo. It would be hard to obtain such a response from an orchestra if the solo were improvised. Computers are much better than humans at following precise complex musical instructions to be performed in real time on material input during a performance. However, the task of delegating performance-time compositional tasks to a computer requires sophisticated programming techniques. This section introduces one such technique: dynamic programming (DP). DP has been successfully used to build interactive music systems (Dannenberg 2000), and it is particularly good for implementing systems for intelligent accompaniment, phrase-matching tasks, and, of course, score following.

DP is a standard algorithmic technique in computer science and is particularly useful for problems known as sequence alignment. The motto of DP is "divide and conquer." The technique works by dividing a problem into smaller sub-problems. Then the sub-problems are solved and the solutions are stored for use in solving the larger problem. Thus, the central idea of DP is to break a large problem down into incremental steps so that, at any given stage, optimal solutions are known to solve sub-problems. When the problem-solving technique is applicable, this condition can be extended incrementally without having to alter previously computed optimal solutions to sub-problems. Eventually the condition applies to all of the data and, if the formulation is correct, this, together with the fact that nothing remains untreated, gives the desired answer to the complete problem.

DP is efficient at finding optimal solutions for cases involving a great deal of overlapping sub-problems because it solves problems by combining solutions to sub-problems, when the sub-problems themselves may share sub-sub-problems, and so on. In order to avoid solving these sub-sub-problems several times, their results are gradually computed and memorized, starting from the simpler problems, until the overall problem itself is solved.

In order to illustrate the functioning of DP, let us imagine the following problem: a trader has to cross a river to take his merchandise to a market, but his boat has a limited capacity. How does he choose which items to take to the market in order to maximize profit? For example, assume that there are four different boxes of goods, as shown in Table 5.1.

Table 5.1
Goods to be taken to a market across the river.

Box	Size	Value
1	1.2 m^2	$2,000.00
2	0.5 m^2	$ 800.00
3	0.3 m^2	$1,000.00
4	0.6 m^2	$1,000.00

If the capacity of the boat is 1.2 m^2, then the trader should clearly take box number 1 first and leave the rest for later. But the choice would not be so straightforward if the boat had a capacity of 1.5 m^2. In this case it would probably be better to leave the large box and take smaller ones first.

As with most things in computer programming, the DP approach to solving this problem is not very intuitive. Assuming N is the size of the particular boat in question, DP works by calculating the best combination of boxes for all possible boat sizes up to N. The algorithm for doing this is as follows (B = number of boxes and N = size of the boat in question):

```
FOR j = 1 TO B
FOR i = 1 TO N
IF i > = size(j) THEN
   { IF cost(i) < (cost(i - size(j)) + value(j)) THEN
          { cost(i) = cost(i - size(j)) + value(j)
            best(i) = j }
   }
```

The algorithm assumes that there are a number of boxes of given size and value stored in an array. The highest value that can be achieved with a boat of capacity i is represented by cost(i), and the last item that was added to achieve this maximum is represented by best(i). The algorithm starts by calculating the value it can achieve with box 1 (j = 1). Then it uses this result to calculate the value it can achieve with boxes 1 and 2, and so on. When considering a new item, the revised computation of cost(n) considers the value of items that the trader would be able to take if enough boxes were removed to leave room for the new box: cost(i − size(j)). If that value plus the value of the item that they were considering adding was greater than the old cost just with all the old boxes then the old boxes would be replaced by the new one. To illustrate this, let us consider a simple abstract example as follows, considering a boat of size = 4, as shown in Table 5.2.

Table 5.2
An abstract example.

Box	Size	Value
1	3	6
2	2	5
3	1	2

Initially the algorithm considers box 1. The box would not fit in a boat of size 1 and 2. But in boat of size 3 it can fit box 1: cost(3) < (cost (0) + value(1)). Thus cost(3) = 6 and best(3) = 1. Next the algorithm checks for boat size 4. In this case it checks if cost(4) < (cost(1) + value(1)) is true. This is indeed true and so this size also accommodates box 1 as follows: cost(4) = 6 and best(4) = 1.

Next, the algorithm considers box 2. This does not fit in boat size 1, but it would fit in a boat of size 2. It checks if cost(2) < (cost(0) + value(2)). Again this condition is true because box 1 did not fit in the boat, and so the algorithm calculates that the last (and only) box in this boat with cost(2) = 5. Next, when the algorithm checks cost(3) < (cost(1) + value(2)) for boat of size 3, the answer is no, so it proceeds to check if cost(4) < (cost(2) + value(2)) for boat size 4. In this case the answer is yes because cost(4) = 6 and cost(2) is calculated as equal to 5. The previous box is thrown out of the boat and is replaced by box 2. The current status of the computations up to now is:

```
cost(1) = 0
cost(2) = 5
cost(3) = 6
cost(4) = 10
```

With respect to box 3, it fits in a boat of size 1, so cost(1) = 2. It is not worth considering for boat size 2 but for boat size 3 cost(3) < (cost(2) + value(3)). Thus box 3 is the top box for boat size 3. Boat size 4 is not worth considering because the scores will not increase. The final results are:

```
cost(1) = 2          best(1) = 3
cost(2) = 5          best(2) = 2
cost(3) = 7          best(3) = 1
cost(4) = 10         best(4) = 2
```

At the end of the calculations, the best(*n*) array determines the contents of the boat. Suppose that best(*N*) is box *k* of size(*k*). Then the next box in the boat must be the top item for the boat of size(*M*—size(*k*)), and so forth. In the above example best(4) = 2, and so box 2 goes in the boat. Then best(4—size(2)) = best(2) = 2, that is, another box size 2 goes in the boat.

5.3.2 An Example of a Score-oriented System

In the following example DP is used to build an automatic accompaniment system. This example appeared in a chapter by Roger Dannenberg published in Eduardo R. Miranda's book *Readings in Music and Artificial Intelligence* (Dannenberg 2000).

Consider the scenario of a duet where a bass guitar accompanies a solo guitar. This is not a case of improvised music: both guitarists are given a score. The score contains two parts: the solo line and the accompaniment. As the solo guitar plays, the bass guitarist listens to the solo and matches the live guitar with the line on the score. From this matching, and possibly other cues, the bass guitarist derives the tempo and performs the accompaniment according to the score. The objective is to play the accompaniment in synchrony with the soloist. This is not a straightforward task because the soloist should be able to freely articulate the tempo and the phrasing of the piece during the performance. Leaving aside other aspects of such performance (rehearsal, visual cues, etc.), let us consider this strictly as a problem of synchronization: the ability to follow a score and synchronize with a soloist is an essential musical skill in its own right. The following paragraphs demonstrate how Roger Dannenberg employed DP to program the computer with this skill.

The task of an accompanist is to follow the progress of the soloist in the written score. Essentially this is a matching task: the accompanist matches the solo performance to the score. In an ideal world, the solo is performed perfectly and the accompanist has perfect perception. One could just implement a score-following system that started with the first note and advanced to the next each time the soloist played a new note. But in practice errors are common even amongst the most skilled performers. What if the soloist makes a mistake? In order to design a realistic accompaniment system one needs to take into account that errors may occur. One way to deal with such errors is to accept incomplete matches between the solo and the score.

The algorithm should be able to compare a sequence of performed pitches with a predetermined sequence of pitches in order to determine the best match; this gives the location of the performer in relation to the score. The idea is to think of a performance as being the same as the score, with the exception of omitted, wrong, or extra notes. Starting with the performed sequence, the algorithm has to find a set of corrections consisting of insertions (to correct the omitted notes), alterations (to correct the wrong notes), and deletions (to correct the extra notes) in order to match the pitch sequence of the score. For example, Figure 5.1 shows two sequences with labeled corrections.

One should bear in mind that there are obviously many different corrective procedures that could be applied. For example, the entire performance could be erased and the entire score inserted. However, the objective is to apply only a few essential corrections so that a maximum number of notes can be matched. This is necessary to measure the quality of the match so that one can search all possible sets of corrections for the ones that maximize the result. This gives us an objective that corresponds to the notion of searching

Figure 5.1 A performed sequence and a score sequence. Corrections that would convert the performance into the score are marked.

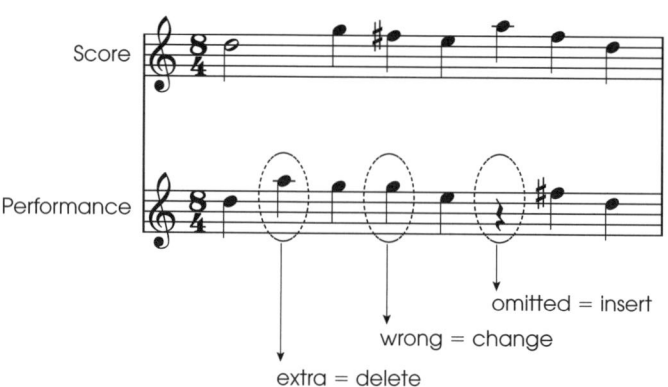

only for a few essential corrections. This measurement can be formalized as follows:

$$Q = \omega_1 M - \omega_2 O - \omega_3 W - \omega_4 E$$

where quality measurement is defined as the number of matched notes M weighted by ω_1 minus the number of omitted notes O weighted by ω_2, the number of wrong notes W weighted by ω_3, and the number of extra notes E weighted by ω_4. This measurement gives the algorithm the means to search all possible sets of corrections for the set(s) that maximize it. By comparing the actual timing of the matched notes to the timing marked in the score, an accompaniment system can determine the location and tempo of the performance. It is not straightforward to find a good match: the number of assignments of matched, omitted, wrong, and extra notes is exponential.

In order to illustrate the functioning of the DP algorithm in more detail, let us ignore the real-time requirement of an interactive system in the first instance. The DP algorithm constructs a two-dimensional array and computes a solution element by element. The rows of the table in Figure 5.2 represent the notes in the score, and the columns represent the notes in the performance. Assume that $\omega_1 = 1$ and $\omega_2 = \omega_3 = \omega_4 = 0$. The number 2 at the lower right of the shaded area represents the number of matches between the sequence {D, A, G} of the performance and the sequence {D, G, F#, E} of the score. In this case notes D and G match, so the value is 2. Each entry on the table corresponds to a possible pair of notes; the lower right-hand corner corresponds to the comparison of the entire performance to the entire score.

Each element of the array can be computed in terms of a few neighboring elements without a global, exponential search. For example, Figure 5.3 illustrates a small section of a larger array. In order to calculate the element with the question mark, we take the values to the left, above, and to the upper left and consider whether or not the performance and score match at this location. The new

Figure 5.2 Data structure for the dynamic programming approach to matching.

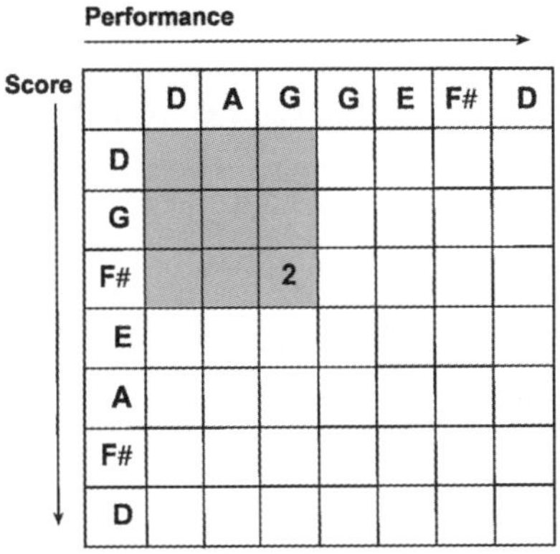

Figure 5.3 Calculating an element of the array.

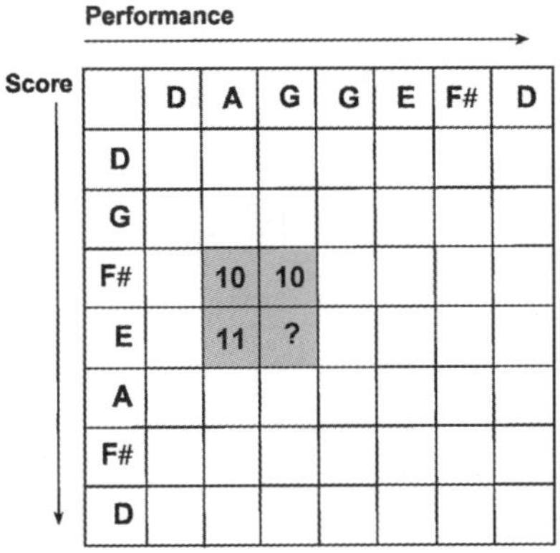

element counts the number of matches between performance and score notes. This is calculated by considering the following:

a. Adding a new note at the end of the performance sequence will never decrease the number of matches. Therefore the value must be at least as great as the number to the left (that is, 11).

b. Similarly, adding a new note to the score sequence will never decrease the number of matches. Therefore the number must be at least as great as the number above (that is, 10).

c. Extending both the score and the performance sequences by matching notes will increase the number of matches by 1. If there is a match, then the number in question will be greater than the number to the upper left.

Because the algorithm is looking for the best match, it simply takes the maximum of the three choices. If $Q(s, p)$ is the value at the row s (score) and column p (performance), then:

$$Q(s, p) = \max(Q(s, p - 1), Q(s - 1, p), Q(s - 1, p - 1) + c)$$

where $c = 1$ if note s in the score matches note p in the performance, and $c = 0$ otherwise.

Assuming that the score and performance notes are numbered starting with 1, we also need to define $Q(0, p) = Q(s, 0) = 0$. The array is computed one column at a time from left to right, starting each column at the top and working down (Figure 5.4). The DP method takes roughly $N \times N$ steps, making it considerably quicker than the 2^N steps of a pure combinatorial approach.

Figure 5.4 Complete evaluation of the array.

Score \ Performance	D	A	G	G	E	F#	D
D	1	1	1	1	1	1	1
G	1	1	2	2	2	2	2
F#	1	1	2	2	2	3	1
E	1	1	2	2	3	3	3
A	1	2	2	2	3	3	3
F#	1	2	2	2	3	4	4
D	1	2	2	2	3	4	5

Any set of weights can be used in the evaluation functions. Referring back to Figure 5.3, extending the performance sequence by one note corresponds to an extra note, so we can say that the value in question is at least as great as the number to the left minus ω_4. Extending the score sequence by one note corresponds to an omitted note, so the value should be as great as the number above minus ω_2. If both performance and score sequences are extended by matching notes, the value is at least as great as the number above and left plus ω_1. If the notes do not match, then we have a wrong note, and in this case the value would be as great as the number above and left minus ω_3, the penalty for wrong notes. These are calculated as follows:

$$Q(s, p) = \max(Q(s, p - 1), -\omega_4, Q(s - 1, p), -\omega_2, Q(s - 1, p - 1) + c)$$

where $c = \omega_1$ if note s in the score matches note p in the performance and $c = -\omega_3$ otherwise. Initially $Q(0, p) = -p \times \omega_4$ and $Q(s, 0) = -s \times \omega_2$.

The corrections to make in the performance sequence are derived by working backward from the lower right corner of the array. That is, the best match between the performance and the score can be determined only by examining the entire performance. This is not acceptable for live performance, but the problem can be overcome by a simple heuristic to guess which notes match. If the heuristic generates an incorrect guess, then the error becomes apparent as the performance progresses. In practice, incorrect guesses are rare. If they occur at all it is because they may correspond to some ambiguity that would also have caused problems for humans. Dannenberg's heuristic works as follows: As values are calculated, the algorithm keeps track of the greatest value seen so far. Whenever a new value in location (s, p) is greater, it assumes that the performed note p is a performance of the score note s; see underlined matches in Figure 5.5.

Note in Figure 5.5 that the second performed note is reported as matching the fifth note in the score (the note A). Later it is discovered that the fifth performed note matches the fourth note in the score (the note E). This means that a note performed later matches an earlier score note; that is, there has been an error somewhere. It occurred because with only two notes (D and A) in the initial performance, the algorithm looked ahead in the score and found a matching note A. The error was later detected and corrected.

In a performance situation the computer needs to calculate a whole column of the array for every performed note. An alternative

Figure 5.5 Complete evaluation of the array with matches underlined.

	D	A	G	G	E	F#	D
D	(1)	1	1	1	1	1	1
G	1	1	2	2	2	2	2
F#	1	1	2	2	2	3	1
E	1	1	2	2	(3)	3	3
A	1	(2)	2	2	3	3	3
F#	1	2	2	2	3	(4)	4
D	1	2	2	2	3	4	(5)

(Performance across columns; Score down rows.)

to optimize this process is to compute a sliding window of values rather than an entire column; only the previous window is saved for calculating the next window.

Once matches have been determined, the system uses them to synchronize the accompaniment. In the system created by Roger Dannenberg, the solo and accompaniment scores are stored as events with time stamps, representing the real performance time, in milliseconds, of each event in a nominal performance. Notated tempo and tempo changes are already factored into these time steps. All that remains is to make slight adjustments to compensate for variations in the live performance.

Each match conveys the current location. By looking at the time stamp of the matched solo note, we obtain the current score time. Tempo can be estimated by looking at successive matches. For example, suppose there is a match at performance time 20,000 ms and at score time 10,000 ms, and the next match is at performance time 21,000 ms and score time 10,800 ms. The tempo is then 800/1000, which is 80% of nominal tempo.

DP works rather well to find matches between a preexisting score and the sequential notes of a live performance. The basic matching algorithm is simple and flexible, and it can be used with various features (e.g., pitch and duration), matching functions (e.g., exact match, approximate match, etc.), and weights. The speed of the algorithm allows it to be applied over large intervals of the full score, which leads to robust matching systems.

5.3.3 An Example of a Performer-oriented System

The previous section discussed an example of a score-oriented system using dynamic programming, where both the computer and the performer follow a score. This section introduces Cypher, a performance-oriented system designed by Robert Rowe (1993).

In order to respond to improvised music, computers must be programmed to make some sense of the context around them and to react in accordance with that sense. Programming a computer system to improvise brings us quickly to issues concerned with machine musicianship, as discussed brilliantly by Robert Rowe (2001).

Central to an interactive music system for musical improvisation is the capability to analyze the features of a musical performance. The process of analyzing musical performance involves an important activity: listening.

It is important to bear in mind that the act of listening is not the same as the act of hearing. In the book *Traité des objets musicaux*, Pierre Schaeffer (1966) introduced a thorough discussion on this difference, but for the purposes of this chapter it suffices to consider that hearing is the passive perception of sound, whereas listening implies active mental cognition. For instance, we can hear the sounds of a flute, but we listen to the music played on the flute. We hear the birds, but we listen to birdsong. In this context we could metaphorically consider that although a computer can "hear" streams of MIDI numbers as they come in through a MIDI interface, it needs to be programmed to be able to "listen" to the incoming MIDI data in order to make sense of them. Listening therefore implies some form of understanding.

Music is essentially a time-based art in which elements and structures create coherence in a time flow. A musical composition can be viewed from its largest time structures, with distinct sections that define the overall shape of a piece, to smaller levels, which consist of subsections, phrases within subsections, short motives within phrases, and single notes within motives. One way to define musical understanding by computers is to consider that understanding occurs when musical events can be matched in the memory with identical events or representations of such events. This could be the recognition of simple data, such as a musical note, the matching of a rhythmic pattern, the representation of note intervals, and so forth. In such cases musical memory is referenced to provide insights into the listening activity.

Also important is the ability of the system to respond meaningfully to performance data. For example, the computer may look for a specific note, condition, or other input data to trigger a prerecorded sequence or to begin a compositional process. Playback or processing begins to take place when a specified condition is met. Performers may also have continuous control over specific parameters of a process, such as controlling the dynamic level or the tempo, which continually shapes the musical outcome. The composer may determine the range, scale, and time frame for a performer to influence musical processes. Performer actions may not always have obvious one-to-one correspondence with compositional algorithms; they may be stored, delayed, accumulated, or modified in other ways in order to produce satisfactory musical results. Triggers may even cause a chain reaction of generative music algorithms.

The main difficulty with interactive computer-based music nowadays has not so much to do with the implementation of algorithms to generate musical materials. A plethora of sound synthesis and audio signal processing techniques exists (Cook 2002; Miranda 2002; Zölzer 2002). The main difficulty is organizing musical materials in real time into coherent musical forms with a clear sense of direction and purpose. Composing involves the combination of various parts and elements to form a unified whole. Composers must make decisions on how musical ideas will be presented and developed, how sections will be delineated, how transitions will be made from one section to another, and so forth. Compositional schemes for interactive computer music differ from schemes used for other types of music in the sense that they are governed primarily by the relationship between human performers and computers. A clear concept of how musical ideas will be realized through interactive processes will guide the formation of musical structures. The interplay between musical concepts and modes of interaction will define the unfolding of the composition.

The central idea behind Cypher's design was that an interactive music system required a sophisticated form of artificial intelligence, which could be accomplished through the coordinated action and cross-connected communication of many simple, self-contained, relatively unintelligent software agents. It employed a distributed agent systems architecture, where simple analysis processes were implemented as single agents, and larger operations involving several such agents constitute agencies. Agents were conceived as situated systems in continuous interaction with the outside world. The control structure of Cypher was in many ways inspired by Marvin Minsky's book *The Society of Mind* (1988).

Cypher comprises two main components: the listener and the player. The listener component analyzes MIDI data arriving from some source with the objective of characterizing the data. Then it passes messages relaying the result of this analysis to the player component. Internal musical events are built from incoming MIDI data and can represent either single notes or chords.

The listener component is set to track events arriving on a MIDI channel, apply a number of feature analyzers to incoming events, and store the classifications produced by each of them. Cypher responds to these classifications by channeling the input through various transformation processes in the player component. The user can configure the player to apply specific transformations when particular combinations of feature classification are received. For example, one rule might specify that when major and loud chords are found at the input, the player responds by transforming that material through decelerating and thinning processes. The listener continually analyzes incoming data and sends messages to the player describing what it hears.

The listener component operates on two levels. At the lower level the agents analyze several attributes of the signal: register, interonset interval rate, vertical density, loudness, articulation, and harmony. The results are attached to the event being analyzed and can be simply read from the event by the agents when needed.

At the higher level, the agents characterize the way lower-level classifications change over time. The low-level analysis results that are attached to each event are used to make this characterization, and the new results are added to it. Basically, at the higher level Cypher is looking for regularities in the signal. The listener typifies the behavior of each feature individually in terms of its regularity. If a feature is invariant within the current group (e.g., always loud), it is called regular, but if the feature changes frequently (e.g., alternating between loud and soft), it is called irregular. These regularity-versus-irregularity judgments form the conditions of the rules that the user can specify for the composition. For example, the user may require that irregular articulations within a group should prompt the player to trigger a drone note.

The player component employs a number of different strategies to produce musical responses. It features two sub-modules: the composer and the critic. The former employs three different types of strategies for generating music: strategies for playing sequences, strategies for generating new material, and strategies for transforming received material. The most common and often more effective is the last strategy, which applies such transformations to incoming musical data as accelerando, inversion, delay, and transposition. The player is programmed with rules for choosing transformations and the material for the transformations. The information from the analysis is sent to a process that manages the employment of compositional strategies, making the output of all listener components available for compositional decisions. These strategies can be combined to form composite musical results. In contrast to the parallel nature of the listener component, the player component tends to link compositional strategy processes in sequence, with the music that is generated being passed from one strategy to the next.

As mentioned earlier, the user can configure the operations to be performed by establishing connections between listener messages of the input data and methods for generating the response. Whenever a feature is noticed in an event, the transformation to which it is connected is applied to the event. High-level connections can also be made between listener reports on phrase-length behavior and player methods that affect groups of several events.

The connection between listener messages and compositional methods are programmed as logical expressions of the features and regularities reported by the listener. For instance:

```
IF register = high OR loudness = loud THEN trill
```

In this case, if the current event is either of a high register or loud then the algorithm to make a trill is employed. The user specifies the generative strategies to be activated by the composer sub-module in response to listener messages.

The critic sub-module assesses the material the program is about to play. It acts as an internal arbiter of the music and can change this material before it is actually played. The critic includes an independent list of conditional rules. For example, a critic rule might specify that if the program is about to output fast, loud, dense chords in the low register, that material should first be trimmed out, slowed down, and made softer. Cypher is provided with a fully fledged critic module that cannot be changed using scripts or graphic interfaces; the only way to change the critic is to rewrite the programming code.

■ 5.4 INTERACTIVE MUSICAL EVOLUTION WITH GENETIC ALGORITHMS

Genetic algorithms (GA) comprise computing methods inspired by biological processes, most notably those processes that are believed to be the driving forces of the origin and evolution of species, as proposed in the 1850s by Charles Darwin (1859) and more recently by Richard Dawkins (1986). GAs are normally employed to find optimal solutions to engineering and design problems where many alternative solutions may exist, but whose evaluation cannot be ascertained until they have been implemented and tested. In such cases, the optimal solution can be sought by manually generating, implementing, and testing the alternatives or by making gradual improvements to alleged nonoptimal solutions. As the complexity of the problem in question grows, however, these procedures become increasingly unsatisfactory and wasteful. Hence the need for an automated method that explores the capability of the computer to perform voluminous combinatorial tasks. Notwithstanding this, GAs go beyond standard combinatorial processing: they embody powerful mechanisms for targeting only potentially fruitful combinations. These mechanisms resemble aspects of biological evolution such as natural selection based on fitness, crossover of genes, mutation, and so forth; hence the label "genetic algorithms." (The term "genetic programming" is sometimes used when the target solution is a program rather than data. In fact, genetic programming is often thought of as a different field of research altogether.)

The sequence of actions illustrated in Figure 5.6 portrays a typical GA. Initially a population of abstract entities is randomly created. Depending on the application, these entities can represent practically anything, from the fundamental components of an organism to the commands for a robot or the notes of a musical composition. Next, an evaluation procedure is applied to the population in order to test whether it meets the objectives to solve the task or problem in question. As this initial population is bound to fail the evaluation at this stage, the system embarks on the creation of a new generation of entities. Firstly, a number of entities are set apart from the population according to some prescribed criteria. These are often referred to as the fitness-for-reproduction criteria because this subset will undergo a mating-like process in order to produce offspring. The fitness criteria obviously vary from application to application, but in general they indicate which entities from the current generation work best. The chosen entities are then combined (usually in pairs) and give birth to the offspring. During this reproduction process, the formation of the offspring involves a mutation process. Next, the offspring are inserted in the population, replacing their parents (totally or partially). The fate of the remaining entities of the population not selected for reproduction may vary, but they usually die out without causing any effect. At this point we say that

Figure 5.6 The sequence of actions of a typical GA.

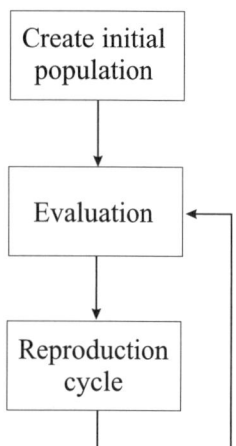

a new generation of the population has evolved. The evaluation procedure is now applied to the new generation. If the population still does not meet the objectives, then the system embarks once more on the creation of a new generation. This cycle is repeated until the population passes the evaluation test.

In practice, genetic algorithms normally operate on a set of binary codes that represent the entities of the population. These operations involve three basic classes of process: *recombination*, *mutation*, and *selection*. The recombination process causes the exchange of information between a pair of codes; the mutation process alters the value of single bits in a code. Recombination produces offspring codes by combining the information contained in the codes of their parents. Depending on the form of the representation of the codes, two types of recombination can be applied: real-valued recombination or binary-valued crossover.

In order to illustrate a typical genetic algorithm in action, consider a population P of n entities represented as 8-bit codes as follows: P = {11010110, 10010111, 01001001, . . .}. Then, suppose that at a certain point in the evolutionary process, the following pair of codes is selected to reproduce: p_7 = 11000101 and p_{11} = 01111001. Reproduction in this example is defined as a process whereby the couple exchange the last three digits of their codes, followed by a mutation process. In this case, the pair p_7 and p_{11} will exchange the last three digits of their code, as follows:

p_7:   11000[101] → 11000[001]
p_{11}: 01111[001] → 01111[101]

Next, the mutation process takes place; mutation usually occurs according to a probabilistic scheme. In this example, a designated probability determines the likelihood of shifting the state of a bit from zero to one, or vice versa, as the code string is scanned. Mutation is important for introducing diversity in the population, but one should always bear in mind that higher mutation probabilities reduce the effectiveness of the selective process because they tend to produce offspring with little resemblance with their parents. In this example, the third bit of p_7 and the fourth bit of p_{11} were mutated:

p_7:   11[0]00001 → 11[1]00001
p_{11}: 011[1]1101 → 011[0]1101

The new offspring of p_7 and p_{11} are 11100001 and 01101101, respectively.

In order to make effective use of genetic algorithms one has to devise suitable methods both to codify the population and to associate the behavior of the evolutionary process with the application domain, which in this case is music. The rule of thumb is that one should try to employ the smallest possible coding alphabet to represent the population.

A typical codification method is binary string coding, where a string of some specified length represents each individual; the eight-bit coding illustrated above is a typical example of binary string coding. This coding method is interesting because each digit of the code, or groups of digits, can be associated with a different attribute of the individual (Figure 5.7).

A number of variations of binary string coding may be devised. For example, one could devise codes using large binary strings divided into words of a fixed length; each word would correspond to a decimal value. In this case, the code is a decimal string, but the actual computing of the genetic algorithm processes occurs at their corresponding binary representation.

Figure 5.7 Binary string coding.

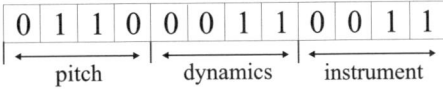

The mechanism for selecting the population subset for reproduction varies according to the application of the genetic algorithm. This mechanism generally involves the combination of a fitness assignment method and a probability scheme. One of the simplest selection mechanisms is the stochastic sampling selection. In order to visualize how this selection mechanism works, imagine that the whole population is projected onto a line made of continuous segments of variable lengths. Each individual is tied to a different segment whose length represents its fitness value (Figure 5.8). Then, random numbers whose maximum value is equal to the length of the whole line are generated; those individuals whose segments cover the values of the random numbers are selected.

Another widely used selection mechanism is local neighborhood selection. In this case, individuals are constrained to interact only within the scope of a limited neighborhood. The neighborhood therefore defines groups of potential parents. In order to render this process more effective, the algorithm firstly selects a group of fit candidates (using stochastic sampling, for example) and then a local neighborhood is defined for every candidate. The mating partner is selected from within this neighborhood according to its fitness criteria. The neighborhood schemes that are commonly used are ring, two-dimensional, and three-dimensional neighborhood (Figure 5.9), but more complex schemes may also be devised.

Figure 5.8 Stochastic sampling selection mechanism.

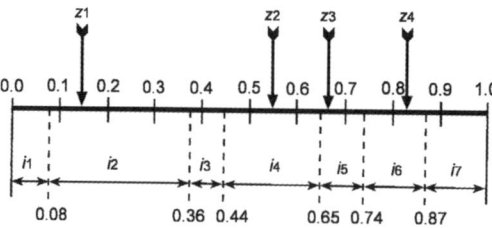

Figure 5.9 Ring, two dimensional, and three-dimensional neighborhood schemes.

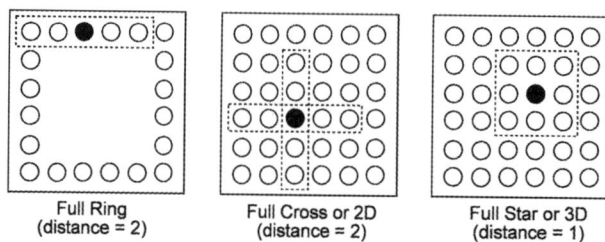

Many more selection methods exist but it is impracticable to consider all of them here. Successful applications of genetic algorithms often use selection mechanisms tailored specifically to the task at hand.

The selection operation is responsible for choosing the best possible codes according to a certain predetermined fitness criterion. There are applications, however, in which the user is required to interact with the system during the search process. In the case of an interactive musical system, for example, a number of musical passages may be presented to the user, who then assigns fitness values to them based either on aesthetic judgments or on the subjective sense of how close these passages are to specific musical targets.

As an interesting example of a GA-based interactive music system we cite Al Biles's GenJam (Biles 2002). GenJam improvises solos and performs interactive and collective improvisation with a performer. It "listens" to what a performer plays, maps the information onto its internal chromosome representation, and uses GA-like mutation and crossover to develop its response.

The basic architecture of the system is shown in Figure 5.10. In order to perform a tune, GenJam reads several files that describe the tune and its arrangement. Then it either reads or builds two populations of musical ideas and interacts with the performer in a number of ways during the performance.

Figure 5.10 The basic architecture of GenJam.

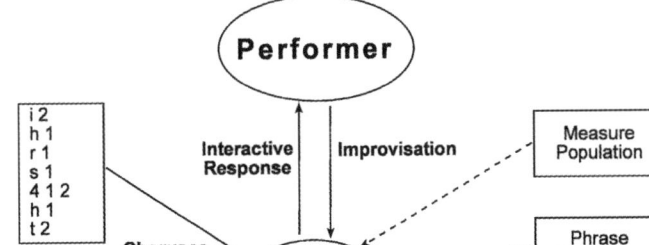

The "Chord Progression" file contains information about the tune to be performed: the octave range (the "4" in the first line), the tempo (the "160" in the first line), whether to use swings (the "S" in the first line), and the chord progression of the tune (one measure per line, up to two chords per measure). The "Choruses" file describes how each cycle of the form described in "Chord Progression" should be performed. Most jazz performances involve variations on a theme, where the soloists perform the original tune in the first and last choruses and improvise in the middle choruses. The improvisation can be full-chorus solos by one soloist, trading fours or eights (where soloists take turns every four or eight bars), or collective (where soloists improvise simultaneously). The "Rhythm" and the "Head Sequence" files are standard MIDI files that provide the rhythm section accompaniment and arrange harmony parts for the first and last choruses. The "MIDI Parameters" file contains configuration information for the synthesizer module (instruments, loudness, etc.). The "Measure Populations" and "Phrase Populations" files contain data structures representing musical ideas for making improvisations. These populations are either read directly from files or built internally from a database of licks. Below is an example illustrating a four-measure phrase, referred to by Al Biles as GenJam Normal Form (GJNF).

In Figure 5.11 is a phrase embedded in the measure and phrase populations: phrase number 23 (out of a population of 48 phrases). This phrase has a fitness of –12, which means that it is regarded as a "bad" phrase. The other four numbers in the "chromosome" of measure 23 were pointers to the measure population. This was indicating that phrase 23 consisted of measure 57 played twice, followed by measures 11 and 38. The measure population contains 64 sequences of eighth-note-length events, in this case 8 events (notes and/or rests) per measure. Pitch is determined using the event number as an offset into a determined octave range associated with the current chord in the progression. Thus, although measure 57 is repeated in the first two measures, the resulting notes may be different if the respective chords are different. In this example, measure 57 has a fitness of 22, which means that it is regarded as a "good" measure. The reason a "good" measure can appear in a "bad" phrase is that a given measure can occur in more than one phrase.

When GenJam trades four with a soloist, it listens to the performer's last four measures. Next, it creates the corresponding GJNF representation and mutates some (or all) of the chromosomes of the data. Then it plays back the mutated phrase as its response in the next four measures, and so forth. The interesting aspect of GenJam

TOWARD INTELLIGENT MUSICAL INSTRUMENTS 247

Figure 5.11 A phrase embedded in the measure and phrase populations.

						11	6	9	7	0	5	7	8	7	5
23	-12	57	57	11	38										
						38	-4	7	8	7	7	15	15	15	0
		Phase Population				57	22	9	7	0	5	7	15	15	0
									Measure Population						

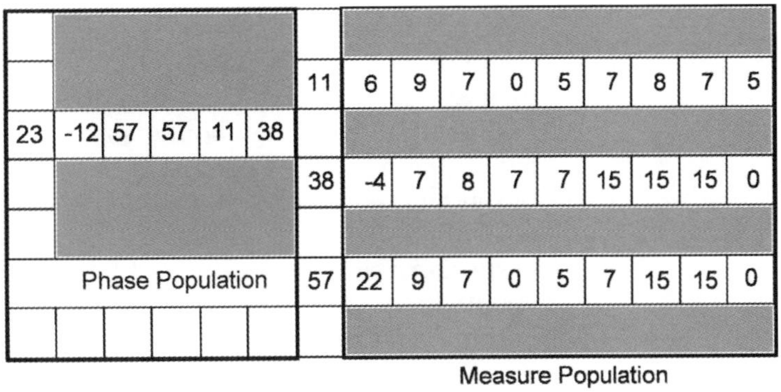

is that the mutations are musically meaningful in the sense that the operation includes musical operations such as reversing the sequence, turning it upside down, transposing, sorting, and so forth.

The populations of measures are produced by means of an interactive GA, which requires a human critic to provide the fitness for each individual. To train GenJam, the critic creates an arrangement for a tune in which every chorus is a GenJan-generated solo. As the system generates the solos, the critic listens and provides feedback in real time by typing "g" for "good" and "b" for "bad." Each time the critic types a "g," the fitness for the corresponding measure and phrases is increased by one, and vice versa. A typical trained section begins with randomly generated initial populations and continues with a sequence of tunes, each of which results in a new generation. Measure and phrase populations generate offspring from the best individuals, replacing worse individuals.

A subsequent version of GenJam eliminates the fitness evaluation in order to bypass the notorious problem of fitness bottleneck. Fitness bottleneck is caused by the need for the critic to hear each measure and phrase in order to evaluate its fitness. It is questionable whether GenJam can still be considered an evolutionary system in this case, but such debate is beyond the scope of this book.

■ 5.5 IMPROVISING WITH SWARM INTELLIGENCE

Flocks of birds, swarms of insects, and shoals of fish are examples of systems that develop global properties from low-level interaction. These systems have no high-level central control or organizing plan.

The self-organizing behavior of swarms can be explained by the behavior of relatively simple individuals interacting locally with near neighbors; self-organization is not due to any centralized control. For instance, a swarm of insects has a persistent shape and may suddenly change the direction of flight, with every member seemingly responding spontaneously. Yet they do so without collision. This behavior appears to be controlled centrally by a leader, but in fact mere local interactions between adjacent flock members are sufficient to account for this behavior. This phenomenon suggests remarkable similarities with musical structures emerging from spontaneous improvisation among the members of a free-jazz ensemble, each of whom listens to what the others are doing and responds in real time.

Tim Blackwell's Swarmusic is a system inspired by the behavior of insect swarms (Blackwell 2003). The individuals in Swarmusic, however, are not bees or termites, but musical events. Insect swarms have a remarkable ability to organize themselves despite the simplicity of each individual and despite being leaderless. This phenomenon is called self-organization, and Swarmusic demonstrates that these principles can also apply to music. A musical event in Swarmusic inhabits a music parameter space where each dimension corresponds to a musical variable. Events are attracted to each other and to events left behind by other swarms. And like real swarms, the individuals also take care not to bump into each other. As the events move around each other, constantly varying melodies, harmonies, and rhythms are produced. Attracting events captured from an external source enable human performers to interact with the swarm.

In technical terms, Swarmusic employs particle swarm optimization, an evolutionary computation technique whereby candidate solutions for a particular optimization problem are "flown" through the space of all possible solutions. Convergence toward a global solution is obtained by the attraction of each particle to the best solution attained by the swarm as a whole and the best solution achieved by that individual particle. The development of the particle swarm optimization technique mirrors other biologically inspired algorithms in a field that is known as swarm intelligence. The idea is to adapt models of self-organizing natural systems so that they may be applied to difficult problems, such as routing problems in telecommunications, to cite but one example.

A basic swarm model can be defined with three simple steering behaviors, which describe how an individual moves based on the positions and velocities of its nearby swarm-mates: *separation, align-*

ment, and *cohesion*. Whereas separation means to steer in order to avoid crowding local swarm-mates (Figure 5.12), alignment means to steer toward the average direction of local swarm-mates (Figure 5.13). Cohesion means to steer in order to move toward the average position of local swarm-mates (Figure 5.14).

Figure 5.12 Swarm separation behavior.

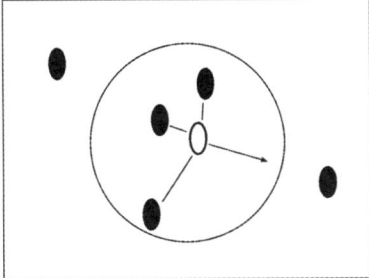

Figure 5.13 Swarm alignment behavior.

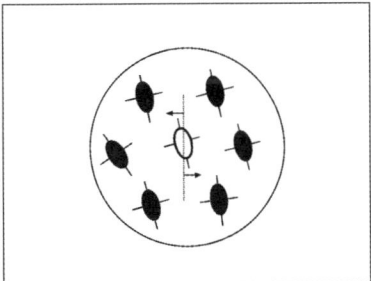

Figure 5.14 Swarm cohesion behavior.

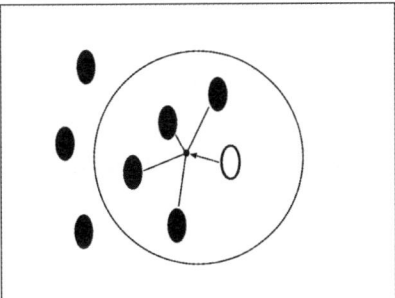

Each individual has direct access to a description of the whole scene, but swarms require that each individual react only to swarm-mates within a certain small neighborhood around itself. A distance and an angle characterize the neighborhood. Swarm-mates outside this local neighborhood are ignored. The neighborhood could be considered a model of limited perception (e.g., limited vision in foggy weather), but it is probably more correct to think of it as defining the region in which swarm-mates influence individual steering.

A group of improvising musicians might be subject to similar steering behavior, where the emergent structure would be musical forms. Musicians respond in an expressive way to the current musical environment, trying to match current parameters such as pitch range, dynamic level, and density of events. Periodically, the position of each particle is translated into musical notes or chords, which are played back to the musician a beat or so later. Just by following basic steering behavior, such as "move toward the center of the swarm" and "do not bump into any other members of the swarm," the software generates music. Consider an improvised melody where the succession of notes may move around a key center with a characteristic form. Melodic variations can be visualized as gradual changes in this form. Musical structure would then emerge from the swarm-like interaction of the participants. For example, particles of a musical swarm may interact with other particles by trying to cluster together without colliding and by moving toward one or more external attractors. The placement of notes in time gives a pattern, and notes may avoid collisions. There may be attraction to a beat, resulting in a simple organized pattern with an implied degree of collision avoidance.

There are three main processes in Swarmusic: *animation, interpretation*, and *scripting*. The heart of the animation process is the particle update algorithm. This algorithm is based on the dynamics of charged and neutral particles and consists of a set of equations that determine the acceleration of each particle in the swarm. (A detailed account of the animation algorithm can be found in Blackwell and Bentley 2002.) In short, each particle might experience one or more of four accelerations, indexed by k, as follows:

- $k = 1$: Attractive acceleration toward the center mass of the particle swarm
- $k = 2$: Attractive acceleration toward the center mass of the target swarm
- $k = 3$: Attractive acceleration toward a particular target
- $k = 4$: Repulsive acceleration (if charged) away from any other charged particle

A swarm might move in an *n*-dimensional space, but only three-dimensional position coordinates are used for the system's music space. The music space is constituted by musical events, each of which corresponds to a note played at a certain time and with a definite loudness. The three coordinates of the music space are loudness, pulse (or beat), and pitch (Figure 5.15). The pitch coordinate can be remapped onto different scales, such as major, minor, pentatonic, and so forth.

The interpretation process is responsible for mapping particle positions onto MIDI events and scheduling times. Each snapshot of the swarm after a completed update represents a succession of events played in some predetermined order and occupying a time interval equal to the sum of the individual times of each event. Any underlying rhythm can arise as an emergent property of the swarm, depending on the spatial relationship between the particles and not on the absolute position.

Information about timbre can be placed in the internal state of each particle. For example, different particles can correspond to different instruments, or spectral information parsed from captured events can be placed in the internal state, and this information can be used to adjust the parameters for a synthesizer.

Figure 5.15 An event in Swarmusic's music space corresponding to the note A3 played at loudness 120 (MIDI key velocity) and sounding at a time interval corresponding to a beat of 120 bpm after a preceding event.

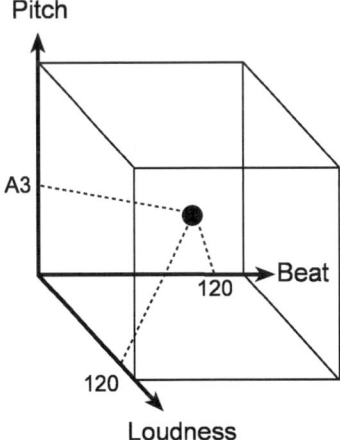

After interpretation, many control options exist for playback. For instance, events can be queued and played in block as a chord, or they can be queued and played in order of pitch, and so on.

The scripting process determines how the captured events are analyzed and used as strategies. External events can be either audio or MIDI. They are captured and parsed for pitch, loudness, duration, and time interval between events. The system examines these parameters and establishes the targets for the particle swarms. These targets are essentially other swarms, called target swarms, which are updated interactively by the performer.

The particle swarm interacts with a swarm of targets, where each target represents an external musical event. This interaction enables the swarm to respond to external events, where the target swarm provides a dynamic environment for the particle swarm. The targets influence particles, but targets are not influenced by the particles. The interaction generates melodies by associating musical parameters with the positions of the particles in the virtual swarm space. A second swarm of targets provides a representation of live music from an external source. Interactions between the target swarm and the particle swarm enable Swarmusic to respond to external events and to take part in a musical dialog.

A number of swarms are used in Swarmusic, each corresponding to a musical performer. Swarms themselves interact by a process known as stigmergy. For example, insects may interact directly by smell and also indirectly by making modifications to the environment that others respond to at a later time. This indirect or stigmergetic interaction is responsible for termite task coordination and nest building. In Swarmusic, each swarm leaves behind markers that become attractors for other swarms.

The system is intended to be controlled interactively, but it can function autonomously. In controlled interaction, the user can influence and direct the improvisations. In this case, the software interacts with a performer who plays a MIDI controller or an acoustic instrument with a microphone connected to the computer's MIDI or audio interface. In the case of an audio input, an event-capture routine uses pulse-height analysis to determine when a musical event, such as a single note or chord, has started or stopped and then channels the signal through a fast Fourier transform algorithm to determine its position in the musical space.

In the absence of control interaction, a script can be written to manage the swarms. For example, the system can begin by positioning the targets randomly in the target space. Then the swarms are released from a random position, and the particles are drawn toward the targets. Once the swarm center of mass is within a specified distance from the target center of mass, the targets are again randomized.

After the user specifies various parameters, such as initial central key and preferred scales, a performance starts with a few randomly generated notes. Subsequent notes are then generated within the music space according to the swarming model and user settings. The MIDI data associated with each note is sent to a synthesizer.

■ 5.6 FURTHER READING

For information about the applications of artificial intelligence in music, the following publications present collections of fundamental texts written by top researchers in the field:

- M. Balaban, K. Ebcioglu, and O. Laske, eds. (1992), *Understanding Music with AI* (Cambridge, MA: MIT Press). This book is relatively old but presents a number of important fundamental chapters.

- E. R. Miranda, ed. (2000), *Readings in Music and Artificial Intelligence* (Amsterdam: Harwood Academic). This book also introduces a number of fundamental issues in music and AI. It is more digestible than the first one because it was intended to introduce students and musicians to the field. Roger Dannemberg's original text on dynamic programming, which was presented extensively in this chapter, can be found in this book.

- C. Anagnostopoulou, M. Ferrand, and A. Smaill, eds. (2002), *Music and Artificial Intelligence*, Proceedings of the 2nd International Conference, ICMAI 2002, Lecture Notes on Artificial Intelligence 2445 (Berlin: Springer-Verlag). This more recent publication includes proceedings of ICMAI, the only international conference dedicated entirely to the topic of AI and music. It features interesting papers on a number of topics, mostly on pattern matching of symbolic musical information.

As for the topic on interactive music systems, we recommend:

- R. Rowe (1993), *Interactive Music Systems* (Cambridge, MA: MIT Press). This book introduces the Cypher system and provided inspiration for most of the concepts on interactivity discussed in this chapter. A fundamental reading for those interested in musical interaction.

- T. Winkler (1998), *Composing Interactive Music* (Cambridge, MA: MIT Press). This is a good hands-on introduction to implementing interactive systems using Max. It presents a good introduction to Max programming. Note, however, that this book focuses on Max only; that is, on MIDI-based processing. It does not touch upon audio processing (MSP) issues.
- R. Rowe (2001), *Machine Musicianship* (Cambridge, MA: MIT Press). This book can be considered a follow-up of Rowe's previous book. It is more general in that it discusses a number of methods for implementing musical processes such as segmentation, pattern processing, and interactive improvisation in computer programs.
- R. Dean (2003), *Hyperimprovisation: Computer-Interactive Sound Improvisation* (Middleton, WI: A-R Editions). This publication constitutes an excellent complementary reading to this book for those interested in the potentials of computer-interactive sound improvisation. It is also part of the Computer Music and Digital Audio Series.

Apart from the above books, there have been a number of papers discussing the issue of intelligent musical instruments in various journals, most notably in *Computer Music Journal, Journal of New Music Research*, and *Organised Sound*. The proceedings of the various editions of the *International Computer Music Conference* (ICMC) often feature papers on this topic.

Epilogue

This book presents the art of new digital instrument design. It introduces a number of developments on new types of controllers for sound and music and their underlying technology, with a view to informing researchers and musicians interested in designing new digital musical instruments. It also discusses the possibility of using biosignals to control sound and music and the provision of artificial intelligence to render such new musical instruments interactive.

The difficulty with writing a pioneering book on emerging musical practices and associated technology is avoiding the danger of rapid obsolescence. We started writing this book approximately three years ago, and the final result is substantially different from the original proposal. We thank our commissioning editor for granting us such flexibility.

It is worth mentioning that since we completed the book, a number of interesting developments have emerged in the field of collaborative and Web-based controllers, some of which are documented in two recent journal issues: *Contemporary Music Review*, 24(6), special issue, *Internet Music*; and *Organised Sound*, 10(3), dedicated to the topic of networked music.

At the beginning of the book we suggested that the art of new digital instrument design involves more than engineering clever audio signal processing or synthesis algorithms. It also requires careful thinking about how such algorithms could be controlled by the performers. And in the case of an interactive instrument, much consideration is required as to how to furnish such an instrument with intelligence for musical interaction. This book is intended to be a source of inspiration and technical information for the development of exciting new digital musical instruments for control and interaction beyond the piano-like keyboard paradigm.

References

Note: Some citations refer to conference proceedings, which do not always have page numbers.

Adrian, E. D., and Matthews, B. H. C. (1934). "The Berger Rhythm: Potential Changes from the Occipital Lobes in Man." *Brain*, 57(4):355–85.

Allison, J., and Place, T. (2003). "SensorBox: A Practical Audio Interface for Gestural Performance." *Proceedings of the 2003 International Conference on New Interfaces for Musical Expression (NIME'03)*, Montreal, Canada, pp. 208–9. Montreal: McGill University.

Anderson, C., and Sijercic, Z. (1996). "Classification of EEG Signals from Four Subjects during Five Mental Tasks." *Solving Engineering Problems with Neural Networks: Proceedings of the Conference on Engineering Applications in Neural Networks (EANN'96)*, London, pp. 307–414. London: King's College and Kingston University.

Arfib, D., Couturier, J.-M., Kessus, L., and Verfaille, V. (2002). "Strategies of Mapping between Gesture Data and Synthesis Model Parameters using Perceptual Spaces." *Organised Sound*, 7(2):127–44.

Auzet, R. (2000). "Gesture-Following Devices for Percussionists." In M. Wanderley and M. Battier (Eds.), *Trends in Gestural Control of Music*. Paris: IRCAM—Centre Pompidou, pp. 391–97.

Bahn, C., and Trueman, D. (2001). "Interface: Electronic Chamber Ensemble." *Online Proceedings of CHI 2001 Workshop of New Interfaces for Musical Expression*, Seattle, WA. http://hct.ece.ubc.ca/nime/2001/ (accessed 12 October 2005).

Bailey, N., Purvis, A., Bowler, I. W., and Manning, P. D. (1993). "Applications of the Phase Vocoder in the Control of Real-Time Electronic Musical Instruments." *Interface* 22:259–75.

Balakrishnan, R., Fitzmaurice, G., Kurtenbach, G., and Singh, K. (1999). "Exploring Interactive Curve and Surface Manipulation Using a Bend and Twist Sensitive Input Strip." *Proceedings of the*

1999 Symposium on Interactive 3D Graphics, Atlanta, GA, pp. 111–18. New York: ACM Press.

Bauer, W., and Foss, B. (1992). "GAMS: An Integrated Media Controller System." *Computer Music Journal*, 16(1):19–24.

Bayle, F. (1993). *Musique acousmatique*. Paris: INA-GRM/Buchet-Chastel.

Beauregard, G. (1991). "Rethinking the Design of Wind Controllers." Master's thesis, Dartmouth College.

Bencina, R. (2005). "The Metasurface: Applying Natural Neighbor Interpolation to Two-to-many Mapping." *Proceedings of the 2005 International Conference on New Interfaces for Musical Expression (NIME'05)*, Vancouver, Canada, pp. 101–4. Vancouver: University of British Columbia.

Berger, H. (1929). "Über das Elektrenkephalogramm des Menschen." *Archiv für Psychiatrie und Nervenkrankheiten*, 87(1929):527–70.

Berger, H. (1969). "On the Electroencephalogram of Man." *The Fourteen Original Reports on the Human Electroencephalogram, Electroencephalography and Clinical Neurophysiology*, Supplement No. 28. Amsterdam: Elsevier.

Bertini, G., and Carosi, P. (1992). "Light Baton: A System for Conducting Computer Music Performance." *Proceedings of the 1992 International Computer Music Conference (ICMC'92)*, San Jose, CA, pp. 73–76. San Francisco: International Computer Music Association.

Bevilacqua, F., Muller, R., and Schnell, N. (2005). "MnM: A Mzx/MSP Mapping Toolbox." *Proceedings of the 2005 International Conference on New Interfaces for Musical Expression (NIME'05)*, Vancouver, Canada, pp. 85–88. Vancouver: University of British Columbia.

Biles, J. A. (2002). "GenJam: Evolutionary Computation Gets a Gig." *Proceedings of the 2002 Conference for Information Technology Curriculum*. Rochester: Society for Information Technology Generation. http://www.it.rit.edu/~jab/CITC3/paper.html (accessed 17 December 2005).

Birbaumer, N., Ghanayin, N., Hinterberger, T., Iversen, I., Kotchoubey, B., Kubler, A., Perelmeouter, J., Taub, E., and Flor, H. (1999). "A Spelling Device for the Paralysed." *Nature*, 398:297–98.

Birnbaum, D., Fiebrink, R., Malloch, J., and Wanderley, M. M. (2005). "Towards a Dimension Space for Musical Devices." *Proceedings of the 2005 International Conference on New Interfaces for Musical Expression (NIME'05)*, Vancouver, Canada, pp. 192–95. Vancouver: University of British Columbia.

Bishop, C. M. (1995). *Neural Networks for Pattern Recognition*. Oxford: Oxford University Press.

Blackwell, T. M. (2003). "Self-organising Music with Swarms." *Newsletter for the Society for the Study of Artificial Intelligence and Simulation of Behaviour*, 113:5.

Blackwell, T. M., and Bentley, P. J. (2002). "Improvised Music with Swarms." *Proceedings of the 2002 Congress on Evolutionary Computation*, Honolulu, HI, pp. 1462–67. Washington: IEEE Computer Society.

Blaine, T., and Fels, S. (2003). "Contexts of Collaborative Musical Experiences." *Proceedings of the 2003 International Conference on New Interfaces for Musical Expression—NIME 03*, Montreal, Canada, pp. 129–34.

Blaine, T., and Perkins, T. (2000). "Jam-O-Drum: A Study in Interaction Design." *Proceedings of the ACM Conference on Designing Interactive Systems*, New York. New York: ACM Press.

Bongers, B. (1998a). "An Interview with Sensorband." *Computer Music Journal*, 22(1):13–24.

Bongers, B. (1998b). "Tactual Display of Sound Properties in Electronic Musical Instruments." *Displays*, 18:129–33.

Bongers, B. (2000). "Physical Interfaces in the Electronic Arts Interaction Theory and Interfacing Techniques for Real-time Performance." In M. Wanderley and M. Battier (Eds.), *Trends in Gestural Control of Music*. Paris: IRCAM—Centre Pompidou, pp. 41–70.

Bongers, B., and Harris, J. (2002). "A Structured Instrument Design Approach: The Video-Organ." *Proceedings of the 2002 International Conference on New Interfaces for Musical Expression (NIME'02)*, Dublin, Ireland, pp. 86–91. Dublin: Media Lab Europe.

Bowler, I., Manning, P., Purvis, A., and Bailey, N. (1990). "New Techniques for a Real-Time Phase Vocoder." *Proceedings of the 1990 International Computer Music Conference*. Glasgow, Scotland, pp. 178–80. San Francisco: ICMA.

Bromwich, M. A. (1997). "The Metabone: An Interactive Sensory Control Mechanism for Virtuoso Trombone." *Proceedings of the 1997 International Computer Music Conference (ICMC'97)*, Thessaloniki, Greece, pp. 473–75. San Francisco: ICMA.

Bromwich, M. A., and Wilson, J. (1998). "Bodycoder: A SensoEr Suit and Vocal Performance Mechanism for Real-time Performance." *Proceedings of the 1998 International Computer Music Conference*, Ann Arbor, MI, pp. 292–95. San Francisco: ICMA.

Bugnacki, M., Pyle, J., and Emerald, P. (2001). "A Micromachined Thermal Accelerometer for Motion, Inclination and Vibration Measurement." *Sensors Online*, vol. 18, no. 6. http://www.sensorsmag.com/articles/0601/index.htm (accessed 17 October 2005).

Burdea, G. (1996). *Force and Touch Feedback for Virtual Reality*. John Wiley and Sons.

Burdea, G., and Coiffet, P. (2003). *Virtual Reality Technology*. 2nd ed. John Wiley and Sons.

Burtner, M. (2002). "Noisegate 76 for Metasaxophone: Composition and Performance Considerations of a New Computer Music Controllers." *Proceedings of the 2002 International Conference on New Interfaces for Musical Expression (NIME'02)*, Dublin, Ireland, pp. 71–76. Dublin: Media Lab Europe.

Buxton, W., Dannenberg, R., and Vercoe, B. (1986). "The Computer as Accompanist." *Proceedings of Conference on Computer and Human Interaction—CHI'86*, Boston, MA, pp. 41–43. New York: ACM Press.

Buxton, W., Reeves, W., Fedorkow, G., Smith, K. C., and Baecker, R. (1980). "A Microcomputer-based Conducting System." *Computer Music Journal*, 4(1), 8–21.

Cadoz, C. (1988). "Instrumental Gesture and Music Composition." *Proceedings of the 1988 International Computer Music Conference (ICMC'88)*, Cologne, Germany, pp. 1–12. San Francisco: ICMA.

Cadoz, C., Lisowski, L., and Florens, J. L. (1990). "A Modular Feedback Keyboard Design." *Computer Music Journal*, 14(2):47–51.

Cadoz, C., Luciani, A., and Florens, J. L. (1984). "Responsive Input Devices and Sound Synthesis by Simulation of Instrumental Mechanisms: The CORDIS System." *Computer Music Journal*, 8(3):60–73.

Cadoz, C., Luciani, A., Florens, J. L., and Castagné, N. (2003). "ACROE-ICA: Artistic Creation and Computer Interactive Multisensory Simulation Force Feedback Gesture Transducers." *Proceedings of the 2003 International Conference on New Interfaces for Musical Expression (NIME '03)*, Montreal, Canada, pp. 235–46. Montreal: McGill University.

Cadoz, C., and Wanderley, M. M. (2000). "Gesture-Music," In M. Wanderley and M. Bartier (Eds.), *Trends in Gestural Control of Music*. Paris: IRCAM-Centre Georges Pompidou, pp. 71–93.

Camurri, A. (1995). "Interactive Dance/Music Systems." *Proceedings of the 1995 International Computer Music Conference (ICMC'95)*, Banff, Canada, pp. 245–52. San Francisco: ICMA.

Cannon, C., Hughes, S., and O'Modhrain, S. (2003). "EpipE: Exploration of the Uilleann Pipes as a Potential Controller for Computer-Based Music." *Proceedings of the 2003 International Conference on New Interfaces for Musical Expression (NIME'03)*, Montreal, Canada, pp. 3–8. Montreal: McGill University.

Cardoso, J.-F. (1999). "High-order Contrasts for Independent Component Analysis." *Neural Computation*, 11(1):157–92.

Cariou, B. (1994). "The aXi0 MIDI Controller." *Proceedings of the 1994 International Computer Music Conference (ICMC'94)*, Aarhus, Denmark, pp. 163–66. San Francisco: ICMA.

Carr, J. J. (1993). *Sensors and Circuits: Sensors, Transducers, and Supporting Circuits for Electronic Instrumentation, Measurement, and Control.* Upper Saddle River, NJ: Prentice-Hall.

Carr, J. J. (1997). *Electronic Circuit Guidebook.* Vol. 1, *Sensors.* Indianapolis: Prompt Publications.

Chadabe, J. (1997). *Electric Sound: The Past and Promise of Electronic Music.* Upper Saddle River, NJ: Prentice-Hall.

Chadabe, J. (2002). "The Limitations of Mapping as a Structural Descriptive in Electronic Musical Instruments." *Proceedings of the 2002 International Conference on New Interfaces for Musical Expression (NIME'02)*, Dublin, Ireland, pp. XXX. Dublin: Media Lab Europe.

Choi, I. (2000). "Gestural Primitives and the Context for Computational Processing in an Interactive Performance System." In M. Wanderley and M. Battier (Eds.), *Trends in Gestural Control of Music.* Paris: IRCAM—Centre Pompidou, pp. 139–72.

Choi, I., and Ricci, C. (1997). "Foot-mounted Gesture Detection and Its Application in a Virtual Environment." *Proceedings of the 1997 IEEE International Conference on Systems, Man and Cybernetics*, Orlando, FL, pp. 5:4248–53. Washington, DC: IEEE Computer Society.

Collinge, D. J., and Parkinson, S. M. (1988). "The Oculus Ranae." *Proceedings of the 1988 International Computer Music Conference (ICMC'88)*, Cologne, Germany. San Francisco: ICMA, pp. 15–19.

Collins, N. (1991). "Low Brass: The Evolution of Trombone-propelled Electronics." *Leonardo Music Journal*, 1(1):41–44.

Collins, N. (2003). "Generative Music and Laptop Performance." *Contemporary Music Review*, 22(4):67–79.

Cook, P. (1992). "A Meta-wind-instrument Physical Model, and a Meta-controller for Real Time Performance Control." *Proceedings of the 1992 International Computer Music Conference (ICMC'92)*, San Jose, CA, pp. 273–76. San Francisco: ICMA.

Cook, P. (2001). "Principles for Designing Computer Music Controllers." *On-line Proceedings of New Interfaces for Musical Expression Workshop (NIME'01)*, Seattle, WA, 2001. New York: ACM Press.

Cook, P. (2002). *Real Sound Synthesis for Interactive Applications.* Natick, MA: A. K. Peters.

Cook, P., and Morrill, D. (1989). "Hardware, Software, and Compositional Tools for a Real Time Improvised Solo Trumpet Work." *Proceedings of the International Computer Music Conference (ICMC'89)*, Ohio. San Francisco: ICMA.

Cook, P., and Scavone, G. (1999). "The Synthesis Toolkit (STK)." *Proceedings of the 1999 International Computer Music Conference (ICMC'99)*, Beijing, China, pp. 164–66. San Francisco: ICMA.

Cope, D. (1991). *Computers and Musical Style*. Madison, WI: A-R Editions.

Cope, D. (1996). *Experiments in Musical Intelligence*. Madison, WI: A-R Editions.

Cope, D. (2000). *The Algorithmic Composer*. Madison, WI: A-R Editions.

Couturier, J.-M., and Arfib, D. (2003). "Pointing Fingers: Using Multiple Direct Interactions with Visual Objects to Perform Music." *Proceedings of the 2003 International Conference on New Interfaces for Musical Expression (NIME'03)*, Montreal, Canada, pp. 184–87. Montreal: McGill University.

D'Arcangelo, G. (2001). "Creating Contexts of Creativity: Musical Composition with Modular Components." *Proceedings of New Interfaces for Musical Expression Workshop (NIME'01)*, Seattle, WA, 2001. New York: ACM Press.

Daryanani, G. (1976). *Principles of Active Network Synthesis and Design*. New York: John Wiley and Sons.

Dannenberg, R. (2000). "Dynamic Programming for Interactive Music Systems." In E. R. Miranda (Ed.), *Readings in Music and Artificial Intelligence*. Amsterdam: Harwood Academic, pp. 189–206.

Dannenberg, R., and Bookstein, K. (1991). "Practical Aspects of a MIDI Conducting System." *Proceedings of the 1991 International Computer Music Conference (ICMC'91)*, Montreal, Canada, pp. 537–40. Montreal: McGill University.

Darwin, C. (1859). *On the Origin of Species by Means of Natural Selection*. London: John Murray.

da Silva, A. R., Wanderley, M. M., and Scavone, G. (2005). "On the Use of Flute Air Jet as a Musical Control Variable." *Proceedings of the 2005 International Conference on New Interfaces for Musical Expression (NIME'05)*, Vancouver, Canada. Vancouver: University of British Columbia.

Davidson, J. W. (1993). "Visual Perception of Performance Manner in the Movements of Solo Musicians." *Psychology of Music*, 21: 103–13.

Davidson, J. W. (1994). "Expressive Movements in Musical Performance." *Conference Proceedings of the Third International Conference on Music Cognition* (ESCOM), Liege, Belgium, pp. 327–29. Liege: ESCOM.

Dawkins, R. (1986). *The Blind Watchmaker*. New York: Norton.

Dean, R. (2003). *Hyperimprovisation: Computer-interactive Sound Improvisation*. Middleton, WI: A-R Editions.

de Cecco, M., Lindeman, E., and Puckette, M. (1992). "The IRCAM Signal Processing Workstation Prototyping Environment." *Proceedings of SIGCHI Conference on Human Factors in Computing Systems*, Monterey, CA, pp. 639–40.

Delalande, F. (1988). "La gestique de Gould: Elements pour une semiologie du geste musical." In G. Guertin (Ed.), *Glenn Gould, Pluriel*. Montreal: Louise Courteau Editrice, pp. 83–111.

de Laubier, S. (1998). "The Meta-instrument." *Computer Music Journal*, 22(1):25–29.

de Laubier, S. (2000). "The Méta-instrument: How the Project Started." In M. Wanderley and M. Battier (Eds.), *Trends in Gestural Control of Music*. Paris: IRCAM—Centre Pompidou, pp. 175–82.

Depalle, P., Tassart, S., and Wanderley, M. (1997). "Instruments virtuels." *Résonance*, 12:5–8.

Di Giugno, G., and Armand, J. P. (1991). "Studio Report IRIS." *Proceedings of the IX Colloquio di Informatica Musicale*, Genoa, Italy, pp. 358–62. Genoa: Dist. Università di Genova.

Di Giugno, G., Kott, J., and Gerzso, A. (1981). "Progess Report on the 4X Machine and Its Use." *Proceedings of the International Computer Music Conference*, Denton, TX. San Francisco: ICMA.

Dobrian, C., and Bevilacqua, F. (2003). "Gestural Control of Music Using the Vicon 8 Motion Capture System." *NIME 2003 Online Proceedings*, www.music.mcgill.ca/musictech/nime/onlineproceedings/TOC.html (accessed 12 August 2005).

Dodge, C., and Jerse, T. (1985). *Computer Music: Synthesis, Composition and Performance*. New York: Schirmer Books.

Dodge, C., and Jerse, T. (1997). *Computer Music: Synthesis, Composition and Performance*. 2nd edition. New York: Schirmer Books.

Doornbusch, P. (2002). "Composers' Views on Mapping in Algorithmic Composition." *Organised Sound*, 7(2):145–56.

Duncan, A. (2001). "EEG Pattern Recognition for the Brain-computer Musical Interface." Ph.D. diss., University of Glasgow.

Egozy, E. B. (1995). "Deriving Musical Control Features from a Real-time Timbre Analysis of the Clarinet." Master's thesis, Massachusetts Institute of Technology.

Favilla, S. (1994). "The LDR Controller." *Proceedings of the 1994 International Computer Music Conference (ICMC'94)*, Aarhus, Denmark, pp. 177–80. San Francisco: ICMA.

Fels, S. (1994). "Glove Talk II: Mapping Hand Gestures to Speech Using Neural Networks." Ph.D. diss., University of Toronto.

Fels, S., Gadd, A., and Mulder, A. (2002). "Mapping Transparency through Metaphor: Towards More Expressive Musical Instruments." *Organised Sound*, 7(2):109–26.

Fels, S., Kaastra, L., Takahashi, S., and McCaig, G. (2004). "Evolving Tooka: from Experiment to Instrument." *Proceedings of the 2004 International Conference on New Interfaces for Musical Expression (NIME'04)*, Hamamatsu, Japan, pp. 1–6. Hamamatsu: Shizuoka University of Art and Culture.

Fels, S., and Vogt, F. (2002). "Tooka: Exploration of Two Person Instruments." *Proceedings of the 2002 International Conference on New Interfaces for Musical Expression (NIME'02)*, Dublin, Ireland, pp. 116–21. Dublin: Media Lab Europe.

Feyereisen, P., and Lannoy, J.-D. de (1991). *Gestures and Speech*. Cambridge: Cambridge University Press.

Fléty, E. (2000). "3D Gesture Acquisition Using Ultrasonic Sensors." In M. Wanderley and M. Battier (Eds.), *Trends in Gestural Control of Music*. Paris: IRCAM—Centre Pompidou, pp. 193–207.

Fléty, E. (2001). "Interactive Devices for Gestural Acquisition in Musical Live Performance Context." *Proceedings of the 5th World Multi-conference on Systemics, Cybernetics and Informatics (SCI 2001)*, Orlando, FL, pp. 535–40. Orlando, FL: International Institute of Informatics and Systemics.

Florens, J. L. (1978). "Coupleur gestuel interactif pour la commande et le contrôle de sons synthétisés en temps-réel." Ph.D. diss., Institut National Polytechnique de Grenoble.

Florens, J. L., and Henry, C. (2001). "Bowed String Synthesis with Force-Feedback Gesture Interaction." *Proceedings of the 2001 International Computer Music Conference (ICMC01)*, Havana, Cuba, pp. 115–18. San Francisco: ICMA.

Florens, J. L., Razafindrakoto, A., Luciani, A., and Cadoz, C. (1986). "Optimized Real-time Simulation of Objects for Musical Synthesis and Animated Image Synthesis." *Proceedings of the 1986 International Computer Music Conference (ICMC'86)*, The Hague, Netherlands, pp. 65–70. San Francisco: ICMA.

Fraden, J. (2004). *Handbook of Modern Sensors: Physics, Design and Applications*. 3rd ed. London: Springer-Verlag.

Fuchs, P. (1999). *Les interfaces de la réalité virtuelle*. Paris: AJIIMD/Presses de l'Ecole des Mines de Paris.

Garrett, P. H. (1994). *Advanced Instrumentation and Computer I/O Design: Real-time System Computer Interface Engineering*. Washington, DC: IEEE Computer Society.

Gaye, L., Mazé, R., and Holmquist, L. E. (2003). "Sonic City: The Urban Environment as a Musical Interface." *Proceedings of the 2003 International Conference on New Interfaces for Musical Expression (NIME'03)*, Montreal, Canada, pp. 109–15. Montreal: McGill University.

Gillespie, B. (1992a). "Dynamical Modeling of the Grand Piano Action." *Proceedings of the 1992 International Computer Music Conference (ICMC'92)*, San Jose, CA, pp. 447–448. San Francisco: ICMA.

Gillespie, B. (1992b). "The Touchback Keyboard." *Proceedings of the 1992 International Computer Music Conference (ICMC'92)*, San Jose, CA, pp. 77–80. San Francisco: ICMA.

Gillespie, B. (1999a). "Haptics." In P. Cook (Ed.), *Music, Cognition and Computerized Sound: An Introduction to Psychoacoustics.* Cambridge, MA: MIT Press, pp. 229–45.

Gillespie, B. (1999b). "Haptics in Manipulation." In P. Cook (Ed.), *Music, Cognition and Computerized Sound: An Introduction to Psychoacoustics.* Cambridge, MA: MIT Press, pp. 247–60.

Goldin-Meadow, S. (2003). *Hearing Gesture: How Our Hands Help Us Think.* Cambridge, MA: Harvard University Press.

Goncharova, I. I., and Barlow, J. S. (1990). "Changes in EEG Mean Frequency and Spectral Purity during Spontaneous Alpha Blocking." *Electroencephalography and Clinical Neurophysiology*, 76:197–204.

Goto, S. (2000). "Virtual Musical Instruments: Technological Aspects and Interactive Performance Issues." In M. Wanderley and M. Battier (Eds.), *Trends in Gestural Control of Music.* Paris: IRCAM—Centre Pompidou, pp. 217–29.

Goudeseune, C. (2001). "Composing with Parameters for Synthetic Instruments." Ph.D. diss., University of Illinois at Urbana-Champaign.

Goudeseune, C. (2002). "Interpolated Mappings for Musical Instruments." *Organised Sound*, 7(2):85–96.

Griffith, N., and Fernström, M. (1998). "LiteFoot: A Floor Space for Recording Dance and Controlling Media." *Proceedings of the 1998 International Computer Music Conference (ICMC'98)*, Ann Arbor, MI, pp. 475–81. San Francisco: ICMA.

Guiard, Y. (1987). "Asymmetric Division of Labor in Human Skilled Bimanual Action: The Kinematic Chain as a Model." *Journal of Motor Behavior*, 19(4):486–517.

Gunther, E., Davenport, G., and O'Modrain, S. (2002). "Cutaneous Grooves: Composing for the Sense of Touch." *Proceedings of the 2002 International Conference on New Interfaces for Musical Expression (NIME'02)*, Dublin, Ireland, pp. 37–42. Dublin: Media Lab Europe.

Gurevich, M., and von Muehlen, S. (2001). "The Accordiatron: A MIDI Controller For Interactive Music." *Proceedings of New Interfaces for Musical Expression Workshop (NIME'01)*, Seattle, WA, 2001. New York: AMC Press.

Gurney, K. (1997). *An Introduction to Neural Networks.* London: Routledge.

Haflich, S., and Burns, M. (1983). "Following a Conductor: the Engineering of an Input Device." *Proceedings of the International Computer Music Conference (ICMC'83)*, Rochester, NY. San Francisco: ICMA.

Haken, L., Abdullah, R., and Smart, M. (1992). "The Continuum: A Continuous Music Keyboard." *Proceedings of the 1992 International Computer Music Conference (ICMC'92)*, San Jose, CA, pp. 81–84. San Francisco: ICMA.

Haken, L., Tellman, E., and Wolfe, P. (1998). "An Indiscrete Music Keyboard." *Computer Music Journal*, 22(1):30–48.

Hamming, R. W. (1989). *Digital Filters.* Prentice Hall Signal Processing Series. Upper Saddle River, NJ, Prentice Hall.

Hapipis, T. (2005). "Interacting with a Singing Computer by Means of a Lip-reading System." Master's thesis, University of Plymouth.

Hasan, L., Paradiso, J., and Yu, N. (2002). "The Termenova: A Hybrid Free-gesture Interface." *Proceedings of the 2002 International Conference on New Interfaces for Musical Expression (NIME'02)*, Dublin, Ireland, pp. 122–27. Dublin: Media Lab Europe.

Hatanaka, M. (2003). "Ergonomic Design of a Portable Musical Instrument." *Proceedings of the 2003 International Conference on New Interfaces for Musical Expression (NIME'03)*, Montreal, Canada, pp. 77–82. Montreal: McGill University.

Hayward, V., and Armstrong, B. (2000). "A New Computational Model of Friction Applied to Haptic Rendering." In P. Corke and J. Trevelyan (Eds.), *Experimental Robotics VI.* New York: Springer Verlag, pp. 404–12.

Hewitt, D., and Stevenson, I. (2003). "E-Mic: Extended Mic-stand Interface Controller." *Proceedings of the 2003 International Conference on New Interfaces for Musical Expression (NIME'03)*, Montreal, Canada, pp. 122–28. Montreal: McGill University.

Hjorth, B. (1970). "EEG Analysis Based on Time Domain Properties." *Electroencephalography and Clinical Neurophysiology*, 29:306–10.

Hsiao, K.-y., and Paradiso, J. (1999). "A New Continuous Multimodal Musical Controller using Wireless Magnetic Tags." *Proceedings of the 1999 International Computer Music Conference (ICMC'99)*, Beijing, China, pp. 24–27. San Francisco: ICMA.

Hughes, S., Cannon, C., and O'Modhrain, S. (2004). "Epipe: A Novel Electronic Woodwind Controller." *Proceedings of the 2004 International Conference on New Interfaces for Musical Expression (NIME'04)*, Hamamatsu, Japan. Hamamatsu: Shizuoka University of Arts and Culture.

Hughes, S., Oakley, I., and O'Modhrain, S. (2004). "MESH: Supporting Mobile Multi-modal Interfaces." Paper presented at *UIST 04 Conference*, Santa Fe, NM.

Hummels, C., Smets, G., and Overbeeke, K. (1998). "An Intuitive Two-handed Gestural Interface for Computer Supported Product Design." In I. Wachsmuth and M. Fröhlich (Eds.), *Gesture and Sign Language in Human-computer Interaction: Proceedings of the II Gesture Workshop.* Heidelberg: Springer-Verlag, pp. 197–208.

Hunt, A. (1999). "Radical Musical Interfaces for Real-time Musical Control." Ph.D. diss., University of York.

Hunt, A., and Kirk, R. (2000). "Mapping Strategies for Musical Performance." In M. Wanderley and M. Battier (Eds.), *Trends in Gestural Control of Music.* Paris: IRCAM—Centre Pompidou, pp. 231–58.

Hunt, A., and Wanderley, M. M. (2002). "Mapping Performer Parameters to Synthesis Engines." *Organised Sound*, 7(2):97–108.

Hunt, A., Wanderley, M. M., and Kirk, R. (2000). "Towards a Model for Instrumental Mapping in Expert Musical Interactions." *Proceedings of the 2000 International Computer Music Conference (ICMC 2000),* Berlin, Germany, pp. 209–212. San Francisco: ICMA.

Hunt, A., Wanderley, M. M., and Paradiso, M. (2003). "The Importance of Mapping in Electronic Instrument Design." *Journal of New Music Research*, 32(4):429–40.

Huott, R. (2002). "An Interface for Precise Musical Control." *Proceedings of the 2002 International Conference on New Interfaces for Musical Expression (NIME'02)*, Dublin, Ireland, pp. 1–5. Dublin: Media Lab Europe.

Hurbain. P. (2004). "Demystifying the Sharp IR Ranger." Acroname Articles Online, www.acroname.com/robotics/info/articles/sharp/sharp.html (accessed 29 October 2004).

Iazzetta, F. (2000). "Meaning in Musical Gesture." In M. Wanderley and M. Battier (Eds.), *Trends in Gestural Control of Music.* Paris: IRCAM—Centre Pompidou, pp. 259–68.

Ilmonen, T., and Takala, T. (1999). "Conductor Following with Artificial Neural Networks." *Proceedings of the 1999 International Computer Music Conference (ICMC'99)*, Beijing, China, pp. 367–70. San Francisco: ICMA.

Impett, J. (1994). "A Meta-Trumpet(er)." *Proceedings of the 1994 International Computer Music Conference (ICMC'94)*, Aarhus, Denmark, pp. 147–50. San Francisco: ICMA.

Jensenius, A. R., Godøy, R. I., and Wanderley, M. M. (2005). "Developing Tools for Studying Musical Gestures Within the Max/MSP/Jitter Environment." *Proceedings of the 2005 International Com-

puter Music Conference (ICMC'05), Barcelona, Spain, pp. 282–85. San Francisco: ICMA.

Jensenius, A. R., Koehly, R., and Wanderley, M. M. (2005). "Building Low-Cost Music Controllers." *Proceedings of the 2005 International Conference on Computer Music Modeling and Retrieval (CMMR05)*, Pisa, Italy, pp. 252–56. San Francisco: ICMA.

Johnstone, E. (1985). "The Rolky: A Poly-touch Controller for Electronic Music." *Proceedings of the 1985 International Computer Music Conference (ICMC'85)*, Burnaby, Canada, pp. 291–95. San Francisco: ICMA.

Johnstone, E. (1991). "A MIDI Foot Controller: The PodoBoard." *Proceedings of the 1991 International Computer Music Conference (ICMC'91)*, Montreal, Canada, pp. 123–26. San Francisco: ICMA.

Jordà, S. (2002). "Afasia: The Ultimate Homeric One-man-multimedia-band." *Proceedings of the 2002 International Conference on New Interfaces for Musical Expression (NIME'02)*, Dublin, Ireland, pp. 132–37. Dublin: Media Lab Europe.

Jordà, S. (2004). "Digital Instruments and Players, Part I: Efficiency and Apprenticeship." *Proceedings of the 2004 International Conference on New Interfaces for Musical Expression (NIME'04)*, Hamamatsu, Japan, pp. 59–63. Hamamatsu: Shizuoka University of Arts and Culture.

Jordà, S. (2005). "Multi-user Instruments: Models, Examples and Promises." *Proceedings of the 2005 International Conference on New Interfaces for Musical Expression (NIME'05),* Vancouver, Canada, pp. 23–26. Vancouver: University of British Columbia.

Kanamori, T., Katayose, H., Simura, S., and Inokuchi, S. (1993). "Gesture Sensor in Virtual Performer." *Proceedings of the 1993 International Computer Music Conference (ICMC'93)*, Tokyo, Japan, pp. 127–29. San Francisco: ICMA.

Kanamori, T., Katayose, H., Aono, Y., Inokuchi, S. and Sakaguchi, T. (1995). "Sensor Integration for Interactive Digital Art." *Proceedings of the 1995 International Computer Music Conference (ICMC'95)*, Banff, Canada, pp. 265–68. San Francisco: International Computer Music Association.

Kay, S. M. (1988). *Modern Spectral Estimation.* Upper Saddle River, NJ. Prentice Hall.

Keane, D., and Gross, P. (1989). "The MIDI Baton." *Proceedings of the 1989 International Computer Music Conference (ICMC'89)*, Columbus, OH, pp. 151–54. San Francisco: ICMA.

Kendon, A. (2004). *Gesture: Visible Action as Utterance.* Cambridge and New York: Cambridge University Press.

Koehly, R. (2005). "A Study of Various Technologies for Home-made Sensors." Masters' thesis. ACROE, Grenoble, France.

Kolesnik, P. (2004). "Conducting Gesture Recognition, Analysis and Performance System." Master's thesis, McGill University.

Kolesnik, P., and Wanderley, M. M. (2004). "Recognition, Analysis and Performance with Expressive Conducting Gestures." *Proceedings of the 2004 International Computer Music Conference (ICMC'04)*, Miami, FL, pp. 572–75. San Francisco: ICMA.

Kurtenbach, G., and Hulteen, E. (1990). "Gestures in Human Communication." In B. Laurel (Ed.), *The Art of Human-computer Interface Design*. Reading, PA: Addison-Wesley, pp. 309–17.

Laibowitz, M. (2003). "BASIS: A Genesis in Musical Interfaces." *Proceedings of the 2003 International Conference on New Interfaces for Musical Expression (NIME'03)*, Montreal, Canada, pp. 216–17. Montreal: McGill University.

Lee, M., and Wessel, D. (1992). "Connectionist Models for Real-time Control of Synthesis and Compositional Algorithms." *Proceedings of the 1992 International Computer Music Conference (ICMC'92)*, San Jose, CA, pp. 277–80. San Francisco: ICMA.

L'Estrange, P. R., Rowell, J., and Stokes, M. J. (1993). "Acoustic Myography in the Assessment of the Human Masseter Muscle." *Journal of Rehabilitation*, 20:353–62.

Lima, G., Maes, M., Bonfim, M., Lamar, M. V., and Wanderley, M. M. (1996). "Dance-music Interface Based on Ultrasound Sensors and Computers." *Proceedings of the 3rd Brazilian Symposium on Computer Music*, Recife, Brazil, pp. 12–16. Porto Alegre: Sociedade Brasileira de Computação.

Livingstone, D., and Miranda, E. (2004). "Composition for Ubiquitous Responsive Sound Environments." *Proceedings of the International Computer Music Conference (ICMC'04)*, Miami, FL. San Francisco: ICMA.

Livingstone, D., and Miranda, E. R. (2005). "Orb-3: Musical Robots with an Adaptive Social Composition System." *Proceedings of the 2005 International Computer Music Conference*, Barcelona, pp. 543–46. San Francisco: ICMA.

Lucier, A. (1976). "Statement On: Music for Solo Performer." In D. Rosenboom (Ed.), *Biofeedback and the Arts: Results of Early Experiments*. Vancouver: Aesthetic Research Center of Canada Publications, pp. 60–61.

Lucier, A. (1980). *Chambers*. Middletown, CT: Wesleyan University Press.

Lusted, H. S., and Knapp, R. B. (1996). "Controlling Computers with Neural Signals." *Scientific American*, October: 82–87.

Lyons, M. J., Haehnel, M., and Tetsutani, N. (2003). "Designing, Playing and Performing with a Vision-based Mouth Interface." *Proceedings of the 2003 International Conference on New Interfaces for*

Musical Expression (NIME'03), Montreal, Canada, pp. 116–21. Montreal: McGill University.

Machover, T. (1992). *Hyperinstruments: A Progress Report, 1987–1991*. Technical report, Massachusetts Institute of Technology, Boston, MA.

Machover, T., and Chung, J. (1989). "Hyperinstruments: Musically Intelligent and Interactive Performance and Creativity Systems." *Proceedings of the 1989 International Computer Music Conference (ICMC'89)*, Ohio, pp. 186–90. San Francisco: ICMA.

Maconie, R. (1976). *The Works of Stockhausen*. London: Marion Boyars.

Manning, P. (2004). *Electronic and Computer Music*. 3rd ed. Oxford: Oxford University Press.

Marrin, T. (1999). "Inside the Conductor's Jacket: Analysis, Interpretation and Musical Synthesis of Expressive Gesture." Ph.D. diss., Massachusetts Institute of Technology.

Marrin, T. (2000). "Searching for Meaning in Gestural Data. Interpretive Feature Extraction and Signal Processing for Affective and Expressive Content." In M. Wanderley and M. Battier (Eds.), *Trends in Gestural Control of Music*. Paris: IRCAM—Centre Pompidou, pp. 269–99.

Marrin, T. (2002). "Synthesizing Expressive Music through the Language of Conducting." *Journal of New Music Research*, 31(1):11–26.

Marrin, T. and Paradiso, J. (1997). "The Digital Baton: A Versatile Performance Instrument." *Proceedings of the 1997 International Computer Music Conference (ICMC'97)*, Thessaloniki, Greece, pp. 313–16. San Francisco: ICMA.

Marrin, T., and Picard, R. (1998). "The "Conductor's Jacket": A Device for Recording Expressive Musical Gestures." *Proceedings of the 1998 International Computer Music Conference (ICMC'98)*, Ann Arbor, MI, pp. 215–19. San Francisco: ICMA.

Marshall, M., Moynihan, B., and Rath, M. (2002). "The Virtual Bodhran: The Vodhran; An Interface for Musical Control." *Proceedings of the 2002 International Conference on New Interfaces for Musical Expression (NIME'02)*, Dublin, Ireland, pp. 179–80. Dublin: Media Lab Europe.

Mathews, M. V. (1976). "The Conductor Program." *Proceedings of the 1976 International Computer Music Conference (ICMC'76)*, Cambridge, MA. San Francisco: ICMA.

Mathews, M. V. (1980). *The Sequential Drum*. Rapports IRCAM 27/80. Paris: IRCAM.

Mathews, M. V. (1989). "The Conductor Program and Mechanical Baton." In M. V. Mathews and J. R. Pierce (Eds.), *Current Directions in Computer Music Research.* Cambridge, MA: MIT Press, pp. 263–81.

Mathews, M. V. (1991). "The Radio Baton and the Conductor Program, or: Pitch, the Most Important and Least Expressive Part of Music." *Computer Music Journal*, 15(4):37–46.

Mathews, M. V. (2000). *Radio-Baton Instruction Manual.* Preliminary ed. San Francisco: MARMAX.

Mathews, M. V., and Abbott, C. (1980). "The Sequential Drum." *Computer Music Journal*, 4(4):45–59.

Mathews, M. V., and Bennett, G. (1978). *Real-time Synthesizer Control.* Technical Report 5/78. Paris: IRCAM.

McElligott, L., Dillon, M., and Dixon, E. (2002). "PegLeg in Music: Processing the Effort Generated by Levels of Expressive Gesturing in Music." *Proceedings of the 2002 International Conference on New Interfaces for Musical Expression (NIME'02)*, Dublin, Ireland, pp. 6–10. Dublin: Media Lab Europe.

McNeill, D. (1992). *Hand and Mind: What Gestures Reveal about Thought.* Chicago: University of Chicago Press.

McNeill, D. (Ed.) (2000). *Language and Gesture.* Cambridge: Cambridge University Press.

Minsky, M. (1988). *The Society of Mind.* Riverside, CA: Simon & Schuster.

Miranda, E. R. (1998). *Computer Sound Synthesis for the Electronic Musician.* Oxford: Focal Press.

Miranda, E. R. (2002). *Computer Sound Design: Synthesis Techniques and Programming.* 2nd ed. Oxford: Elsevier Science/Focal Press.

Miranda, E. R., and Brouse, A. (2005). "Interfacing the Brain Directly with Musical Systems: On Developing Systems for Making Music with Brain Signals," *Leonardo*, 38(4):331–336.

Miranda, E. R., Sharman, K., Kilborn, K., and Duncan, A. (2003). "On Harnessing the Electroencephalogram for the Musical Braincap." *Computer Music Journal*, 27(2):80–102.

Miranda, E. R. (Ed.) (2000). *Readings in Music and Artificial Intelligence.* Amsterdam: Harwood Academic.

Misulis, K. E. (1997). *Essentials of Clinical Neurophysiology.* Boston, MA: Butterworth-Heinemann.

Mitchell, T. (1997). *Machine Learning.* New York: McGraw-Hill.

Miyashita, H., and Nishimoto, K. (2004a). "Developing a Non-visual Output Device for Musical Performers." *Proceedings of the 2004 Sound and Music Computing Conference*, Paris, pp. 251–55. Paris: IRCAM—Centre Pompidou.

Miyashita, H., and Nishimoto, K. (2004b). "Thermoscore: A New-type Musical Score with Temperature Sensation." *Proceedings of the*

2004 International Conference on New Interfaces for Musical Expression (NIME'04), Hamamatsu, Japan, pp. 104–7. Hamamatsu: Shizuoka University of Arts and Culture.

Modler, P. (2000). "Neural Networks for Mapping Gestures to Sound Synthesis." In M. Wanderley and M. Battier (Eds.), *Trends in Gestural Control of Music*. Paris: IRCAM—Centre Pompidou, pp. 301–14.

Modler, P., and Zannos, I. (1997). "Emotional Aspects of Gesture Recognition by a Neural Network, Using Dedicated Input Devices." *Proceedings of the AIMI International Workshop Kansei: The Technology of Emotion*, Genoa, Italy,

Moog, R. A. (1982). "A Multiply Touch-sensitive Clavier for Computer Music Systems." *Proceedings of the 1982 International Computer Music Conference (ICMC'82)*, Venice, Italy, pp. 601–05. San Francisco: ICMC.

Moog, R. A. (2005). *The Moog PianoBar.* www.moogmusic.com/detail.php?main_product_id=71 (accessed 31 March 2005).

Moog, R. A., and Rhea, T. (1990). "Evolution of the Keyboard Interface: The Bösendorfer 290 SE Recording Piano and the Moog Multiply-touch-sensitive Keyboard." *Computer Music Journal*, 14(2): 52–60.

Moore, F. R. (1987). "The Dysfunctions of MIDI." *Proceedings of the 1987 International Computer Music Conference (ICMC'87)*, Champaign-Urbana, IL, pp. 256–63. San Francisco: ICMC.

Moore, F. R. (1988). "The Dysfunctions of MIDI." *Computer Music Journal*, 12(1):19–28.

Morita, H., Otheru, S., and Hashimoto, S. (1989). "Computer Music System Which Follows a Human Conductor." *Proceedings of the 1989 International Computer Music Conference (ICMC'89)*, Columbus, OH, pp. 207–10. San Francisco: ICMC.

Morris, G. C., Leitman, S., and Kassianidou, M. (2004). "SillyTone Squish Factory." *Proceedings of the 2004 International Conference on New Interfaces for Musical Expression (NIME'04)*, Hamamatsu, Japan. Hamamatsu: Shizuoka University of Arts and Culture.

Mulder, A. (1994a). "How to Build an Instrumented Glove Based on the Powerglove Flex Sensors." *PCVR Magazine*, 16:10–14.

Mulder, A. (1994b). "Virtual Musical Instruments: Accessing the Sound Synthesis Universe and a Performer." *I Simpósio Brasilieiro de Computacao e Musica*, Caxambu, Brazil, pp. 243–50. Porto Alegre: Sociedade Brasileira de Computação.

Mulder, A. (1998). "Design of Virtual Three-dimensional Instruments for Sound Control." Ph.D. diss., Simon Fraser University.

Mulder, A. (2000). "Towards a Choice of Gestural Constraints for Instrumental Performers." In M. Wanderley and M. Battier (Eds.),

Trends in Gestural Control of Music. Paris: IRCAM—Centre Pompidou, pp. 315–35.

Mumma, G. (1975). "Live-electronic Music." In J. H. Appleton and R. C. Perera (Eds.), *The Development and Practice of Electronic Music.* Englewood Cliffs, NJ: Prentice-Hall, pp. 286–335.

Murphy, D., Andersen, T. H., and Jensen, K. (2003). "Conducting Audio Files via Computer Vision." *Proceedings of the 2003 International Gesture Workshop,* Genoa, Italy. Genoa: Dist. Università di Genova.

Nagashima, Y. (1998). "Biosensorfusion: New Interfaces for Interactive Multimedia Art." *Proceedings of the International Computer Music Conference (ICMC'98)*, Ann Arbor, MI, pp. 129–32. San Francisco: ICMA.

Nagashima, Y., and Ito, T. T. (1999). "It's SHO Time: An Interactive Environment for SHO (Sheng) Performance." *Proceedings of International Computer Music Conference (ICMC'99)*, Montreal, Canada, pp. 32–35. San Francisco: ICMA.

Neapolitan, R. E. (2004). *Learning Bayesian Networks.* Upper Saddle River, NJ: Prentice Hall.

Niedermeyer, E., and Lopes da Silva, F. H. (Eds.) (1987). *Electroencephalography.* 2nd ed. Munich: Urban and Schwartzenberg.

Ng, K. (2004). "Music via Motion: Transdomain Mapping of Motion and Sound for Interactive Performances." *Proceedings of the IEEE*, 92(4):645–55.

Nichols, C. (2000). "The vBow: A Haptic Musical Controller Human-computer Interface." *Proceedings of the 2000 International Computer Music Conference (ICMC'00)*, Berlin, Germany, pp. 274–76. San Francisco: ICMA.

Nichols, C. (2002). "The vBow: Development of a Virtual Violin Bow Haptic Human-computer Interface." *Proceedings of the 2002 International Conference on New Interfaces for Musical Expression (NIME'02)*, Dublin, Ireland, pp. 29–32. Dublin: Media Lab Europe.

Nichols, C. (2003). "The vBow: An Expressive Musical Controller Haptic Human-computer Interface." Ph.D. diss., Stanford University.

Nyce, D. S. (2004). *Linear Position Sensors: Theory and Application.* Hoboken, NJ: John Wiley and Sons.

Oboe, R., and De Poli, G. (2002). "Multi-instrument Virtual Keyboard: The MIKEY Project." *Proceedings of the 2002 International Conference on New Interfaces for Musical Expression (NIME'02)*, Dublin, Ireland, pp. 23–28. Dublin: Media Lab Europe.

O'Modhrain, S., and Chafe, C. (2000). "The Performer-Instrument Interaction: A Sensory Motor Perspective." *Proceedings of the 2000 International Computer Music Conference (ICMC'00)*, Berlin, Germany, pp. 145–48. San Francisco: ICMA.

O'Modhrain, S., and Essl, G. (2004). "PebbleBox and CrumbleBag: Tactile Interfaces for Granular Synthesis." *Proceedings of the 2004 International Conference on New Interfaces for Musical Expression (NIME'04)*, Hamamatsu, Japan, pp. 74–79. Hamamatsu: Shiziuoka University of Art and Culture.

O'Modhrain, S., and Gillespie, B. (1996). "The Moose: A Haptic User Interface for Blind Persons." Internal report, Stanford Center for Computer Research in Music and Acoustics, Stanford, CA.

O'Modhrain, S., Serafin, S., Chafe, C., and Smith, J. O. (2000). "Qualitative and Quantitative Assessment of a Virtual Bowed String Instrument." *Proceedings of the 2000 International Computer Music Conference (ICMC'00)*, Berlin, Germany. San Francisco, International Computer Music Association, pp. 66–69.

Orio, N. (1997). "A Gestural Interface Controlled by the Oral Cavity." *Proceedings of the 1997 International Computer Music Conference (ICMC'97)*, Thessaloniki, Greece, pp. 141–44. San Francisco: ICMA.

Orio, N. (1999). "A Model for Human-computer Interaction Based on the Recognition of Musical Gestures." *Proceedings of IEEE Conference on Systems, Men and Cybernetics*, 1999, Tokyo, Japan, pp. 333–38. Washington, DC: IEEE Computer Society.

Overholt, D. (2001). "The MATRIX: A Novel Controller for Musical." *Proceedings of New Interfaces for Musical Expression Workshop (NIME'01)*, Seattle, WA, 2001. New York: ACM Press.

Overholt, D. (2005). "The Overtone Violin." *Proceedings of the 2005 International Conference on New Interfaces for Musical Expression (NIME'05)*, Vancouver, Canada, pp. 34–37. Vancouver: University of British Columbia.

Palacio-Quintin, C. (2003). "The Hyper-flute." *Proceedings of the 2003 International Conference on New Interfaces for Musical Expression (NIME'03)*, Montreal, Canada, pp. 206–7. Montreal: McGill University.

Pallàs-Areny, R., and Webster, J. G. (2001). *Sensors and Signal Conditioning*. 2nd ed. New York: Wiley Interscience.

Paradiso, J. (1999). "The Brain Opera Technology: New Instruments and Gestural Sensors for Musical Interaction and Performance." *Journal of New Music Research*, 28(2):130–49.

Paradiso, J. (2003). "Dual-use Technologies for Electronic Music Controllers: A Personal Perspective." *Proceedings of the 2003 International Conference on New Interfaces for Musical Expression (NIME'03)*, Montreal, Canada, pp. 228–34. Montreal: McGill University.

Paradiso, J., Abler, C., Hsiao, K., and Reynolds, M. (1997). "The Magic Carpet: Physical Sensing for Immersive Environments." *CHI'97*

Electronic Publications: Late-Breaking/Short Demonstrations. http://sigchi.org/chi97/proceedings/short-demo/jp.htm (accessed 12 August 2005).

Paradiso, J., and Gershenfeld, N. (1997). "Musical Applications of Electric Field Sensing." *Computer Music Journal*, 21(2):69–89.

Paradiso, J., Hsiao, K.-y., and Hu, E. (1999). "Interactive Music for Instrumented Dancing Shoes." *Proceedings of the 1999 International Computer Music Conference (ICMC'99)*, Beijing, China, pp. 453–56. San Francisco: ICMA.

Paradiso, J., Leo, C. K., Checka, N., and Hsiao, K. (2002). "Passive Acoustic Knock Tracking for Interactive Windows." *Proceedings of the CHI'02 Conference on Human Factors in Computing* Systems, Minneapolis, MN, pp. 732–33. New York: ACM Press.

Pardue, L., and Paradiso, J. (2002). "Musical Navigatrics: New Musical Interactions with Passive Magnetic Tags." *Proceedings of the 2002 International Conference on New Interfaces for Musical Expression (NIME'02)*, Dublin, Ireland, pp. 168–69. Dublin: Media Lab Europe.

Pascal, M. (1999). "Le studio instrumental: Les données d'une virtuosité à l'intérieur meme du son." In H. Genevois and R. de Vivo (Eds.), *Les nouveaux gestes de la musique.* Marseille: Editions Parentheses, pp. 157–68.

Penny, W. D., Roberts, S. J., Curran, E., and Stokes, M. (1999). "EEG-based Communication: A Pattern Recognition Approach." *IEEE Transactions on Rehabilitation Engineering*, 20(5):214–16.

Peters, B. O., Pfurtscheller, G., and Flyvberg, H. (1997). "Prompt Recognition of Brain States by their EEG Signals." *Theory in Biosciences*, 116:290–301.

Petsche, H., and Etlinger, S. C. (1998). *EEG and Thinking.* Vienna: Verlag der Österreichischen Akademie der Wissenschaften.

Pinkston, R., Kerkhoff, J., and McQuilken, M. (1995). "A Touch Sensitive Dance Floor/MIDI Controller." *Proceedings of the 1995 International Computer Music Conference (ICMC'95)*, Banff, Canada, pp. 224–25. San Francisco: ICMA.

Piringer, J. (2001). "Elektronische Musik und Interaktivität. Prinzipien, Konzepte, Anwendungen." Master's thesis, Technical University of Vienna.

Pousset, D. (1992). "La flute-MIDI : L'histoire et quelques Applications." Master's thesis, University of Paris-Sorbonne.

Pressing, J. (1990). "Cybernetic Issues in Interactive Performance Systems." *Computer Music Journal*, 14(2):12–25.

Prevot, P. (1986). "Tele-Detection and Large Dimension Gestual Control." *Proceedings of the 1986 International Computer Music*

Conference (ICMC'86), The Hague, Netherlands, pp. 95–97. San Francisco: ICMA.

Quek, F., McNeill, D., Bryll, R., Duncan, S., Ma, X.-F., Kirbas, C., McCullough, K. E., and Ansari, R. (2002). "Multimodal Human Discourse: Gesture and Speech." *ACM Transactions on Computer-Human Interaction*, 9:171–93.

Rabiner, L. (1989). "A Tutorial on Hidden Markov Models and Selected Applications in Speech Recognition." *Proceedings of the IEEE*, 77(2):257–286.

Ramstein, C. (1991). "Analyse, representation et traitement du geste instrumental." Ph.D. diss., Institut National Polytechnique de Grenoble.

Reighley, K. B. (2000). *Looking for the Perfect Beat: The Art and Culture of the DJ*. Riverside, CA: Simon & Schuster/MTV Books.

Rhatigan, B. A., Mylrea, K., Lonsdale, E., and Stern, L. Z. (1986). "Investigations of Sounds Produced by Healthy and Diseased Human Muscular Contraction." *IEEE Transactions on Biomedical Engineering*, 33(10):967–71.

Richardson, B., Leydon, K., Fernström, M., and Paradiso, J. A. (2004). "Z-Tiles: Building Blocks for Modular, Pressure-sensing Floorspaces." *Proceedings of the CHI'04 Conference on Human factors in Computing Systems*, Vienna, Austria, pp. 1529–32. New York: ACM Press.

Risset, J. C., and Duyne, S. V. (1996). "Real-time Performance Interaction with a Computer-Controlled Acoustic Piano." *Computer Music Journal*, 20(1):62–75.

Roads, C. (1996). *Computer Music Tutorial*. Cambridge, MA: MIT Press.

Robbins, J. (2000). *A Symphony in the Brain: The Evolution of the New Brain Wave Biofeedback*. New York: Grove Press.

Roberts, S. J., and Penny, W. (2000). "Real-time Brain Computer Interfacing: A Preliminary Study Using Bayesian Learning." *Medical & Biological Engineering and Computing*, 38(1):56–61.

Ronen, M., and Lipman, A. (1991). "The V-scope." *Physics Teacher*, 29:289–302.

Rosenbaum, D. (1990). *Human Motor Control*. San Diego, CA: Academic Press.

Rosenboom, D. (1990a). *Extended Musical Interface with the Human Nervous System*, Leonardo Monograph Series No. 1. Berkeley, CA: International Society for the Arts, Science and Technology (ISAST).

Rosenboom, D. (1990b). "The Performing Brain." *Computer Music Journal*, 14(1):48–65.

Rovan, J., and Hayward, V. (2000). "Typology of Tactile Sounds and their Synthesis in Gesture-Driven Computer Music Performance." In M. Wanderley and M. Battier (Eds.), *Trends in Gestural Control of Music*. Paris: IRCAM—Centre Pompidou, pp. 355–68.

Rovan, J., Wanderley, M. M., Dubnov, S., and Depalle, P. (1997). "Instrumental Gestural Mapping Strategies as Expressivity Determinants in Computer Music Performance." *Proceedings of the AIMI International Workshop Kansei: The Technology of Emotion*, Genoa, Italy, pp. 68–73. Genoa: University of Genoa and Associazione di Informatiga Musicale Italiana.

Rowe, R. (1993). *Interactive Music Systems*. Cambridge, MA: MIT Press.

Rowe, R. (2001). *Machine Musicianship*. Cambridge, MA: MIT Press.

Rubine, D., and McAvinney, P. (1988). "The VideoHarp." *Proceedings of the 1988 International Computer Music Conference (ICMC'88)*, Cologne, Germany, pp. 49–55. San Francisco: ICMA.

Rudolph, M. (1950). *The Grammar of Conducting*. New York: Schirmer Books.

Sawada, H., Onoe, N., and Hashimoto, S. (1997). "Sounds in Hands: A Sound Modifier using Datagloves and Twiddle Interface." *Proceedings of the 1997 International Computer Music Conference (ICMC'97)*, Thessaloniki, Greece, pp. 309–12. San Francisco: ICMA.

Sawada, H., Onoe, N., and Hashimoto, S. (1996). "Acceleration Sensor as an Input Device for Musical Environment." *Proceedings of the 1996 International Computer Music Conference (ICMC'96)*, Hong Kong, pp. 421–24. San Francisco: ICMA.

Sawada, H., Ohkura, S., and Hashimoto, S. (1995). "Gesture Analysis Using 3D Acceleration Sensor for Music Control." *Proceedings of the 1995 International Computer Music Conference (ICMC'95)*, Banff, Canada, pp. 257–60. San Francisco: ICMA.

Scavone, G. (2003). "The PIPE: Explorations with Breath Control." *Proceedings of the 2003 International Conference on New Interfaces for Musical Expression (NIME'03)*, Montreal, Canada, pp. 15–18. Montreal: McGill University.

Schaeffer, P. (1966). *Traité des objets musicaux*. Paris: Seuil.

Schloss, W. A. (1990). "Recent Advances in the Coupling of the Language MAX with the Matthew-Boie Radio Drum." *Proceedings of the 1990 International Computer Music Conference (ICMC'90)*, Glasgow, UK, pp. 398–400. San Francisco: ICMA.

Schloss, W. A., and Driessen, P. (2001). "Towards a Virtual Membrane: New Algorithms for Analyzing Gestural Data." *Proceedings of the 2001 International Computer Music Conference (ICMC'01)*, Havana, Cuba. San Francisco: ICMA.

Serafin, S., Vergez, C., and Rodet, X. (1999). "Friction and Application to Real-time Physical Modeling of a Violin." *Proceedings of the 1999 International Computer Music Conference (ICMC'99)*, Beijing, China, pp. 216–19. San Francisco: ICMA.

Sheehan, B. (2004). "The Squiggle: A Digital Musical Instrument." *Proceedings of the 2004 International Conference on New Interfaces for Musical Expression (NIME'04)*, Hamamatsu, Japan, pp. 92–95. Hamamatsu: Shizuoka University of Arts and Culture.

Shiraiwa, H., Segnini, R., and Woo, V. (2003). "Sound Kitchen: Designing an Chemically Controlled Musical Performance." *Proceedings of the 2003 International Conference on New Interfaces for Musical Expression (NIME'03)*, Montreal, Canada, pp. 83–86. Montreal: McGill University.

Siegel, W., and Jacobsen, J. (1998). "The Challenges of Interactive Dance: An Overview and Case Study." *Computer Music Journal*, 22(4):29–43.

Singer, E. (2003). "Sonic Banana: A Novel Bend-sensor-based MIDI Controller." *Proceedings of the 2003 International Conference on New Interfaces for Musical Expression (NIME'03)*, Montreal, Canada, pp. 220–21. Montreal: McGill University.

Sinyor, E., and Wanderley, M. M. (2005). "Gyrotyre. A Hand-held Dynamic Computer-music Controller Based on a Spinning Wheel." *Proceedings of the 2005 International Conference on New Interfaces for Musical Expression (NIME'05)*, Vancouver, Canada, pp. 42–45. Vancouver: University of British Columbia.

Smith, R. L. (1993). "Sensors." In R. C. Dorf (Ed.), *The Electrical Engineering Handbook*. London: CRC Press, pp. 1255–64.

Snell, J. (1983). "Sensors for Playing Computer Music with Expression." *Proceedings of the 1983 International Computer Music Conference (ICMC'83)*, Rochester, NY, pp. 113–26. San Francisco: ICMA.

Starkier, M., and Prevot, P. (1986). "Real-Time Gestural Control." *Proceedings of the 1986 International Computer Music Conference (ICMC'86)*, The Hague, Netherlands, pp. 423–26. San Francisco: ICMA.

Smyth, T., and Smith, J. (2003). "A Musical Controller Inspired by the Cicada's Efficient Buckling Mechanism." *Journal of New Music Research*, 32(4):361–68.

Steiner, H.-C. (2005). "[Hid] Toolkit: A Unified Framework for Instrument Design." *Proceedings of the 2005 International Conference on New Interfaces for Musical Expression (NIME'05)*, Vancouver, Canada, pp. 140–43. Vancouver: University of British Columbia.

Stokes, M. J., and Blythe, G. M. (2001). *Muscle Sounds in Physiology, Sports Science and Clinical Investigation: Applications and History of Mechanomyography*. Oxford: Medintel Publications.

Sutherland, R. (1994). *New Perspectives in Music.* London: Sun Tavern Fields.

Taelman, J. (2002). "A Low-cost Sonar for Unobtrusive Man-machine Interfacing." *Proceedings of the 2002 International Conference on New Interfaces for Musical Expression (NIME'02),* Dublin, Ireland, pp. 92–95. Dublin: Media Lab Europe.

Tanaka, A. (1993). "Musical Technical Issues in Using Interactive Instrument Technology with Application to the BioMuse." *Proceedings of the 1993 International Computer Music Conference (ICMC'93),* Tokyo, Japan, pp. 124–26. San Francisco: ICMA.

Tanaka, A. (2000). "Musical Performance Practice on Sensor-based Instruments." In M. Wanderley and M. Battier (Eds.), *Trends in Gestural Control of Music.* Paris: IRCAM—Centre Pompidou, pp. 398–405.

Tanaka, A., and Bongers, B. (2001). "Global String: A Musical Instrument for Hybrid Space." *Proceedings of Cast01: Living in Mixed Realities,* Sankt Augustin, Germany, pp. 177–81. Sankt Augustin: Fraunhofer Institut für Medienkommunikation.

Tanaka, A., and Knapp, R. B. (2002). "Multimodal Interaction in Music Using the Electromyogram and Relative Position Sensing." *Proceedings of the 2002 International Conference on New Interfaces for Musical Expression (NIME'02),* Dublin, Ireland, pp. 43–48. Dublin: Media Lab Europe.

Teitelbaum, R. (1976). "In Tune: Some Early Experiments in Biofeedback Music (1966–1974)." In D. Rosenboom (Ed.), *Biofeedback and the Arts: Results of Early Experiments.* Vancouver: Aesthetic Research Center of Canada Publications, pp. 35–56.

Traube, C., Depalle, P. and Wanderley, M. M. (2003). "Indirect Acquisition of Instrumental Gesture Based on Signal, Physical and Perceptual Information." *Proceedings of the 2003 International Conference on New Interfaces for Musical Expression (NIME'03),* pp. 42–47. Montreal: McGill University.

Trochimczyk, M. (2001). "From Circles to Nets: On the Signification of Spatial Sound Imagery in New Music." *Computer Music Journal,* 25(4):39–56.

Trueman, D., and Cook, P. (1999). "BoSSA: The Deconstructed Violin Reconstructed." *Proceedings of the 1999 International Computer Music Conference (ICMC'99),* Beijing, China, pp. 232–39. San Francisco: ICMA.

Usa, S., and Mochida, Y. (1998). "A Multi-Modal Conducting Simulator." *Proceedings of the 1998 International Computer Music Conference (ICMC'98),* Ann Arbor, MI, pp. 25–32. San Francisco: ICMA.

Van Nort, D., Wanderley, M. M., and Depalle, P. (2004). "On the Choice of Mappings Based on Geometric Properties." *Proceedings* of the 2004 International Conference on New Interfaces for Musical Expression (NIME'04), Hamamatsu, Japan, pp. 87–91. Hamamatsu: Shizuoka University of Arts and Culture.

van Schutterhoef, A. (2005). *STRATIFIER: A Multi-dimensional Controller for the Performance of Live Electro-Acoustic Music.* http://www.xs4all.nl/~schreck/eng/html/strat.html (accessed 28 March 2005).

Vecchi, F., Freschi, C., Micera, S., Sabatini, A. M., Dario, P., and Sacchetti, R. (2000). "Experimental Evaluation of Two Commercial Force Sensors for Applications in Biomechanics and Motor Control." *Proceedings of the 5th Annual Conference of the International Functional Electrical Stimulation Society*, Aalborg, Denmark. Aalborg: International Functional Electrical Stimulation Society.

Vercoe, B. (1984). "The Synthetic Performer in the Context of Live Performance." *Proceedings of the 1984 International Computer Music Conference (ICMC'84)*, Paris, France, pp. 199–200. San Francisco: ICMA.

Verplaetse, C. (1996). "Inertial Proprioceptive Devices: Self-Motion-Sensing Toys and Tools." *IBM Systems Journal*, 35(3–4):639–50.

Verplank, W., Sapp, C., and Mathews, M. (2001). "A Course on Controllers." *Proceedings of the Workshop New Interfaces for Musical Expression (NIME'01)*, Seattle, WA. New York: ACM Press.

Vertegaal, R., Ungvary, T., and Kieslinger, M. (1996). "Towards a Musician's Cockpit: Transducer, Feedback and Musical Function." *Proceedings of the 1996 International Computer Music Conference (ICMC'96)*, Hong Kong, pp. 308–11. San Francisco: ICMA.

Vidal, J. J. (1973). "Toward Direct Brain-Computer Communication." *Annual Review of Biophysics and Bioengineering* 2:157–80.

Vogt, F., McCaig, G., Ali, M. A., and Feld, S. (2002). "Tongue 'n' Groove." *Proceedings of the 2002 International Conference on New Interfaces for Musical Expression (NIME'02)*, Dublin, Ireland, pp. 60–64. Dublin: Media Lab Europe.

Waisvisz, M. (1985). "The Hands: A Set of Remote MIDI-controllers." *Proceedings of the 1985 International Computer Music Conference (ICMC'85)*, Vancouver, Canada, pp. 313–18. San Francisco: ICMA.

Waisvisz, M. (1989). "Now the Hands II." The Michel Waisvisz Archive. http://www.crackle.org/ (accessed 28 March 2005).

Waisvisz, M. (1996). "Small Web." The Michel Waisvisz Archive. http://www.crackle.org/ (accessed 12 October 2005).

Wanderley, M. M. (Ed.) (2002a). "Mapping Strategies in Realtime Computer Music." *Organised Sound*, 7(2).

Wanderley, M. M. (2002b). "Quantitative Analysis of Non-obvious Performer Gestures." In I. Wachsmuth and T. Sowa (Eds.), *Gesture and Sign Language in Human-computer Interaction*. Berlin: Springer Verlag, pp. 241–53.

Wanderley, M. M., and Battier, M. (Eds.) (2000). *Trends in Gestural Control of Music*. CD-ROM. Paris: IRCAM—Centre Pompidou.

Wanderley, M. M., and Depalle, P. (2004). "Gestural Control of Sound Synthesis." *Proceedings of the IEEE*, 92(4):632–644.

Wanderley, M. M., and Koehly, R. (N.d.). "Methods for the In-house Development of Sensors for Musical Applications." Unpublished manuscript.

Wanderley, M. M., and Orio, N. (2002). "Evaluation of Input Devices for Musical Expression: Borrowing Tools from HCI." *Computer Music Journal*, 26(3):62–76.

Wanderley, M. M., Vines, B., Middleton, N., McKay, C., and Hatch, W. (2005). "The Musical Significance of Clarinetists' Ancillary Gestures: An Exploration of the Field." *Journal of New Music Research*, 34(1):97–113.

Wanderley, M. M., Viollet, J.-P., Isart, F., and Rodet, X. (2000). "On the Choice of Transducer Technologies for Specific Musical Functions." *Proceedings of the 2000 International Computer Music Conference (ICMC'00)*, Berlin, Germany, pp. 244–47. San Francisco: ICMA.

Webster, J. (Ed.) (1999). *The Measurement, Instrumentation and Sensors Handbook*. Boca Raton, FL: CRC Press.

Weinberg, G., Aimi, R., and Jennings, K. (2002). "The Beatbug Network: A Rhythmic System for Interdependent Group Collaboration." *Proceedings of the 2002 International Conference on New Interfaces for Musical Expression (NIME'02)*, Dublin, Ireland, pp. 107–11. Dublin: Media Lab Europe.

Wessel, D. (1991). "Instruments That Learn, Refined Controllers, and Source Model Loudspeakers." *Computer Music Journal*, 15(4):82–86.

Wessel, D., and Wright, M. (2002). "Problems and Prospects for Intimate Musical Control of Computers." *Computer Music Journal*, 26(3):11–22.

Wiener, N. (1948). *Cybernetics, or Control and Communication in the Animal and the Machine*. Cambridge, MA: MIT Press.

Wilkerson, C., Ng, K., and Serafin, S. (2002). "The Mutha Rubboard Controller." *Proceedings of the 2002 International Conference on New Interfaces for Musical Expression (NIME'02)*, Dublin, Ireland, pp. 82–85. Dublin: Media Lab Europe.

Wilson, S., Gurevich, M., Verplank, B., and Stang, P. (2003). "Microcontrollers in Music HCI Instruction: Reflections on our Switch to the Atmel AVR Platform." *NIME 2003 Online Proceedings*, http://www.music.mcgill.ca/musictech/nime/onlineproceedings/TOC.html (accessed 12 August 2005).

Wiggins, G., Miranda, E., Smaill, A., and Harris, M. (1993). "A Framework for the Evaluation of Music Representation Systems." *Computer Music Journal*, 17(3):31–42.

Windsor, W. L. (1995). "A Perceptual Approach to the Description and Analysis of Acousmatic Music." Ph.D. diss., City University, London.

Wright, M. (1998). "Implementation and Performance Issues with Open Sound Control." *Proceedings of the 1998 International Computer Music Conference (ICMC'98)*, Ann Arbor, MI, pp. 224–27. San Francisco: ICMA.

Wright, M., and Freed, A. (1997). "Open Sound Control: A New Protocol for Communicating with Sound Synthesizers." *Proceedings of the 1997 International Computer Music Conference (ICMC'97)*, Thessaloniki, Greece, pp. 101–4. San Francisco: ICMA.

Wright, M., Freed, A., and Momeni, A. (2003). "Open Sound Control: State of the Art 2003." *Proceedings of the 2003 International Conference on New Interfaces for Musical Expression (NIME'03)*, Montreal, Canada, pp. 153–60. Montreal: McGill University.

Wright, M., Wessel, D., and Freed, A. (1997). "New Musical Control Structures from Standard Gestural Controllers." *Proceedings of the 1997 International Computer Music Conference (ICMC'97)*, Thessaloniki, Greece, pp. 387–90. San Francisco: ICMA.

Yokono, J., and Hashimoto, S. (1998). "Center of Gravity Sensing for Motion Interface." *Proceedings of the IEEE International Conference on Systems, Man and Cybernetics (SMC'98)*, pp. 1113–18. Washington, DC: ICCC Computer Society.

Young, D. (2002). "The Hyperbow Controller: Real-time Dynamics Measurement of Violin Performance." *Proceedings of the 2002 International Conference on New Interfaces for Musical Expression (NIME'02)*, Dublin, Ireland, pp. 65–70. Dublin: Media Lab Europe.

Young, D., and Essl, G. (2003). "HyperPuja: A Tibetan Singing Bowl Controller." *Proceedings of the 2003 International Conference on New Interfaces for Musical Expression (NIME'03)*, Montreal, Canada, pp. 9–14. Montreal: McGill University.

Young, G. (1984). "Hugh Le Caine's 1948 Sackbut Synthesizer: Performance Mode of Electronic Instruments." *Proceedings of the 1984 International Computer Music Conference (ICMC'84)*, Paris, France, pp. 101–104. San Francisco: ICMA.

Young, G. (1989). *The Sackbut Blues: Hugh Le Caine, Pioneer in Electronic Music.* Ottawa: National Museum of Science and Technology.

Ystad, S. (1998). *Sound Modeling Using a Combination of Physical and Signal Models*. Ph.D. diss., University of Aix-Marseille II.

Ystad, S., and Voinier, T. (1999). "Design of a Flute Interface to Control Synthesis Models." *Proceedings of the 1999 International Computer Music Conference (ICMC'99)*, Beijing, China, pp. 228–31. San Francisco: ICMA.

Ystad, S., and Voinier, T. (2001). "A Virtually Real Flute." *Computer Music Journal*, 25(2):13–24.

Yunik, M., Borys, M., and Swift, G. W. (1983). "A Microprocessor Based Digital Flute." *Proceedings of the 1983 International Computer Music Conference (ICMC'83)*, Rochester, NY, pp. 127–36. San Francisco: ICMA.

Yunik, M., Borys, M., and Swift, G. W. (1985). "A Digital Flute." *Computer Music Journal,* 9(2):49–52.

Zölzer, U. (Ed.) 2002. *DAFX: Digital Audio Effects*. Hoboken, NJ: John Wiley & Sons.

Appendix: The Accompanying CD-ROM

The accompanying CD-ROM contains short movies to demonstrate examples of functioning sensors. All the videos can be played with QuickTime Player on Macintosh computers (tested with version 6.5.1 under OSX 10.3.5) and on Windows machines (.mov files, tested with version 6.5.2). On Windows machines, the Windows Media Player should be used to play .avi and .mpg files (tested with series 9 version under Windows XP version 2002). The CD-ROM has two folders: Demos and Sensors. The Demos folder contains 4 film clips, and the Sensors folder has 15 film clips.

■ DEMOS FOLDER

- Andre Brouse Performance [AndrewBrouse.mov] This video features Andrew Brouse performing his version of Alvin Lucier's piece *Music for Solo Performer*, with robotic percussion instruments designed by Maxime Rioux. Lucier is known for his pioneering work in many areas of music composition, such as the use of EEG in live music performance. See chapter 4, section 4.6.2, for more information on Brain-Computer Music Interface (BCMI).
- BCMI-Piano System [BCMI_Piano.mov] This clip features a demonstration of the BCMI-Piano system developed at the Interdisciplinary Centre for Computer Music Research (ICCMR) at the University of Plymouth. More information on this system can be found in chapter 4, section 4.6.2.
- Conductors Jacket [ConductorsJacket.mpg] This movie features Teresa Marrin performing with her conductor's jacket system.

For more information about the conductor's jacket, please refer to chapter 4, section 4.6.1.

- Global String [GlobalString.mov] This movie features the Global String network music installation created by Atau Tanaka, Bert Bongers, and Kasper Toeplitz. Refer to chapter 2, section 2.7, for more information on Global String.

■ SENSORS FOLDER

The Sensors folder contains fifteen film clips showing examples of various sensors discussed in chapter 3.

Sensor Type	File	Discussed in text:
Accelerometer	accel.avi	Chapter 3, section 3.3.15
Air pressure sensor	air_pressure.avi	Chapter 3, section 3.3.18
Capacitive sensing (using a metal can)	capacit_can.mov	Chapter 3, section 3.3.14
Capacitive sensing (using foil paper)	capacit_foil.mov	Chapter 3, section 3.3.14
Capacitive sensing (using a mirror)	capacit_mirror.mov	Chapter 3, section 3.3.14
Capacitive sensing (using a coil)	capacit_ring.mov	Chapter 3, section 3.3.14
Magnetoresistive sensor or compass	compass.mov	Chapter 3, section 3.3.13
Bend sensor	flexion.avi	Chapter 3, section 3.3.3
Force-sensitive resistor (FSR)	fsr.avi	Chapter 3, section 3.3.1
Force-sensitive resistor (additional example)	fsr155.avi	Chapter 3, section 3.3.1
Gyroscope	gyro.avi	Chapter 3, section 3.3.16
Hall effect sensor	hall.avi	Chapter 3, section 3.3.11
Infrared (IR) sensor	infrared.avi	Chapter 3, section 3.3.9
Strain gauge sensor	strain.mov	Chapter 3, section 3.3.2
Ultrasound sensors	ultrasound.mov	Chapter 3, section 3.3.8

Index

A

Abrasion, 174
Acceleration, 103
Accelerometer(s), 22–23, 44–45, 53, 59, 69, 109, 113, 123, 143, 147, 181, 182
Accents, 69
Accordiatron, 28
ACH-04-08-05, 145
Acoustic waves, 124
ACROE (Association pour la Création et la Recherche sur les Outils d'Expression), 75, 77, 153, 160
Acroname (company), 125
Actions
  blowing, 10
  bowing, 10
  grasping, 5
  manipulation, 5
  plucking, 10
  striking, 10
  walking, 10
Active listening, 193
Actuator(s), 71, 91, 104, 149
ADC (analog-to-digital converter), 160
ADXL105, 144
ADXL202, 144, 150
ADXRS300, 148
Aftertouch, 29
Agent systems, 238
Air Drums, 147
Air pressure, 51
Airflow, 51
Akai (company), 26
Akai EWI, 26
Algorithm(s)
  DSP, 201
  Matching, 236
  synthesis, 4
Algorithmic composition, 15
Allison, Jesse, 164
Alpha rhythm(s), 188, 199, 209, 211
Alto saxophone, 26
Ambient light, 85, 108
Analog Devices (company), 145, 148
Analog synthesizers, 121
Analog-to-MIDI, 161
Analog-to-OSC, 163
Anderson, Chuck, 208
Anodized aluminium, 143
AR (auto-regression), 190
Articulation, 25, 69
Artificial Intelligence, 191, 223
Artificial limbs, 180
Ascension Technology (company), 84
Atmel, 158, 163
AtoMIC Pro Interface, 159, 162
Audio, 90, 92
Augmented instruments, 21
  flute, 47, 150
  transverse flute, 24
  trombone, 29
  trumpets, 24
  violin, 135
aXi0 Controller, 37

B

Bahn, Curtis, 22, 122
Bailey, Nicolas, 14
Balakrishnan, Ravin, 117
Barlow, John, 189
Barlow analysis, 189
Basic Stamp (microcontroller), 23, 163, 171
Basis, 37
Bauer, Will, 127
Bayesian networks, 191
BCI (brain-computer interface), 190, 206, 208
BCMI (brain-computer music interfacing), 193, 206
BCMI-Piano, 200, 209
Beatbugs, 88, 124
Beauregard, Gerald, 28, 54, 59
Beauregard, Lawrence, 45, 52–53
Beethoven, Ludwig van, 215
Bell Labs, 222
BendMicro, 116
BendMini, 116
BendShort, 116
Berger, Hans, 206
Berkeley, 160
Beta rhythm(s), 188, 212
Bevilacqua, Frederic, 86
Beyls, Peter, 22
Biceps branchii, 181
Biceps muscle, 202–3
BigEye, 151
Biles, Al, 245
Bimanual manipulation, 36
Binary string code, 243
Biofeedback, 199
Biological processes, 240
BioMuse (system), 14, 19, 53, 200
Biosensor, 19
Biosignal(s), 14, 173, 201
  conditioning, 184
  processing, 184, 216
Birds, 237
Birdsong, 237
Bishop, Christopher, 192
Blackwell, Tim, 248
Blaine, Tina, 90

Bleauregard, 28, 53, 59
Blythe, 182
Body postures, 103
Body suit, 31, 43, 76
Boehm flute, 51
Boie, Bob, 38
Bois-Reymond, Emil Heinrich du, 173
Bonge, 44
Bongers, Bert, 22, 24, 41, 43, 90, 110, 147
Bösendorfer 290 SE, 22, 138, 159
Boskamp, Bram, 212
BoSSa, 43–44, 147
Boulez, Pierre, 8, 46
Bowed string instruments, 82
Brain Conductor, 193–94
Brain Soloist, 193
Brainwaves, 10
Breath
    intensity, 69
    stream, 25, 51
Bromwich, Mark, 28
Brouse, Andrew, 216
BTS SpA (company), 86
Buchla, Donald, 21, 40–41
Buchla Lighting II, 40–41, 135
Buchla Thunder, 33
Burdea, Grigore, 17
Burtner, Mathew, 21–22
Butterworth filter, 186

C

Cadoz, Claude, 9, 80
Cage, John, 137
California (University of), *see* University of California
Camera(s), 32, 59, 66, 69, 85
Capacitive sensing, 39, 40
Capacitors, 105
Cardoso, Jean-François, 187
Carious, Brad, 37
Carr, Joseph, 158, 171
Catchments, 6
CCD (charge-coupled device) array, 131, 151
CCRMA (Centre for Computer Research in Music and Acoustics), 134, 163, 200
Celloboard, 114
Cellophone, 122, 124
Cerebral cortex, 183

Chafe, Chris, 76
Cheapstick, 168
Choi, Insook, 60
Chromasone, 37
Chu, Lonny, 74
Clackage, 62, 124
Clarinet, 4, 14, 17–18, 53
Close, 132
CNMAT (Centre for New Music and Audio Technology), 160
Coffee mug, 31
Cognitive schemes, 224
Coiffet, Philippe, 17
Collins, Nicholas, 28
Compositional
    schemes, 238
    strategies, 240
Computer-mediated performance, 222
Concertina, 28
Conductance, 110
Conducting gesture systems, 68, 201
Conductive
    foam, 111
    gel, 174
    rubber, 30, 70, 143
Conductor
    follower, 67
    movements, 151
    program, 67, 223
Conductor's jacket, 200–1
Connectionism, 191
Contact microphone(s), 22, 27, 182
Continuum, 30, 32, 70, 98
Control
    continuous, 238
    fingering, 57
    knobs, 28
    linear slide, 57
    real-time EEG, 213
    score-following, 52
    surface, 3
    valve, 57
Controller(s)
    adaptive, 90, 92
    alternate, 21, 30, 45
    alternative, 21
    biosignal, 184
    breath, 56, 150
    collaborative, 88
    ecologically-inspired, 36
    EMG, 53

    expanded-range, 31
    external, 31
    gestural, 3, 95
    hand-held, 128
    haptic, 72
    harp-inspired, 28
    immersive, 31, 43
    instrument-inspired, 27, 45
    instrument-like, 21, 25–26
    internal, 31
    MIDI, 222
    open-air, 11
    partially immersive, 32
    performance, 3
    ribbon, 122
    symbolic, 31
    three-dimensional, 33
    totally immersive, 32
    touch, 31–32, 36
    trombone-inspired, 28
    violin-inspired, 119
    Web-based, 88, 90
    wind, 53, 58
    wind instrument, 26
Cook, Perry, 24, 44, 57, 59, 98
Cope, David, 210–11
Copper foil, 111
CORDIS-ANIMA, 80
Coriolis acceleration, 148
Corporeal activity, 19
CRT display, 32
CrumbleBag, 36, 153
Cunningham, Merce, 137
Current leakage, 174
Cutaneous Grooves, 76, 108
CyberBoots, 60, 111
Cybernetics, 207
Cybersonic Console, 221
Cycling '74 (company), 152
Cypher, 237–38

D

Dance floor, 62
Dancer, 43
Dannenberg, Roger, 226, 230–31, 235–36
D'Arcangelo, Gideon, 90
Darwin, Charles, 241
Data
    acquisition, 103
    reduction, 190
Data gloves, 31, 43

Datasuit, 69
Davidson, Jane, 10
Dawkins, Richard, 241
De Poli, Giovanni, 77
Delalande, François, 8
Delta rhythm, 188
Deltoid muscles, 202
DIEM (Danish Institute for Electronic Music), 43, 117
Differentiator, 157
Digital
  audio effects, 51
  flute, 28
  musical instruments, 1
  sound synthesis methods, 1
Digital Dance Interface, 43, 117
Dimension Bean, 134
Diodes, 105, 157
Direct acquisition, 25
Disklavier (piano), 22
DIST (Department of Communications, Computer and System Science), 131, 151
Distance, 52
DJ culture, 220
DMI (Digital Musical Instruments), 1, 3
Dobrian, Christopher, 86
Doepfer Musikelektronik, 162
Doppler radars, 63, 65, 110, 153
Double-bass, 22
Driessen, Peter, 40, 164
Driving wheels, 73
DSP (digital signal processing), 82
Ducoureau, Michel, 45, 52
Duncan, Alexander, 186, 196
Dynamic programming, 226–27
Dynamics, 69

E

E-Mic, 134
Ear lobe, 183
ECG (electrocardiogram or electrocardiography), 175, 177, 207
EDR (electrodermal response), 176
EEG (electroencephalogram), 14, 183, 185–86, 188, 190–91, 198, 200–1, 207–8, 210
Effectors, 104
Egozy, Eran, 14, 18
Einthoven, Willem, 178
Einthoven's Triangle, 178

EKG (electrocardiogram), 176
Electric field sensing, 39–40
Electrical
  conductivity, 174
  resistance, 110
  safety, 174
Electrically resistive film, 30
Electroacoustic music, 220
  acousmatic, 219
  live electronics, 219–20
Electrode(s), 39, 173
  active, 180
  ground, 180
  monopolar, 180
  needle, 180
  non-invasive, 180
  recording, 180
  reference, 180
  surface, 180
Electromagnet, 91
Electronic sackbut, 29, 143
Electrophysiology, 173
Electrotap, 165, 169
Embouchure, 25, 51
Emergent
  behavior, 94
  property, 248
Emerson, Keith, 122
Emission (of information), 9
EMG (electromyogram or electromyography), 14, 69, 175, 180, 200–1, 204
ENC-03M, 148
Envelope following, 24
EoBody, 162
EOG (electrooculogram), 14, 175, 200
Eowave (company), 121, 162, 169
EpipE, 143
Epistemic (hand gesture), 9
Ergotic (hand gesture), 9
Eroktronix (company), 162
Essl, Georg, 22, 36, 53, 139, 149
Ethersense, 163
EVI (electronic valve instrument), 26
Exo's Dexterous, 43
ExoSinger, 65–66
Exoskeleton (device by Seri Jordà), 43, 150
Exoskeletons, 73
Expression
  facial, 10, 65
  semiotic (hand gesture), 9

Expressivity, 95
Extensor muscle, 202
Eyeblinks, 183
Eyebrows, 65
EyeCon, 151
EyesWeb, 66, 151

F

Fabeck, Walter, 37
Fangerbored, 44
Far Reach, 130
Feature
  analysis, 187
  extraction, 15
Feedback, 95
  active, 11
  auditory, 11
  force, 71, 75
  haptic, 18, 71–72, 75, 104
  modalities, 4
  passive, 11
  passive-force, 25
  primary, 11
  secondary, 11
  tactile, 4, 71, 104
  tactile-kinesthetic, 11
  visual, 11
Feet, 7
Fels, Sidney, 18, 90, 151
Fernström, Mikael, 63, 165
Feyereisen, Pierre, 5
Fiber-optic, 32, 116
FilterPro software, 158
Finger
  muscles, 25
  position(s), 23, 27
Finger electrodes, 176
Fingerboard, 44
Fingering, 25
  alternative, 28
  information, 4, 46–47, 50
  intuitive, 54
  invalid, 28
  schemes, 53
FingerprintR knob, 36
Fingertips, 7
Fitness criteria, 241, 245
Fléty, Emmanuel, 22, 133
Flexiforce (sensor), 110
Flexpoint (company), 114
Flock of Birds, 84, 247
Florens, Jean-Loup, 77, 82

Flute, 22, 46, 50–51, 139, 237
Foot
   movements, 59
   pedals, 24
Foot-pedal switches, 39
Force, 123
Force-feedback
   devices, 72
   joysticks, 73
Force-sensitive floor, 111
Forearm, 203
Fortier, Pierre-Yves, 112, 120, 134
Foss, Bruce, 127
Fourier transform, 188
Fraden, Jacob, 106, 109, 131, 144
Fredericks Company, 150
FSR (force-sensing resistor), 22–23, 33, 44, 50, 52, 58, 60, 62, 64–65, 109–10, 114, 154
FSR Glove, 43
Fujikura, 150

G

GA (genetic algorithms), 240
Galvanometer, 173
Gamepads, 74
Games, 73
Gamma rhythm, 188
GAMS, 127, 130
Generative
   engine, 213
   music, 209
Genetic programming, 241
GenJam, 245
Genoa (University of), *see* University of Genoa
Gershenfeld, Neil, 142
Gesticulation, 9, 11
Gesticulator, 130
Gestural
   channel, 9
   vocabularies, 27
Gestural controller(s), 19
   Internet-based, 20
   mechanical, 19
   nonmechanical, 19
   nonphysical, 19
   physical, 19
Gesture(s), 5
   accompanist, 9, 10
   ancillary, 10
   audio, 76
   beats, 6
   capture strategies, 4
   conducting-like, 67
   conductor's, 8
   contact, 6
   crumbling, 37
   deictic, 6
   descriptive, 7
   dropping, 37
   effective, 9
   empty-handed, 6–7, 9, 10
   ergotic, 6
   excitation, 7
   expressive, 69
   figurative, 9
   finger, 37
   free, 6
   functional, 7
   grabbing, 37
   hand, 9, 33
   haptic, 6
   iconic, 6
   instrumental, 6–9
   intrinsic, 7
   manipulative, 6–7, 32
   metaphoric, 6
   musical, 8
   naked, 6
   natural, 9
   non-contact, 6
   parametric, 8
   parametric modification, 7
   performance, 8, 25, 28
   phenomenological, 7
   rolling, 37
   semaphoric, 7
   semiotic, 6
   shuffling, 37
   symbolic, 8
   tapping, 37
   violin-like, 45
Gesture acquisition
   direct, 12
   indirect, 12–13
   physiological, 12
Gesture Construction, 201, 204
Gesture Frame, 143
GForce2D, 146
GForce3D, 146
Gillespie, Brent, 77, 81
Glasgow (University of), *see* University of Glasgow
Global String, 90
Goldin-Meadow, Susan, 17
Goncharova, Irina, 189
Goto, Suguru, 43–44, 119
Goudeseune, Camille, 18
Gould, Glen, 9
GP2D12 IR, 105
Granular materials, 36
GraspMIDI, 151
Grass-Telefactor, 124
Gray code, 53
Griffith, Nial, 63
Grip, 11
Groove system, 222
GSR (galvanic skin response), 14, 110, 153, 201, 203
Guitar
   acoustic, 14, 18, 22, 72
   electric, 22
Gugger Technologies, 210
Gunther, Eric, 76
Gurevich, Michael, 28
Gyroscope(s), 53, 110, 148–49
Gyroscopic precession, 38
GyroTyre, 38, 134

H

Haken, Lippold, 29–30, 70
Hall effect, 52, 91
Halogen lamp, 32
Hammond organ, 81
Hand-held wands, 40
Handfield, François, 122, 124
Hands (device), 41, 130, 147, 150, 152
Hapipis, Thanasis, 65-66
Haptic
   knobs, 74
   mouse, 74
Harmonic coloration, 69
Harp sensor, 28
Harpsichord, 74, 81
Hashimoto, Shuji, 114
Hatanaka, Motohide, 37
Hayward, Vincent, 72, 75–76
Headphones, 123
Heart
   rate, 177, 180
   rhythm, 177
Heartbeat, 183
Heide, Edwin van der, 41
Henry, Cyrille, 82
HID interface, 163

Hirn, 57, 59
Hjorth, Bo, 189
Hjorth analysis, 189
Holbrook, Geof, 128
Honeywell HMC1023, 141
Honeywell HOA1397, 132
Horn, 221
Hot, 152
Hot&Humid, 152
HPD15 HandSonic Percussion Controller, 134
HPF (high-pass filter), 157
Hsiao, Kai-yuh, 140
Human-computer interaction, 95
Hunt, Andy, 18
Huott, Robert, 37
Hurny, Martin, 21, 26
Hybrid instruments, 21
Hyper-bow, 114
Hyper-cello, 22
Hyper-flute, 47, 50, 52, 111, 130, 150
Hyper-puja, 53, 139
Hyper-viola, 22
Hyper-violin, 22
Hyperinstrument, 21

I

ICA (independent component analysis), 187
ICCMR (Interdisciplinary Centre for Computer Music Research), 92, 200, 206
I-Cube, 160–61, 169
IDMIL (Input Devices and Music Interaction Laboratory), 86, 168
IEE (International Electronics and Engineering)
IEEE (Institute of Electrical and Electronic Engineers), 170
Igoe, Tom, 171
Intelligent
  behavior, 224
  interactive systems, 225
Immersion, 95
Impedance adapter, 155
Impet, Jonathan, 24, 139
Improvisation systems, 151, 226
Inclination, 52, 103
Inclinometers, 149
Indirect acquisition, 25
Inductors, 105
Infrared, 41, 85

Infusion Systems (company), 112, 116, 121, 125, 130, 132, 141, 146, 149, 152, 161, 169
Insects, 31
Instrumented dancing shoes, 65, 141, 147, 149
Integrator, 157
Interactif Spatio-musical, 137
Interactive
  installations, 88, 108
  laboratory, 225
  music, 52, 201, 222
Interface(s)
  biosignal, 201
  collaborative, 20, 88
  dance-music, 131
  DIY (do-it-yourself), 163
  haptic, 223
  sensor-to-MIDI, 131
  OSC, 131
  wind instruments, 57
Interlink FRS, 110
IR LED (integrated infrared light-emitting diode), 63, 65, 85, 133–34, 136
IR violin, 22
IRCAM (Institut de Recherche et Coordination Acoustique/Musique), 22, 24, 44–45, 127, 153, 159, 162–63, 222
IRIS (Instituto di Ricerca per l'Industria dello Spettacolo), 222
Isometric activity, 53
ISPW (IRCAM Signal Processing Workstation), 222
Ito, Tanami Tonu, 23

J

Jacobsen, Jens, 43
Jaffe, David, 22
Jam-O-Drum, 88
Java MUG, 111
Jazz Mutant, 32
Jensenius, Alexander, 152, 168
Jitter, 152
Johnstone, Eric, 32, 62, 70, 124
Jordà, Sergi, 43, 150
Joystick(s), 36, 223

K

Kagel, Mauricio, 220
Kanamori, Tsutomu, 130, 146, 148

Kedon, Adam, 17
Kendon's Continuum, 6
Keyboard(s)
  Carillon, 81
  electronic, 21
  instrument, 25
  modular force-feedback, 77
  numerical, 45
  piano, 21, 81
  synthesizers, 150
  thermodisplay, 74
  touchback, 81
Kinesthetic, 71
KitPAiA, 162
Koehly, Rodolphe, 165, 168
Klüver, Billy, 137
KMZ51 (Philips semiconductor), 141
KMZ52 (Philips semiconductor), 141
Knapp, Benjamin, 22, 53, 148, 200
Kroonde, 163

L

La Kitchen (company), 163, 169
La Touché, 77
Lady's Glove, 43, 115, 130, 139, 147
Laibowitz, Mat, 37
Lamar, Marcus, 60
LaMontaigne, Alain, 62
Lannoy, Jacques-Dominique de, 5
Laplace filter, 186
Laubier, Serge, 42, 71
Le Caine, Hugh, 29, 137, 143
LCD (liquid crystal display), 36
LDR (light-dependent resistors), 50, 136
LDR Controller, 137
LED (light-emitting diode), 29, 36, 85, 92
Lemur, 32
Light Baton, 151
Light-sensitive memory cells, 27
LinPot, 119
Lips, 65
Listening, 237
LiteFoot, 63, 65, 138
Livingstone, Dan, 92
LMA flute, 47, 50, 52
Loudspeaker(s), 71, 74, 104, 123
Low brass, 28
LPF (low-pass filter), 157, 186
Lucier, Alvin, 207
LuSense (company), 110–11, 119, 121

Lusted, Hugh, 200
LVDT (linear variable differential transformer), 78, 110, 153
Lyons, Michael, 65

M

Machine learning, 190–91, 210
Machover, Tod, 22, 43
Magic Carpet, 63, 65, 153
Magnetic tags, 110, 139
Magnetic trackers, 84
Magnets, 36, 45
Making Things (company), 163
Malloch, Joseph, 114
Manoury, Philippe, 46
Mapping, 4
    layer, 3
    strategies, 15
Markov models, 191, 212
Marrin, Teresa, 201
Mars workstation, 222
Marshall, Mark, 163
Martenot, Maurice, 2
Masseter, 182
Mathews, Max, 27, 223
Matrix, 33
Max/MSP, 164
McAvinney, 27
McGill University, 51, 86, 112, 122, 134, 168
MCM (Motion Capture Music), 86
McNeill, David, 17
Measurand (company), 116
Measurement Specialties (company), 145
Mechanical vibrations, 105
Mechanoreceptors, 71
Memsic 2125GL, 145
M.E.S.H., 149
Meta-instrument, 42, 71
Meta-saxophone, 21–22, 111
Meta-trombone, 28-29
Meta-trumpet, 24, 130, 139, 147
Meter, 69
Miburi, 31
Microchip (company), 158
MicroLab, 130, 161
Microphone(s), 13, 28, 36, 47, 52, 104, 110, 128, 153, 181, 221
MIDI, 103
    continuous parameter, 56
    flute, 24, 45, 50, 52

    horn, 55–56
    program number, 56
MidiBox, 162
MIDICompass, 141
MidiConductor, 41, 130
MIDICreator, 162
MIDI Dance Floor, 62, 65
MIDI foot controller, 124
MIDI Horn, 59
Midiman (company), 33
MidiTron, 162
MIKEY (multi-instrument virtual keyboard), 75, 81
MindPeak (company), 201
MiniDig, 161
Minsky, Marvin, 238
Miranda, Eduardo, 17, 230
MIT Media Lab, 141, 143, 149, 201
Mitchell, Tom, 191
Mixing console, 36, 220
Miyashita, Homei, 74
MLP (multi-layer perceptron), 191
MMG (mechanomyogram), 181
Modified shoes, 62
Modular Feedback Keyboard, 75
Montage, 184
    bipolar, 184, 187, 209
    referential, 184
Moog, Robert, 21, 28–29, 138, 207
Moog synthesiser, 122
Moose, 74, 76, 83
Morril, Dexter, 24
Motion Analysis (company), 86
Motion tracking, 43, 84
Motor(s), 75, 78, 104
Motorola 33794, 142, 150
MOTU 828 mkII interface, 128
Mouth cavity, 65
Mouthpiece, 51
Mouthsizer, 65, 66
Movement(s)
    arms, 103
    body, 5
    dance, 10
    empty-handed, 5
    expressive, 10
    eyes, 103
    feet, 103
    fingers, 103
    hands, 103
    head, 103
    legs, 103

    non-contact, 5
    optical, 85
    rotary, 153
    voluntary, 5
MoveOn, 132
MPXV5010, 150
MTC Express Pad, 32
Muehlen, Stephan von, 28
Mulder, Axel, 18, 31, 36, 115
Multiply-touch-sensitive clavier, 21, 29, 143
Mumma, Gordon, 221
Murata (company), 148
Murphy, Declan, 151
Muscle
    sounds, 182
    vibrations, 181
Muscle tension, 10, 203
Musical instruments, 1
    acoustic, 1
    digital, 1
    electrical, 1
    electronic, 1
    recorder, 59
Musical Navigatrics, 37
Musical styles, 210
Musical Thinkets, 140
Mutha Rubboard, 124, 143

N

Nagashima, Yoichi, 23, 28
NaturalPoint (company), 86
Nelson, Gary Lee, 55
Nervous receptors, 7
Neural
    activity, 183
    networks, 15, 147, 191
Neurons, 183
Ng, Kia, 65, 66
Nichols, Charles, 83
NIME (New Interfaces for Musical Expression), 17
Nishimoto, Kazushi, 74
Non-linguistic cues, 11
Noninverting amplifier, 155
Nonmusicians, 90
Northern Digital (company), 85, 135
Nose, 183
Notam, 162
Nyce, David, 104
Nyquist theorem, 159

O

O'Modhrain, Sile, 36, 76, 83, 149, 153
Oboe, Roberto, 77, 81
Oculus Renae, 151
Ondes martenot, 1
Op amp, 157
Operational amplifiers, 105, 156–57
Opponens policis, 204
Optical encoders, 81
OptiTrack, 86
Optotrak 3020, 85, 135
Optotrak Certus, 135
Orb-3, 92
Organ, 74
Orient, 141
Orio, Nicola, 8, 14, 65–66
OSC (open sound control), 103, 160
Overholt, Dan, 33, 136
Overtone Violin, 136

P

Pacom, 36, 153
PaiA Electronics (company), 162
Palacio-Quintin, Cléo, 47
Palindrome, 151
Pallàs-Areny, Ramon, 107, 109
Pantomime, 9
Paradiso, Joe, 37, 63, 140, 142, 153
Pardue, Laurel, 37
Pascal, Michel, 25
Passive listening, 193
Pattern recognition, 15
PebbleBox, 36, 153
Peltier devices, 74
Percussion instrument, 39
Performer
    expert, 88
    nonexpert, 54
Phanton Omni, 73
Phase vocoder, 14
PhoeniX Technologies (company), 85
Photodetector, 133–34
Photodiodes, 63, 136
Phototransistor, 29, 136
Physical modelling, 80
Piano, 22, 25, 74–75
Piano Bar, 21
Pierrot, Patrice, 44, 115, 119
Piezo transducer, 91
Piezoelectric
    cables, 65
    crystal(s), 123–24
    effect, 113
    films, 62, 123
Pinkston, Russell, 62
Pipe, 58–59
Pitch bend wheel, 27
Pitch identification, 25
Plank, 74–75
Plexiglas, 32
Plymouth (University of), *see* University of Plymouth
Pressure-sensitive keys, 42
Prevot, Philippe, 36
Pringer, Jörg, 32
Place, Timothy, 164
Plubber, 165
Pocket Electronics (company), 162
PodoBoard, 60–61
Pointing Fingers, 84
Polaroid sensor, 125
Polhemus Fastrak, 84
Pollution, 108
Polyethylene foam, 62
Polyphone, 137
Postures, 5
    adjustments, 10
Potentiometers, 24, 36, 39, 41, 43, 59
Power Glove (Mattel's), 43, 114
Pressure
    air, 150
    blow, 28
    breath, 27, 57, 150
    keys, 152
    lateral finger, 29
    lip, 57
    lower lip, 26
Prevot, Philippe, 130
Protocol
    active listening, 196
    auditory stimulus, 196
    passive listening, 197
Pushbuttons, 56
PVDF (polyvinylidene fluoride), 123–24

Q

Quantum Research Group, 142
Quek, Francis, 6
QSlide, 142
QTouch, 142
QWheel, 142

R

Radiation, 104
Radio Baton, 38–40, 45, 143, 164
Radio Drum, 38, 164
RF (radio frequency), 85
Ramstein, Christoph, 7
ReachClose, 132
Receiver, 125
Reception (of information), 9
Resistor, 105, 154
Ricci, Carlos, 60
Risset, Jean-Claude, 22
Roads, Curtis, 17
Robotics, 72, 92
Rokeby, David, 151
Roland (company), 134
Rolky Asproyd, 32, 70
Rollerblade Wheel Encoder, 134
Rosenboom, David, 199, 207
Rotary encoders, 110, 153
Rotary potentiometers, 22
Rotation, 52
Rovan, Joseph "Butch," 43, 72, 75–76, 92, 112–13
Rowe, Robert, 237
Rubine, Dean, 27
Rudolph, Max, 201

S

Sampling
    rate, 159
    resolution, 159
Sawada, Hydeyuki, 147, 151
Saxophone, 21–23, 53, 72
SBass, 22, 122
Scavone, Gary, 58–59
Schaeffer, Pierre, 237
Schloss, Andrew, 40, 164
Schumann, Robert, 213, 215
Schutterhoef, Arie van
Score following, 14, 18, 46, 225, 227
Self-organizing behavior, 248
SensAble Technologies (company), 73
Sensing
    continuous, 52
    hand-tilt, 41
    surface(s), 59–60
    ultra-sound, 41
    visible light-sensing, 109
Sensitive floor, 59

Sensor(s)
　absolute, 105
　air pressure, 23, 110
　analog, 105
　bend, 109, 112–14
　breath, 69
　camera-based systems, 151
　capacitive, 110, 141, 144
　complex, 105
　computer-vision systems, 151
　contact, 105
　data, 90
　digital, 105
　direct, 105
　earlobe, 180
　flexion, 22
　galvanic skin response, 69
　gravitational, 149
　Hall effect, 45, 47, 50, 109, 138
　heart rate, 69
　homemade, 165
　humidity, 110, 152
　inclination, 149
　inertial, 53
　interfaces, 158
　IR (infrared), 109, 112, 131, 132
　Light, 50
　linear, 50
　linear position, 44, 121
　linear touch, 36
　LuSense CPS2 155, 44, 109
　magnetic field, 24, 50
　magnetoresistive, 140
　moisture, 152
　motion, 63
　noncontact, 105
　optical proximity, 63
　piezo, 92, 105, 109, 123–124
　piezoelectric, 144
　piezoresistive, 144
　position, 105, 109
　potentiometer, 109
　pressure, 24
　relative, 105
　self-generating, 105
　sliders, 121
　specification, 106
　tactile, 109
　temperature, 69, 110, 152
　tilt, 110, 149
　ultra-sound, 50, 52, 123–25
　vibration, 90

Sensor Mannequin, 143
SensorBand, 41
SensorBox, 164
SensOrg Cyberinstrument, 36
SensorLab (company), 130, 161
Sequential drum, 27, 45, 67, 223
Serrano, Jacques, 137
Shaft encoders, 36
Shakuhachi, 148, 152
Shannon theorem, 159
Shapetape sensor, 116, 119
Sheehan, Brian, 119
Shoals of fish, 247
Shock, 123
Siegel, Wayne, 43, 117
Sign language, 9, 11
Signal(s)
　acquisition (physiological), 14
　brainwaves, 10
　conditioning, 153
　infrared, 40
　MIDI, 26
　muscle, 173
　nerve, 173
　nonmovement, 10
Sijercic, Zlatko, 208
SillyTone Squish Factory, 37, 111
Silva, Andrey da, 51–52, 150
Singer, Eric, 37
Sinyor, Elliot, 134
Ski, 37
Sliders, 36
Snell, John, 29–30
Softwind Instruments (company), 26
Sonami, Laetitia, 43, 115, 139, 147
Sonic Banana, 37
Sonic City, 152
Sound
　amplitude, 52
　diffusion, 220
　generation unit, 3
　modulation, 25
　synthesis, 1, 52, 222, 238
Sound Kitchen, 152
Spectral density, 190–91
Spirit Chair, 143
Squeezebox, 28
Squiggle, 119
Stanford University, 134, 200
Starkier, Michel, 36, 45, 52
STEIM, 151, 158, 161

Steiner, Nyle, 26
Stethoscopes, 182
Stigmergy, 252
STK (Synthesis ToolKit Library), 83
Stockhausen, Karlheinz, 88, 220
Stokes, Maria, 182
Strain gauge(s), 81, 109, 113–14, 150
Stratifier, 33
Sullivan, Dan, 171
Super Polm, 44–45, 119
Surface One, 33
Swarm intelligence, 248
Swarmusic, 248
Swarms of insects, 247
Switches, 24, 28, 36, 40–41
　mercury, 41, 43, 52, 110, 147
　mercury tilt, 50
Synthesis (techniques)
　additive, 14, 92
　FM (frequency modulation), 15
　formant, 15, 66
　granular, 36, 45, 153
　hybrid, 47
　momentary, 59
　physical models, 15
Synthesizer
　4X system, 153, 222
　voltage-controlled, 221
Synthophone, 21, 26, 29

T

Tachometers, 81
Tactex Controls, 32
Tactile
　gloves, 111–12, 120
　information, 108
　receptors, 108
　stimulators, 71–73
Taelman, Johannes, 128, 131
Talbert, 55
Tam-Tam, 220–21
Tanaka, Atau, 19, 22, 53, 90, 148
Tchaikovsky, Piotr Ilyitch, 204
Teabox, 165
Teitelbaum, Richard, 207
Tekscan, 110
Teleo modules, 163
Temperature, 103, 114
Temperature display, 74
Tempo, 69
Temporal features, 11
Termen, Lev, 2

T

Termenova, 143
Terrier, Alain, 44, 115, 119
Texas Instruments, 158
TGR (transducteur gestuel rétroactif), 77, 153, 160
Theremin, 2, 76, 142
Thermistor(s), 92, 152
Thermoelectric coolers, 74
Theta rhythm, 188
Tibetan singing bowls, 53
Tilt2D, 146
TiltOn, 149
Toaster, 163
Toeplitz, Kasper, 90
Tongue, 25, 65
Tooka, 88, 117, 151
Touch-screen, 36
    surface, 32
Touch sensitive organ, 29
TouchSound, 74
Touch switches, 23
Trackballs, 36
Trackers
    active, 85
    passive infrared, 85
    video, 92
Transducer(s), 104
Transistor(s), 105, 136
Transition networks, 212
Transmitters, 125
Transverse flute, 28, 45
Trapezius muscle, 204
Traube, Caroline, 14
Trautonium, 2
Trautwein, Friedrich, 2
Trible, 124
Triceps muscle, 202–3
Trombone, 22, 57
Trombone propelled electronics, 28–29
Trueman, Dan, 44
Trumpet, 22, 24, 57

U

Ultrasound
    transmitters, 24
    wave, 127
University of California, 160
University of Genoa, 131
University of Glasgow, 186
University of Plymouth, 66, 92, 206, 209
University of York, 125, 130, 141, 162, 169
USB cameras, 86

V

V-scope, 131
Valve trombone, 24
vBow, 83
Vecci, Fabricio, 110
Vercoe, Barry, 14, 45
Verplank, Bill, 163
Vertegaal, Roel, 36
Very Nervous System, 151
Vibration, 123
Vibrotactile displays, 74
Vicon Motion System (company), 86
Vidal, Jacques, 207
Video, 90, 92
VideoHarp, 27, 138
Violin, 7, 22, 44–45, 74
    augmented, 22
Virtual Bodhrán, 84
Virtual-reality, 43, 72
Visio-based systems, 110
Vision System (company), 151
Visualeyez, 85
Vodhrán, 84
Voinier, Thierry, 47
Voltage
    divider, 153
    limiter, 157
VPL Dataglove, 43
VR/TX (virtual texture) system, 74, 76

W

Wacom tablet, 111, 119
Waizvisz, Michel, 37, 41, 139
Wanderley, Marcelo, 18, 115, 165
Wands, 40
Wasserman, Gil, 22
WaveRider, 200–1
Web (device), 37, 139
Webster, John, 107, 109
Wessel, David, 88–89
Wheatstone bridge, 155
Wi-miniDig, 161
Wired batons, 41
Wireless technology, 42
Wireless wands, 41
Woodwinds, 57
Wright, Matt, 88–89, 160
Wrist, 202
Wynnchuk, Jordan, 66

X

XFGN-6, 150

Y

Yamaha (company), 26
Yamaha WX series, 26
    WX5, 55, 150
    WX7, 150
Yokono, Jun, 114
York Electronics Centre, 125, 169
York (University of), *see* University of York
Young, Diana, 22, 53, 114, 139, 149
Ystad, Sølvi, 47

Z

Z-Tiles, 64–65
Zadel, Mark, 117